331.11
M82p

72626

DATE DUE			
Oct 9 '74			

GAYLORD M-2   PRINTED IN U.S.A.

Contents

INTRODUCTION

What is required for economic growth and prosperity? Is it a sufficient number of entrepreneurs who will assemble resources and provide jobs
for others? Is it a stable government that will enforce the performance of
contracts and assure freedom from arbitrary change of rules? Is it that the
country has natural advantages or outside help that enable it to reach the
"take-off" point, or controls international trade properly, or has a banking
system to provide credit, or has sufficient markets for its output, or makes
wise investment in "human capital"? Is it, in part, the energy and flexibility of its millions of citizens making billions of decisions about the allocation of the country's most critical resource--the time, effort, and
ingenuity of its people?

All of the above are essential, and all need to be studied and
promoted. They need to be studied as they differ in time, in different countries, and within countries.

This book studies one of the requisites for economic growth--the
economic behavior of individuals. The study has been made within one country
at one point in history, namely the United States in 1965. The findings are
based on a representative national sample of families interviewed early in
1965. Quantitative measures that can be translated and altered to suit different circumstances are used so that the results of the survey can be used
in making comparisons between countries at different stages of development

or within the same country at different times. To improve such comparisons, we have introduced and measured variables, such as the strength of family ties, that have little economic effect in the United States at present, but may well have great effect in other countries or other times.

The present study builds on nearly two decades of studies done by the Economic Behavior Program of the Survey Research Center on the saving and spending behavior of families. Those studies were supplemented in 1960 by a study of the determinants of family income and of the transmission of econom-ic status from one generation to the next.[1]

But these studies done by the Survey Research Center, like the many other studies of labor force participation and hours of work, really measured neither the total economic effort of families, nor the outside constraints and inner desires that affected that effort, nor the ancillary attitudes and views of people (such as their interest in new products) that might affect the quantity and the efficiency of their work effort.

The present study is a report of such measurements. We present a picture of the hard-working American family, and we attempt to explain and interpret differences within this country in the extent to which families work, plan ahead, accept change, avoid risk, and keep a high and rising, but realizable, set of goals.

This study is a project of the Economic Behavior Program of the Survey Research Center, a division of the Institute for Social Research of the University of Michigan. The Director of the Program is George Katona; of the Center, Angus Campbell; and of the Institute, Rensis Likert.

---

[1]James Morgan, Martin David, Wilbur Cohen, and Harvey Brazer, Income and Welfare in the United States (New York: McGraw-Hill Book Company, Inc., 1962).

The study was supported by a grant from the Carnegie Corporation, for which the authors wish to express their gratitude. The grant provided for an international design conference, and the following persons either attended that conference or provided written comments and suggestions which aided in improving the design of the study:

Conference

Prof. Ojetunji Aboyade	Ibadan, Nigeria
Mr. Lars Berglund	Sweden
Dr. Jose Nieto de Pascual	Mexico
Dr. Abdul Farouk	Dacca, East Pakistan
Prof. Herman Felstehausen	Univ. of Wisconsin (Land Tenure Center)
Prof. Ronald Freedman	Univ. of Michigan (Population Studies Center)
Prof. Gino Germani	Argentina
Prof. Eduardo Hamuy	Chile
Dr. Jose Hernandez Alvarez	Puerto Rico
Prof. Eugene Jacobson	Michigan State University (Asst. Dean for International Research)
Mr. Erling Jørgensen	Denmark
Dr. Anna Koutsoyiannis-Kokkova	Greece
Prof. and Mrs. Ugur Korum	Turkey
Dr. Jorge Ruiz Lara	Colombia
Mr. Dennis L. Lury	Kenya
Mr. Raul Pedro Mentz	Argentina
Dr. Safia K. Mohsen	Egypt
Dr. Frederic A. Mosher	New York (Carnegie Corporation)
Dr. Hollis W. Peter	Univ. of Michigan (Foundation for Research on Human Behavior)
Prof. Everett M. Rogers	Colombia and Michigan State University
Mrs. Ursula Wallberg	Sweden

Other Contributors

Dr. Weitze Eizenga	The Netherlands
Prof. Bert Hoselitz	University of Chicago
Prof. Herbert Hyman	Columbia University
Prof. Alex Inkeles	Harvard
Prof. Nathan Keyfitz	University of Chicago
Prof. David McClelland	Harvard
Dr. Louis Moss	England (The Social Survey)
Prof. Charles Osgood	University of Illinois
Dr. Burkhard Strümpel	West Germany

4

Special thanks are due to Dr. Farouk, whose contributions were most useful and perceptive.

The study also benefited from the assistance of many experts within the Survey Research Center. The questionnaire design was improved greatly by the advice of Prof. Charles Cannell and of the Detroit interviewers who assisted us at the pretest phase of the study. Irene Hess, Head of the Sampling Section, who directed the sampling, devised an economical procedure for dividing local clusters between two surveys which increased the sampling efficiency of both. The coding was supervised by Joan Scheffler, and the data processing by Ralph Bisco, Carl Bixby, and David Schupp. Most of the typing was done by Mildred Dennis and Alice Sano. Thomas Way's editing made things clearer and easier to read.

It is most difficult to specify the important, pervasive, and creative influence of our colleagues in the Economic Behavior Program, and in the rest of the University, but it is certain that the study benefited from the long and close collaboration with Professors George Katona, John Lansing, Eva Mueller, and Mr. John Sonquist. Many of the other members of the Economic Behavior Program also had a hand in the project at one time or another.

Needless to say, we did not always solicit advice when we should have, or heed it when it came, and the resulting product could have benefited from still more collaboration. We shall look forward to suggestions and ideas from our readers.

CHAPTER 1

GENERAL

Findings

The United States is affluent today because its people are hard-working, ambitious, and progressive. Many of them do economically productive work for purposes other than monetary rewards; we estimate that such unpaid work in 1964, if it could be measured, would be found to have increased the country's estimated Gross National Product by 38%. The comparable percentage for other countries is a matter for speculation. Certainly some countries have relatively larger nonmarket sectors; offsetting this, however, their people may well do less volunteer work, and certainly they invest less time in self-education.

This book is a study of the productive use of time among United States citizens. The times spent by husbands, wives, and entire families are studied in detail in separate chapters, as are work rewarded with money and work that saves money or that, like volunteer work, saves the recipients' money. One major variable that constrains work time and is subject to no social control is age: the very young and the very old work less than the middle-aged. Another, subject to change only over long periods, is formal education. But by setting aside uncontrollables such as age, and by looking behind the complex influences of education, one can begin to examine the basic attitudes and motives that affect work behavior within a culture.

These attitudes and motivations can be shown to be affected, in turn, by the results of past behavior. Success reinforces the attitudes that stimulate the behavior that leads to further success in a dynamic process; or, conversely, failure and distress reinforce the attitudes that stimulate the behavior that leads to further failure. (See Appendix D.)

The attitudes and ancillary behaviors which interrelate with economically productive activity are themselves studied in some detail. For simplicity we have given them names such as planning, caution and risk avoidance, use of new products, receptivity to change, mobility, and ambition and aspiration. As much as possible, we have used behavioral indicators rather than purely verbal expressions, since the former can be assessed against a constant absolute standard, whereas people's self-images are often measured against unknown and variable standards.

Hence, although the analysis is based on a single cross-section study, the basic model and implications are dynamic: creative response to progress leads to a more efficient and productive use of time, which then leads to individual economic success and prosperity. That prosperity in turn reinforces the positive response to progress and change.

The most powerful force in this cumulative cycle seems to be formal education, which is itself subject to national policy decisions. Whatever combination education may represent of native intelligence, parental background, initiative, and acquired skills and information, it appears to be a dominant and dynamic force, certainly representing something more than unchangeable inherited differences. It seems clear, then, that the current proposals for greater "investment in human capital" through support for improving education and health are justified not only as methods of increasing potential productivity, but also as affecting the ancillary and related behavior and attitudes that are crucial for economic progress.

Organization of the Book

Productive activity is studied, decision area by decision area, starting with the hours worked for money by heads of families, wives and others in the family, and the journey to work. Unwanted leisure, such as that resulting from illness or unemployment, is analyzed separately. Unpaid productive work--which otherwise someone outside the family would have to do and perhaps be paid for--is then analyzed, first regular housework and then other unpaid productive activities, and finally the receipt of labor from outside the household (work done for the family by someone from outside the family whether received free or paid for). The final two chapters in the first section analyze the total productive time of families and the extent to which they seem to be trying to work more or less.

The second section studies the indexes of related behaviors and attitudes previously used to help explain the productive use of time. Successive chapters treat the forces affecting receptivity to change, planning and time horizon, geographic and occupational mobility, ambition and aspiration, social participation, caution and risk avoidance, closeness of family ties, and attitude toward mothers' working. In a final, capstone chapter, a combined index of concern with progress is analyzed and shown to result in part from the family's own past economic success or difficulty.

In each chapter, then, we try to explain one or more measures of behavior or attitude, or of a mixture of the two. We have tried systematically, first, to present the distribution of that "dependent variable," then to show its relation to one or two of its most important determinants, and finally to move to more complex multivariate analyses. Each chapter concludes with a summary of the results and a brief overview of related research.

The analysis has to be complex because there are multiple causes which sometimes act jointly, and because some factors are logically prior to others in the causal process. By logically prior, we mean that they can alter the other causal forces, but cannot be altered by them. Most logically prior variables are also predetermined earlier in time, such as a man's age which is determined by his year of birth. But it is logical priority, not temporal priority, that matters. Some factors determined long ago such as religion, past mobility, or parent's education, are treated as representing current motivations and attitudes rather than as basic constraints.

We first remove the effects of these constraints and logically prior factors, in whatever complex way they operate. This usually takes account of extreme behavior that results from such things as advanced age or very little education. We then try to explain the remaining variation by examining further for the influences of economic and other currently operating motivations.

We have attempted to keep to a minimum the description of our analytic techniques and our negative findings, and to make it as easy as possible for the reader to see the main positive results--what really matters. For those interested in particular hypotheses, however, we provide lists of variables included in each analysis. The reader will be able to see not only which variables proved important, but which ones, perhaps contrary to expectations, proved to have little or no effect. Indeed the analytic procedure used allows us to say that a variable not only had no effect over the whole sample, but also had no effect on any major subgroup of the sample or no effect once the influence of background variables and constraints was taken into account.

Implications for the Future

Any piece of social research builds on the past, and becomes more and more useful if future work is in turn built upon it. The present study was designed to facilitate a variety of comparative studies here and in other countries. To insure that we were not "culture-bound" but were including variables that might be important in other countries, even if they were not important in the United States, we held an international conference at which social scientists from nearly a dozen countries participated in the design of the study. These social scientists concluded that it was particularly important to study the constraints of various sorts that limited people's freedom of action. They also agreed that comparative studies might be most productive if they adapted the basic concepts into the situation of each country, rather than translating the questionnaire word for word.

The study will also provide a basis for assessment of changes in this country over the years. The year 1964 was a prosperous one, coming after many years of relative prosperity for most people. On the other hand, the full effects of the attempts to achieve full employment, of the War on Poverty, and of the expansion stimulated by the war in Viet Nam, had not yet been felt. Hence there were still some people affected by unemployment, and many others working long hours at low hourly earnings trying to achieve an acceptable standard of living. The effects of the more recent upward pressures on wages and prices, of the War on Poverty, and of the extensions of welfare legislation may well affect people's attitudes and behavior in the future.

Whether the comparisons to be made are between countries or between different years in the same country, the great virtue of richly detailed survey data is that they make possible a sophisticated "within-between" analysis.

Differences <u>between</u> countries, or between epochs can be explained better when we also have explained differences <u>within</u> each country at each point in time. Differences between countries or between epochs can be attributed as follows:

1. They result from differences in levels of the explanatory factors, with little difference in the way these factors affect people.

2. They result from differences in the way in which the variables affect behavior. Different variables may be important in different places or times.

3. Both of the first two may be true. For instance, education may affect people more in one time or place than at another, and the educational levels of the populations may also differ.

4. Neither of the first two may be true. There may be differences between countries that cannot be accounted for either by differences in the average levels of explanatory forces, nor by differences in the way they operate. In this case one is reduced to comparisons between countries as units, with little possibility of discrimination between alternative hypotheses. <u>Samples</u> of countries are difficult to draw, and in addition to the inter-country differences in the kinds of variables that affect individual behavior, there are all the global differences traditionally of concern to economists such as natural resources, balance of payments problems, capital accumulation, and the like. [1]

But there are vast differences among subcultures within any one country, as in the United States and differences in many things between countries, so it seems likely that much of the overall difference between countries can be attributed to differences in the situations people face or the ways they react to them.

---

[1] For some interesting hypotheses about global cultural differences between countries, see Conrad M. Arensberg and Arthur H. Niehoff, <u>Introducing Social Change</u> (Chicago: Aldine Publishing Co., 1964), pp. 163-167; Yusif A. Sayigh, "Cultural Problems and the Economic Development of the Arab World," in <u>Religion and Progress in Modern Asia</u>, ed. Robert N. Bellah (New York: The Free Press, 1965), p. 65; and Raul S. Manglapus, "Philippine Culture and Modernization," <u>ibid.</u>, pp. 37-38. For an opposite view which discounts such differences, see H. DeLa Costa, "The Concept of Progress and Traditional Values in a Christian Society," <u>ibid.</u>, pp. 25-26.

What is required, particularly in studies in underdeveloped countries, is the wisdom to use survey research flexibly and progressively, not merely and rigidly copying the expenditure surveys of western countries, but focusing attention on the very basic economic activities crucial to economic growth-- productive use of time, receptivity to change, planning ahead--and on the effectiveness of government programs in influencing these behaviors. This in turn requires that nationals of these countries be trained in the broad concepts of survey research as well as in details of procedure, so that they will be able to adapt their designs to the needs and the resources at hand. Since the subject of study is such basic economic behavior in such universal units as productive use of time or receptivity to current changes, not only should the design be easier, but the results should be more useful, both for improving economic development programs and policies, and for more long-range comparative studies of behavior.

But we must turn aside from these speculations to the immediate task of relating what we have found about the United States in the mid-sixties.

CHAPTER 2

HOURS OF WORK FOR MONEY
BY HEADS OF FAMILIES

Introduction

In a market economy with extensive division of labor, such as the
United States, the major economic contribution most people make is paid for
in money by an employer or customers. Hence it seems appropriate to begin a
study of people's productive work with an examination of the work heads of
families do for money. This will be followed by an analysis of the work for
money by wives, and by other family members.

Overall Findings

If we take a forty-hour week as standard, with two weeks vacation,
then nearly half of all the heads of families surveyed, and well _over_ half of
those under sixty-five years old, said they worked more than that standard.
Aside from the ill or unemployed, few worked less than forty hours.
Table 2-1 shows the distributions, annual hours being estimated by multiplying
reported weeks of work by reported hours per week when working.

Of those who reported working more than an average of forty hours per
week in 1964, only 15 per cent had second jobs; the rest did overtime or
extra work on their main jobs. Extra work is not stable in amount from month
to month: nearly two-thirds (65 per cent) of those working reported that they
sometimes had overtime work or short work weeks; and a three-year panel study

12

TABLE 2-1

A: HOURS OF WORK FOR MONEY BY HEADS OF FAMILIES IN 1964
(For all 2214 heads of families)

Hours worked for money	Per cent of cases
None	17
1-1000	7
1001-2000	30
2001-3000	36
3001 or more	10
Total	100
Number of cases	2214

B: HOURS WORKED PER WEEK BY HEADS OF FAMILIES IN 1964
(For all 1789 heads of families who worked
and whose hours worked per week were known)

Hours worked per week	Per cent of cases
Fewer than 35	7
35 - 40	43
41-48	20
49-59	17
60 or more	13
Total	100
Number of cases	1789

conducted by the Survey Research Center showed that such variations in work do not even average out over the year.[1] That study reports very frequent year-to-year changes in income, even among those who "worked a full year"-- that is, fifty weeks.

Aside from the ill or unemployed, few worked less than the standard forty-hour work week, but many worked more. Half said they worked more than forty hours a week, and 30 per cent said they worked more than forty-eight hours a week.

At the other end there are people who do not work at all, or work less than full time. The chief reasons seem to be powerful constraints such as advanced age, disability, illness, or unemployment, rather than any free economic choice between leisure and more money.

Constraints and Pressures

The impacts of illness, unemployment, being a woman, advanced age, or extreme youth are shown clearly in Figure 2-1.[2]

The heads of families who did not work at all in 1964, comprising 17 per cent of those analyzed, are excluded from the figure. Most of these were old people. Among those analyzed, it is clear that the chief reasons why some heads of families work less than full time are extreme age, long-term

---

[1] See Richard Kosobud and James Morgan (eds.), Consumer Behavior over Two and Three Years, Monograph 36 (Ann Arbor: Survey Research Center, University of Michigan, 1964), Chapter 3, pp. 18-41.

[2] The chart results from an automated search for homogeneous population groups that differ widely from one another, yet are large enough so that isolating them makes it easier to explain and predict hours of work. The method is explained in detail in Appendix E. All the reader needs to keep in mind is that any of the allowable factors could have taken over at any splitting stage, but would have left more unexplained variation in hours of work.

FIGURE 2-1

HOURS OF WORK FOR MONEY IN 1964 BY HEADS OF FAMILIES
(For all 1833 heads of families who worked for money in 1964)

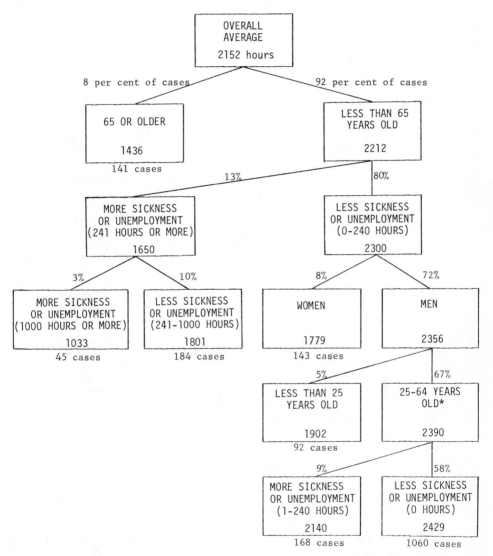

*This group of 1228 cases is analyzed further in Figure 2-2, and, after exclud-
ing 12 cases working less than 700 hours and 10 cases working more than 4780
hours, in Figure 2-3.

MTR 201

illness, unemployment, or being a woman. Most women who are heads of families are widows or have children at home but no husband, and they frequently have some other source of income. Many of them are also poor.

The explanatory variables used in the multivariate analysis (search process), whose results are shown in Figure 2-1, are listed below in order of their importance if used to make a single division of the whole sample.

* Age of head of family
* Sex of head of family
* Hours lost from work in 1964 by head of family from illness and unemployment

---

Whether head of family was disabled

Asterisked variables are those used in Figure 2-1. They explained 22 per cent of the variance. The overall standard deviation is 809 hours. The variable below the line could not explain as much as 0.5 per cent of the total sum of squares by a single division of the whole sample.

An earlier analysis using the four variables plus several others -- whether the family head grew up on a farm, size of place (town) where the family lives, race, location of residence relative to nearest large city, education of head of family, and whether the county was an economically depressed area -- produced a figure very similar to Figure 2-1. The main difference was that disability of the head and location of residence relative to nearest large city were actually used. It was decided to use the simpler Figure 2-1 but to analyze its two main subgroups separately, using a still wider variety of variables.

Figure 2-1 suggests that working heads of families can be divided into two major groups: (a) a main group of men (the starred group at the lower right of the figure) comprising the two-thirds of heads of families subject to no severe constraints against working, and (b) the rest, who were working in the face of various constraints and pressures on their total hours.

In Figure 2-2 the work times of the two groups of heads of families are compared, age group by age group. It is clear that the "standard" forty-hour week is not so standard as one might think. The very young may not be handicapped, but some are still going to school part-time or entered the labor force during the year.

We next analyze the work time of the two subgroups separately, in more detail, since we have reason to believe that different forces will affect the work hours of the two groups.

Motives and Incentives: Men with no Severe Constraints on Their Work Time

We turn now to the two-thirds of the working heads of families who were men twenty-five to sixty-four years old and who reported less than 241 hours of illness or unemployment, no disabilities, and no extremely low or high totals of work hours.[3] Can we account for what variations there are in their work hours? Figure 2-3 shows the first part of a multivariate analysis.

The variables used, in order of their explanatory power if used to make a single division of the whole group, were as follows:

---

[3]Heads of families reporting less than 700 hours or more than 4780 hours of work during 1964 were excluded, chiefly for statistical reasons: a few cases so extreme tend to dominate any results obtained by least-squares procedures. The 12 cases reporting less than 700 hours were such persons as students; those who were half-retired, such as older farmers, painters, plumbers, or music teachers; and a retired sailor with an apartment house to run.

The 10 cases reporting more than 4780 hours either had their own business or farm, or worked at a job involving a good deal of waiting time such as managing a restaurant, a hotel, or a small store.

FIGURE 2-2

HOURS OF WORK FOR MONEY BY HEADS OF FAMILIES IN 1964, BY AGE OF HEAD
OF FAMILY
(For all 1833 heads of families who worked for money in 1964)

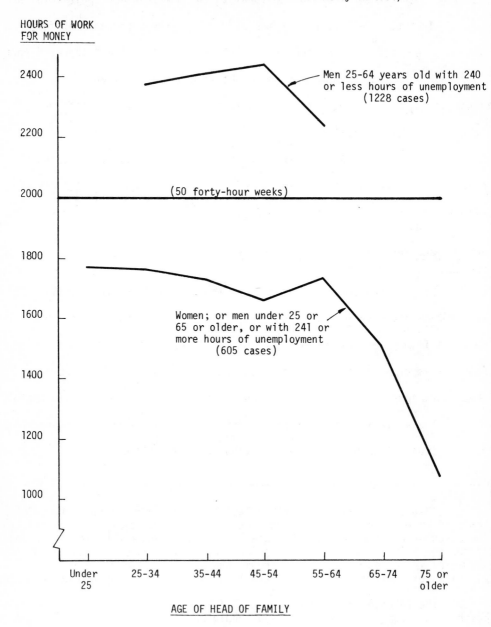

MTR 201

FIGURE 2-3

HOURS OF WORK FOR MONEY IN 1964 BY HEADS OF FAMILIES WITH NO SEVERE CONSTRAINTS
ON THEIR WORK TIME
(For 1206 heads of families who were male, 25-64 years old,
who had 0-240 hours of unemployment or sickness in 1964,
and who worked between 700 and 4780 hours)

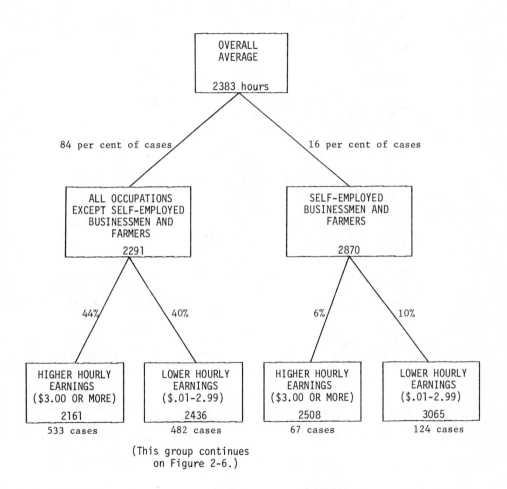

(This group continues
on Figure 2-6.)

MTR 100

*Occupation of head of family (self-employed businessmen work more
   Whether head of family was self-employed
*Hourly earnings of head of family
   Location of residence relative to nearest large city (the farther
      out, the more work)
   Index of planning and time horizon (those who plan least, work
      the longest)
   Number of people in family (more people to support, more work)
   Housing status (home ownership) (homeowners work a little more,
      those who neither own nor rent work most)
   Whether any child of the head of the family is currently in
      college

Age of head of family (younger people work more)
   Education of head of family
   Attitude toward mothers' working
*Religious preference of head of family
   Whether head of family has held a number of different jobs
   Index of ambition and aspiration
   Index of social participation
   Index of achievement orientation
   Index of mobility experience
   Difference in education between head of family and wife
   Index of caution and risk avoidance
   Index of closeness of family ties
*Index of receptivity to change
*Number of brothers and sisters older than head of family
   Attitude toward importance of luck for financial success
   Number of responses indicating a sense of personal effectiveness

Asterisked variables are those used in Figure 2-3 or 2-6. They
explained 21 per cent of the variance. The overall standard deviation
for the 1206 cases is 590 hours. None of the variables below the line
could explain as much as 0.5 per cent of the total sum of squares by a
single division of the whole sample of 1206.

A recapitulation of the total variance in hours worked by the head
may be useful. Of the full sample of 2214 cases, 55 per cent is accounted
for by eliminating the 17 per cent who did not work at all; 25 per cent is
accounted for by omitting the 28 per cent who worked but were under twenty-
five, sixty-five or older, ill or unemployed for more than 240 hours, or
women; 4 per cent is accounted for by 22 extreme cases removed from the analysis; 3 per cent is accounted for by separating the 191 self-employed businessmen and farmers; and 1 per cent is accounted for by dividing the two

occupation groups according to hourly earnings in Figure 2-3. This leaves
12 per cent, of which 2 per cent is accounted for by the further divisions
in Figure 2-6 below.

Main Factors

The most important explanatory variable out of the very large number
of possible ones was whether the person was a businessman or a farmer, as
Figure 2-3 shows. Self-employment as such was less important than actually
owning a business or farm. Including a few self-employed artisans with the
farmers and businessmen would have reduced the difference in hours. From
this we infer, though we cannot be sure, that ownership and entrepreneurial
opportunity, rather than the freedom to choose one's own hours, is what makes
the difference. The convention of the "standard" forty-hour work week, as we
have already seen, has less effect than one would expect even on those employed
by others.

Those with low hourly earnings worked more hours. This finding, like
earlier ones herein, is based on figures for healthy, employed men, since
including figures for disabled or unemployed ones would have distorted the
picture. (The disadvantaged have both lower wages and fewer hours of work.)
The obvious explanation for the main finding is that those whose wages are
low must work more hours to achieve the minimum living standards to which
they aspire.[4]

---

[4]There is no reason to suspect systematic errors in reporting either
income or hours of work. However, random errors in reporting either hours or
earned income would produce a biased tendency toward a negative relation of
hours to hourly earnings, since hourly earnings are estimated by dividing
earnings by hours. It does not seem likely that such errors could be large
enough to account for the negative relation reported here.

The relation of hours worked to hourly earnings is roughly the same
for the two occupation groups, and the difference in hours is almost constant.
It is interesting to see the relation over the entire range of hourly earnings shown in Figure 2-4. The increase in hours at low earning rates is
greater than sampling error would account for, though the slight tendency of
persons at the highest hourly earnings to work a little more is not; that
tendency, by the way, is seen mostly among self-employed businessmen and
farmers.[5]

Since Figure 2-4 is a truncated or "gee whiz type" graph, it is important to note that the actual decrease of effort relative to a 1 per cent
increase in earning rate is rather small, around 0.15 per cent and reasonably
constant. No one is likely to quit working entirely when his wages are
raised.[6]

The notion that people work to achieve a desired income--that is,
that people prefer more leisure to more work as their hourly earnings rise--
is reinforced by the tendency for people with larger families to work more.

---

[5]See Appendix A for a discussion of sampling variability and details
on computing sampling errors for the estimates reported in this book.

[6]An international comparison of work effort as it relates to incomes
or manufacturing wage rates shows a similar negative relationship that seems
to be linear in a log-log form or a reciprocal form. This would seem to
agree with our findings within this country; see Gordon C. Winston, "An International Comparison of Income and Hours of Work," Review of Economics and Statistics, XLVIII (February 1966), pp. 28-39.
    In 1932, Lazare Teper reported in his study of hours of labor in some
American industries that: "there is a tendency for the hourly rates of wages
to vary inversely with the number of hours of work." He also reported a downward trend of working hours during the period from 1890 to 1928; see Lazare
Teper, "Hours of Labor," Johns Hopkins University Studies in Historical and
Political Science, Vol. L (Baltimore: Johns Hopkins Press, 1932), pp. 24, 54.

FIGURE 2-4

HOURS OF WORK FOR MONEY BY HEADS OF FAMILIES IN 1964, BY HOURLY
EARNINGS OF HEAD OF FAMILY
(For 1206 men 25-64 years old with 240 or less hours of unemploy-
ment who worked between 700 and 4780 hours for money in 1964)

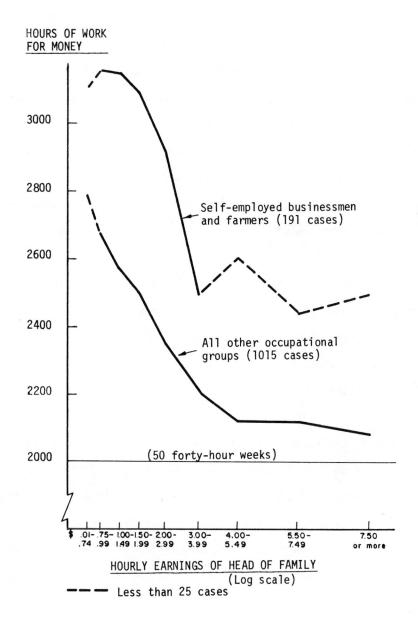

MTR 100

This is graphed in Figure 2-5; and, as the line for self-employed businessmen and farmers shows, they are the ones who contribute most to this tendency. Again, however, the differences are not large.

It was possible to gain a little explanatory power by further analysis of one of the four groups at the bottom of Figure 2-3: those who had no business or farm and whose hourly earnings were less than $3.00. There were not enough businessmen and farmers to warrant more analysis, and the variations in hours worked by others with hourly earnings of $3.00 or more were both small and uncorrelated with the explanatory factors we could measure. We therefore continue our analysis for the group of families whose heads earn less than $3.00 an hour and are not businessmen or farmers (the group second from the left at the bottom of Figure 2-3). The results are shown in Figure 2-6.

It is no surprise that professionals and managers work longer hours than clerical or blue-collar workers. They are under the pressures of their responsibilities. This single division accounts for more than a tenth of the variance within the select group. The professionals and managers divide in turn into the non-fundamentalist Protestants and all other religious affiliations. This is not the pattern over most of the sample, where religious preference made no difference, or had a different effect. Indeed, in the hardest-working group isolated previously in Figure 2-3--the self-employed businessmen and farmers making less than $3.00 an hour--there is a small group of 14 Catholics who average 3592 hours. The pressure on those with low hourly earnings to make enough income by working longer hours appears again among the remaining occupations on the left of Figure 2-6. For one group of

FIGURE 2-5

HOURS OF WORK FOR MONEY BY HEADS OF FAMILIES IN 1964, BY NUMBER OF PEOPLE IN FAMILY
(For 1206 men 25-64 years old with 240 or less hours of unemployment who
worked between 700 and 4780 hours for money in 1964)

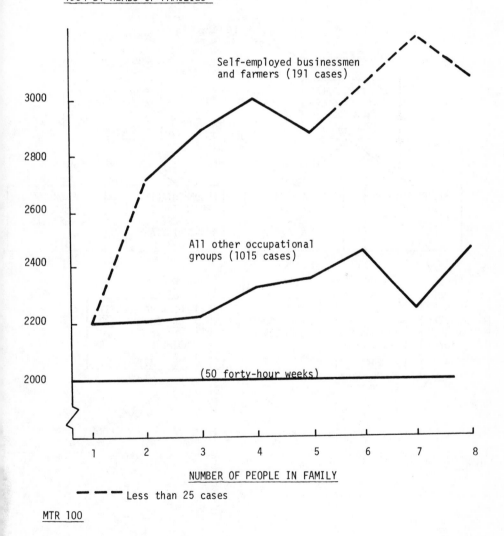

MTR 100

26

FIGURE 2-6

HOURS OF WORK FOR MONEY IN 1964 BY HEADS OF FAMILIES FROM A SELECT GROUP
OF FIGURE 2-3

(For 482 heads of families whose hourly earnings were less than $3.00,
and who were not self-employed businessmen or farmers,
who were male 25-64 years, who had 0-240 hours of unemployment
or sickness in 1964, and who worked between 700 and 4780 hours)

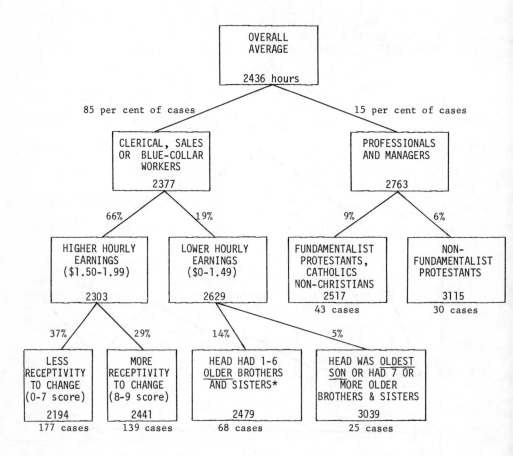

*Includes 4 heads of families who were the only child in their families.

MTR 100

moderately paid employees, receptivity to change appears to lead to working more hours for money.[7]

Two major components of the index of receptivity to change are the use of and interest in new products. Hence we have some confirmation for the hypothesis that interest in new products may stimulate hard work, a notion which led the Russians, it is reported, to decide to increase their output of consumer goods as a stimulus to production.

Finally, for one group of low-paid blue collar and clerical workers, there appears a tendency for people who were the oldest sons when they were growing up (or one of the younger children in large families) to work harder now. This is one of very few places where we have been able to find any appreciable differences in behavior or attitudes according to birth order, about which there is a very large psychological and sociological literature.[8]

---

[7]The construction of the index of receptivity to change is discussed in Appendix D. The index is also treated as a dependent variable in Chapter 13.

[8]For a summary of the findings and an exhaustive bibliography, see Edward E. Sampson, "A Study of Ordinal Position: Antecedents and Outcomes" (mimeo, September 1964), to appear in Vol. 2 of Progress in Experimental Personality Research. Sampson's summary of the findings on achievement are: "On the basis of this survey, it appears rather consistently that the first born child (and probably, especially the first born male) is more likely to achieve social and intellectual eminence. The firstborn indeed may not only be holding the expectations of his parents to achieve social status and success, but also may have been subjected to other conditions which are (1) absence of a sibling for a period of time with the consequent orientation towards the adult world; (2) the accelerated verbal and intellectual training; (3) the early demands for responsibility; (4) the early period of complete attention and then its sudden withdrawal, setting the person on his own to strive to win the high level of approval and affection he once held; (5) the inconsistency in training which on the beneficial side may increase the first child's ability to tolerate novelty, variation, and ambiguity, while at the same time he seeks its elimination, a condition possibly requisite to a scientific approach."
He concludes in spite of the "overwhelming array of inconsistency

We could have explained almost as much, however, by dividing the group by education rather than birth order, and by formulating a simple economic interpretation: Within the narrow range of hourly earnings ($1.50-$2.99), those with more education, and presumably higher desired and expected standards of living, were induced to work longer hours.

Other Factors of Some Importance

Some factors were not powerful enough to be used in competition with the ones already discussed, but would have come in if we had continued the branching beyond the point where each split reduced the unexplained variance by less than one per cent.

The location of a man's residence relative to the nearest large city actually appeared in Figure 2-1, but when the two groups were recombined and analyzed further so that other variables could operate, location appeared far less important in producing longer hours of work than having an entrepreneurial occupation or low hourly earnings. However, a small but persistent tendency for those "farther out" to report more hours of work in each of the groups of Figure 2-3 and 2-6 would indicate that there is some real relationship, not just a spurious correlation through occupation or hourly earnings.

The size of the family has already been discussed in conjunction with the effect of low hourly earnings on work, as imposing another kind of pressure to come up to the society's minimum standards. More dependents require more money, which requires more work.

---

that emerges across the entire spectrum of research" that ordinal position should be explored further. For another summary and criticism see Edith Chen and Sidney Cobb, "Family Structure in Relation to Health and Disease," Journal of Chronic Diseases, 12 (November 1960).

For a summary of birth-order associations throughout this study, see Appendix D.

A tendency to plan ahead can lead to more work if it means that a man's horizons and desires are continually expanding. But it might also mean less work if it leads a man to make better decisions, so that he enters the right occupation and gets ahead by brains rather than brawn. The pooled deviations from Figure 2-1 seem to show both effects, with longer hours being reported at both ends of the planning index. But the main group of family heads analyzed in Figure 2-3 shows extra hours only for the low-planners, and moreover the index itself has to allow middle scores for the very old and young and those without children; so the whole curved effect may be only an artifact. But it may still be true that the less educated people who do not plan ahead work longer hours because they have to, to make up for their lack of foresight.

Nonwhites said they worked somewhat less, but the differences were not large enough, nor were the numbers of nonwhites great enough, to make race a major predictor. For all heads of families, including those who didn't work at all, whites worked an average of 289 hours more than non-whites. Counting only those who worked, whites worked 312 hours more than nonwhites; this indicated that more white people were completely retired. But among men who were twenty-five to sixty-four years old and not ill or unemployed more than 240 hours (if we exclude some extreme cases as in Figure 2-3), whites worked only 177 hours more than nonwhites. For employees making less than $3.00 an hour (see Figure 2-3) the difference was 196 hours, statistically significant for the 504 and 74 cases involved. In that sub-group, however, both whites and Negroes were working more than 2200 hours a year, the actual averages being 2465 and 2269 hours.

Homeowners worked a little more than renters, but those who neither owned nor rented worked still more. The differences were small in the first case, and the group small in the second. Homeowners were expected to be more ambitious, but perhaps those who neither own nor rent were the most anxious to escape from their dependency on those providing the free housing. Some of them were farm laborers.

Having children in college made no appreciable difference in the hours worked by the head of the family, a difference of 19 hours more for those with children in college being inconclusive. In the next chapter it will appear that the wife is not more likely to work when there are children in college either. The differences between those with and without children were more important. In other words, if children increase the pressure to work and earn, they do so from birth on, not just when they are in college.

Once we restrict ourselves to men aged twenty-five through sixty-four, and eliminate extreme cases and ill or unemployed, age of the head of the family does not affect hours of work. Men aged fifty-five through sixty-four, however, are more likely to report illness or unemployment.

Formal education is highly correlated with hourly earnings, and with stability of employment. When residuals from the means of Figure 2-1 are pooled, it seems that more work is reported by those with 9 to 12 grades of school, or with an advanced or professional college degree. Perhaps the former need the money and are offsetting low hourly earnings, whereas the latter have other pressures to work. When we look only at the relatively unconstrained group that starts Figure 2-3, the education differences follow the same pattern, but are not significant.

There is still a difference of opinion about whether a mother should work, particularly if her children are all in school--that is, when the reasons for her staying home are present but not overwhelming. The small but meaningful pattern that emerges can be summarized by saying that those who oppose the idea of mothers' working and also are earning less than $3.00 an hour, work more hours than those who are not opposed. Among the self-employed businessmen, farmers, and professional and managerial men making less than $2.00 an hour, the average difference is still greater; those opposing wives' working tend to work 511 hours more per year than those who favor the idea. Among those earning more than $3.00 per hour the differences are, if anything, reverse, with those who oppose wives' working tending to work less themselves.

Attitudinal indexes, such as social participation, ambition, caution, and closeness of family ties, had no important relation to hours worked.

Neither an index of mobility experience nor a report on whether the individual had had a number of different jobs appeared to affect his current hours of work. Nor were work hours affected by an index built by counting how many responses to three questions indicated a sense of personal effec-tiveness.

These negative findings apply to pooled residuals from the pattern of Figure 2-1, to the main group of Figure 2-3, and to all the main subgroups generated in Figures 2-3 and 2-6. They are, then, pretty conclusive, but with-in limits: that is, they do not mean that there is no relation between ambi-tion and work; they mean only that with the measures we used, no relation appeared between work hours and the other unused variables on the list on page 20.

It has frequently been suggested that the wife sets the living stan-dards of the family, and that hence if a wife has more education than her hus-band, he might find it difficult to earn enough to meet that standard without working overtime. On the other hand, the more education the wife has, the easier it is for her to work and earn money. At any rate such an educational difference shows no relation to the head's work hours. In the next two chapters we shall find that it has no effect on whether the wife works or on how many hours working wives work.

The motivational index that seemed in advance the most likely to be related to work was a measure of <u>achievement orientation</u>.[9]

Since theory says that achievement motivation affects work only if the individual also sees work, not luck, as the path to success, the response to a question about the <u>importance of luck</u> was introduced in the same analysis. No such joint effect or interaction emerged. One small group of low-earning Protestant self-employed businessmen and farmers who thought luck was important were working less, but not enough to justify a division of that subgroup. The achievement orientation index does have some relation to work hours in the expected direction for the low-wage employees and even for the whole main group of men twenty-five to sixty-four years old. The differences are small, however, and there is a curious reversal by which a few at the very top of the scale have lower average work hours than any other group.

Since other measures of achievement orientation have produced significant findings in other studies, we can only say that the measure of achievement orientation we used did not help explain hours of family heads.

Motives and Incentives: All Women and Men
with Severe Constraints on Their Work

We turn now to the one-third of the working heads of families who were either men who were very old or very young, or had more than 240 hours of

[9]See Appendix D for details of how the index of achievement orientation was constructed.

illness or unemployment, or reported working less than 700 hours during 1964, or were women. We concluded in the last section that motivational forces contributed nothing towards explaining differences in hours of work done by the main group of people who were not facing serious constraints or pressure. Figure 2-7 shows, for both groups, the relationship between hours of work for money and an index of concern with progress which is a combination of four motivational indexes, namely, achievement orientation, receptivity to change, ambition and aspiration, and planning and time horizon.[10] The upper line in Figure 2-7 confirms our previous conclusion about motivational forces and hours worked by men with no severe constraints on their work: there is no systematic relation between hours of work and the score on the combined index of concern with progress. The lower line of the figure, however, shows that for women, and for men with severe constraints on their work, hours of work are generally greater for people with higher scores on the index of concern with progress.

The figure shows the hours only for those who worked during 1964. The marginal groups (women and very young or old men) also tend to be more likely to work at least a little if they have a high index of concern with progress. The line could have been made to look more dramatic by including those with zero work hours in the averages, but at least some of it would have been spurious since some of the components of the index were relevant only for people who were working.

Is it possible to conclude from Figure 2-7 that when people are faced with real constraints and pressures, their goals become more difficult and

---

[10]See Chapter 20 for details on the construction and further discussion of the combined index of concern with progress. It is important to remember that the name given the index is for convenience - a short-hand description of its content.

34

FIGURE 2-7

HOURS OF WORK FOR MONEY BY HEADS OF FAMILIES IN 1964, BY
SCORE ON INDEX OF CONCERN WITH PROGRESS
(For 1206 men 25-64 years old with 240 or less hours of unemployment who worked between
700 and 4780 hours for money in 1964; and 605 women, or men under 25, or 65 or older
or with 241 hours or more of unemployment who worked between 1 and 4779 hours of
work for money)

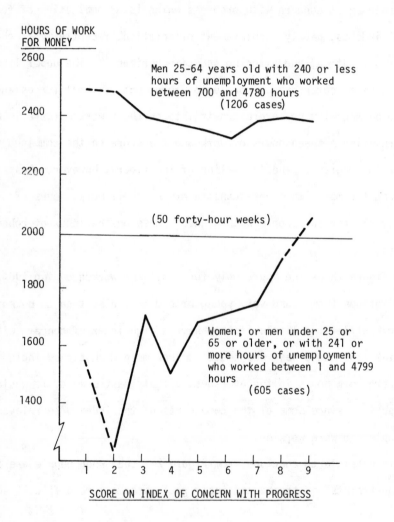

MTR's 193,195,199

challenging, and their actual behavior is affected greatly by differences in their personalities? Perhaps--but the relationship shown in Figure 2-7 is a gross one. It does not take account of differences in constraints among the group, as shown in our earlier analysis and in Figure 2-1. Nor does it take account of other economic motives and forces which might compete or interact with the index of concern with progress.

A logical step is to make a more complex two-stage analysis for the group of men and women with severe constraints on their work. This is done by taking the differences from the end-group averages of Figure 2-1 (excluding the two-thirds of the people who are men with no severe constraints on their work), pooling them, and using the newly created variable (the residuals) as our dependent variable in a multivariate analysis. This removes the main effects of illness, unemployment, disability, and sex, and asks: "Given all that, then what other variables will explain further differences in hours of work, and who it is who works more if he is concerned with progress?"

The following explanatory variables were used in the second-stage multivariate analysis of pooled differences from expected hours worked by those who worked in spite of some disadvantages. They are listed below in order of their importance if used to make a single division of the whole sample:

> *Sex and marital status of head of family
> *Whether family owns a business or farm
> *Hourly earnings of head of family
> Education of head of family
> *Combined index of concern with progress (bracketed, see Appendix D)
> Age of head of family

> Race
> Family head's birth order and family size
> Religious preference

Asterisked variables are those used in Figure 2-8. They
explained 12.5 per cent of the variance. The overall standard
deviation is 823 hours. None of the variables below the line could
explain as much as 0.5 per cent of the total sum of squares if used
to make a single division of the whole subsample.

The findings in Figure 2-8 are straightforward and clear. Single men

work fewer hours for money than the rest. It should be noted that 22 of

these 61 single men were under twenty-five years old. Those who own a busi-

ness or farm work more than others in the constrained group. Half of them

are sixty-five or older. Actually the entrepreneurial group nearly split off

at the two earlier divisions. It is mostly those earning less than $.75 an

hour as owners of businesses or farms who account for the long hours.

But finally, having set aside those groups, we find for the three-

fourths who remain that higher levels of the combined index of concern with

progress are indeed associated with working more hours. And the detailed

effect of the index is very similar to the pattern of the lower line of

Figure 2-7.

We are left with 414 men who made $7.49 per hour or less who owned no

business or farm and who did not score very low on the index of concern for

progress; these account for nearly half the variance of these 600 or so cases.

None of our variables can explain any more of their differences in work time.

As for other variables included in the analysis but not used in the

figure, Protestants appeared to work more hours than the others, except for a

small group of Catholics who owned businesses or farms, who worked a great

deal. Nonwhites worked less, but not enough less to justify establishing a

division for such a small group. The extremes in both age and education

worked less. Single men who were the oldest among their siblings worked less

than other single men in this constrained group. On the other hand, married

FIGURE 2-8

HOURS OF WORK FOR MONEY IN 1964 BY HEADS OF FAMILIES WITH SEVERE CONSTRAINTS
ON THEIR WORK TIME: ANALYSIS OF DIFFERENCES FROM END-GROUP AVERAGES
OF FIGURE 2-1

(For 613 family heads who were under 25, or 65 or older, or had 241 or more
hours of unemployment or sickness in 1964, or were female and who worked
for money in 1964)

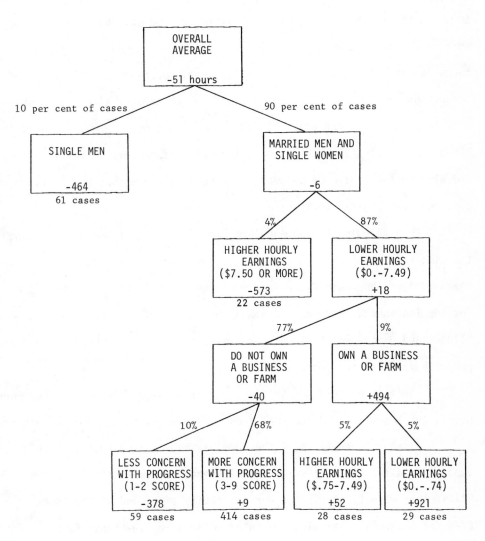

MTR 212

men and single women who were the oldest child, worked more than the others, regardless of the numbers of brothers and sisters they had.

Summary

We find, then, that after dealing with the most important constraints on work, the remaining interpersonal differences among the main group of workers depend largely upon the need for a decent standard of living that makes people with large families or low hourly earnings work longer, and on the demands of a business, farm, profession, or managerial position which lead to more work. And after all this, we find some marginal evidence for a bit of the "Protestant ethic" among the non-fundamentalist Protestants who are also professionals or managers, and some evidence that those with more concern with progress work more.

Even allowing for some natural tendency for respondents to exaggerate the time spent on such a worthy activity as work, it is apparent that the standard forty-hour work week is commonly exceeded, and that averages which include the young, the old, the women who head families, and those subject to illness and unemployment, tend to be lower than those for healthy middle-aged men with families to support.

There is no evidence that above-average wages lead to reduced work hours, but there is evidence that substandard wages force some to work more.

A separate analysis of the marginal people--the young, the old, those subject to extensive illness or unemployment, or women without husbands--suggests some effects of birth order and family size, and of the index of concern for progress, that might be interpreted as motivational forces. Motivational differences may have their strongest effects among those subject to

counter pressures tending to reduce work hours. Since it is shifts at the
margin that matter, in economics as elsewhere, the implication is that motivational forces may still be important, even if they affect only those on
the fringes of the labor market.

Other Research

In addition to the many sociological studies of the working man, which
contain only rudimentary quantification or which study small special groups,
there have been a number of studies of hours of work. The main statistics
are those on which the Bureau of the Census and the Bureau of Labor Statistics
have based their estimates of the "average work week." In nonagricultural
activities, the work week appears to have decreased by several hours in the
last two decades, and then risen in the last few years, to around 38 hours a
week at present.[11]

But as Sebastian de Grazia has pointed out, if one excludes the part-
time and peripherally attached workers and concentrates on the full-time male
workers, the work week looks longer: "And when we add up their hours (regular and overtime) they come not to 39 or 40 but to 46 or 47."[12]

De Grazia also provides some data from an unpublished study based on
a national sample and diaries for a two-day period from overlapped subsamples.
That study shows an average work week of 42 hours for men (plus nearly ten

---

[11]See U.S. Bureau of the Census, Current Population Reports: Labor
Force Series P-50 through 1959, and Bureau of Labor Statistics, Employment and
Earnings, and Monthly Report on the Labor Force since 1959.

[12]Sebastian de Grazia, Of Time Work and Leisure (New York: The Twentieth Century Fund, 1962), p. 69. His exclusion of those working less than
35 hours a week is considerably cruder than our segregation of the old, young,
ill or unemployed, etc.

hours of traveling).[13]

T. Aldrich Finegan used occupational groups as the unit of analysis and found a negative coefficient of -.08 between median hourly earnings and average hours worked per week.[14]

Once a year, in the February Current Population Survey, the Census interviewers ask questions, not just about work last week, but about employment experience for the whole previous year, and the distributions are given by age, sex, race and occupation.[15] During 1963 some 17 per cent were unemployed at one time or another.

Studies of "moonlighting" (second jobs) in local areas have been focused on married men.[16] More recently, correlations of changes in the makeup of the labor force with changes in economic opportunity have indicated that females and very old or very young men are those most likely to be affected by changes in economic conditions: a high level of unemployment tends to discourage men from working, whereas wives tend to seek jobs when hard times create a need to increase the family's income.[17]

---

[13]Ibid., pp. 73, 444-445.

[14]T. Aldrich Finegan, "Hours of Work in the United States: A Cross-Sectional Analysis," Journal of Political Economy, LXX (October 1962), pp. 452-470.

[15]Samuel Saben, "Work Experience of the Population in 1963," Monthly Labor Review, 88 (January 1965), pp. 8-16.

[16]Harold L. Wilensky, "The Moonlighter, A Product of Relative Deprivation," Industrial Relations, 3 (October 1963), pp. 105-124; Leete A. Thompson, "Motives and Practices of Moonlighters," University of Washington Business Review, XXI (October 1961), pp. 5-21.

[17]See for example, Thomas Dernburg and Kenneth Strand, "Hidden Unemployment 1953-1962: A Quantitative Analysis by Age and Sex," American Economic Review, 56 (March 1966), pp. 71-75; Strand and Dernburg, "Cyclical Variation in Civilian Labor Force Participation," Review of Economics and Statistics, 46 (November 1964), pp. 378-391.

The most detailed analysis comes from a 1960 study by the Survey Research Center, on hours of work during 1959. The data were collected much as were those reported in the present study: each of a national probability sample of household heads was asked how many weeks he had worked in the previous year, and how many hours per week he had worked when he was working. Subjects were not asked first, as in this study, about vacation or illness or unemployment, but if they reported less than 49 weeks of full-time work, they were asked what they were doing the rest of the time.[18]

Several factors make comparisons difficult, however. First, the 1960 study accounted separately for each head of a spending unit, including some secondary units living with relatives but keeping separate finances. Second, the analysis was originally in a multiple regression format assuming a set of additive effects except where interactions were explicitly introduced. Third, some different attitudinal and motivational variables were used. In general, however, these data too gave the impression that constraints such as extreme age or disability reduced hours of work, and that a number of dependents to feed or low hourly earnings forced more work. Plans to help children or parents in the future, a measure of achievement motivation, a belief that hard work pays off, and church attendance, all proxy measures of motivation, showed significant positive association with longer hours of work. The difference in education between husband and wife had no effect on the heads' hours, however, just as in the current study.

In a secondary analysis made by the search procedure used in the present study, the 1960 data were analyzed in two stages. The results

[18]For a fuller report of both methods and findings, see James Morgan et al., Income and Welfare in the United States (New York: McGraw-Hill Book Company, Inc., 1962).

produced a similar impression that middle-aged married men who were not disabled worked much more than full time. The residuals were affected by the opportunities and incentives connected with being a self-employed businessman or farmer, and by the pressures of low wages.[19]

Since the analyses are somewhat disparate, we have recalculated some of the data from this earlier study—those on work hours for major groups—to make possible a comparison of the findings for 1959 and 1964. The results of the comparison are shown in Table 2-2. Tables similar to Table 2-2 but excluding those working less than some minimum number of hours, showed closely similar results for the two studies.

Clearly, the number of hours worked has increased. This is not surprising in view of the reduction in unemployment between 1959 and 1964. It is also clear that the increases in hours within each earning rate is greater than the overall increase, because an increasing proportion of workers are in the higher rates where the average hours are less. Remaining in the same wage rate during this period meant, of course, relative deprivation, since unless a man worked more he would find that his income was not keeping up with those of his fellow citizens.

Cost of living does not affect this last statement as much as one might think, since during this period it rose much less than average hourly earnings. Median earnings of the main subgroup of men twenty-five to sixty-four years old, other than self-employed businessmen or farmers, went up from $2.54 to $3.00, while the consumer price index went up from 102.2 to 108.9 from January 1960 to January 1965, less than a third as fast.

---

[19]See James N. Morgan, "Time, Work and Welfare," in M. J. Brennan, ed., Patterns of Market Behavior (Providence: Brown University Press, 1965).

TABLE 2-2

HOURS OF WORK FOR MONEY IN 1959 AND 1964
BY HEADS OF FAMILIES

(For all 1833 heads of families who worked for money and in 1964
and 2370 heads of families who worked for money in 1959)

Characteristics of heads of families	Hours of work for money		Per cent of cases	
	1959	1964	1959	1964
Under 25, or 65 or older	1646	1595	13	14
25-64 years old:				
Women heads of families	1703	1729	11	9
Self-employed businessmen or farmers	2711	2856	12	12
Remainder: employed men who were not self-employed businessmen or farmers (See below for this group)	2166	2202	64	65
All cases	2118	2152	100	100
Hourly earnings of employed men who were not self-employed businessmen or farmers who were 25-64 years old				
Less than $1.00	2357	2489	6	6
$1.00-1.99	2263	2290	24	16
$2.00-2.99	2142	2296	37	29
$3.00-3.99	2083	2134	20	25
$4.00-4.99	2011	2082	7	12
$5.00 or more	2180	2031	6	13
All cases	2166	2202	100	100

MTRs 134,136

CHAPTER 3

WIVES WHO WORK FOR MONEY

Introduction

The dramatic increase since 1942 in the proportion of wives who work outside the home for money has been documented, discussed, and studied. The present study thus builds upon considerable earlier analysis, but carries it forward in several ways, by making clearer the distinctions among constraints, pressures, and the more discretionary motives, and by documenting the relation between work for money and other economic activities of the household.

Nearly three-quarters of the family units studied in this survey include wives, and nearly half of these wives--more than 20 million--worked for money during at least part of 1964. Averages hide important differences among wives of different ages, of course. Only 12 per cent of the wives sixty-five or older worked at all in 1964, but nearly 60 per cent of those under twenty-five worked. Indeed, more than three-fourths of the wives who married in 1964 worked during the year. Figure 3-1 shows the proportions who worked in each age group. It is apparent that advanced age or young children at home are the two main constraints that keep wives from working. Indeed, most of the remaining differences in labor force participation for wives sixty-five or older are explained by further differences in their age: only 4 per cent of those seventy-five and older worked in 1964.

As for wives under sixty-five years old, the main forces affecting

44

45

PER CENT OF WIVES WHO WORKED FOR MONEY IN 1964, BY AGE OF WIFE
(For all 1640 wives)

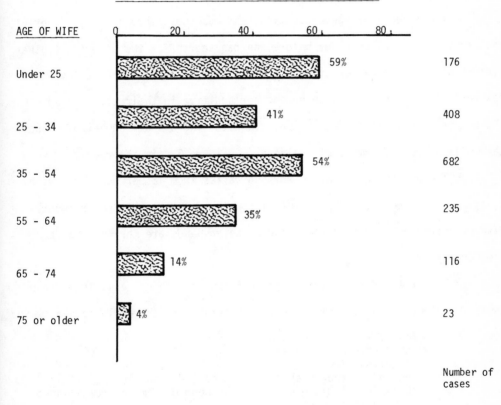

PER CENT OF WIVES WHO WORKED FOR MONEY IN 1964

AGE OF WIFE	0 20 40 60 80		Number of cases
Under 25	59%		176
25 - 34	41%		408
35 - 54	54%		682
55 - 64	35%		235
65 - 74	14%		116
75 or older	4%		23

MTR 98

whether they worked outside the home were their own formal education, since more education makes pleasant, well-paying jobs available, and their husbands' income, which, if high enough, makes a job unnecessary. Figures 3-2 and 3-3 show these effects, which are not independent, since women with more education marry men with more education and they in turn earn higher incomes Hence both effects are underestimated.

Constraints and Pressures

The effects of age, education, and husbands' income are so powerful that they must be allowed for before one can search for the effects of other factors without the danger of making spurious correlations. Since even these few variables are neither independent nor additive in their effects, we use the search process described in Appendix E to find a small number of groups that will account for most of the effect. Figure 3-4 is the result.

The percentage of wives working varies from 12 per cent, for wives sixty-five or older, to 83 per cent, for well-educated wives under twenty-five or thirty-five to fifty-four and whose husbands are making less than $10,000 a year.

The explanatory factors allowed in the search process, in order of their importance if used to make a single division of the whole sample, were:

* Age of wife
* Total income of husband
* Education of wife
  Who, other than husband, was disabled (usually the wife)
  Hours lost from work in 1964 by head of family from illness and unemployment
  Race

Whether there were any children under 5 in family
Number of children of head living at home (includes those 18 or older)
Size of place (town) where family lives
Location of residence relative to nearest largest city
Number of adults in family
Whether husband was disabled
Whether county was a depressed area

47

FIGURE 3-2

PER CENT OF WIVES WHO WORKED FOR MONEY IN 1964, BY EDUCATION OF WIFE
(For 1494 wives uder 65 for whom education was ascertained)

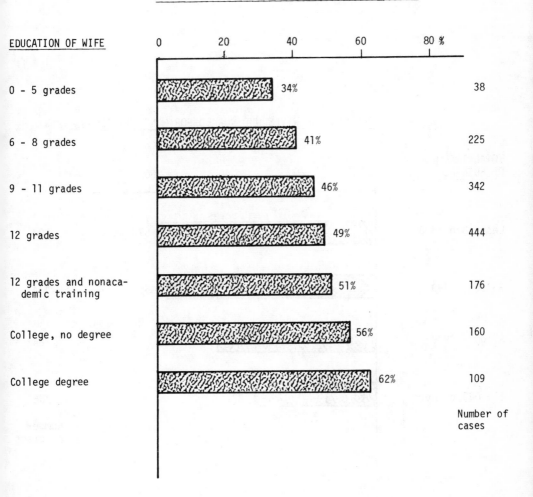

PER CENT OF WIVES WHO WORKED FOR MONEY IN 1964

MTR 98

48

FIGURE 3-3

PER CENT OF WIVES WHO WORKED FOR MONEY IN 1964, BY
TOTAL INCOME OF HUSBAND
(For all 1501 wives under 65 years old)

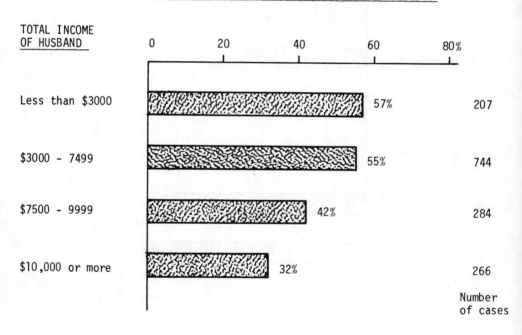

PER CENT OF WIVES WHO WORKED FOR MONEY IN 1964

MTR 98

49

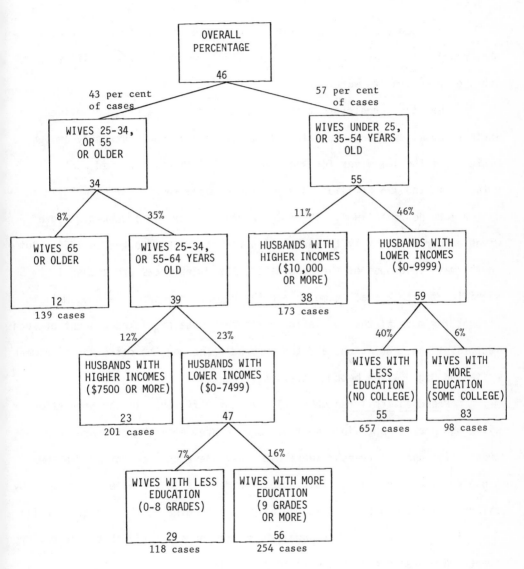

FIGURE 3-4

WHETHER WIFE WORKED FOR MONEY IN 1964
(For all 1640 wives)

MTR 98

Asterisked variables are those used in Figure 3-4. They explained 13 per cent of the variance. The overall standard deviation of the proportion is 0.5. None of the variables below the line could explain as much as 0.5 per cent of the total sum of squares by a single division of the whole sample.

The theory behind the three factors used in the figure is clear: they represent either hindrances to the wife's working, opportunities for jobs, or pressures to work.

The other predictors tried but not used had the expected effects on whether the wife worked, but did not affect enough people strongly enough to matter. Of the 107 wives for whom some disability was reported, only 24 worked. In the 195 families in which the husband was ill or unemployed for 241 or more hours in 1964, 115 of the wives (59 per cent) worked. Negro wives appear more likely to work: 61 per cent of them worked in 1964. But in the main subgroups of the population, the differences are too small to be significant with a small sample, and the number of Negroes is too small to account for much of the population variance. Once one takes account of such factors as age, education, and the husband's income, the differences between white and Negro wives become very small anyway.

Preschool children make a 7 per cent difference in the proportion of wives who worked, but since most wives with preschool children are between twenty-five and thirty-four years old, they are accounted for by the age groupings. Another way of looking at the demands on the wife's time made by children at home is to look at the effects according to the number of children living at home, as in Figure 3-5, which shows clearly that more children create more pressure on the wife to stay home.

But these differences were not great enough to be taken into account in Figure 3-4. The same is true for the size of place (town) where the

51

FIGURE 3-5

PER CENT OF WIVES WHO WORKED FOR MONEY IN 1964, BY
NUMBER OF CHILDREN LIVING AT HOME
(For all 1266 wives under 55 years old)

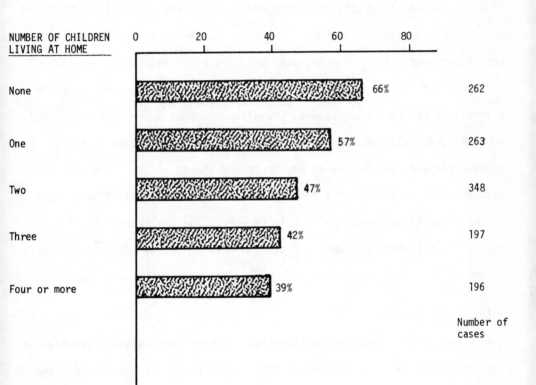

PER CENT OF WIVES WHO WORKED FOR MONEY IN 1964

NUMBER OF CHILDREN LIVING AT HOME	Per cent	Number of cases
None	66%	262
One	57%	263
Two	47%	348
Three	42%	197
Four or more	39%	196

MTR 98

family lives. Wives living in standard metropolitan areas of 50,000 or more,
but not in the twelve largest of them, were about 10 per cent more likely to
work, probably because such places offer more opportunities for women's
employment. Almost the same group is identified by classifying people according to location of residence relative to the nearest large city.

The final three factors allowed in the search had no appreciable
effects--number of adults, disability of husband, and living in a depressed
area. Other variables which we did not include in this search process have
some importance, in an expected way, but only a few people are actually
affected. If the husband had been unemployed for more than two months at a
time within the past two decades, the wife was about 8 per cent more likely
to work, presumably because of the uncertainty of her husband's income, or
because she went to work in an emergency and stayed at it. If the husband
had been seriously ill for a month or more between three and five years ago,
the wife was 10 per cent more likely to work. The implication is that illness or unemployment probably affects the wife's work immediately, but most
of the effect of illness wears off, while that of unemployment does not.

Motives and Desires

All these findings are expected, and have been shown, separately or
two at a time, in other studies. Figure 3-4, however, shows the most important combinations of the basic constraints and pressures, and we can now take
the differences from the expected proportions in the final groups of that
figure, pool them, and examine them for the effects of other forces.[1]

---

[1]In practice, we assign to each wife a probability of working depending upon her group in Figure 3-4; if she worked, her "difference" is 1.0

Some of the explanatory factors used in the first search were reintroduced into the second stage to see whether they might modify the effects of the other second-stage variables. For instance, the wife's age, education, or race might alter the extent to which the husband's disapproval of mothers' working actually deterred her from working.

Although some of the factors in the second stage seem similar to those in the first, they serve a different purpose. In the first stage, the husband's income represented the (prior) decision to increase the family's income by having the husband work more hours rather than of letting the wife work. In the second stage the husband's hourly earnings are used to represent the adequacy of his earning capacity, whatever his hours of work. In the first stage, again, the presence of preschool children and the number of children at home represented demands on the wife to stay at home and take care of them, whereas in the second stage the total number of people in the family is used to reflect the need for additional family income or the help of other income earners. Similarly, living in a depressed county might make

---

minus the proportion working in her group, and if she did not work, her difference is 0 plus that proportion. The average of such differences for any group is the difference between the average expected proportion and the actual proportion for the whole group.

A group's appearing in the residual analysis with an average of, say, -5 per cent is to be taken as meaning that it is made up of people who, whatever group they were in in the first analysis, tended to be 5 per cent less likely to work than the average for their subgroup.

It must be remembered that any second-stage analysis will underestimate the influence of the second-stage variables to the extent that they are correlated with the variables used in the first stage. For a brief explanation, see James N. Morgan, "Consumer Investment Expenditures," American Economic Review, XLVIII (December 1958), 874-902. For a more formal treatment see A. Goldberger, "Stepwise Least Squares, Residual Analysis and Specification Error," Journal of the American Statistical Association, 56 (December 1961), 998-1000.

jobs for wives scarce, but living in one with a high median income might induce them to want to work because the local standards of living, or cost of living, required additional money.

The explanatory factors used in analyzing the residuals, in order of their power to discriminate in a single division over the whole sample of pooled residuals, were as follows:

*Husband's attitude toward mothers' working
*Whether husband was self-employed (and whether he worked)
Whether any child of the head of the family is currently in college
*Number of people in family
Who, other than husband, was disabled
*Education of wife
Difference between education of husband and wife

Husband's index of closeness of family ties
Race
Husband's index of planning and time horizon
*Religious preference of husband
*Husband's index of achievement orientation
Husband's index of caution and risk avoidance
Husband's index of ambition and aspiration
*Husband's hourly earnings (and whether he worked for money in 1964)
Number of brothers and sisters of wife
Husband's index of receptivity to change
Number of rooms in home (large house to care for?)
Husband's index of social participation
Median income in the county (standards and cost of living)
Husband's attitude toward importance of luck for financial success
Husband's index of mobility experience
Home ownership (housing status)
*Age of wife

Asterisked variables are those used in Figure 3-6. They explained 9 per cent of the variance. The overall standard deviation of the proportion is 0.5. None of the variables below the line could explain as much as 0.5 per cent of the total sum of squares by a single division of the whole sample.

Figure 3-6 (a, b and c) shows the most important discriminants producing further differences in the likelihood of the wife to work. It explains an additional 11 per cent of the total variance.

FIGURE 3-6-a

WHETHER WIFE WORKED FOR MONEY IN 1964: ANALYSIS OF DIFFERENCES
FROM END-GROUP AVERAGES OF FIGURE 3-4
(For all 1640 wives)

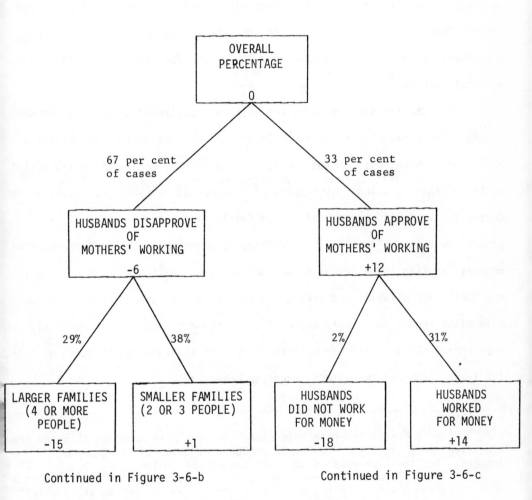

Continued in Figure 3-6-b   Continued in Figure 3-6-c

MTR 98

The first part of Figure 3-6 (3-6-a) shows that the husband's attitude about whether it was a good idea for mothers to work made an 18 per cent
difference in the probability of his own wife's working. There is always the
possibility that the husband adapts his view to his own family situation and
rationalizes it. However, there were some who opposed mothers' working even
when their own wives were working, and others who favored it when their wives
were not working.[2]

For the families in which the husband disapproved of mothers' working,
Figure 3-6-b shows that a large family of four or more further inhibits the
wife from working, except when the pressure of home responsibility was offset
by the husband's having a high level of achievement orientation. Perhaps the
desire for economic advancement of the family offset the disapproval of
mothers' working. Even in small families in which the husband disapproved of
mothers' working, older wives tended not to work, particularly if someone in
the family was disabled and needed constant care. On the other hand, a young
wife often tended to work in spite of the husband's disapproval, particularly
when there were no children; here the husband's attitude can be taken as less
likely to influence the wife's immediate behavior.

---

[2]The question asked in this study was made more explicit than the one
used five years earlier, in order to reduce the number of "it depends"
answers. The question asked five years ago was as follows:
"There are many wives who have jobs these days. Do you think it is a
good thing for a wife to work, or a bad thing, or what? Why do you say so?"
See   James N. Morgan, et al., Income and Welfare in the United States (New
York: McGraw-Hill Book Company, Inc., 1962). It was clear from the earlier
study that the family whose children were all in school was the one in which
the other forces were most nearly in balance; hence the question asked in
this study was: "Suppose a family has children but they are all in school--
would you say it is a good thing for the wife to take a job, or a bad thing,
or what?"

FIGURE 3-6-b
(CONTINUATION OF FIGURE 3-6-a)

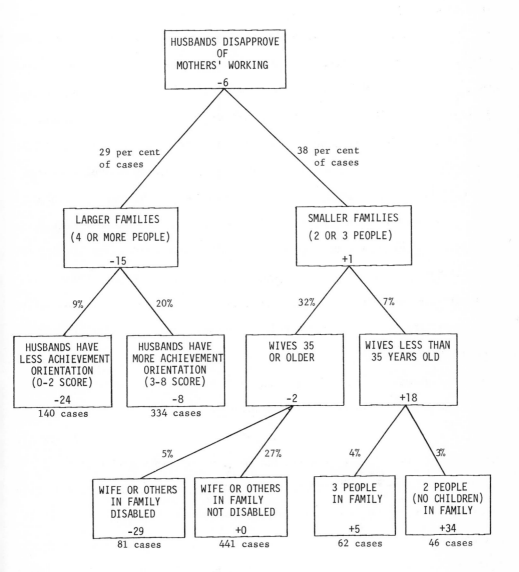

MTR 98

For the 33 per cent of families in which the husbands approved of mothers' working, Figure 3-6-c shows that the few cases, mostly of old couples, in which the husband did not work, the wife was less likely to work too. Beyond that the husband's approval seems to have had less effect for younger wives, many of whom presumably have preschool children. The younger wives with approving husbands appear more likely to work, the "other things" of Figure 3-4 aside, if they are Catholics or fundamentalist Protestants. (Over most of the rest of the sample, the Catholic wives were the least likely to be working.) The middle-aged wives with approving husbands were particularly likely to work if they had some education beyond high school.

In summary, when a wife has children at home and a husband who does not approve of mothers' working, she is usually discouraged from working beyond what one would expect from her age and education and her husband's income, already accounted for. The effect of the husband's disapproval is stronger if the husband is not highly achievement-oriented. The husband's approval also has more effect if his index of achievement orientation is low, though the effect was not strong enough to show up in Figure 3-6-c.

Some factors seemed important over the whole sample of residuals but were not powerful enough to appear in Figure 3-6. The wives of self-employed husbands were less likely to work; but many of them worked without pay in the family business or farm. Interestingly, however, the simple hypothesis that uncertainty of income from self-employment might press the wife to work, is not borne out. Of course, the facts are that, in general, the self-employed have stabler incomes than most semi-skilled and unskilled workers who suffer intermittent unemployment. Wives were more likely to work if there was a child currently going to college. A high score on the index of closeness of

59

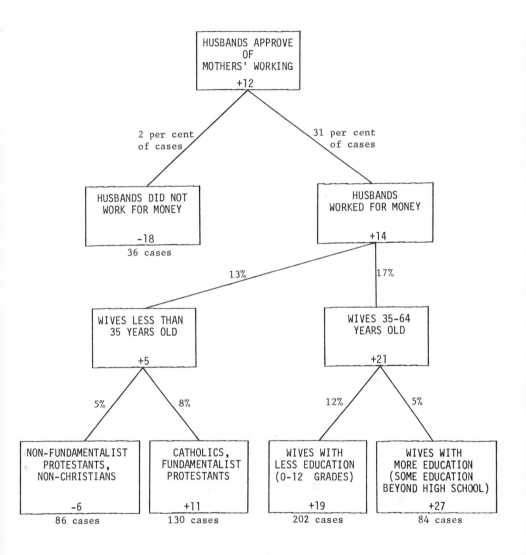

FIGURE 3-6-c
(CONTINUATION OF FIGURE 3-6-a)

MTR 98

family ties did seem to discourage some younger wives from working even when the husband approved of mothers' working, but the religious preference made still more difference and hence appears in Figure 3-6-c. The index of closeness of family ties does include reports of actual volunteer work for relatives, however, so that it may have been the productive use of time in that way that discouraged the wife from working for pay.

Nonwhites were more than twice as likely as whites to approve of mothers' working, but race was never powerful enough to divide the sample.

The index of planning never came close to making a discrimination, and none of the remaining predictors made any difference. Wives were not more likely to work where the husband had a high score on the ambition and aspiration index, nor where he scored high on the index of receptivity to change nor where the county had a high median income and hence high living standards, nor where the family owned its home. And wives did not seem to be less likely to work for money where the head of the family had a high score on the index of social participation, or where there was a large home to care for, or where the wife had a large number of brothers or sisters.

Since none of the other variables on the list mattered, either for the whole sample or for any of its major subgroups, we can be reasonably sure that, as measured, they did not matter. One might feel that some were operating through the other variables used, particularly those used in the first stage, but it is doubtful that they could be considered prior in their causation.

We are left with only three effective explanatory forces that could be considered individual motives rather than outside forces or constraints or opportunities: the husband's attitude toward mothers' working, his score on the index of achievement orientation, and his religious preference. A few others seemed on the verge of showing through the more powerful but less interesting forces. For example, the difference in education between husband and wife seemed to show an effect even after the wife's education had been taken into account, though it may still reflect finer differences in the wife's absolute education, rather than her educational difference from her husband.

Related Research

A complex analysis of labor force participation of wives was published as part of the study which served as one of the taking-off points for the present study.[3] The data from that analysis were reworked into the more flexible format that has been used in this study, with similar results, except that the earlier study showed that wives whose husbands had grown up in the Deep South were more likely to work.[4]

Since the publication of Income and Welfare in the United States, analyses of other data have appeared. Jacob Mincer has reanalyzed data from the 1950 Bureau of Labor Statistics Survey as well as community average data from the 1950 Census and the 1956 Current Population Survey Data, interpreted in the permanent-transitory income model; the patterns he found were basically the same as those reported here.[5]

---

[3]James N. Morgan, et al., Income and Welfare in the United States (New York: The McGraw-Hill Book Company, Inc., 1962), especially pp. 106-109.

[4]James N. Morgan, "Time, Work and Welfare," in M. Brennan, ed., Patterns of Market Behavior (Providence: Brown University Press, 1965), pp. 89-107.

[5]Jacob Mincer, "Labor Force Participation of Married Women: A Study of Labor Supply," in Aspects of Labor Economics (Princeton: National Bureau of Economic Research, Princeton University Press, 1962), pp. 63-105.

62

Two chapters in a book on the employed mother focus on her decision to work. One uses Survey Research Center data, and the other uses data from a study of the growth of American families done by the Survey Research Center for Professors R. Freedman, P. Whelpton, and A. Campbell.[6]

Finally, a recent small study of college-educated mothers indicated that those among them who worked were less satisfied with their marriages or their lives, were brighter, and had lower family incomes than those who did not work.[7]

Three empirical studies of working women in other countries showed that women in England work because they need the money, and that women in Pakistan are restrained from working by "purdah."[8] A Hungarian study, based on 1960 data, focuses on the housework time and who does it, as affected by the family size and whether the wife works outside the income.[9] Of wives aged fifteen through fifty-five whose husbands were employed workers in Budapest and a few other Hungarian cities, 61 per cent were employed. And the husbands were much more likely to help around the house if the wives worked:

---

[6]Marion G. Sobol, "Commitment to Work," and Lois Hoffman, "The Decision to Work," both in F. Ivan Nye and Lois Hoffman, eds., The Employed Mother in America (Chicago: Rand-McNally and Company, 1963). Data used in the latter article were taken from Ronald Freedman, et al., Family Planning, Sterility, and Population Growth (New York: McGraw-Hill Book Company, Inc., 1959).

[7]Jack E. Rossmann and David P. Campbell, "Why College-Trained Mothers Work," Personnel and Guidance Journal (June 1965), pp. 986-992.

[8]F. Zweig, Women's Life and Labour (London: Victor Gollancz, 1952); Viola Klein, Working Wives (London: Institute of Personnel Management, 1959); A. F. A. Husain, Employment of Middle Class Women in Dacca (Dacca, East Pakistan: University of Dacca, Socio-Economic Research Board, 1958). The "purdah" is a religious custom prohibiting women from appearing in public unless they are veiled.

[9]Hungarian Central Statistical Office, Women in Employment and at Home (English supplement) (Budapest, Hungary: 1962).

35 per cent of them, as against 15 per cent of those whose wives did not work. The employed Hungarian wife worked between six and seven hours per day, regardless of the number of children in the family.

Russian urban workers were studied in 1924 and again in 1959. These studies show that women spend as much time in "productive work" as the men, as well as devoting additional time to housework. The two startling findings are the small changes between 1924 and 1959, and the increase in "lost time" spent getting to work and back, shopping, and waiting in lines, which jumped from 1.17 to 2.30 hours per day for men and from 1.06 to 1.95 hours per day for women.[10]

---

[10]Prudensky, ed., "Vnerabochee vremya" (Nobosibirsk, U.S.S.R.: 1961), p. 34 (courtesy of Professor Alexander Szalai).

CHAPTER 4

WIVES' HOURS OF WORK FOR MONEY

Introduction

Of the 747 working wives in sample families, 7 reported the wife was working more than 3,000 hours, and 68 reported she was working 120 hours or less. The former were mostly working in a family business, or in a business of their own, but there were two unskilled working wives whose jobs demanded many hours. The wives who worked only a few hours during the year were no different from other working wives except that somewhat more of them had pre-school children.

With these extreme cases eliminated, the distribution of the rest of working wives was as follows:

Hours worked for money by wives in 1964	Per cent of working wives (excluding extreme cases)
121-240	8
241-1000	26
1001-2000	48
2001-3000	18
Total	100
Number of cases	672

Constraints and Pressures

The most important force restraining working wives from working long hours was, of course, the presence of preschool children. Child care for children under five is expensive. Children of five or older, however, are

64

65

generally in school, and somewhere around age thirteen they are likely to have lunch at school too.

The data on whether the wife worked, and the data on the average hours worked for money by those who worked, are affected in opposite directions by a few women who worked only a few hours. By eliminating those who worked 120 or fewer hours, however, we can proceed to analyze average hours worked undisturbed by variations in the numbers of those reporting very small amounts of work.

Figure 4-1 shows that working wives under sixty-five with either no children or one child five or older (in school) worked an average of 1538 hours in 1964, and that working wives with preschool children averaged 1029 hours (978 if we exclude six extreme cases).

The variables used in the analysis, in order of their importance if used to make a single division of the whole sample of working wives, were as follows:

> *Whether there were any children under 5 in family
> *Number of children of head living at home (includes those
>   18 or older)
> *Age of wife
> Who, other than husband, was disabled
> Education of wife

> Race
> Number of adults in family
> *Total income of husband
> Whether husband was disabled
> Location of residence relative to nearest large city
> Hours lost from work by husband in 1964 from illness or
>   unemployment
> Size of place (town) where family lives
> Whether county was a depressed area

Asterisked variables are those used in Figure 4-1. They explained 12 per cent of the variance. The overall standard deviation is 730 hours. None of the variables below the line could explain as much as 0.5 per cent of the total sum of squares by a single division of the whole sample.

FIGURE 4-1

HOURS OF WORK FOR MONEY IN 1964 BY WORKING WIVES

(For all 672 wives who worked between 121 and 3000 hours
for money in 1964)

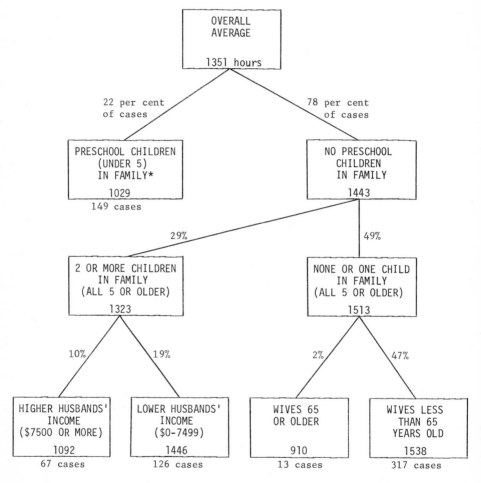

*The automatic process split off three small groups of three, two, and one case
respectively, each with more than 2000 hours worked, and by treating them as
separate groups, removed their extremeness from the residuals. Without them, the
mean for working wives with preschool children was 978 hours.

MTR 99

Several factors, such as the <u>education of the wife</u> and the <u>income of</u> <u>the husband</u>, though they affected whether the wife worked, had very little effect on the hours she worked. The only exception was that mothers with two or more children but no preschoolers worked longer if their husbands earned less.

<u>Negro wives</u> had been shown to be more likely to work than white ones, but they worked somewhat fewer hours; 1244 for Negro wives versus 1358 for white. The overall average, including nonworking wives, still leaves Negro wives doing more work for money.

A few <u>disabled wives</u>, or wives in families in which someone else was disabled, worked fewer hours. But none of the other factors amounted to any-thing over the whole sample or for any of its major subgroups in Figure 4-1.

Motives and Incentives

Taking the end-group averages of Figure 4-1 as reflecting differences in hours produced by pressures or constraints, we can pool the individual differences from these averages, use them as our new dependent variable, and examine their relation to a much wider range of explanatory variables that reflect more positive motives and incentives.

The variables used in this second-stage analysis are given below in order of their importance if used to make an optimal single division of the whole sample:

    *Husband's attitude toward mothers' working (when children
      are in school)
    *Husband's attitude toward importance of luck for financial
      success
    *Housing status (home ownership)
     Husband's index of achievement orientation
    *Husband's index of planning and time horizon
     Husband's hourly earnings (and whether he worked in 1964)
    *Husband's index of social participation

68

Husband's index of caution and risk avoidance
Husband's index of closeness of family ties

---

*Number of rooms in home (large house to care for)
Who, other than husband, was disabled
Education of wife
Difference between education of husband and wife
Whether any child of the head of the family is currently in
    college
Husband's index of ambition and aspiration
Husband's index of mobility experience
Number of brothers and sisters of wife
*Median county income (standards and costs of living)
Number of people in family
Age of wife
Husband's index of receptivity to change
Whether husband was self-employed
Religious preference of husband
Race

Asterisked variables are those used in Figure 4-2. They explained an additional 11 per cent of the variance. The overall standard deviation is 684 hours. None of the variables below the line could explain as much as 0.5 per cent of the total sum of squares by a single division of the whole sample.

The distribution of the differences contains a few relatively large numbers (is skewed) and hence a number of very small groups of fewer than 25 cases were isolated. Such small groups have been excluded from Figure 4-2, except in three places where later divisions were important and the smaller group contained ten cases or more.

The most important single factor at this stage affecting the wife's hours of work turns out to be the husband's attitude toward mothers' of school-age children working at all. There may well be something circular about the husband's attitude; that is, it may reflect an adaptation to reality rather than an independent force shaping it. However, the relation between the husband's attitude toward mothers' working when the children are all in school was strongly related both to whether the wife worked and to the hours she worked, even after taking account of the family situation.

69

FIGURE 4-2

HOURS OF WORK FOR MONEY IN 1964 BY WIVES: ANALYSIS OF DIFFERENCES
FROM END-GROUP AVERAGES OF FIGURE 4-1
(For all 672 wives who worked between 121 and 3000 hours for money in 1964)

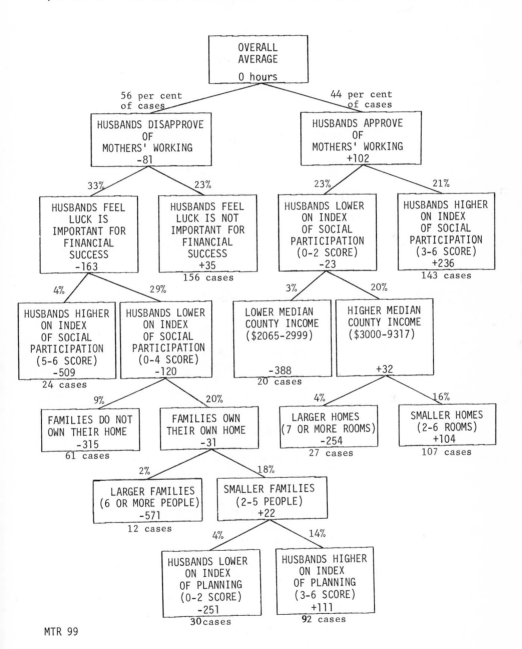

MTR 99

Our data indicate that husbands who disapprove are more likely to be non-fundamentalist Protestants, white, forty-five or older, with small families (one child or none at home), self-employed, and to have low hourly earnings or to not even be working at all. It must be remembered, however, that in dividing the sample in Figure 4-2, none of these variables was powerful enough to compete with husband's disapproval of mothers' working.

Why should the wife work more hours if her husband feels that luck is not important to getting ahead in this world? The alternative to luck in most people's mind is hard work and enterprise, and Professor Atkinson's model of the impact of achievement orientation on behavior suggests that that motive leads to action only when there is a high subjective probability that the action will lead toward some goal.[3] If most husbands in our culture are already achievement-oriented, then less belief in luck (and more trust in the efficacy of hard work) could lead to more work by the husband, and also by the wife.

Figure 4-3 shows in more detail (than Figure 4-2) that the husband's score on the index of social participation affects the wife's hours of work for money in different ways according to the husband's attitude toward mothers' working. If the husband thinks that mothers should not work, then social participation seems to compete with the wife's work--the more social participation, the fewer hours the wife works. A reasonable interpretation of this is that husbands who object to mothers' working also have high standards for housework and think the wife should be at home a goodly amount of time. This would put real constraints on her ability to be active both

---

[3] John Atkinson, "Motivational Determinants of Risk-taking Behavior," Psychological Review, 64 (November 1957), 359-372.

FIGURE 4-3

HOURS OF WORK FOR MONEY BY WIVES: DIFFERENCES FROM END-GROUP
AVERAGES OF HUSBAND'S SCORE ON INDEX OF SOCIAL PARTICIPATION
(For 672 wives who worked between 121 and 3000 hours for money in 1964)

HOURS OF WORK FOR MONEY BY WIVES:
DIFFERENCES FROM END-GROUP AVERAGES OF FIGURE 4-1

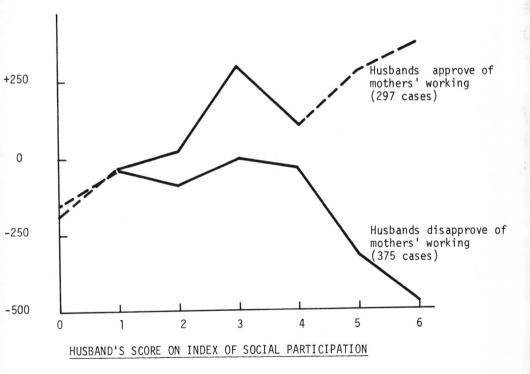

HUSBAND'S SCORE ON INDEX OF SOCIAL PARTICIPATION

— — — Less than 25 cases

MTR 99

socially and on a job. On the other hand, where the husband is more permissive and flexible about mothers' working, he may also be more flexible about her housework. In this case energetic wives could work for money and also be active socially.

For the group on the left in Figure 4-2 in which the husbands feel that luck is important for financial success and in which the families are not active socially, three alternative forces seem to reduce the wife's work hours: not owning a home, having a large family of six or more people, and the husband's having a low score on the index of planning. Stated another way, those who own their homes and have small families and plan ahead, have wives who work more.

For the group of families on the right, with approving husbands, and low social participation, either a large home or living in a low-income county seems to decrease the wife's work hours. To state it the other way, wives who live in high-income counties and have smaller homes to care for often work more hours away from home for money. It is not clear whether a high median income in the county has its effect through better employment opportunities for wives or higher community standards of living that increase her desire for money.

Four of the variables used in the second-stage analysis had been used in the first-stage analysis. They were reintroduced in case they might have a combined effect with the others in the second-stage list; but they showed no important joint effects: wife's education, wife's age, race, and whether anyone other than the husband was disabled.

The rest of the variables used in the second-stage analysis made little difference. Each of them, however, was introduced with some hypothesis

73

in mind. And since those which did not appear were important neither for the whole sample nor for any major subgroup thereof, we must conclude that, at least as measured, they did not matter.

Indeed, the list of variables which proved unimportant in explaining either whether the wife worked or how many hours she worked is very long, and includes such enticing variables as:

Race
Whether husband was disabled
Who, other than husband, was disabled (usually the wife)
Hours lost from work by husband in 1964 from illness or unemployment
Size of place (town) where family lives
Husband's index of caution and risk avoidance
Difference between education of husband and wife
Husband's index of closeness of family ties
Whether any child of the head of the family is currently in college
Husband's index of ambition and aspiration
Husband's index of mobility experience
Number of brothers and sisters of wife
Husband's index of receptivity to change

Summary

It must be concluded that having once taken account in the first-stage analysis of the main and fairly obvious pressures, such as preschool children, a husband who earns insufficient income, the presence of many children, or advanced age of the wife, the second-stage analysis focused on intermediate rather than basic forces: husband's attitudes, and the husband's index of social participation. It also focused on other indicators of pressures to work, such as owning a home or living in a high-income county, and on pressures not to work, such as having a large family or a large home to care for. Perhaps the intermediate attitudes took over as the transmitting mechanism of more basic motives. This may have been the fate of such variables as the difference in education between husband and wife and the ambition and aspiration index. On the other hand, the presumably basic index of achievement orientation did not even have an effect that was systematic in direction. Perhaps the husband's achievement orientation leads, not to more hours of work by either spouse, but to more energetic or resourceful use of that time.

CHAPTER 5

THE JOURNEY TO WORK

Overall Findings

Whatever one may say about the possibilities of reducing the time of wasteful traveling to work and back, we must count that time as part of a man's work time, and a necessary part of his contribution to output. If we could locate people's homes closer to their places of work, or somehow decrease the time they spend getting to work and back, we would reduce the hours needed to produce a given output; that is, we would increase people's efficiency.

The journey to work is not at all useless, if it is required in order to have the kind of privacy or space the family wants. Such privacy and space are often to be found at reasonable price only in the suburbs or in some location distant from where one works. A choice has to be made between living close to work to save commuting time and expense, or living in a more desirable neighborhood. Any reduction in the hours of traveling required to secure privacy, space, and a nice neighborhood, whether by increasing speeds or locating things better, would clearly be an economic gain.

The workers are not all trying to live as far out from the center of town as possible. Many of them work outside the very center. Furthermore, speeds of travel are much greater in the less densely populated areas. The net result, as we shall see, is that it is those living closest to the

centers of the largest cities who must spend the most time getting to work
and back. Their travel is slower and they do not live that much closer to
where they work.

We have not included commuting time in the hours of work for money,
nor used it in calculating average hourly earnings, partly because of tradition and partly because work hours on the job and dollars earned per hour on
the job are themselves important concepts to measure and study.

The distribution among families of the number of hours so spent getting to work and back is affected by the fact that some families have working
wives who also journey to work and back. The hours spent in 1964 by husbands
and wives getting to work and back were distributed as follows for families
whose heads were in the labor force at the time of the interview.

Hours spent going to work and back by heads of families and wives	Per cent of cases (for families where head of family was in the labor force in early 1965)
None	2
1-40	7
41-120	23
121-240	31
241-1000	37
1001 or more	0
Total	100
Number of cases	1639

One hour per day, five days a week, for fifty weeks, would be 250
hours. Even with a full-time working wife, the total hours spent would not
exceed 500 for most families.

The journey to work is a function of both distance and speed. Big
cities have both more traffic congestion and perhaps better and faster public

transportation. Density of population does not necessarily mean that a man

lives closer to his work; it may merely slow him down in getting there.

Indeed, the most important single variable in accounting for differences in

the time spent on the journey to work, aside from having a working wife, is

the location of the family's residence relative to the center of the nearest

large city. And the effect is the reverse of common expectations: the far-

ther out from the center of a metropolitan area, the less time spent getting

to work and back. Table 5-1 shows the averages. One reason is that persons

closer to the center of large cities are more likely to use public transpor-

tation, which is much slower.[1]

The only other thing that has much effect on the time spent on the

journey to work is age. People under twenty-five have slightly lower average

hours of commuting, perhaps because they have had less chance to change resi-

dences or jobs. More important, people sixty-five or older reported less

than half as many hours as others, except for a few cases in which the wife

was working too. Presumably they were working fewer hours, and the total was

small because they went to work fewer times in a year, though they might well

also have been working at a place closer to home. Perhaps those with a con-

venient location were less likely to retire.[2]

---

[1]For evidence, see John Lansing, Residential Location and Urban Mobility: The Second Wave of Interviews (Ann Arbor: Survey Research Center, The
University of Michigan, 1966).
For an example of the common, but erroneous, assumption that those
farther out are paying for it in more travel time, see Bernard J. Frieden,
The Future of Old Neighborhoods (Cambridge: Massachusetts Institute of Tech-
nology Press, 1964), p. 64.

[2]A forthcoming study of the retirement decision by the Survey
Research Center will throw some light on this possibility.

TABLE 5-1

HOURS SPENT GETTING TO WORK AND BACK IN 1964 OF HEADS OF FAMILIES AND WIVES
DISTRIBUTED BY LOCATION OF RESIDENCE RELATIVE TO NEAREST LARGE CITY

(For all 1833 heads of families who worked for money in 1964,
and their wives)

Location of residence relative to nearest large city	Head of family only --no working wife		Head of family and working wife	
	Number of cases	Hours	Number of cases	Hours
Within central cities of the 12 largest metropolitan areas	167	243	73	387
Suburbs of the 12 largest metropolitan areas	182	202	94	312
Within central cities of other metropolitan areas (50,000 or more population)	177	139	129	291
Suburbs of other metropolitan areas	171	149	108	264
Areas adjacent to metropolitan areas	177	134	146	266
Outlying areas (areas not adjacent to metropolitan areas)	252	82	157	166

MTR 64,54

The most dramatic difference was among families without a working wife, who lived in adjacent or outlying areas or in suburban areas of one of the smaller standard metropolitan areas. Here, those under sixty-five averaged 129 hours a year in getting to work and back, and those sixty-five or older averaged 31 hours.

Annual hours are a product of the daily commuting time and the number of days worked per year, and, when they are calculated for husband and wife,

are also affected by whether the wife works. Table 5-2 shows, for heads and
wives, the distribution of hours per day spent getting to work and back.
There is clearly quite a range.

Table 5-3 shows that the head's daily journey to work is also related
to where he lives. A separate tabulation for the New York area in Table 5-3
shows it to be closely similar to the distribution for all twelve of the
largest metropolitan areas including New York.

There were only a few farmers in the sample, but seven-tenths of them
reported that it took them no time to get to work, since they lived right on
their own farms. In general, the skilled and semiskilled workers were the
most likely to report a really time-consuming journey to work.

TABLE 5-2

DAILY JOURNEY TO WORK OF HEADS OF FAMILIES AND WIVES
(For 1639 heads of families and 747 wives
working for money in early 1965)

Daily journey to work	Heads of families	Wives
None (lives where works)	9	9
1-22 minutes	24	35
23-38 minutes	19	17
39-52 minutes	11	12
53-75 minutes	20	15
76-119 minutes	6	5
120 minutes or more	8	4
Not ascertained	3	3
Total	100	100
Number of cases	1639	747

MTR 25, Decks 6 and 3

TABLE 5-3

DAILY JOURNEY TO WORK OF HEADS OF FAMILIES BY LOCATION OF RESIDENCE RELATIVE TO NEAREST LARGE CITY

(For heads of families working for money in early 1965)

Daily journey to work	New York-Northeastern New Jersey Consolidated area	Within 12 Largest metropolitan areas other than New York		Within other metropolitan areas		Outside metropolitan areas	
		Central cities	Suburbs	Central cities	Suburbs	Adjacent areas	Outlying areas
None (lives where works)	3	2	1	5	5	16	20
1-22 minutes	13	13	23	24	19	28	37
23-38 minutes	18	20	13	26	21	12	19
39-52 minutes	7	13	16	13	22	6	8
53-75 minutes	26	26	24	21	23	19	8
76-119 minutes	10	12	13	4	3	7	1
120 minutes or more	20	11	8	5	4	8	3
Not ascertained	3	3	2	2	3	4	4
Total	100	100	100	100	100	100	100
Number of cases	209	120	166	281	260	260	343
Median daily journey to work in minutes	43	53	50	35	41	27	17
Average daily journey to work in minutes	68	59	55	42	43	42	25

Location of residence relative to nearest large city

MTR 152

Multivariate Analysis: Journey to Work by Heads of Families and Wives

Even though hours getting to work and back are affected by whether the wife works, a multivariate analysis was made, since the search process would divide the sample first by whether there was a working wife and allow further analysis of the two groups.

The variables used in the programmed search are listed below in order of their importance if used to make a single division of the whole sample of families whose heads worked in 1964:

> *Whether family includes a working wife
> *Location of residence relative to nearest large city
> Size of place (town) where family lives
> *Age of head of family
> Region of country
> Race

> Housing status (home ownership)
> Education of head of family

Asterisked variables are those used in Figure 5-1. They explained 17 per cent of the variance. The overall standard deviation is 185 hours. None of the variables below the line could explain as much as 0.5 per cent of the total sum of squares by a single division of the whole sample.

Size of place and location of residence relative to nearest large city measure nearly the same thing, each of them containing a classification for the rural areas and one for the central cities of the twelve largest metropolitan areas. Hence, once we had taken account of the more powerful of the two variables, location of residence relative to nearest large city, the second variable, size of place, became unimportant. Some of the same inter-correlation is true of region and race, and of race and housing status. The results are given in Figure 5-1.

FIGURE 5-1

HOURS SPENT GETTING TO WORK AND BACK IN 1964 OF HEADS OF FAMILIES AND WIVES
(For all 1833 heads of families who worked for money in 1964)

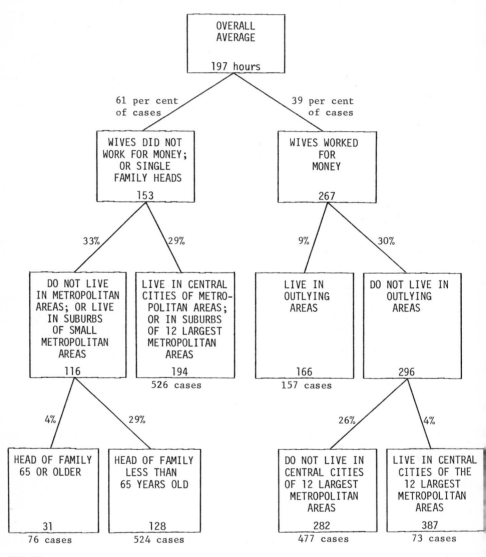

MTR 54

The original hypothesis about housing status was that homeowners might be reluctant to move when their place of employment changed, and hence would travel farther to work. However, in practice it was those who neither owned nor rented, many of whom were older, who had the lowest journey to work time. (There were very few such people, however.)

It was also felt that highly educated people would have fewer choices of place of work because of their specialization and might therefore travel farther, but in practice educational level made little difference, and what there was seemed to show that those in the middle education range traveled more.

Journey to Work by Heads of Families Only

Finally, a multivariate analysis on the time spent by family heads alone (excluding wives) on their journey to work was made. The same variables used in the previous analysis were used, but hours worked for money by family heads were substituted for whether the wife worked.

Figure 5-2 shows the result. People living farther out spent less time getting to work and back, and older people spent less time because they also take fewer journeys, as mentioned before. Figure 5-2 also indicates that those with less than full-time jobs spent the least hours on their journey to work.

The variables used in the multivariate analysis are listed below in order of their importance if used to make a single division of the whole sample of family heads who worked in 1964:

    *Location of residence relative to nearest large city
    *Hours of work for money by head of family in 1964
    Size of place (town) where family lives

84

FIGURE 5-2

HOURS SPENT GETTING TO WORK AND BACK IN 1964 OF HEADS OF FAMILIES
(For all 1833 heads of families who worked for money in 1964)

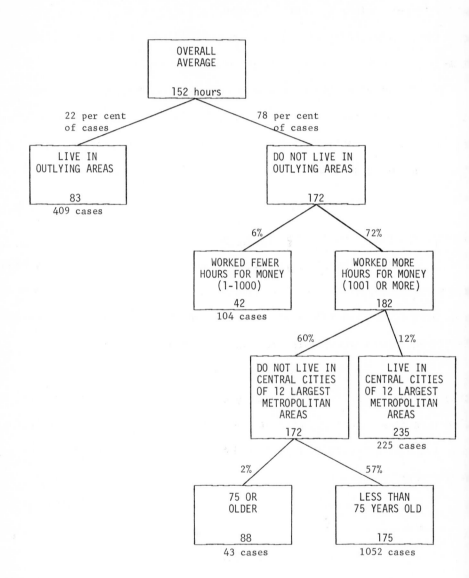

MTR 208

*Age of head of family
Region of country
Housing status (home ownership)
Sex of head of family

Education of head of family
Race

Asterisked variables are those used in Figure 5-2. They explained 12 per cent of the variance. The overall standard deviation is 153 hours. None of the variables below the line could explain as much as 0.5 per cent of the total sum of squares by a single division of the whole sample.

Summary

The strongest positive finding about the time people spend in getting to work and back is that it remains a clear cost of the large urban agglomeration. The larger the concentration of people, and the closer to its center the family lives, the more time they must spend just getting to work and back. The chances are that other journeys take longer too. Other advantages of the city presumably offset this wasteful absorption of time.

CHAPTER 6

OTHER EARNERS IN FAMILIES

A family may well contain earners other than the head of the family

and his wife. The sizes of families, and the alacrity with which young peo-

ple leave home as soon as they can earn enough to support themselves, vary in

different countries and at different times. Economic adversity or housing

shortages can encourage the formation of compound families even in the face

of a preponderant dislike, at least in this country, of having aged parents

or grown children living with their relatives.[1]

Minor children can earn money, of course, and survey data may well

underestimate the amounts involved. Of all the families sampled in the United

States, however, only a relatively small proportion reported any extensive

earnings from work by anyone other than the head and his wife. By converting

these earnings into estimated hours, we get the following distribution[2]:

---

[1]For an analysis of the economic impact of living with relatives and
of attitudes toward it, see James Morgan, Martin David, Wilbur Cohen, and Harvey Brazer, Income and Welfare in the United States (New York: McGraw-Hill
Book Company, Inc., 1962), Chapter 14, pp. 158-178.

[2]Hours for family members other than the head and his wife were estimated from their reported earned incomes by assuming that on the average
their hourly earnings were $1.25, and restricting each member to a maximum of
2000 hours.

Hours of work for money by family members other than head and wife	Per cent of cases
None	81
1-40	1
41-120	2
121-240	2
241-1000	5
1001-2000	7
2001-3000	1
3001 or more hours	1
Total	100
Number of cases	2214

Most commonly, extra wage-earners in a family are either children still living at home, or parents of the head of the family or his wife; but grown children are somewhat more likely to work than aged parents. Hence, the total hours of work for money by extra earners are greatest when the family head is middle-aged, and can have either children or parents or both living with him. And they are least when the family head is young and is likely, if he provides housing for any relatives, to provide it for parents. The head of a family is usually defined as the major earner, so that if a fifty-five year old father and a thirty year old son are living together, the father is more likely to be considered the head of the family than the son.

Table 6-1 shows the average hours of work for money by extra earners according to the head's age. The averages are dominated, of course, by the proportion of families with no extra earners at all, being an average of many zeroes and a few substantial contributions. The 417 families in the sample having extra earners reported an average of 1230 hours per family worked by these people.

Even casual accounts of other cultures and other periods in our own

TABLE 6-1

HOURS OF WORK FOR MONEY IN 1964 BY FAMILY MEMBERS
OTHER THAN THE HEAD OF THE FAMILY AND WIFE
BY AGE OF HEAD OF FAMILY

(For all 2214 families)

Age of head of family	Number of cases	Per cent of cases with extra earners	Hours of work for money (averages include zero cases)
Under 25	130	3	67
25-34	360	3	34
35-44	445	22	144
45-54	476	36	473
55-64	387	18	308
65-74	277	10	198
75 or older	139	12	210
All cases	2214	19	232

MTR 135

history make it clear that the typical family in the United States is about
as close to a purely nuclear family as one finds. The sense of family obli-
gation, as reflected either in providing homes for needy relatives or in
interfamily aid is not extensive, and growing demands for more extensive welfare programs imply a continued shrinkage of responsibility for relatives.
The stronger family responsibilities in other cultures raise questions about
the disincentive effects on those whose main gain from added work and accumulation may be added responsibilities.

The economic contribution of extra earners is a somewhat smaller fraction of the total than their hours, since they tend to be younger or older and to earn less per hour. This was reflected in our assumption that they worked an hour for every $1.25 they earned. Finally, their presence, even in the small proportions of the present-day United States, affects estimates of income distribution and income inequality. These distortions can be minimized either by separating families into nuclear family units (married couples and their children, single adults), or by relating income to a standard of needs.[3] Such calculations are crucial in comparing different countries or different time periods, where the amounts of "doubling-up" vary greatly. Even in the United States dividing families into nuclear units, and dividing joint incomes and estimating transfers such as free rent, will increase estimates of inequality by one-sixth, a substantial change in such a stable measure.[4]

The amount of hidden poverty which could be uncovered by undoubling families in other countries is almost certainly much larger than in the United States. It must be remembered, however, that where the cultural sense of extended family responsibility is strong, the nuclear definition of poverty may be inappropriate.

There remains one final component of the family's hours of work for money--hours they would like to have worked but were prevented by illness or unemployment--to which we now turn.

---

[3]Morgan et al., Chapter 20.

[4]Ibid., p. 315.

CHAPTER 7

UNEMPLOYMENT AND ILLNESS--"UNWANTED LEISURE"

In much of our analysis of work we have purposely excluded those subject to the constraints of severe illness or unemployment, or have removed the
effects of these constraints early in the analysis so that more positive motivations could show through. But any analysis, including any interpretation of
the distribution of income, must account for the difference between desired
and undesired "leisure."

Morgan et al. concluded, after extensive study, that the interpretation of income distributions was clouded by the fact that families with higher
incomes were working more hours--which meant that data on income exaggerated
how much better off they were and hence the inequality of real welfare. And
matters are complicated still further by the fact that some people with low
incomes who seemed to have more leisure were not enjoying that leisure: they
called it unemployment, and hence their having more free time did not really
make them better off than high-income families. Since low-income people commonly say they want more work than they have, and also report more illness and
unemployment, it seems likely that, at least at the bottom of the income scale
inequality is underestimated by looking only at incomes.

We have several measures of the extent to which people are working
less than they would like:

91

Historical

"Have you ever been out of a job or on strike for two months or more at one time? When was the last time that happened?"

"Have you ever had a major illness that laid you up for a month or more? When was that?"

"Do you sometimes have overtime work, or short work weeks?"

Recent

"How many weeks were there last year when you weren't working because of illness or unemployment?"

Attitudinal

"Some people would like to work more hours a week if they could be paid for it. Others would prefer to work fewer hours a week even if they earned less. How do you feel about this?"

One head of family in ten had been out of work or on strike for two months or more at a time at some time within the last five years, and nearly one in six had been laid up sick for a month or more within the last five years. Among the family heads under thirty-five who did not graduate from high school, two-fifths reported such extensive unemployment within the last ten years. The combination of low education and no seniority or experience was apparently quite devastating.

Although these extreme situations affect only a small minority, particularly in any one year, overtime or short work weeks are not rare. Among those currently working, nearly two-thirds said they sometimes had overtime work or short work weeks. As mentioned at the outset, the "standard" forty-hour week is apparently the exception rather than the rule when it comes to actual work hours.

A fifth of the heads of families reported losing some work time during

1964 because of illness or unemployment (a fourth of those who worked). Some
7 per cent of those who worked reported losing more than a month (four weeks)
through illness and unemployment.

But loss of work through illness or unemployment becomes an inadequate
measure of unwanted leisure when people are working overtime, have second jobs
and the like. Hence it is useful and instructive to ask people directly
whether they wanted more work than they had. The two measures overlap imper-
fectly, of course, since some who were ill would not say they wanted more work
and many who were neither ill nor unemployed wanted more work.

At any rate, people were asked whether they would like more work at
more pay, or fewer hours at less pay (nearly everyone would like less work for
the same pay, presumably). The detailed answers are given in Appendix C; here
we can say that over a third of those who worked at all (35 per cent) said
they would like more work, and only 13 per cent said they would like less work
even at less pay.

Of course, it was those in the blue-collar and clerical and sales
occupations who were most likely to say they wanted more work (Table 7-1).
Formal education distinguishes them even more clearly. Table 7-2 shows the
effect of education within age groups since younger people also usually prefer
to work more hours. The fraction of people who prefer to work more is lower
for those with more education. Better-educated people were more likely to
report that they would prefer to work fewer hours even at lower wages. This
was especially true among young people with at least some college training (or
more). Does this mean that there is a new generation of educated young people
with high incomes who prefer more leisure? Our data do not permit us to veri-
fy such a dynamic assertion; only time and further testing could give us the
answer.

93

TABLE 7-1

WHETHER HEAD OF FAMILY WOULD PREFER TO WORK MORE OR FEWER HOURS BY
OCCUPATION OF HEAD OF FAMILY
(For all 1639 heads of families who were working in early 1965)

WHETHER WOULD PREFER TO WORK MORE OR FEWER HOURS

OCCUPATION	Prefer more work more pay	Satisfied with present situation or don't know	Prefer less work less pay	Total	Number of cases
Professional and technical	25	62	13	100	218
Managers and officials	14	68	18	100	140
Self-employed businessmen	24	52	24	100	159
Clerical and sales workers	35	57	8	100	211
Skilled workers	38	49	13	100	310
Semi-skilled workers	52	38	10	100	270
Unskilled laborers and service workers	43	45	12	100	186
Farmers	27	59	15	100	95
Miscellaneous groups	50	40	10	100	50
ALL OCCUPATIONS	35	52	13	100	1639

MTR 73

94

TABLE 7-2

WHETHER HEAD OF FAMILY WOULD PREFER TO WORK MORE OR FEWER HOURS BY
AGE AND EDUCATION OF HEAD OF FAMILY
(For all 1639 heads of families who were working in early 1965)

WHETHER WOULD PREFER TO WORK MORE OR FEWER HOURS

AGE AND EDUCATION	Prefer more work more pay	Satisfied with present situation or don't know	Prefer less work less pay	Total	Number of cases
Less than 35 years old					
0 - 11 grades	62	31	7	100	112
12 grades or more but no college	56	38	6	100	174
Some college	38	34	29	100	140
35 - 54 years old					
0 - 11 grades	40	48	12	100	348
12 grades or more but no college	31	55	15	100	275
Some college	26	59	15	100	217
55 or older					
0 - 11 grades	23	60	18	100	235
12 grades or more but no college	18	61	22	100	64
Some college	13	68	20	100	71
ALL AGES AND EDUCATION LEVELS	35	52	13	100	1639

Hand tabulation

Actual hours of work do not measure the supply of effort that would be
available if people were not restrained by illness or unemployment, any more
than the actual work output approximates the potential output. In this chapter we limit ourselves to an analysis of unwanted leisure, without attempting
to separate illness from unemployment, even though the remedies necessary to
remove the constraints on the individual are different. One reason is that
it is not always easy to separate the two. Another is that there are extensive data on unemployment and more recently on morbidity, but little attention
to their combined effect, even though they tend to affect the same groups in
the population.

The hours of illness or unemployment reported for family heads, for
wives, and for both combined are given in Table 7-3.

TABLE 7-3

HOURS LOST FROM WORK IN 1964 BY HEADS OF FAMILIES,
WIVES, AND HEADS OF FAMILIES AND WIVES COMBINED
FROM ILLNESS OR UNEMPLOYMENT

(For all 2214 families)

Hours lost from work in 1964 from illness or unemployment	Per cent of cases for:		
	Heads of families	Wives	Heads of families and wives combined
None	78	93	74
1-40	2	1	2
41-120	5	2	5
121-240	4	1	4
241-1000	9	2	10
1001-2000	2	1	4
2001 or more	*	*	1
Total	100	100	100
Number of cases	2214	2214	2214

*Less than 0.5 per cent.

The actual questions were:

"How many weeks were there last year when you weren't working because of illness or unemployment? On the average, about how many hours a week did you work when you were working?"

We can summarize people's experience by treating the bracket code of Table 7-3 as a number--which produces a kind of crude logarithmic transformation so that averages will be more stable. Excluding those who did not work at all in 1964 and omitting eight cases where the bracket code is greater than five, the dramatic association between lack of formal education and unwanted leisure is shown in Figure 7-1. This is not just a spurious association resulting from the fact that most of the uneducated are older people. The overall age effect is shown in Figure 7-2. But Table 7-4 shows that illness and unemployment have their greatest impact on uneducated people regardless of their age, while the youngest family heads suffered the most from their lack of education.

A multivariate analysis was run with this same group and with the index as the dependent variable. It showed no powerful effects beyond those of education and age, except perhaps for race: nonwhites had an average index of 1.31, against 0.77 for whites, after allowing for education and age effects.

Reports of illness and unemployment may exaggerate the extent to which better health and more opportunities would increase people's productive output but it seems clear that there is a substantial reservoir of potential work, first in people's desire for more work, even if they are fully employed by usual standards, and second in the possible further reduction of illness and unemployment.

FIGURE 7-1

HOURS LOST FROM WORK IN 1964 BY HEADS OF FAMILIES FROM ILLNESS
AND UNEMPLOYMENT, BY EDUCATION OF HEAD OF FAMILY
(For 1824 heads of families who worked for money in 1964, for whom education was
ascertained, but excluding those with 2001 hours of unemployment or more)

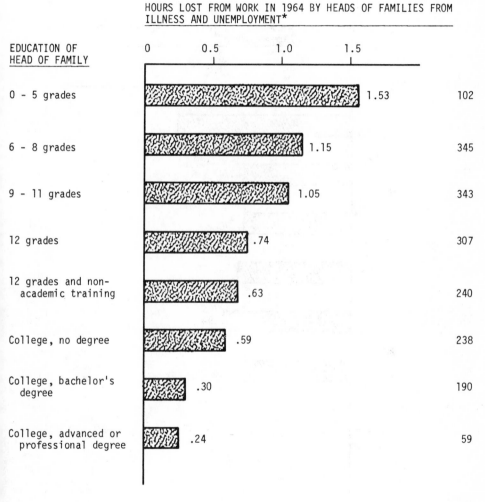

MTR 148

*The above is an index of hours where 1 means 1 - 40 hours, 2 means 41 - 120 hours,
3 means 121 - 240 hours, 4 means 241 - 1000 hours, and 5 means 1001 - 2000 hours.

FIGURE 7-2

HOURS LOST FROM WORK IN 1964 BY HEADS OF FAMILIES FROM
ILLNESS AND UNEMPLOYMENT BY AGE OF HEAD OF FAMILY
(For 1826 heads of families who worked for money in 1964, but excluding
those with 2001 hours of unemployment or more)

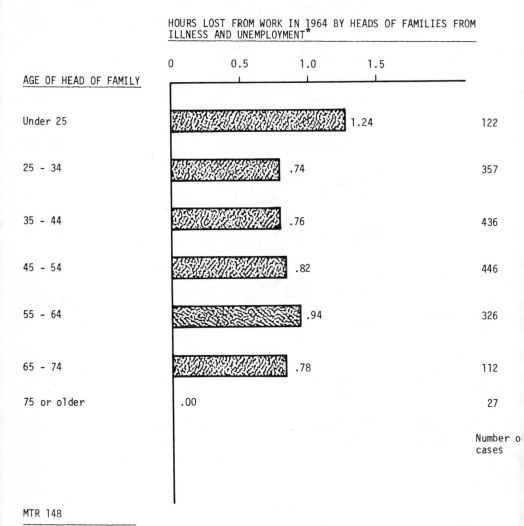

HOURS LOST FROM WORK IN 1964 BY HEADS OF FAMILIES FROM
ILLNESS AND UNEMPLOYMENT*

AGE OF HEAD OF FAMILY		Number of cases
Under 25	1.24	122
25 - 34	.74	357
35 - 44	.76	436
45 - 54	.82	446
55 - 64	.94	326
65 - 74	.78	112
75 or older	.00	27

MTR 148

*The above is an index of hours where 1 means 1 - 40 hours, 2 means 41 - 120 hours,
3 means 121 - 240 hours, 4 means 241 - 1000 hours, and 5 means 1001 - 2000 hours.

99

TABLE 7-4

HOURS LOST FROM WORK IN 1964 BY HEADS OF FAMILIES FROM ILLNESS OR UNEMPLOYMENT
BY AGE AND EDUCATION OF HEAD OF FAMILY
(For all 1833 heads of families who worked for money in 1964)

HOURS LOST IN 1964 FROM ILLNESS OR UNEMPLOYMENT

AGE AND EDUCATION	None	1-120	121 or more	Total	Number of cases
Less than 35 years old					
0 - 11 grades	51	13	36	100	126
12 grades or more but no college	72	11	16	100	184
Some college	89	4	7	100	169
35 - 54 years old					
0 - 11 grades	66	9	25	100	372
12 grades or more but no college	81	7	12	100	287
Some college	82	6	12	100	226
55 or older					
0 - 11 grades	69	9	22	100	305
12 grades or more but no college	74	6	21	100	72
Some college	87	5	8	100	92
ALL AGES AND EDUCATION LEVELS	74	8	18	100	1833

MTR 205

Other Research

The impact of unemployment and illness, unlike some of the other subjects treated in this book, has received so much attention that the sheer volume of work makes unwise any attempt to summarize it or to provide a bibliography. We can say, however, that most of it has been focused on precise measurement of the incidence of unemployment or illness and of its relation to demographic factors like age, sex, race, and area of the country. The search for precision in measuring unemployment has led to a tendency to define away everything except the clearest cases, and to focus on "last week." Our data on the extent of the desire for more work and on the great variability in work hours, which are supplemented in other Survey Research Center studies by data on variability over time, indicate that formal unemployment is only the visible part of a large iceberg.[1]

Morbidity data come from the National Health Survey and from various data on hospital utilization. However, since there are still economic constraints on the use of medical facilities, the best data on the need for hospital care by age and sex may well be the data from Saskatchewan, Canada, where a complete poll-tax-financed hospitalization scheme removes that economic barrier.[2]

A few studies of how hard the unemployed look for work, and of the effect of exhaustion of unemployment compensation exist, but will not be discussed here.

---

[1] See Richard Kosobud and James Morgan, eds., Consumer Behavior over Two and Three Years, Monograph 36 (Ann Arbor: Survey Research Center, University of Michigan, 1964); also a forthcoming report of a panel study on the impact of the tax cut of 1964.

[2] See, for instance, Annual Report of the Saskatchewan Hospital Service Plan (Saskatoon: Department of Public Health, Province of Saskatchewan, 1965), pp. 16-17.

II: UNPAID PRODUCTIVE WORK

American people spend as much time on unpaid productive activities as they do on work for pay. In Part I we examined families' work for pay; in this section we offer a general view of families' productive activities for no pay. These latter include those which either save the family money or increase the value of its assets, including nontangible ones such as human capital.

Chapter 8 analyzes our findings on regular housework. Chapter 9 deals with other unpaid work, including time spent on doing volunteer work and getting further education. And Chapter 10 deals with the other side of the family's productive-time balance sheets--work done _for_ our sample families by others, whether received free or paid for. Chapter 10 concludes with a survey of the literature on unpaid productive activity.

CHAPTER 8

REGULAR HOUSEWORK[1]

General Findings

American women--especially the married ones with children--tend to do most of the housework.[2] For wives in general, it is a full-time job. They reported spending an average of 40 hours per week doing housework during 1964. And their aggregate hours accounted for 70 per cent of housework done by all family members. If we add their work for money, we find that their aggregate productive hours exceeded the productive hours reported by male heads of families. Figure 8-1 shows the relative time contribution of the various

---

[1]Research related to unpaid work in general is cited at the end of Chapter 10.

[2]In this study, housework includes meal preparation, regular cleaning, child care, straightening up, and other time spent working around the house. The main problems involved in ascertaining hours of regular housework are those of classification and measurement. For example, some activities, like cleaning and meal preparation, can be done in the same time period. For others, like child care, it is difficult to report exactly the time spent on them. Furthermore, time devoted to housework activities is not the same for all days or seasons.

Our objective is not the measurement of efficiency or time budgeting but the measurement of the aggregate hours of input devoted to all such activities. And, we did not ask about hours spent on individual activities, but left to each respondent the problem of summarizing for us the allocation of his own time. We simply asked the following question:

"We'd like to know about how much of your (WIFE) time is spent on work around the house, such as preparing meals, cleaning, and straightening up. On the average about how much of your (WIFE) time is spent working around the house?"

Assuming that a day has a maximum of 16 working hours, we were able to estimate hours of housework even when the individual stated, "20 per cent of my time." Details on editing and coding procedures are given in Appendix B.

FIGURE 8-1

AGGREGATE HOURS OF REGULAR HOUSEWORK AND WORK FOR MONEY DONE
BY VARIOUS FAMILY MEMBERS IN 1964
(Aggregates based on all 2214 families)

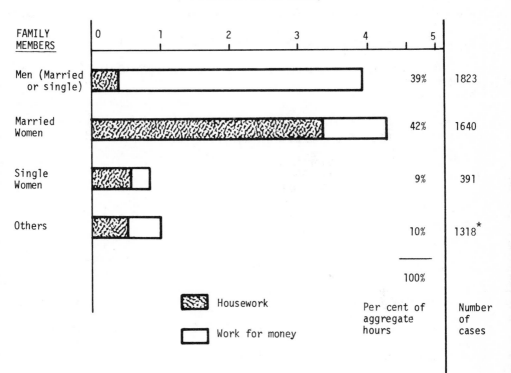

HOURS OF HOUSEWORK AND WORK FOR MONEY DONE IN 1964
(in millions of hours)

MTR's 46,92,145

*This refers to the number of families having members in addition to family
heads (and wives).

members of the family to housework and work for money. In this chapter, however, we analyze only the time spent by heads of families and wives on their
housework activities.

In average hours of regular housework, husbands' contributions were
only 4 hours per week. Our study showed that single women with families spent
6 hours per week less on regular housework than married women did. Finally,
single women who lived alone spent, on the average, only 20 hours per week on
housework; this was more than double the amount done by single men.

The distribution of hours of housework for heads of families and wives
is as follows:

Hours of regular housework done in 1964 by heads of families and wives	Per cent of cases
Fewer than 241	5
241-1000	17
1001-2000	37
2001-3000	26
3001-4500	11
4501 or more	4
Total	100
Number of cases	2214

The differences in average hours of housework between groups of different sex and marital status are shown clearly in Figure 8-2. In families
containing members other than the head of the family and his wife, the children and any other adult members helped around the house. Their average
contribution amounted to 7 hours per week. However, a larger family means
more people and usually more living space. These two factors create their
own pressures on wives' work efforts. Families living in larger homes tended
to spend more time on housework. Whereas it took about 9 hours per week to
care for a one-room place, it took more than 35 hours for a four- or five-room
place. Figure 8-3 shows that more rooms made for more hours of housework, but
not in proportion to the number of rooms. This might suggest that there are

FIGURE 8-2

HOURS OF REGULAR HOUSEWORK DONE BY VARIOUS FAMILY MEMBERS IN 1964
(For all 2214 families)

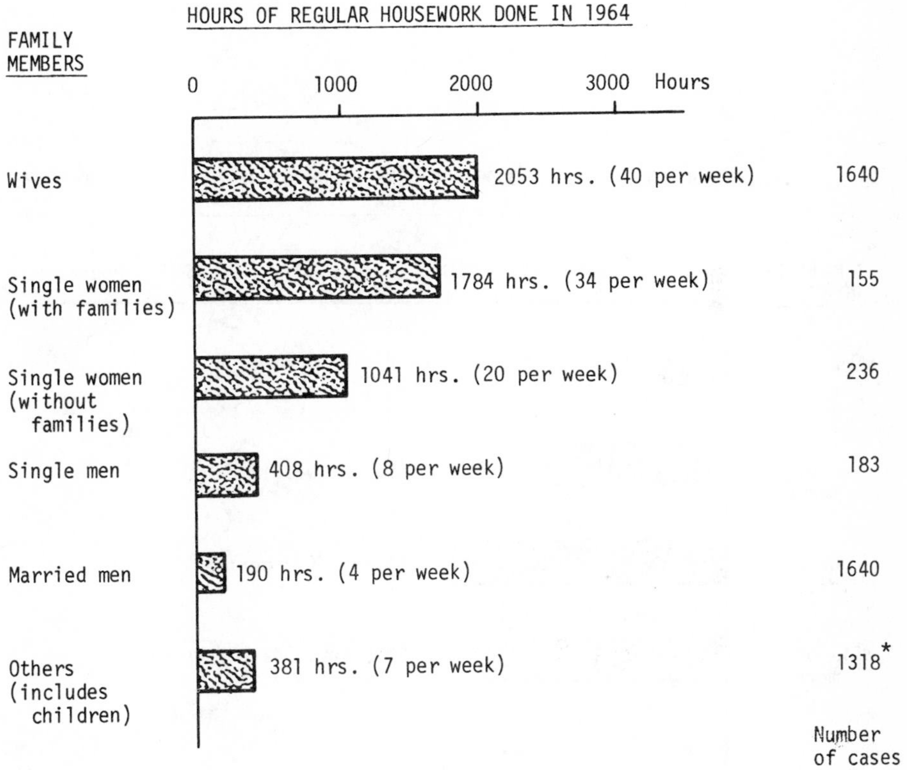

HOURS OF REGULAR HOUSEWORK DONE IN 1964

FAMILY
MEMBERS

	0	1000	2000	3000 Hours	

Wives — 2053 hrs. (40 per week) — 1640

Single women (with families) — 1784 hrs. (34 per week) — 155

Single women (without families) — 1041 hrs. (20 per week) — 236

Single men — 408 hrs. (8 per week) — 183

Married men — 190 hrs. (4 per week) — 1640

Others (includes children) — 381 hrs. (7 per week) — 1318*

Number of cases

*This refers to the number of families having members in addition to heads (and wives).

MTR's 92,133,135,137,138

FIGURE 8-3

HOURS OF REGULAR HOUSEWORK DONE BY HEADS OF FAMILIES AND WIVES
IN 1964 BY NUMBER OF ROOMS IN HOUSE
(For all 2210 families where heads of families and wives did between,
0 and 6500 hours of regular housework in 1964)

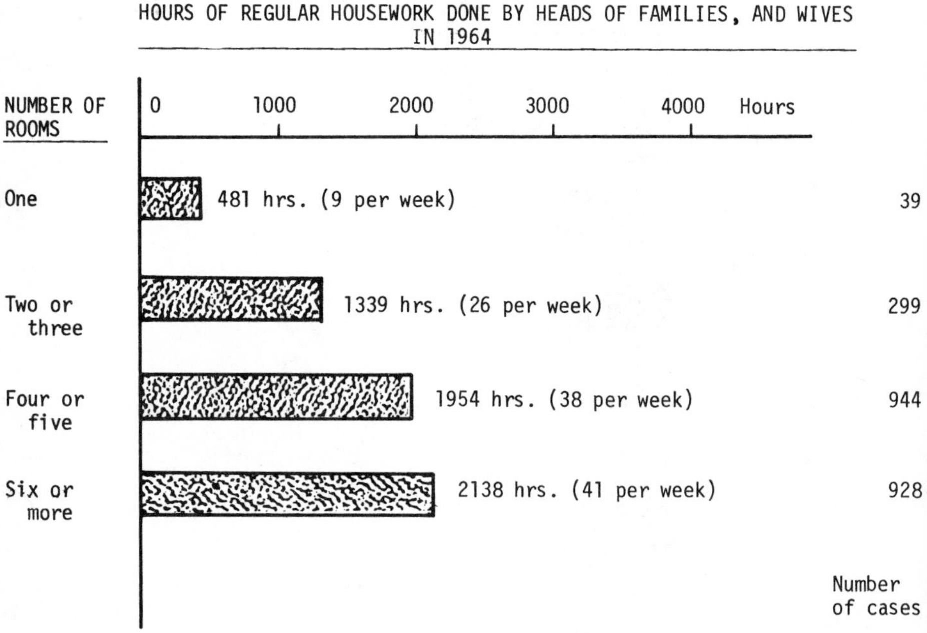

HOURS OF REGULAR HOUSEWORK DONE BY HEADS OF FAMILIES, AND WIVES
IN 1964

NUMBER OF ROOMS	0	1000	2000	3000	4000	Hours	
One		481 hrs. (9 per week)					39
Two or three		1339 hrs. (26 per week)					299
Four or five		1954 hrs. (38 per week)					944
Six or more		2138 hrs. (41 per week)					928

Number
of cases

MTR 92

some economies in the amount of housework effort required for larger homes. On the other hand, the number of rooms and the number of people in the family were highly correlated so that a bigger house contains more people to care for.

Other pressures cause some people to do more housework--for example, the presence of very young children or disabled persons. We believe that any analysis of the motives affecting the choice between leisure and more housework should first consider such pressures and constraints. In what follows, we will consider mainly the pooled time spent by family heads and wives on their housework activities. This assumes that there is a family decision about housework standards, whoever does the work, and that contributions by other members to housework are of secondary importance to the main decision process. In other words, people other than family head and wife generally contribute very few hours of housework, and probably offset it by equivalent demands. The allocation of the rest of the housework between husband and wife presumably depends on a number of things, such as whether the wife works for money. Before looking at that, however, we analyze the total housework done by husband and wife.

Constraints and Pressures

What determines the amount of time family heads and wives together devote to regular housework? Figure 8-4 shows the results of a multivariate analysis.[3] Clearly, situational constraints and pressures dominated the situation. Single men do little housework, and families with preschool children do

---

[3]Figure 8-4 is a result of a systematic search process described in detail in Appendix E. As mentioned before, among all variables used, at each step of the analysis, only that variable which provides the most clearcut explanation of variation in hours of housework is selected and appears in the figure.

FIGURE 8-4

HOURS OF REGULAR HOUSEWORK DONE IN 1964 BY HEADS OF FAMILIES AND WIVES
(For all 2210 families who did between 0 and 6500 hours
of regular housework in 1964)

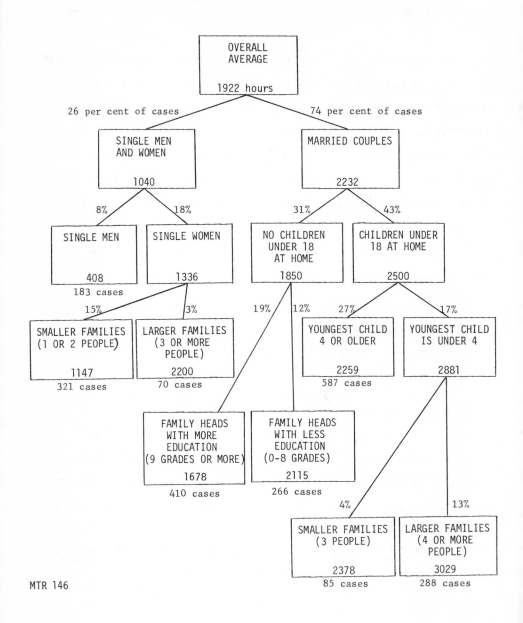

MTR 146

109

uch. The groups of Figure 8-4 accounted for 33 per cent of the total vari-
nce, which is a great deal in explaining individual differences.

The explanatory factors used in the search process of Figure 8-4 are
isted below in the order of their importance if used to make a single divi-
ion of the whole sample:

>   *Sex and marital status of head of family
>   *Number of people in family
>   *Age of youngest child under 18 living at home
>   Number of rooms in home
>   Number of automatic home appliances
>   Age of head of family
>   Hours of work for money in 1964 by all members of family
>   Type of structure in which family lives
>   Hours lost from work in 1964 by head of family and wife
>   from illness or unemployment
>   Size of place (town) where family lives
>   Whether it was difficult to hire outside help for work
>   around the house
>   *Education of head of family
>   Number of years lived in present home

>   Whether family could do some of the work for which they
>   hired help
>   Number of disabled persons in family
>   Whether county was a depressed area
>   Race

Asterisked variables are those used in Figure 8-4. They explained
33 per cent of the variance. The overall standard deviation is 1228
hours. None of the variables below the line could explain as much as
0.5 per cent of the total sum of squares by a single division of the
whole sample.

The theory behind these measures is clear: they are either pressures
 the families to do more housework, or constraints on their productive work
 general. The first three, as well as education of the head of the family
re used, and their effects will be discussed below. As mentioned before,
e fourth variable, number of rooms in the home, was highly correlated with
e number of people in the family and the age of the youngest child in the

family. Its overall effect on housework time diminished considerably after allowing for the effects of these two variables, and so it was never actually used.

Family Structure

Married and single people with many or young children present at home (especially preschool children) reported spending more hours on their regular housework. Figure 8-4 illustrates that married couples with at least one child under four reported doing 50 per cent more hours of housework than the overall average. Our data also indicate that single people having preschool children tend to do more housework than single people without preschool children. One reason, obviously, is that young children require more parental care and attention. Another explanation is that mothers with young children tend to stay at home rather than seek outside employment, and presence at home increases the hours they have for housework.[4]

Education

Figure 8-4 also shows that a married couple in which there are no young children and the husband has less than nine grades of education tends to spend more time doing regular housework. One possible reason for this finding is that husbands with low education are likely to marry women of about the same educational level or lower,[5] and the tendency of these wives to work for money is below the overall average.[6] As a result, they have more free time or

---

[4] See for example our findings in Chapters 3 and 4.

[5] In our sample, this was true of about 70 per cent of all couples.

[6] See Figure 3-2.

their hands which might make it easy to do more housework. Furthermore, the
family income is generally not high enough to encourage paying someone else to
do it. Another explanation is that wives with more education, who generally
have husbands with more education, both do their housework more efficiently,
and have more other activities to occupy their time, so that they compress
their housework into fewer hours.

But the education of family heads is also correlated with the age and
number of people in the family. For example, in Figure 8-4, for the 12 per
cent of all families consisting only of a husband with little education, a wife,
and no children under eighteen, we find that 80 per cent of the family heads
in that group were fifty-five or older; this is 25 per cent higher than in the
whole sample. Also, couples with young children are young themselves and
hence, have more education than the average.

Automatic Home Appliances

Figure 8-5 shows that, if we look at the whole sample, there is no
apparent tendency for the family with more automatic home appliances to spend
less time on housework activities.[7] However, there are two opposing forces
behind that general pattern. Most probably having an automatic washer or
clothes dryer saves housework time. But people buy such appliances while their
families are growing and their required housework is greatest.[8] Families who

---

[7]We shall see later that those with appliances do in fact do more
volunteer work. See Chapter 9.

[8]Some findings, based on restrictive assumptions about household dura-
ble-expenditure behavior, have shown that there is a priority pattern in the
demand for household durable goods. See, for example, F. G. Pyatt, Priority
Patterns and the Demand for Household Durable Goods (Cambridge: Cambridge University Press, 1964).
Our data show that if a family owns a single appliance, it is most

acquire small children and household appliances about the same time are not likely to find themselves spending less time on housework. Also, most of the mothers in this subgroup do not work, and to the extent that they define their housework standards in terms of time spent, their total work time would not be decreased by time-saving appliances.[9] Single people, on the other hand, have no such accumulated pressures. For them, the net time-saving feature of having a washing machine, clothes dryer, or dishwasher is quite apparent in Figure 8-5. Acquiring the first appliance is a time saver for families with young children but not for the single person, since for the latter it results in a new housework activity not otherwise done at home--washing, for example. It is also reasonably clear that some appliances save more time than others. It is doubtful that a dishwasher saves any time over hand washing and drying. A clothes dryer, on the other hand, saves a great deal of time, as well as reducing time constraints. A washing machine saves less time than it formerly did, since the alternative now is the neighborhood automatic laundry.

Age

Married couples do less housework as they get older since many elderly couples live by themselves in small homes. However, single people, especially those living alone, show a reversed age effect. Being alone at home might encourage "busy work" (Figure 8-6). Also most older one-person families are women, often widows left with large homes to care for.

---

likely to be a washing machine, the second most likely, a clothes dryer, and the third, an automatic dishwasher.

[9]Marie G. Gage, "The Work Load and Its Value for 50 Homemakers in Tompkins County, New York" (unpublished Ph.D. dissertation, Cornell University, 1960).

FIGURE 8-5

HOURS OF REGULAR HOUSEWORK DONE BY HEADS OF FAMILIES AND WIVES
IN 1964 BY NUMBER OF AUTOMATIC HOME APPLIANCES
(For all 2210 families where heads of families and wives did
between 0 and 6500 hours of regular housework in 1964)

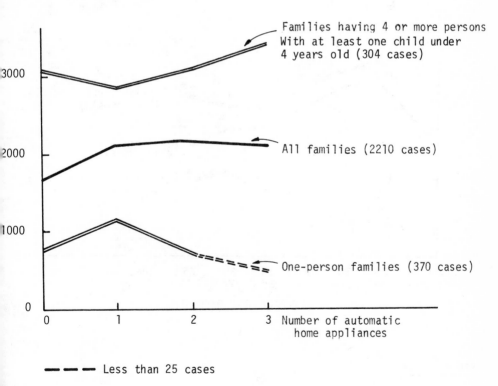

HOURS OF REGULAR HOUSEWORK

Families having 4 or more persons
With at least one child under
4 years old (304 cases)

All families (2210 cases)

One-person families (370 cases)

Number of automatic
home appliances

— — — Less than 25 cases

MTR 92

FIGURE 8-6

HOURS OF REGULAR HOUSEWORK OF HEADS OF FAMILIES AND WIVES IN 1964,
BY AGE OF HEAD OF FAMILY
(For all 2210 families who did between 0 and 6500 hours of regular
housework in 1964)

HOURS OF REGULAR HOUSEWORK

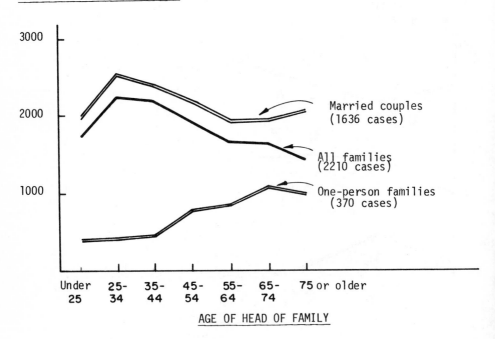

ours Worked for Money by the Family

    Time is clearly a constraint on how much people can do. A family has
o decide either to do more productive work or to have more leisure time. We
ight expect that people who work longer hours for money, would tend to spend
ess time on housework, probably either doing the housework more efficiently
r getting outside help, without reducing their leisure time. This is not al-
ays the case, however, since most housework is done by wives and not all of
he wives have outside employment.

    Nonworking mothers, especially those with children under eighteen,
end to do more housework as their husbands work more hours for money. Equal
articipation in increasing the real welfare of the family is an understanda-
le motive for nonworking wives, and would explain this finding. For families
ith working wives, on the other hand, spending more hours on work for money
eans spending fewer hours on housework, regardless of the number and ages of
he children. Families with working wives tend to reallocate their time be-
ween housework and work for money, without changing many of their leisure
abits, as Figure 8-7 shows. However, this trade-off between hours of outside
mployment and hours of housework done by families with working wives was not
owerful enough to show in the previous multivariate analysis of this chapter.
he results of that analysis were dominated by the powerful effects of the
asic constraints and pressures of family structure and other demographic
actors.

    In our next analysis step, however, hours of work for money will be
ntroduced once more, as an economic motive, to explain further differences in
ousework behavior after the effects of the basic constraints and pressures
re removed.

116

FIGURE 8-7

HOURS OF REGULAR HOUSEWORK DONE BY HEADS OF HEADS OF FAMILIES AND WIVES
IN 1964, BY HOURS OF WORK FOR MONEY BY ALL FAMILY MEMBERS
(For 1019 married couples with selected characteristics who did between
0 and 6500 hours of regular housework in 1964)

HOURS OF REGULAR HOUSEWORK

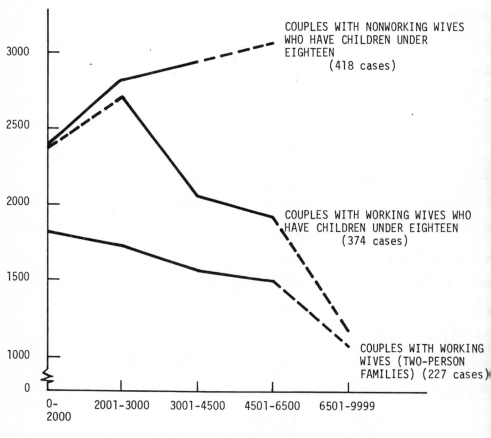

HOURS OF WORK FOR MONEY BY ALL FAMILY MEMBERS

— — — — Less than 25 cases

MTR 143

Other Constraints and Pressure

None of the remaining explanatory variables, listed earlier and used in the analysis, showed any important effects in explaining differences in hours of housework, either for the sample as a whole or for the subgroups of families shown in Figure 8-4. However, our data show that families who lived in apartments or trailers did 35 per cent less housework than families who lived in houses. Also, couples who had many weeks of illness or unemployment did less housework on the average. It is evident that, for the latter families, any apparent increase in their leisure time is merely involuntary.

Motives and Desires

We have already shown the most important combinations of the basic contraints and pressures. Our next step is to examine whether there is still any room for free choice so that motives and incentives might have additional ffects on families' housework behavior. This was done by taking as our ependent variable the unexplained pooled differences in housework hours pooled residuals from Figure 8-4), and analyzing them further.

Figure 8-8 shows the relation between the unexplained differences in ours of housework and the hours spent in working for money by all family memers. If working couples spent more time on their outside employment, because f higher wages or perhaps in order to acquire an acceptable level of income given their physical and institutional constraints), we should expect these ouples to hire outside help for their housework, or do their housework more fficiently, or do less other unpaid productive activities or have less eisure.[10] Figure 8-8 shows that this is indeed true. And it also shows again

---

[10]In some less affluent societies, people cannot afford to buy their
(continued on next page)

that where the wife does not work, or there is no wife, more work for money is associated with <u>more</u> time spent on housework. Hence, the findings of Figure 8-7 were not spurious, or really the result of differences in family size or age of children, since those forces had already been accounted for in calculating the residuals of Figure 8-8. Devoting less time to housework may mean doing it less well, doing it more efficiently, or paying someone else to do it. The effect on the family's standard of living will depend on which of the three is true. More efficient housework may make the family better off.[11] If someone else is paid to do some of the work, then some of the apparent benefit from working outside the home is offset by the costs of hiring someone to do some of the housework. Paying someone else to do it would produce only small effects from the substitution. At least some of the effect does result from this use of the money earned to pay others to do the housework.

Our analysis in Chapter 10 below will show that families with working wives actually do tend to have more outside help.[12] Nonworking wives, however, do <u>more</u> regular housework as their husbands work more hours for money. Economic variables do not help much in explaining further differences in hours of housework for the latter group. What is needed is more theory from family sociology, and some new explanatory variables.

Twenty-six variables were used in the full second-stage analysis to explain further differences in housework behavior. The dependent variable is

---

own time back. Working wives tend to give up their leisure time for their hours of working for money without reducing their time devoted to housework activities. This was the case reported in a Hungarian study of time use. See, Hungarian Central Statistical Office, The Twenty-four Hours of the Day (Budapest, 1965) (English version).

[11]If the gain in efficiency was a result of new investment in automatic household appliances, we might have to adjust for hours spent earning the income that financed those investments.

[12]Chapter 10, Figure 10-2.

FIGURE 8-8

HOURS OF REGULAR HOUSEWORK DONE BY HEADS OF FAMILIES AND WIVES IN 1964,
DIFFERENCES FROM END-GROUP AVERAGES OF FIGURE 8-1 BY HOURS OF WORK
FOR MONEY DONE BY ALL FAMILY MEMBERS
(For all 2210 families where heads of families and wives did between
0 and 6500 hours of regular housework in 1964)

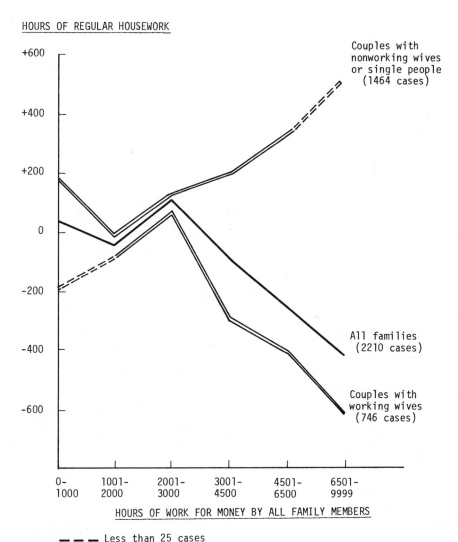

HOURS OF REGULAR HOUSEWORK

Couples with
nonworking wives
or single people
(1464 cases)

All families
(2210 cases)

Couples with
working wives
(746 cases)

HOURS OF WORK FOR MONEY BY ALL FAMILY MEMBERS

— — — Less than 25 cases

MTR 146

the pooled differences of the end-group averages of Figure 8-4. The results

are given in Figure 8-9.[13] These variables are listed below in order of thei

power to discriminate in a single division over the whole sample of pooled

residuals.[14]

*Whether wife worked for money
*Hours of work for money in 1964 by all members of family
*Number of people in family (represents presence of children
    or aged parents at home)
*Per cent of adults in county who completed high school
    (standards and costs of living)
*Region of country
 Index of caution and risk avoidance
 Education of head of family
 Attitude toward mothers' working

Number of calls required to secure interview
Age of youngest child under 18 living at home
Church attendance
Hourly earnings of head of family (alternative costs of
    housework)
Index of achievement orientation
*Religious preference
Whether head of family was self-employed
Number of disabled persons in family
Housing status (home ownership)
Index of mobility experience
Whether head of family grew up on a farm
*Age of head of family
Index of receptivity to change
Index of ambition and aspiration
Index of closeness of family ties
Sex and marital status of head of family

Asterisked variables are those used in Figure 8-9. They explaine
an additional 6 per cent of the variance. The overall standard devia
tion is 1008 hours. None of the variables below the line could expla
as much as 0.5 per cent of the total sum of squares by a single division of the whole sample.

---

[13]To allow for further interactions, where the effect of one variable
was relevant only for a subgroup of the population, some of the main explanatory variables used in the first analysis of Figure 8-4 were reintroduced int
the second stage.

[14]For further technical information about analyzing residuals, see
Appendix E.

121

FIGURE 8-9

HOURS OF REGULAR HOUSEWORK DONE IN 1964 BY HEADS OF FAMILIES AND WIVES:
ANALYSIS OF DIFFERENCES FROM END-GROUP AVERAGES OF FIGURE 8-4
(For all 2210 families who did between 0 and 6500 hours of regular housework
in 1964)

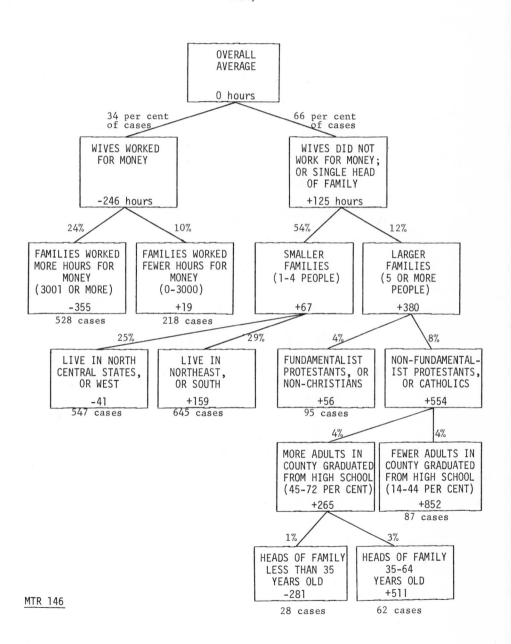

MTR 146

122

Variables Used in Figure 8-9

The first findings in Figure 8-9 had been anticipated. Families with working wives tended to do less housework, and the more hours the wives worked for money, the fewer hours they spent on housework.[15]

Size of family has already been accounted for as a constraint and pressure. However, the presence of many children at home may also have acted as a motive for mothers to do more around the house. In the group of single people and couples in which the wives did not work for money (66 per cent of the cases), those with larger families reported about 6 hours more housework per week than those families with fewer than five persons.

Although this latter group of small families included single as well as married people, the difference according to marital status was not so significant in this residual analysis as were the regional differences. Single people and small families with nonworking wives living in the Northeast or the South did about 4 hours more of housework per week (200 hours per year) than families of the same type living in the North Central states or the West.

One might speculate that people living in the West have modern and newer homes which require less housework, or that families living there have more interesting social or outdoor activities which motivate them to save on their housework time. Another line of reasoning might be that highly educated people are more efficient in doing their housework, and the data show that among families living in the West and North Central states there are twice as

---

[15]The wife's decision to work for money rather than at housework was left to the second stage, because it is clearly a family decision, not a situational constraint such as having small children who need attention. The family can be thought of as making a set of decisions about how much housework is required for its standards, whether the wife should work, and how much time should be saved by paying to have things done.

123

many people with at least some college education as in the South or Northeast.
Education was the second in power only to region in explaining differences in
housework time for the group of single people and small families with nonworking wives. Regional differences, however, invite interesting lines of inquiry
which we do not pursue. For example, our data show that almost the same
regional pattern illustrated in Figure 8-9 also persists for the regions where
wives grew up.

Figure 8-9 also shows that for the 12 per cent of families with five
or more members but no working wife, Catholics and non-fundamentalist Protestants did about 10 hours more housework per week than fundamentalist Protestants and non-Christians in that group. Among the Catholics and non-fundamentalist Protestants who say they do so much housework, there is a tendency to
do still more if they live in a county where the level of education is low, or
to do less housework if the head of the family is less than thirty-five years
old.

Other Explanatory Variables

Among all other explanatory variables used in the multivariate analysis, none of them really mattered much in explaining further differences in
housework done by American families.

Hourly earnings of the head of the family showed no significant effect
either for the sample as a whole or for any major subgroup. An increase in
hourly earnings means both an increase in the family's income and a change in
the relative price of work and leisure for all members of the family. The
decision about reallocation of time within the family is complex, and the outcome is difficult to predict. The data indicate, however, that when wives

work, an increase in husbands' hourly earnings results in somewhat less house-work. There is no clear conclusion about the effect of hourly earnings for the group made up of single people and families with nonworking wives.

We also find that cautious people according to our index do less house work than noncautious people. This might be because 16 per cent more of the wives of men classified as cautious have outside employment, as our data reveal.

As mentioned in Chapter 3, we found that more wives worked for money i their husbands approved of mothers' working. Our data show the opposite effect on hours of housework. If the head of the family approves of mothers' working, then that family does less housework.

CHAPTER 9

OTHER UNPAID PRODUCTIVE ACTIVITIES

Introduction

About nine out of every ten American families engage in unpaid productive activity other than regular housework. The average family spends about 7 hours per week, or 350 hours per year, at such work. Figure 9-1 shows the per cent of men and women who engage in it. The distribution of hours, for family heads and wives, is as follows:

Hours of unpaid work (other than regular housework) done in 1964 by heads of families and wives	Per cent of cases
None	7
1-40	14
41-120	18
121-240	20
241-1000	33
1001 or more	8
Total	100
Number of cases	2214

Some of these activities, usually called home production, are specialized work around the home, such as sewing, canning, gardening, and repairing.[1] On the average, American families spent 4 hours per week on

---

[1]Notice that our definition of home production includes services as well as the production of tangible results. Respondents were asked various questions in order to estimate their time spent on various activities. For details on questions asked and codes, see Appendix C.

FIGURE 9-1

PER CENT OF MEN AND WOMEN DOING UNPAID WORK IN 1964 OTHER THAN
REGULAR HOUSEWORK, BY TYPE OF WORK
(For all 2214 families)

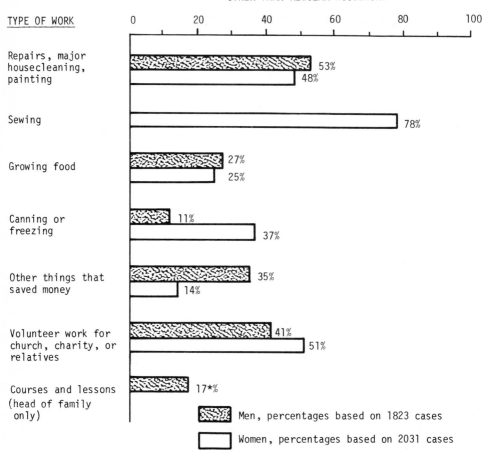

PER CENT OF MEN AND WOMEN DOING UNPAID WORK IN 1964
OTHER THAN REGULAR HOUSEWORK

* Includes 36 female family heads (2 per cent)

MTR 25

home production in 1964. Note that many families today are doing painting, repair work, and other "do-it-yourself" activities to save money. We also include volunteer work done by family heads and wives for relatives, and volunteer participation in religious, charitable, and other organizations. Finally, we include time spent by heads of families in getting more education.[2]

There are different types of behavior patterns with respect to unpaid work, however. For example, elderly women may do lots of baby sitting for their grandchildren, but they are not quite so able as younger people to repair their homes or cars. Even more important for a given family is that home production saves them money, whereas the hours they devote to volunteer work do not. Volunteer work, however, does save the recipients money and accordingly is considered a productive activity for the society as a whole.

We first analyze separately the time spent on home production, volunteer work, and furthering one's education. Then we examine the combined hours spent on these activities.

Home Production: Constraints and Pressures

What determines the amount of time heads and wives together devote to home production? Figure 9-2 shows the results of a multivariate analysis.[3]

---

[2]We have made no attempt in this study to estimate wives' time spent on taking courses or lessons.

[3]Figure 9-2 is a result of a systematic search process described in detail in Appendix E. As mentioned before, among all variables used, only that variable which, at each step of the analysis, explains more of the variation in hours of home production than any of the others is selected and appears in the figure.

FIGURE 9-2

HOURS OF HOME PRODUCTION DONE IN 1964 BY HEADS OF FAMILIES AND WIVES*
(For all 2214 families)

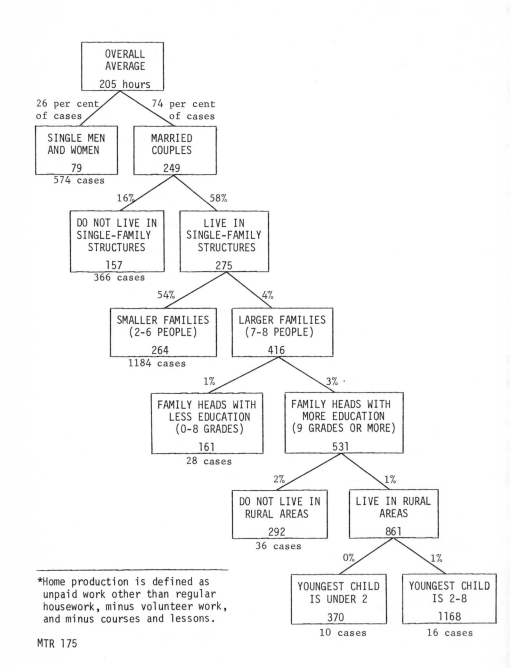

*Home production is defined as
unpaid work other than regular
housework, minus volunteer work,
and minus courses and lessons.

MTR 175

ituational constraints and pressures clearly dominate the results. After
ll, two persons can do twice as much work as one, if they both have the
ame skill and energy. Also, many types of home production require special
ypes of living places and depend, as well, upon the number of people and
vhether there are any children in the family. People cannot grow their own
ood without having a garden; renters do not usually paint or repair their
apartments[4]; the larger the family, the more pressure to do some sewing or
repairing rips and tears on pants for youngsters; and aged people lack the
energy, and the less educated lack the confidence or skill, for certain
kinds of home production.

The explanatory factors used in the search process of Figure 9-2 are
as follows, in the order of their importance if used to make a single division of the whole sample:

> *Sex and marital status
> *Number of people in family
> *Type of structure in which family lives
> Number of rooms in home
> *Size of place (town) where family lives
> Number of automatic home appliances
> *Age of youngest child under 18 living at home
> Whether it is difficult to hire outside help for work
>   around the house
> Total family income
> Age of head of family
> Race

> *Education of head of family
> Whether family could do some of the work for which it hired help
> Number of years lived in present home

---

[4]The causal relationship between home ownership and time spent on home
production is not clear. People may buy homes because they like doing things
around the house. For this reason, home ownership is used as an explanatory
variable in the second-stage analysis rather than in the first-stage one.

Whether county was a depressed area
Hours lost from work in 1964 by heads of families and wives
   from illness and unemployment
Number of disabled persons in family

Asterisked variables are those used in Figure 9-2. They
explained 11 per cent of the variance. The overall standard deviation is 340 hours. None of the variables below the line could
explain as much as 0.5 per cent of the total sum of squares by a
single division of the whole sample.

Figure 9-2 shows that single people spend about one and one-half
hours per week on home production. This is less than one-third of the time
that married couples spend. Married people, however, differ most with
respect to the time they devote to home production, depending on the type of
structure in which they live. The couples living in apartments reported
about 3 hours of home production per week; the couples living in single-
family structures reported about 5 hours.

Figure 9-2 also indicates that among couples living in single-family
structures, those with very large families, especially when the heads of
families having at least some high school education and live in rural areas
and have no children under two years old at home, devote a large part of
their time to home production. In fact, 16 couples having all the characteristics just mentioned, reported devoting 22 hours per week to home production
Indeed, Figure 9-2 is a classic case of alternative causes in which the
things that discourage home production are substitutes for one another, or
the things that encourage reinforce one another cumulatively, depending on
you prefer to describe the situation.

We turn now to some of the variables that did not quite get into
Figure 9-2. Home production is largely a substitute for marketable goods and
services. It is not easy for every family, however, in the affluent, mass-
production, mass-consumption American society, to find outside help. Such

scarcity might be reflected either in high wages, unorganized markets with delayed responses and a kind of supply rationing (the man doesn't show up), or in no markets at all for such services (no way to find a man to do it). Figure 9-3 indicates that families reported _more_ hours of home production when they also reported that it was difficult for them to find outside help. The families who said they did not know whether outside help was difficult to get, reported the least home production. Perhaps these families did not require much help in the first place.

A low family income could be considered as a constraint on how much outside help a family could substitute for its own effort in home production. Figure 9-4 shows that married couples with incomes of $7500 or more, and single people with incomes of $5000 or more, do somewhat less home production as their income increases. Overall, however, high-income families reported more hours of home production than low-income families. This might be because the heads of families with higher incomes have more education and many of them are middle-aged. And the data do show that middle-aged people do more home production on the average than do younger or older ones (Figure 9-5). It seems clear that such income and age effects as do appear are largely reflections of differences in marital status and family size. Age and income are closely related; so even the small income and age effects shown in Figure 9-4 and 9-5, respectively, might each be an overestimation of their individual net effect.

Finally, nonwhite families appear to devote less time to home production: they reported 2 hours per week, whereas white families reported 4 hours on the average. But this race difference was not powerful enough to allow the use of race in Figure 9-2. The same is true for the amount of

132

FIGURE 9-3

HOURS OF HOME PRODUCTION DONE BY HEADS OF FAMILIES AND WIVES IN 1964
BY WHETHER DIFFICULT TO HIRE OUTSIDE HELP
(For all 2214 families)*

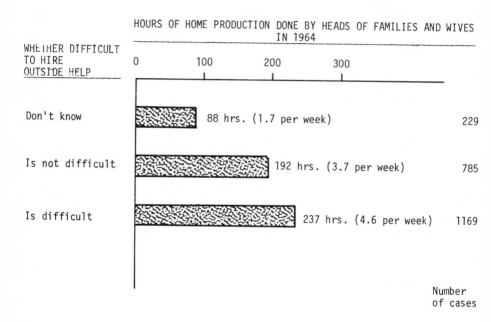

* Excludes 31 cases in which difficulty of hiring outside help was not
ascertained

MTR 175

FIGURE 9-4

HOURS OF HOME PRODUCTION DONE BY HEADS OF FAMILIES AND WIVES IN 1964
BY TOTAL FAMILY INCOME
(For all 2214 families)

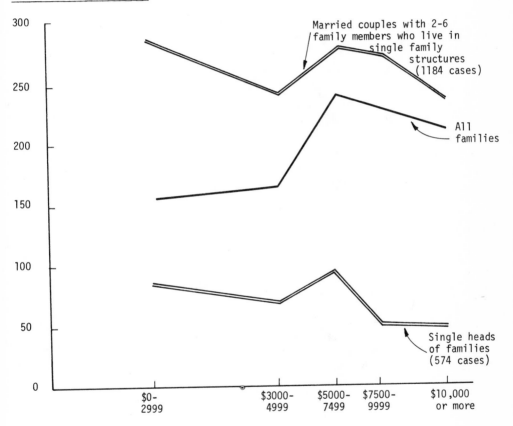

HOURS OF HOME PRODUCTION

TOTAL FAMILY INCOME
(log scale)

MTR 175

134

FIGURE 9-5

HOURS OF HOME PRODUCTION DONE BY HEADS OF FAMILIES AND WIVES
BY AGE OF HEAD OF FAMILY
(For all 2214 families)

HOURS OF HOME PRODUCTION

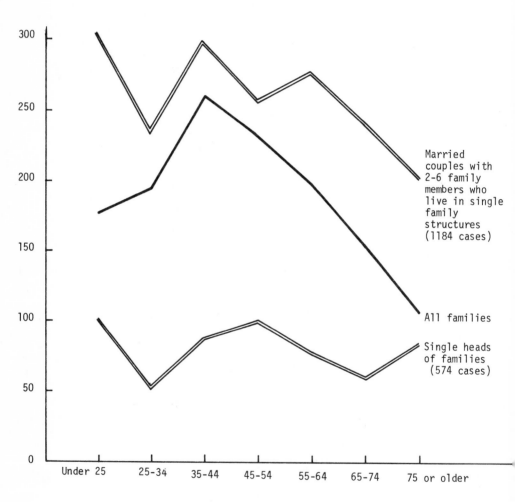

AGE OF HEAD OF FAMILY

MTR 175

<u>outside help</u> engaged by the family for work which the family said it could do itself. Among the 14 per cent of the families who had some outside help, those who reported that they could have done all of that work themselves reported doing more than twice as many hours of other home production by themselves as those who said they could not have done the work themselves. Presumably this merely means that people who have the ability to do things for themselves not only do them, but also report that they could do the other things they are paying to have done.

The <u>last four factors</u> allowed in the search process had no appreciable effects either on the whole sample or on subgroups of it.

Home Production: Motives and Incentives

All the findings so far have been obvious and expected. They show the most important combinations of the basic constraints and pressures. But we can now take the differences from the end-group averages of Figure 9-2, pool them, and examine them further for the effects of other forces. The following twenty-three predictors were used in the second-stage analysis; they are listed in order of their importance over the whole sample.

        *Housing status (home ownership)
         Number of people in family
        *Index of achievement orientation
         Per cent of adults in county who completed high school
___
         Race
         Attitude toward importance of luck for financial success
         Index of caution and risk avoidance
         Index of closeness of family ties
         Attitude toward mothers' working
         Index of receptivity to change
         Whether head of family grew up on farm
         Education of head of family

Number of calls required to secure interview
Age of youngest child under 18 living at home
Church attendance
Index of ambition and aspiration
Index of mobility experience
Whether any child of the head of family had already finished
    college
Whether head of family was self-employed
Hourly earnings of head of family
Number of disabled persons in family
Age of head of family
Sex and marital status of head of family

    Asterisked variables are those used in Figure 9-6. They
explained an additional 2 per cent of the variance. The overall
standard deviation of the residual hours is 320. None of the variables below the line could explain as much as 0.5 per cent of the
total sum of squares by a single division of the whole sample.

Figure 9-6 shows the relationships of the most important factors to

the pooled differences from Figure 9-2. The highly achievement-oriented

home owners do the most home production.

As mentioned earlier, home ownership may well represent not a cause

but an interrelation, since people might buy homes to be able to do more

home production. On the other hand, the 60-hour difference, shown in

Figure 9-6, between those who own and those who do not own their homes might

be underestimated, since part of the real difference has already been

accounted for by eliminating the effect of type of structure in the first-

stage analysis, as shown in Figure 9-2.[5]

Among the homeowners, those who scored three or higher on the index

of achievement orientation did more home production than those with lower

scores. Presumably the more highly achievement--oriented people desire more

---

[5]Our data show a high correlation between home ownership and living
in single-family structures, since 87 per cent of the homeowners, but only
45 per cent of the non-homeowners, live in such structures.

FIGURE 9-6

HOURS OF HOME PRODUCTION DONE IN 1964 BY HEADS OF FAMILIES AND WIVES:
ANALYSIS OF DIFFERENCES FROM END-GROUP AVERAGES OF FIGURE 9-2*
(For all 2214 families)

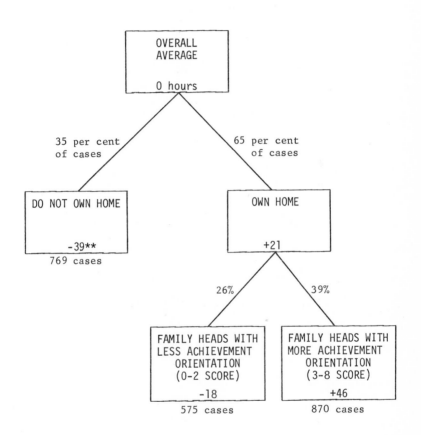

---

*Home production is defined as unpaid work other than regular housework, minus
volunteer work and minus courses and lessons.

**One single woman reporting extremely long hours of home production was elimi-
nated from the residual analysis.

MTR 175

138

goods and services and actually get them by increasing their efforts in home production.[6] Or perhaps they get a feeling of accomplishment from doing the job well, apart from any money they save.

Why did none of the other twenty-one variables seem to matter? Some had already had their main effect removed in Figure 9-2 and were reintroduced only in case they showed further effects in combination with some of the second-stage variables. The education level of the county, which also reflects its income level, did seem to be mildly related to more "do-it-yourself" work. Perhaps higher levels of community education raise community standards, and they in turn affect families' aspirations, inducing them to do more home production like painting and repairing their homes. Perhaps when many families in a community are doing things around their houses, auxiliary services such as equipment rentals appear in the area. Though race seemed important over all the residuals—whites doing more work around the house even after allowing for the differences of Figure 9-2—it dropped in importance once home ownership was taken into account. The same is true of the number of people in the family.

Belief in the importance of luck for a person's financial success was related to hours of home production, in the expected direction. Families who said that luck was important reported doing about 40 fewer hours of home production on the average than those who said that luck was unimportant.

Other indexes representing motives, desires, and attitudes showed progressively less powerful effects over the whole sample of pooled

---

[6]For a discussion of the index of achievement orientation, its components, and its construction, see Appendix D.

residuals.[7] The reader may, however, be curious as to the direction of their effects.

We found that those who scored low on the index of <u>caution and risk avoidance</u> reported doing fewer hours of home production than those scoring higher. Also, those with higher scores on the index of <u>closeness of family ties</u> did more home production; and heads of families who <u>approved of mothers' working</u> reported, along with their wives, doing less hours of home production.

We also found that people who were more <u>receptive to change</u> (i.e., have higher propensity to try, accept, or acquire new products and ideas, both at home and on the job) reported more hours of home production.

The family head's <u>hourly earnings</u> seemed to show no systematic relationship with the time spent on home production, either for the sample of pooled residuals as a whole or for any of the subgroups. Our data indicate that only when hourly earnings are $7.50 or higher do people tend to reduce the time they devote to home production. They probably substitute outside help for their own effort and thus reallocate their time towards more leisure, since Figure 2-4 shows no large increase in hours of work on the job at the higher earning rates.

Volunteer Work

People help one another in several ways: through involuntary means like paying taxes, or insurance, where the lucky help the unlucky, or through voluntary means like contributing money, goods, or effort (time) to relatives, friends, churches, or other charitable and political organizations. In this study we were concerned only with voluntary contributions of time, serving

---

[7] See Appendix D for details on indexes.

people or organizations outside the family unit.[8]

In 1964 American families spent 87 hours of their time, on the average, doing volunteer work, with 57 per cent of all families doing some such work. The full distribution of hours of volunteer work is as follows:

Hours of volunteer work done in 1964 by heads of families and wives	Per cent of cases
None	43
1-40	24
41-120	14
121-240	9
241-1000	8
1001 or more	2
Total	100
Number of cases	2214

Valued at the average hourly earnings of family heads who worked in 1964, the average family's volunteer work was worth more than $260.[9] This calculated value for volunteer work amounts to nearly as much as the $315 of average money contributions to church and charity reported in 1959 by American families in an earlier study.[10] It was reported in that earlier study that income was the most important predictor of money contributions.[1]

---

[8]The total hours of time devoted to such activities were summed from the following questions: "Did you do any volunteer work without pay such as work for church or charity, or helping relatives? What did you do? Altogether, did this take you more than 40 hours last year? About how many hours did it take you?" These questions were asked separately for husbands and wives.

[9]The average hourly earning, $3.07, is for family heads only. It does not include working wives, whose average hourly earnings are lower. The average hourly earnings, however, underestimate the true value of volunteer work, since higher-income people do relatively more volunteer work.

[10]Morgan et al., pp. 257-287.

[11]Ibid., p. 266.

Our findings show that there is also a significant positive relation between family income and hours devoted to volunteer work. Hence, people with higher incomes do not substitute money contributions completely for time devoted to volunteer work. They reported more of both, as Figure 9-7 indicates. That figure suggests further that American philanthropy is deeply rooted among families, regardless of their income: low-income families compensate for their small contributions of money by doing more volunteer work, and high-income families compensate for their "scarce" time by giving more money. Thus, the ratio of total contributions (money and volunteer work) to family income is somewhat higher only for very low-income families and is lower and constant (about 9 per cent) for families with incomes of $3000 or higher. Probably our valuation of all volunteer hours at the average hourly earnings gives too high a value to the time of low-income families, especially since many of them were retired, sick, or unemployed for long periods, resulting in even lower opportunity cost of their time. Theoretically, we could have assumed that the real amount of a family's giving is equal to the value of the time its members contribute, either by doing volunteer work or by earning whatever money they contribute.

The higher a person's income, the higher his marginal income tax rate, and (provided he can itemize his deductions) the lower the cost (after taxes) to him of each extra dollar he gives and of each extra hour he spends on volunteer work instead of earning more money. Hence charitable giving of either time or money might be considered to cost high-income people less, not only relative to their incomes, but absolutely dollar for dollar. Figure 9-8 graphs the effects of deducting tax savings from the gross contributions of Figure 9-7.

142

FIGURE 9-7

VALUE OF VOLUNTEER WORK, AND MONEY CONTRIBUTIONS TO CHURCH AND
CHARITY, BY TOTAL FAMILY INCOME
(For all 2214 families and for all 2800 families
from an earlier study)*

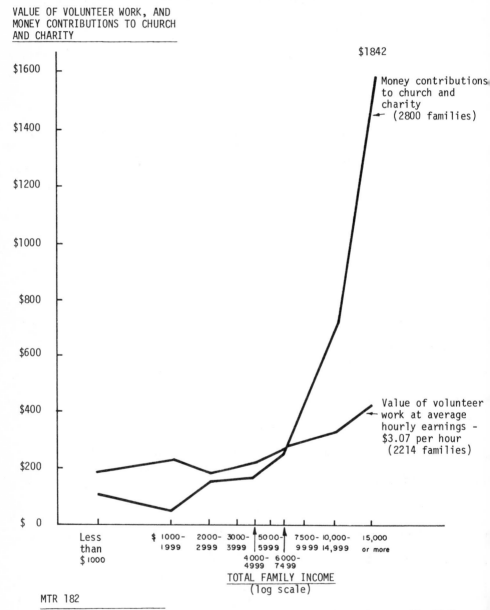

VALUE OF VOLUNTEER WORK, AND
MONEY CONTRIBUTIONS TO CHURCH
AND CHARITY

$1842

Money contributions
to church and
charity
← (2800 families)

Value of volunteer
← work at average
hourly earnings -
$3.07 per hour
(2214 families)

TOTAL FAMILY INCOME
(log scale)

MTR 182

* Morgan et al.,Income and Welfare in the United States,p.267, Table 18-9.

143

FIGURE 9-8

VALUE OF VOLUNTEER WORK AND MONEY CONTRIBUTIONS TO CHURCH AND CHARITY --
ADJUSTED FOR MARGINAL TAX RATE
(For all 2214 families and for 2800 families from an earlier study)*

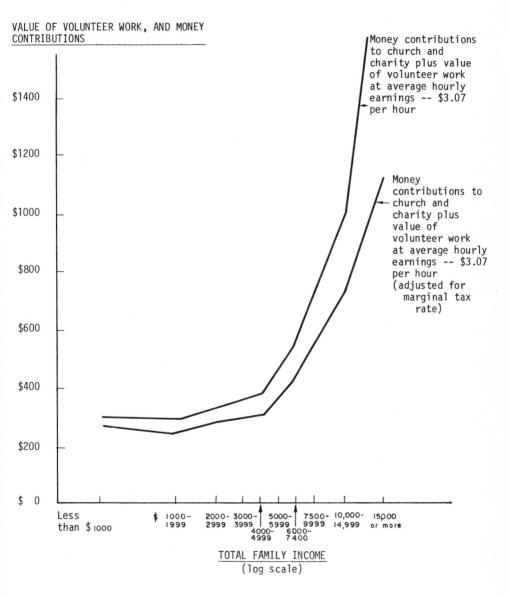

MTR 182

*Morgan et al., p. 267, Table 18-9

On the other hand, taxes are neutral with respect to the <u>choice</u> between the donation of time or money. If a man contributes time, he earns no money to pay tax on. If he gives money, he deducts the amount in computing taxable income; so money earned <u>and</u> given away is "tax free." One might then expect that the <u>proportion</u> of an individual's total philanthropy that is money, rather than time, would not be affected by his marginal income tax rates. But that proportion does vary with family income (as does the tax rate): it rises from one-third to four-fifths as one moves to higher income levels.

Several explanations are possible. One is that though a person with special skills can earn more per hour on the job, the real value of his time when he gives it to a church or charity, is not so much higher than average. Hence, his real contribution to the church can be made larger by giving money, according to the economic principle of comparative advantage. Another explanation may be that lower-income people sometimes do not have opportunities to work as much as they would like for pay and thus find it possible to increase their total output by giving their surplus time, rather than their scarce money, to charity.

More volunteer work is also done by persons at higher educational levels. Figure 9-9 shows the pattern. Income and education are correlated, but we have reason to believe that education is more basic since, aside from its correlation with income and tax considerations, it affects both people's basic motives to do volunteer work, and the demand for their volunteer services.

However, when a number of predictors are used in a multivariate analysis, the best predictor turns out to be neither income nor education

FIGURE 9-9

HOURS OF VOLUNTEER WORK DONE IN 1964 BY HEADS OF FAMILIES AND WIVES,
BY EDUCATION OF HEAD OF FAMILY *
(For all 2206 families doing 2000 or fewer hours of volunteer work)*

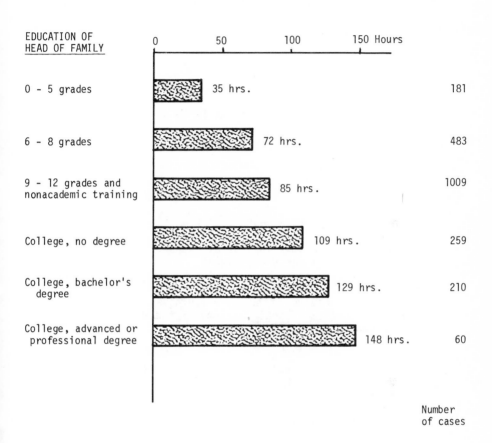

EDUCATION OF HEAD OF FAMILY	Hours	Number of cases
0 - 5 grades	35 hrs.	181
6 - 8 grades	72 hrs.	483
9 - 12 grades and nonacademic training	85 hrs.	1009
College, no degree	109 hrs.	259
College, bachelor's degree	129 hrs.	210
College, advanced or professional degree	148 hrs.	60

MTR 182

*excludes 4 cases in which education of head of family was not ascertained.

146

nor marital status, but whether the family owns at least one of the following automatic home appliances: washer, dryer, or dishwasher (see Figure 9-10). The following variables were used in the multivariate analysis to explain hours of volunteer work:

*Number of automatic home appliances
Total family income
Sex and marital status of head of family
Education of head of family
Size of place (town) where family lives
Number of people in family

Age of head of family
Type of structure in which family lives
Number of years lived in present home
Number of rooms in home
Whether county was a depressed area
Race
Hours lost from work in 1964 by heads of families and wives
    from illness and unemployment
Whether difficult to hire outside help for work around the
    house
Age of youngest child under 18 living at home
Whether the family could do some of the work for which it
    hired help
Number of disabled persons in family

The asterisked variable is that used in Figure 9-10. It explained 1 per cent of the variance. The overall standard deviation is 199 hours. None of the variables below the line could explain as much as 0.5 per cent of the total sum of squares by a single division of the whole sample.

Our previous findings indicate that we cannot explain the findings of Figure 9-10 solely on the grounds that families with automatic home appliances have more free time and consequently could do more volunteer work. What the analysis shows, however, is that having automatic home appliances is a proxy or substitute variable for a large number of other factors, whose combined effect is more powerful than any one of their separate effects.

FIGURE 9-10

HOURS OF VOLUNTEER WORK DONE IN 1964 BY HEADS OF FAMILIES AND WIVES
(For all 2206 families who did less than 2000 hours
of volunteer work in 1964)

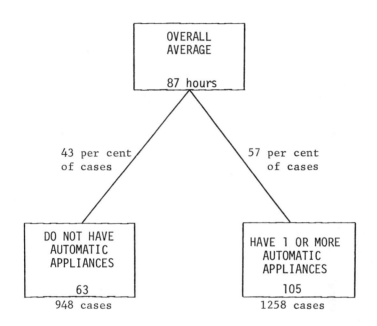

TABLE 9-1

PER CENT OF ALL FAMILIES AND FAMILIES WITH ONE OR MORE AUTOMATIC HOME APPLIANC
HAVING VARIOUS CHARACTERISTICS

(For all 2206 families who did less than 2000 hours
of volunteer work in 1964)

Family characteristics	All families	Per cent of:
		Families with 1 or more automatic home appliance (including automatic washing machine, clothes dryer, or dishwasher
Total family income of $5000 or more	64	82*
Family head with some college education	24	30
Married couple	74	87
Lived in present home for 2 years or more	74	77
Lives in urban places with 2500-49,999 population; or live in rural areas near cities	42	51
Homeowner	65	(76)**
Number of cases	2206	1258

*This should read: "Eighty-two per cent of those with one or more home
appliances have family incomes of $5000 or more, compared with 64 per cent
for all families."

**Estimated.

MTR 182

ble 9-1 indicates that more people with higher incomes and educational
evels have automatic home appliances; and we have already discussed other
nportant effects of income and education.   It also shows that those with
ne or more automatic home appliances are more likely to have a family in-
ome of $5000 or more, to be married, to own a home, and to live in small
rban places or rural areas near cities. And we find, as expected, that
eople living in very small urban places (2500-9999 population) did about
5 per cent more volunteer work than the overall average.

otives and Incentives for Doing
olunteer Work

The most important combinations of the basic constraints and pres-
ures seem to have been accounted for by dividing the sample into two groups:
amilies that own one or more of three automatic home appliances, and fami-
ies that don't. But let us now take the differences from those two group
verages of Figure 9-10, pool them, and examine them for other forces. The
ollowing twenty-two predictors were used in this second-stage analysis; they
re listed in order of their importance over the whole sample:

        *Education of head of family
        Per cent of adults in county who completed high school
        Index of receptivity to change

        Hourly earnings of head of family
        Whether head of family was self-employed
        Index of achievement orientation
        Age of head of family
        Sex and marital status of head of family
        Index of caution and risk avoidance
        Attitude toward mothers' working
        Number of people in family
        Church attendance
        Whether any child of head of family had already finished college
        Housing status (home ownership)

Number of calls required to secure interview
*Index of mobility experience
Age of youngest child under 18 living at home
Race
Index of ambition and aspiration
Attitude toward importance of luck for financial success
Number of disabled persons in family
Whether head of family grew up on farm

Asterisked variables are those used in Figure 9-11. They explained an additional 1.5 per cent of the variance. The overall standard deviation is 198 hours. None of the variables below the line could explain as much as 0.5 per cent of the total sum of squares by a single division of the whole sample.

None of the twenty-two variables, alone or in combination, were able to explain any substantial part of the interpersonal differences in hours of volunteer work. We do conclude, however, that those who have higher levels of education, have some home appliances, and have not moved too often do th most volunteer work.

Volunteer work proved to be associated with education, even after w had partially accounted for its effect in the first-stage analysis.[12] It seems likely that not only do people with higher levels of education face moral pressures from charitable and political organizations to contribute their services, but that they also may be more highly motivated to do volun teer work. Among the educated, those with the lower scores on the index of mobility experience did the most volunteer work. Apparently people start active volunteer participation when they become permanently settled both in their jobs and within a community, are better known, and belong to more organizations.[13]

---

[12]See Table 9-1 and its discussion in the text above.

[13]See Chapter 15 for a discussion of the index of geographic and occupational mobility as a dependent variable.

FIGURE 9-11

HOURS OF VOLUNTEER WORK DONE IN 1964 BY HEADS OF FAMILIES AND WIVES:
ANALYSIS OF DIFFERENCES FROM END-GROUP AVERAGES OF FIGURE 9-10

(For all 2206 families who did less than 2000 hours of
volunteer work in 1964)

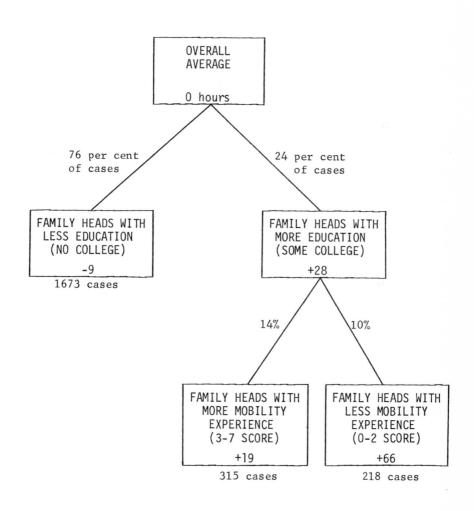

What about the direction of the effects of other less important fac
tors? Among those with higher levels of education and higher mobility
experience (scores of 3-7 on the index), our data show that those who were
more _cautious_ (scores 6-7 on the index) as well did 100 hours more of volun
teer work than the average, perhaps wanting to keep some community ties jus
in case they decided to settle down after all; also, for that same group of
families, those who were raised on a farm or who regularly attended religious services did more volunteer work.

For the 76 per cent of families where the head of the family had no
college education, nothing was important enough to explain further differen
ces in their hours of volunteer work. It seems, however, that families who
live in _counties with a relatively low percentage of high school graduates_
engage in little volunteer work (Figure 9-12). Perhaps there is not much
demand for their services in such communities, though the _need_ might be
greater.

Our data show that for people with lower levels of education, if on
or more of their _children have already finished college_, then those familie
reported devoting more time to volunteer work. Probably such upward educational mobility in the family gives parents a sense of pride and motivates
them towards more social participation in general, and more volunteer work
in particular.

None of the other variables seemed to matter much, except that peop
who scored very high (8 or 9) on the _index of receptivity to change_ reporte
doing more volunteer work. But education of the head of the family, and th
index of receptivity to change, are so closely related that the effect of
the index almost disappeared after the division of the sample by education.

153

FIGURE 9-12

HOURS OF VOLUNTEER WORK DONE IN 1964 BY HEADS OF FAMILIES AND WIVES:
DIFFERENCES FROM END-GROUP AVERAGES OF FIGURE 9-10, BY PER CENT
OF ADULTS IN COUNTY WHO COMPLETED HIGH SCHOOL
(For 1673 families doing 2000 or fewer hours of volunteer work in
which head of family had no college education)

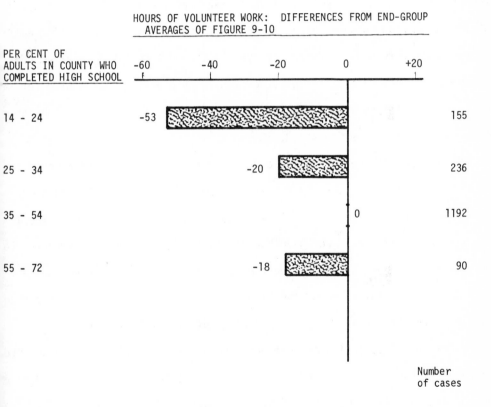

HOURS OF VOLUNTEER WORK: DIFFERENCES FROM END-GROUP
AVERAGES OF FIGURE 9-10

PER CENT OF
ADULTS IN COUNTY WHO
COMPLETED HIGH SCHOOL

	-60	-40	-20	0	+20	
14 - 24	-53					155
25 - 34			-20			236
35 - 54				0		1192
55 - 72			-18			90

Number
of cases

MTR 182

We turn now to the third type of unpaid productive activity--
investing time in one's own education.

Courses and Lessons

One in every six American family heads took some courses or lessons
in 1964. They devoted about 295 hours of their time on the average to
enhance their capabilities as producers and as consumers by "investing in
themselves." About 70 per cent of those heads of families who took courses
or lessons did so in ways likely to increase their economic skills.[14] Half
of those under twenty-five years of age spent some time taking courses and
lessons, and their aggregate hours devoted to this activity accounted for
half of the total as well, even though only 6 per cent of the family heads
were under twenty-five years old.

One might expect that those with lower levels of education would try
to compensate for that lack by educating themselves further. Our data, however, show the opposite. The time devoted to courses and lessons by the 12
per cent of family heads who have bachelor's or advanced degrees amounted to
30 per cent of the total hours spent by all family heads taking courses and
lessons, whereas the share of the 47 per cent of family heads with less than
twelve grades of education was only 7 per cent of the total hours.

Figure 9-13 indicates that both the annual average hours and the pro
portions of people who took courses and lessons increase with higher educational levels. The somewhat high average hours devoted to education by

---

[14]The following questions were asked of family heads only: "Did you
attend any courses, or take lessons of any kind, in the last year? What did
you do? Altogether, did this take you more than 40 hours last year? About
how many hours did it take altogether?" For more details see Appendix C.

155

FIGURE 9-13

HOURS OF COURSES AND LESSONS TAKEN BY HEAD OF FAMILY IN 1964,
BY COMPLETED EDUCATION OF HEAD OF FAMILY
(For all 2214 heads of families)*

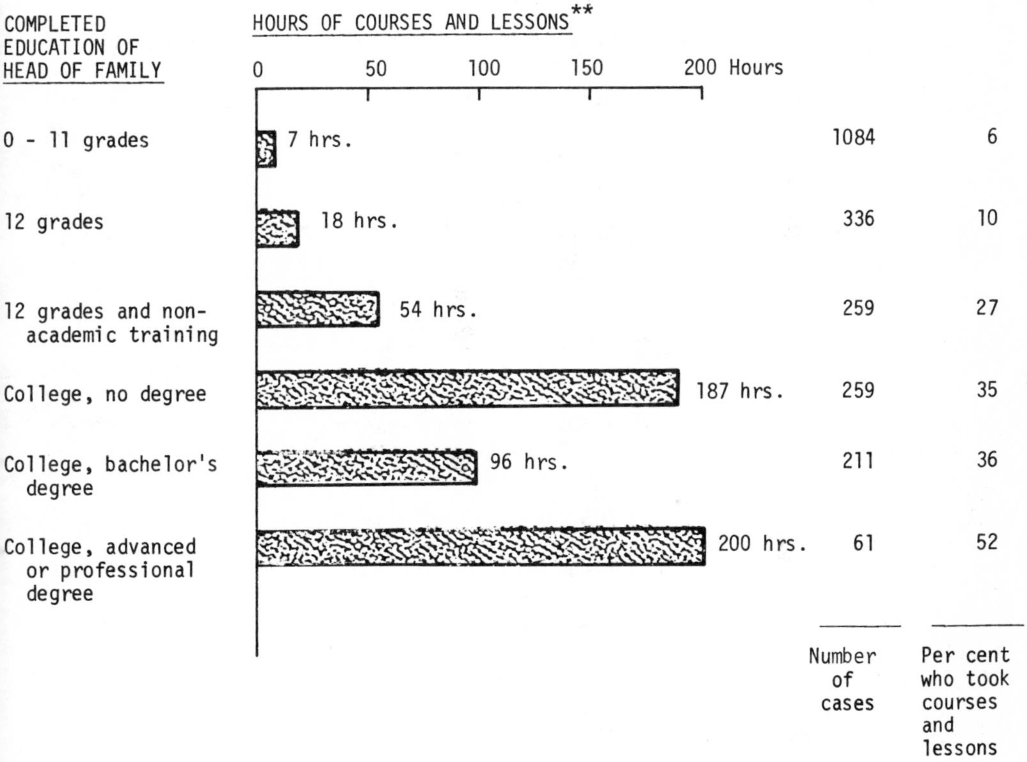

COMPLETED EDUCATION OF HEAD OF FAMILY	HOURS OF COURSES AND LESSONS**	Number of cases	Per cent who took courses and lessons
0 - 11 grades	7 hrs.	1084	6
12 grades	18 hrs.	336	10
12 grades and non-academic training	54 hrs.	259	27
College, no degree	187 hrs.	259	35
College, bachelor's degree	96 hrs.	211	36
College, advanced or professional degree	200 hrs.	61	52

MTR 177
*excludes 4 cases in which education of head of family was not ascertained.
**These averages include those not taking any courses or lessons.

family heads with some college education, but no degree, reflect the fact
that some of them were college students during 1964. Some of those with
college degrees or more, although they might have full-time jobs, were
probably also studying part-time towards higher degrees. But the main and
documented fact is that the "knowledge market" in the United States is an
imperfect one: the educated get more education while the uneducated stay
uneducated![15]

Table 9-2 shows that if we ignore families with less than $3000
annual income, where 10 per cent of these families--mostly students--spent

TABLE 9-2

DISTRIBUTION OF HOURS OF COURSES AND LESSONS OF HEADS OF FAMILIES,
AND PER CENT TAKING COURSES AND LESSONS,
BY TOTAL FAMILY INCOME
(for all 2214 heads of families)

Total family income	Number of cases	Average hours of courses and lessons*	Per cent who took courses and lessons
Less than $1000	100	81	9
$1000-1999	203	114	9
$2000-2999	164	90	12
$3000-3999	175	45	10
$4000-4999	157	56	11
$5000-5999	194	58	16
$6000-7499	304	32	15
$7500-9999	395	30	23
$10,000-14,999	341	29	23
$15,000 and more	181	16	23
All cases	2214	49	17

*Average for all cases including those who did not take any courses or
lessons.
MTR 178

[15]There is accumulating evidence that where adult education is
easily available, it does tend to be used by people farther down the educational scale, and that such use is increasing.
John W. C. Johnstone and Ramon J. Rivera, Volunteers for Learning
(Chicago: Aldine Press, 1965).

1000 hours on the average on courses and lessons, we find a tendency for people with higher incomes to take more courses and lessons but to devote fewer hours of their time.

Analysis of Home Production, Volunteer Work, and Courses and Lessons Combined

Having analyzed home production ("do-it-yourself" work), volunteer work, and adult education separately, we now analyze the three combined. Our dependent variable becomes the aggregate hours of unpaid work, excluding regular housework since it is basically a function of various constraints and pressures. Excluded from this analysis of the aggregate hours were 84 heads of families who spent a substantial amount of their time taking courses and lessons. Most of these were full-time students, whose patterns of allocation of time differ from the average.[16]

The explanatory factors used in the search process of Figure 9-14 are listed below in order of their importance if used to make a single division of the whole sample:

```
*Sex and marital status of head of family
 Number of people in family
*Size of place (town) where family lives
 Type of structure in which family lives
 Number of automatic home appliances
 Number of rooms in home
*Total family income
 Whether it is difficult to hire outside help for work around
    the house
 Age of head of family
```

[16]For statistical reasons, one extreme case was also excluded. This was a couple who reported doing more than 4000 hours of home production and volunteer work.

*Education of head of family
Age of youngest child under 18 living at home
Race

Whether county was a depressed area
Number of years lived in present home
Hours lost from work in 1964 by heads of families and wives
    from illness and unemployment
Whether family could do some of the work for which it hired
    help
Number of disabled persons in family

Asterisked variables are those used in Figure 9-14. They
explained 8 per cent of the variance. The overall standard deviation is 445 hours. None of the variables below the line could
explain as much as 0.5 per cent of the total sum of squares by a
single division of the whole sample.

Married couples who do not live in metropolitan areas and in which

the husband is at least literate (six grades of school or more) do the most

unpaid work, and single men and women do the least. Variables such as num-

ber of people in the family, type of structure in which family lives, and

number of automatic appliances, which mattered for one or more of the com-

ponents, were related to the total hours of unpaid work, but not enough to

justify entering them in Figure 9-14.

Finally, we take the differences of the end-group averages of Figure

9-14, pool them, and examine them to ascertain the effect of variables

representing motives and desires. The explanatory factors used in the

second-stage search process of Figure 9-15 are listed below in order of their

importance if used to make a single division of the whole sample:

*Index of closeness of family ties
*Index of achievement orientation
 Number of people in family
*Per cent of adults in county who completed high school
 Index of caution and risk avoidance
*Housing status (home ownership)

159

FIGURE 9-14

HOURS OF UNPAID WORK OTHER THAN REGULAR HOUSEWORK DONE IN 1964
BY HEADS OF FAMILIES AND WIVES

(For all 2129 families who took less than 241 hours of courses or did less
than 4000 hours of unpaid work other than regular housework in 1964)

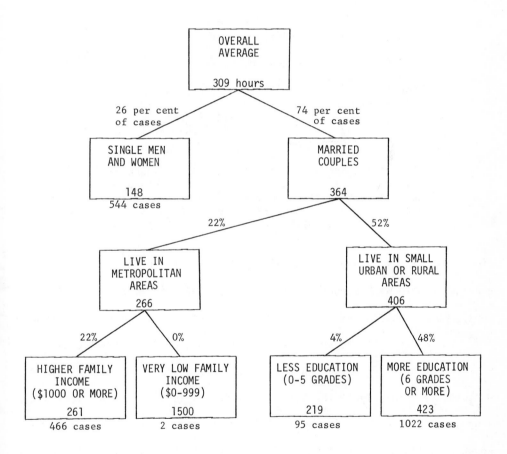

MTR 174

Education of head of family
Attitude toward mothers' working
Index of receptivity to change
Church attendance
*Whether head of family was self-employed (or working at time
    of interview)
Index of ambition and aspiration
Attitude toward importance of luck for financial success
Race
Number of calls required to secure interview
Number of disabled persons in family
Age of youngest child under 18 living at home
Hourly earnings of head of family
Age of head of family
Whether head of family grew up on a farm
Index of mobility experience
Sex and marital status of head of families
Whether any child of the head of the family has already
    finished college

Asterisked variables are those used in Figure 9-15. They explained an additional 5 per cent of the variance. The overall standard deviation is 428 hours. None of the variables below the line could explain as much as 0.5 per cent of the total sum of squares by a single division of the whole sample.

Figure 9-15 shows the results of the analysis of these forces.[17] On the average, people with strong family ties reported doing more hours of such unpaid work. Only 5 per cent of the sample, however, were in that group.

For the rest, we are able to isolate a group with low scores on achievement orientation who do less; and a group who do not own a home who do less, particularly if the head of the family is in the labor force; and a group of home owners in counties of low educational level who do less. Apparently close family ties, or achievement orientation, or home ownership,

[17]As a reminder to the reader, values given in Figure 9-15--and, for that matter, all residual analyses--refer to differences and not to absolute values. What we have in that figure is further adjustments (additions or subtractions) to the findings shown in Figure 9-14. For further technical information about analyzing residuals, see Appendix E.

FIGURE 9-15

HOURS OF UNPAID WORK OTHER THAN REGULAR HOUSEWORK DONE IN 1964
BY HEADS OF FAMILIES AND WIVES: ANALYSIS OF DIFFERENCES
FROM END-GROUP AVERAGES OF FIGURE 9-14

(For all 2129 families who took less than 241 hours of courses or did less
than 4000 hours of unpaid work other than regular housework in 1964)

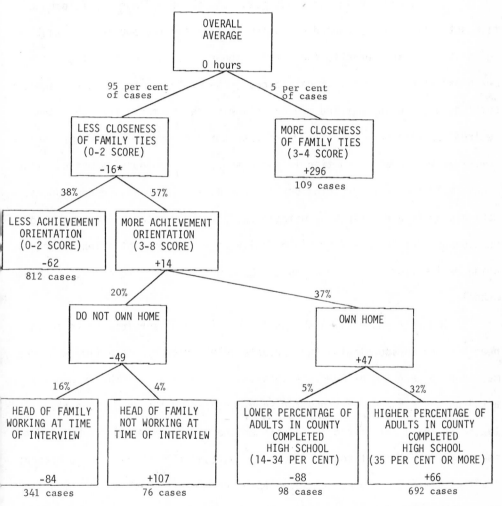

*One extreme case splitting off from this group was eliminated at this point; this
brought the number of cases down to 2128.

MTR 174

_or_ being retired, _or_ living in a county with generally high educational levels, all lead people to do more unpaid work.

Summary

Relatively simple and crude questions about various unpaid productive activities have produced estimates that appear reasonable, and that relate in plausible ways to the various opportunities, constraints, and measures reflecting motivational forces. The well educated, upper-income, settled, home-owning married man and his wife do the most, more than the retired man with more time, and more than twice as much as the single man or single woman. Home production is encouraged by living outside metropolitan areas; volunteer work by being settled and having labor-saving appliances; taking courses and lessons by being already well educated. Total hours of unpaid work are increased by close family ties, achievement orientation, being retired, or living in a county where more people have completed high school.

The vast increase in the public provision of services to those in need has led to speculation that private voluntarism, in both time and money, may tend to decrease or even disappear. And the fact that the income tax is a tax on the exchange of money for services, taxing the income one earns and taxing it again before the house painter one hires can spend it, has led to speculation that do-it-yourself home production will increase. The present crude estimates, we hope, can serve as a benchmark against which comparisons can be made with other countries and with a changed America a few years hence.

CHAPTER 10

OUTSIDE HELP DONE FOR FAMILIES

Introduction

The preceding two chapters have shown how American families differ
in the extent of their unpaid productive work. Now let us look at the
other side of the coin, namely, how much of their time they buy back by
getting outside help, and who does the buying.[1]

Table 10-1 gives the distribution of hours of outside help, whether
free or paid for, received by American families during 1964.[2] The table
indicates that 5 per cent of the families received free help; 87 per cent
paid to have something done. The table also suggests that it is more
appropriate to use the aggregate amount of outside help as the dependent
variable rather than the components separately. After all, even free help
has a cost in the context of the American culture! Something is usually
expected in return.

---

[1]Outside help includes free and paid help. The latter includes
help for regular housework, laundry, child care, painting and repairs
around the house, lawn care, and the time saved by eating out rather than
preparing meals at home. For details on questions and codes, see
Appendix C.

[2]Of the 2214 families in the sample, seven reported receiving 3,000
hours or more of outside help. These extreme cases are eliminated in the
present analysis. These families, however, include two single men.

TABLE 10-1

HOURS OF OUTSIDE HELP RECEIVED BY FAMILIES IN 1964
BY WHETHER FREE OR PAID FOR
(for all 2214 families)

Hours of outside help	All cases	Whether free or paid for		
			Paid for	
		Free	Things other than regular housework*	All paid
None	12	95	13	13
1-40	32	2	33	32
41-120	20	1	22	20
121-240	12	1	13	12
241-1000	18	1	15	17
1001 or more	6	0	4	6
Total	100	100	100	100
Number of cases	2214	2214	2214	2214

*This includes laundry, child care, painting and repairs around the house, lawn care, and the time saved by eating out rather than preparing meals at home.

MTR 25

Which Families Get Outside Help?

On the average, a family gets about 5 hours per week of outside help. Some families, especially those with working wives and young children, average as much as 19 hours per week.

To understand such differences, we start from the premise that people have the choice between doing more productive work around the house, or getting outside help and thus saving their own time. Theoretically, such decisions are based on income-leisure preferences, wage rates or productivity and the price and availability of outside help. For employed parents of young children, an hour of work outside the home by both parents at the same time requires at least one hour of baby sitting. The amount of outside help will then be closely related to the time the mothers spend at work.[3] This close association is not necessarily true for other activities which could be postponed to a more convenient time, or done more skimpily, like much regular housework.

This discussion suggests that three groups of factors affect the amount of outside help: economic factors such as the amount one could make by working more hours for money versus the cost of outside help, constraints such as limited availability of outside help, and peoples' motives and desires. More important, it suggests that the same factors might have different effects on different groups of the population.

Nine predicting characteristics were used in a multivariate analysis of total hours of outside help. Hours of work done for money by family heads and wives, together with education and family head's hourly earnings, represent both economic forces and personal motives. Family size, age of wife, age of youngest child, and the size of the home (number of rooms) represent various constraints and pressures. The following factors, listed in order of their importance if used to make a single division of the whole sample, were used in the systematic search process:

*Hourly earnings of head of family
*Sex and marital status
*Hours of work for money in 1964 by wife
*Education of wife
*Age of wife

---

[3]If the parents have control over their working hours, however, they could arrange their hours such that at least one of them will be at home with the children.

166

Number of rooms in home
*Hours of work for money in 1964 by head of family
*Age of youngest child under 18 living at home

Number of people in family

Asterisked variables are those used in Figure 10-1. They explained 18 per cent of the variance. The overall standard deviation is 453 hours. None of the variables below the line could explain as much as 0.5 per cent of the total sum of squares by a single division of the whole sample.

Figure 10-1 shows that the 4 per cent of the families whose heads had very high hourly earnings bought an average of 13 hours a week of outside help. This is more than two and one-half times the overall average. Furthermore, families whose heads have very high hourly earnings and work more than full-time get more than 18 hours per week of outside help, on the average. Evidently, such differences might be a result of a combination of substitution and an income effect. Higher wages make outside help relatively cheap, and people substitute it for their own efforts. But families with higher hourly earnings are also better able to afford more outside help if they want it.

Single men are very likely to be married later, so that learning how to keep house may not appeal to them as providing future benefits worth the cost in foregone leisure or foregone extra earnings on the job. They average 9 hours per week of outside help, mainly by eating out and having their laundry done. The data also show that single men with high hourly earnings tend to get even more outside help; probably they can afford to hire cleaning help in addition to eating out and having their laundry done. (That difference, however, was not important enough to justify another division in Figure 10-1.)

FIGURE 10-1

HOURS OF HELP RECEIVED IN 1964 BY FAMILIES FROM OUTSIDE FAMILY
(For all 2207 families receiving less than 3000 hours
of help)

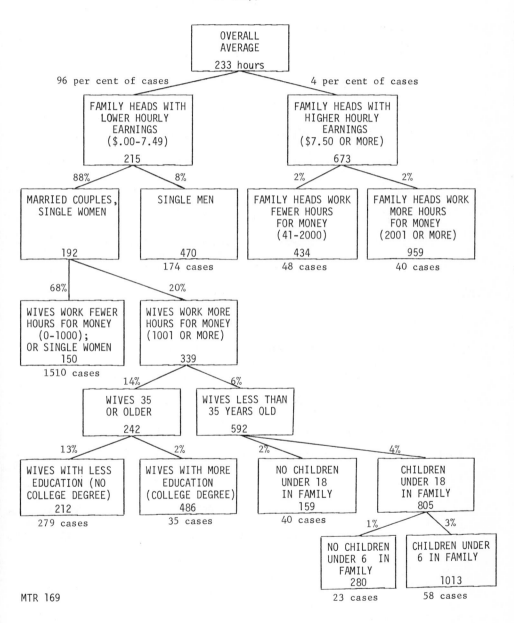

MTR 169

The rest of the story can be seen from Figure 10-1. We are left with a large group of married couples and single women, accounting for about 88 per cent of all families, whose heads were making less than $7.50 per hour. Exploring this group of families, we find that the hours worked for money by the wife was important. Our detailed data show that 53 per cent of the wives in that group did not have outside employment. Their outside help averaged only 2 hours per week. For the rest of that group, outside help increased systematically as wives worked more hours for money. However, the best single division--as Figure 10-1 indicates--seems to be between families with wives working more than half time and the rest: those with wives working less than half time or not at all, and those headed by a single woman.

Continuing further to examine families where the head makes less than $7.50 an hour and the wife works more than half-time, we find that a wife of thirty-five or older relies less on outside help, particularly if she does not have a college degree--and presumably earns little more than she would have to pay for help. The families with younger working wives received more outside help, particularly if there were children under eighteen in the family, and dramatically so if there were children under six at home. The extreme groups of families receiving outside help, then, are those with either a highly paid head who works more than full time, or a wife who is under thirty-five and working more than half time and has children to be cared for. The distinction between families headed by single women, and those with nonworking wives or wives working less or more than half time, is given systematically in Figure 10-2.

These results are all plausible. Single women know how to do things around the house without help, and since they are almost sure to be

169

FIGURE 10-2

HOURS OF HELP RECEIVED IN 1964 BY FAMILIES FROM OUTSIDE FAMILY,
FOR FAMILIES WITH VARIOUS CHARACTERISTICS
(For all 2207 families receiving less than 3000 hours of
help from outside family)

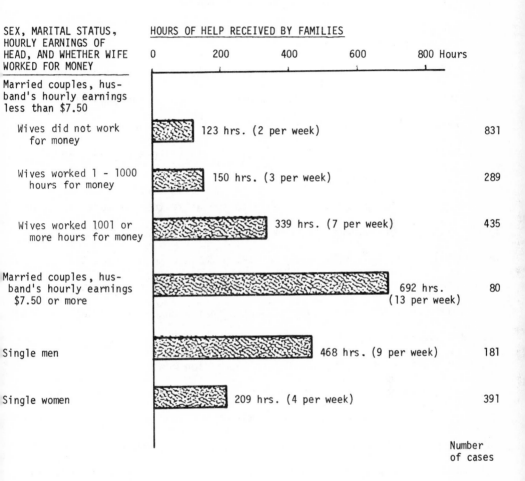

SEX, MARITAL STATUS, HOURLY EARNINGS OF HEAD, AND WHETHER WIFE WORKED FOR MONEY

HOURS OF HELP RECEIVED BY FAMILIES

	Hours	Number of cases
Married couples, husband's hourly earnings less than $7.50		
Wives did not work for money	123 hrs. (2 per week)	831
Wives worked 1 - 1000 hours for money	150 hrs. (3 per week)	289
Wives worked 1001 or more hours for money	339 hrs. (7 per week)	435
Married couples, husband's hourly earnings $7.50 or more	692 hrs. (13 per week)	80
Single men	468 hrs. (9 per week)	181
Single women	209 hrs. (4 per week)	391

married later (unless they are already old), learning how would seem a sound investment in skills. Single men appear more willing to eat in restaurants and to hire outside help.

Some Economic Factors

Our previous analysis would indicate that there is no explanatory variable which has a uniform effect over all groups of the population. In other words, the model of the forces at work is not an additive one. There are powerful interactions, with some factors affecting one group, and different ones affecting another.

But it is important to be able to summarize the possible impact of hourly earnings of husband and wife on their tendency to work for money and buy some of their other time back by paying to have things done that they would otherwise do themselves. One way to do this is to force the data into a more restricted model which assumes that each predictor has a uniform and additive effect over the whole sample, but which takes account of their intercorrelations, that is, a multiple regression model.

To eliminate the worst source of nonadditivity, we restrict our analysis to couples where wives are under sixty-five years old. The set of variables used in the dummy-variable regression is given in Table 10-2 together with the measure of their importance both with and without accounting for their joint effect. They explained 20 per cent of the total variance. The overall average of reported hours of outside help received by this group of couples is 218 hours and the standard deviation is 457 hours.

It appears to be the husband's earnings more than the wife's that matter when it comes to paying others to do things for the family.

TABLE 10-2

VARIABLES USED TO EXPLAIN HOURS OF WORK RECEIVED IN 1964
BY FAMILIES FROM OUTSIDE FAMILY

(For 1469 married couples who received less than 3000 hours of help
and where wives were less than 65 years old

Variables used to explain hours of work received	Relative importance	
	Using unadjusted means	Using adjusted means
	(Eta coefficients)*	(Partial beta coefficients)**
Hourly earnings of husband (and whether he worked for money)	.265	.272
Age of youngest child under 18 living at home	.180	.224
Whether difficult to hire outside for work around the house	.166	.160
Hourly earnings of wife (and whether she worked for money)	.131	.184
Number of rooms in home	.106	.074

*Eta, the correlation ratio, is identical with the multiple correlation coefficient using a set of dummy variables with no overlapping between the groups. Its square is the proportion of variance explained by using the subgroup means of that characteristic to predict the dependent variable.

*This is analogous to the usual partial beta coefficient, except that being based on a set of dummy variable coefficients instead of a variable with an imposed sign, it is always positive.

TR 221

Figure 10-3 shows that as the husbands' hourly earnings rise above $6.00, the family increasingly relies upon outside help, presumably to save the husband's time. Some of it, particularly eating in restaurants and sending out laundry, however, certainly saves the wife's time as well.

Figure 10-4 shows the detailed effect of the second most important factor, the age of the youngest child in the family. Families with pre-school children, but no infant under two, get the most outside help. Those with teen-aged children and none younger get the least, even less than those with no children at all. Apparently teen-aged children do help around the house a little bit! Why do families with infants get so little outside help? Perhaps it is because the mother almost never has an outside job during this period, and because they are unlikely to eat out in restaurants and perhaps are less likely to leave a very small child with baby-sitters.

Figure 10-5 shows that those who said it would be difficult to find someone to do for them the things they now do around the house, are actually receiving less help from outside the family. Hence sheer imperfections in the market--lack of an organized labor supply--are forcing some people to do things for themselves. However, there are two other groups receiving little outside help presumably because they didn't want it--those who say it would be easy to find help but that they have not considered doing so, and those who don't know whether it would be easy or not--presumably because they don't care and haven't tried.

If husband's hourly earnings have to be $6.00 or more before fami-lies start increasing their use of outside help, perhaps because only then can they overcome the income taxes on both salaries (theirs and that of the

FIGURE 10-3

ACTUAL AND ADJUSTED AVERAGE HOURS OF WORK RECEIVED BY FAMILIES IN 1964
FROM OUTSIDE FAMILY, BY HOURLY EARNINGS OF HUSBAND
(For all 1496 married couples where wife is under 65 years old)

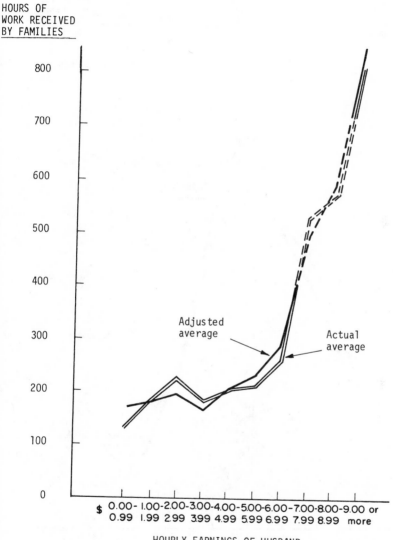

HOURS OF
WORK RECEIVED
BY FAMILIES

HOURLY EARNINGS OF HUSBAND

- - - Less than 25 cases

MTR 221

174

FIGURE 10-4

ACTUAL AND ADJUSTED AVERAGE HOURS OF WORK RECEIVED BY FAMILIES IN 1964 FROM OUTSIDE
FAMILY, BY AGE OF YOUNGEST CHILD UNDER 18 LIVING AT HOME
(For all 1496 married couples where wife is under 65 years old)

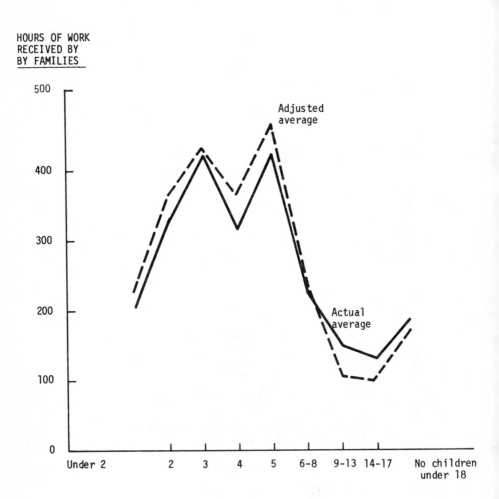

AGE OF YOUNGEST CHILD UNDER 18 LIVING AT HOME

MTR 221

175

FIGURE 10-5

ACTUAL AND ADJUSTED AVERAGE HOURS OF WORK RECEIVED BY FAMILIES IN 1964
FROM OUTSIDE FAMILY, BY WHETHER DIFFICULT TO HIRE OUTSIDE HELP *
(For all 1496 married couples where wife is under 65 years old)*

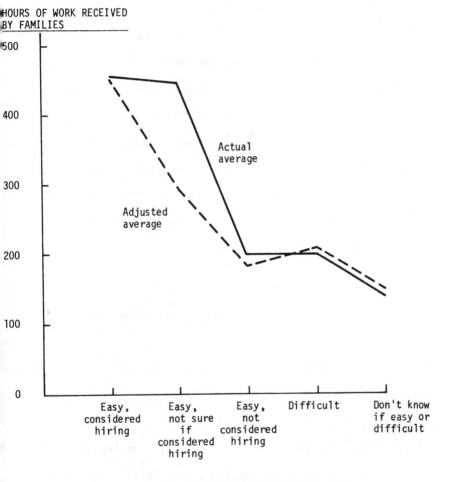

WHETHER DIFFICULT TO HIRE OUTSIDE HELP

MTR 221

*excludes 16 cases in which whether difficult to hire outside help was not
ascertained.

person hired), and the inefficiencies of supervising another, then it is not surprising that the wife's earnings which almost never get that high, have little effect. Figure 10-6 shows that the few families where the wife makes $4.00 an hour or more actually get less outside help, even after taking account of the age of the youngest child and the other variables. The low point at the left of the figure means mostly that families where the wife does not work for money at all, receive less outside help. Those who actually work for less than $1.00 an hour commonly work in family businesses or are so in need of funds that they would hardly consider hiring someone from outside the family to get things done.

Figure 10-7 shows the effect of the least important factor--size of house. Those with very large homes, and those with one or two rooms, are the most likely to pay others to do things, the former because there is so much to do, and the latter probably because there are so few facilities that they eat out and send out their laundry.

Summary

Outside help is a necessity for some and a luxury for others. For single men it is a necessity because they do not know how to do most of the work around the home and often live in places having only limited facilities for cooking and doing laundry. For mothers who have outside employment, it is a necessity especially if they are working long hours and have young children at home since the day has only 24 hours and someone has to take care of their children and do the housework when they are not at home. For the rest of the people, it is only the affluent who actually buy many hours of outside help.

177

FIGURE 10-6

ACTUAL AND ADJUSTED AVERAGE HOURS OF WORK RECEIVED BY FAMILIES IN 1964
FROM OUTSIDE FAMILY, BY HOURLY EARNINGS OF WIFE
(For all 1496 married couples where wife is under 65 years old)[*]

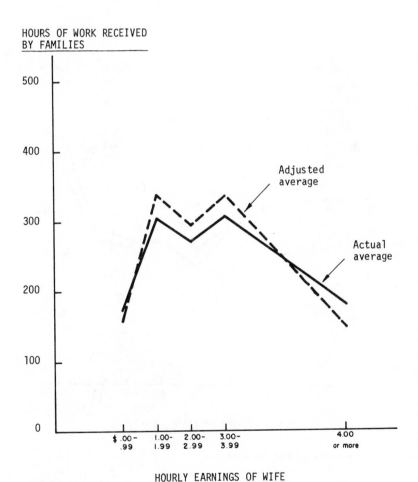

MTR 221

HOURLY EARNINGS OF WIFE

[*]Non-working wives are included in the first bracket of hourly
earnings ($.00 - .99)

FIGURE 10-7

ACTUAL AND ADJUSTED AVERAGE HOURS OF WORK RECEIVED BY FAMILIES IN 1964
FROM OUTSIDE FAMILY, BY NUMBER OF ROOMS IN HOME
(For all 1496 married couples where wife is under 65 years old)*

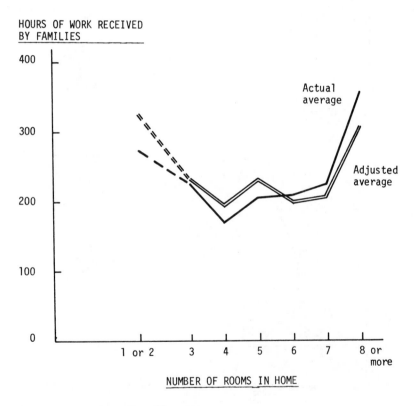

HOURS OF WORK RECEIVED
BY FAMILIES

NUMBER OF ROOMS IN HOME

— — — Less than 25 cases

MTR 221

*excludes 8 cases in which number of rooms in home was not ascertained.

Related Research

No previous studies on the unpaid productive use of time have been done in the United States that are directly comparable to this study. However, many sociological studies of homemakers' use of time have been made, largely from the point of view of efficiency and time budgeting. We refer to a few of them here,[5] but we exclude the vast literature on leisure time and its uses. It is worth noting that as early as about 1917 John B. Leeds had sixty housewives complete a budget of their working time around the house. The average hours of regular housework they reported (our most comparable measure) was over eight hours per day. Wives in that study were also asked if they had done any work besides regular housework for the purpose of saving money or helping out their husbands. About half of them

---

[5]In 1953 May Cowles and Ruth Dietz studied the time spent per week in working by eighty-five Wisconsin rural farm homemakers. They concluded that "the homemakers' time spent in homemaking plus other types of work, increased with the household size." See May L. Cowles and Ruth P. Dietz, Time Spent in Homemaking Activities by a Selected Group of Wisconsin Farm Homemakers," Journal of Home Economics, 48, No. 1 (January 1956), 29-35; see also May L. Cowles, Sara M. Steele, and Mary B. Kishler, "Savings in Distance Walked in Kitchens through Reorganization of Storage and Work Space," Journal of Home Economics, 50, No. 3 (March 1958), 169-174; Francena L. Nolan and Dawn H. Tuttle, Certain Practices, Satisfaction, and Difficulties in Families with Employed Homemakers, Bulletin No. 655 (State College: Pennsylvania State College of Agriculture, August 1959); J. O. Ranking, The Use of Time in Farm Homes, Bulletin No. 230 (Lincoln: University of Nebraska Agricultural Station); Albert Reiss, "Rural-Urban and Status Differences in Interpersonal Contacts," American Journal of Sociology, 75 (September 1959), 182-195; Pitirim A. Sorokin and Clarence Q. Berger, Time-Budget of Human Behavior (Cambridge: Harvard University Press, 1939); E. L. Thorndike, "How We Spend Our Time and What We Spend It For," Scientific Monthly, XLIV (May 1937), 464-469; Kathryn E. Walker, Homemaking Work Units, New York State, Miscellaneous Bulletin No. 28 (Ithaca: Department of Home Economics, Cornell University, February 1958); Grace E. Wasson, Use of Time by South Dakota Farm Homemakers, Bulletin No. 247 (Brookings, South Dakota: Agricultural Experiment Station); Maud Wilson, Use of Time by Oregon Farm Homemakers, Bulletin No. 256 (Eugene: Oregon Agricultural Experimental Station).

answered in the affirmative. The exact hours so spent were not estimated, however.[6]

Some studies have stressed the relation between wives' outside employment and their housework budgeting. They indicate that working wives exercised some saving and efficiency in their housework, and that their hus bands helped out more. Robert O. Blood, Jr., studied a representative sam ple of white married women in Detroit which included 324 families each hav ing at least one child in elementary school. His conclusions were: (1) working mothers participated less than nonworking mothers in household tasks (63 per cent of the nonworking wives have a high share of household tasks, as compared to 33 per cent of working wives, and that their husbands participated more; (2) working mothers made fewer decisions about routine household matters, and their husbands made more; (3) there was no differenc between working and nonworking wives in reported dominance in family deci sion making.[7] A study by F. L. Nolan showed that employed mothers, espe cially in the nonfarm families, tended to redistribute their work load to their husbands and to commercial services.[8] In a study of adolescents, Prodipto Roy reported that high school pupils, especially girls, partici pated more in household chores (had a "high chore score") when their mother

[6]John B. Leeds, The Household Budget (Philadelphia: J. B. Leeds, 1917) (includes time budgets of 60 housewives).

[7]Robert O. Blood, Jr., "The Effects of the Wife's Employment on the Husband-Wife Relationship," The Employed Mother in America, ed. Francis Iva Nye and Lois W. Hoffman (Chicago: Rand-McNally and Co., 1963), pp. 282-305.

[8]Francena L. Nolan, "Rural Employment and Husbands and Wives," in Nye and Hoffman, loc. cit.

worked.[9] Another study, by Pearl Jephcott and others, concluded that "those wives who had to pack a job into their day used the time-honored expedient of getting up earlier . . . and . . . their husbands helped."[10]

Sebastian de Grazia provided some data on housework from an unpublished study based on a national sample. That study showed that, in an average day, women spent about 6 hours on housework, while men spent about 2 hours, and that, on the average, women spent 5 hours on their daily leisure activities, and men 4 1/2.[11]

In a study of the housewife's leisure time, J. Roy Leevy reported (1) that all American housewives have leisure time at their disposal, that this leisure time varies from one-half to 5 hours a day, and that urban wives have more leisure than rural wives; (2) that housewives have leisure time in the afternoon and evening; and (3) that the size of the family has little relationship to the rural housewives' leisure time. On the other hand, the study indicated that urban housewives have smaller families and

---

[9]Prodipto Roy, "Adolescent Roles: Rural-Urban Differentials," in Nye and Hoffman, loc. cit.

[10]Pearl Jephcott, Nancy Sear, and John H. Smith, Married Women Working (London: George Allen and Unwin, 1962); Frances N. Ketchum, "A Study of Homemakers' Values as Reflected in Time Used for Family and Personal Activities" (unpublished Master's thesis, Michigan State Univ., 1961); Alva Myrdal and Viola Klein, Women's Two Roles (London: Routledge and Kegan Paul, Ltd., 1956); Francena L. Nolan and Dawn H. Tuttle, Certain Practices, Satisfactions, and Difficulties in Families with Employed Homemakers, Bulletin No. 655 (State College: Pennsylvania State College of Agriculture, August 1959).

[11]Sebastian de Grazia, Of Time Work and Leisure (New York: The Twentieth Century Fund, 1962), p. 444. In his "The Uses of Time," Aging and Leisure, ed. Robert W. Kleemeier (New York: Oxford University Press, 1961), pp. 121-125, de Grazia reproduced some data from a study done by the Opinion Research Corporation that was based on a national sample which asked people over 15 years old) what leisure activities they had engaged in yesterday.

hence do have more leisure time than rural housewives.[12]

A forthcoming study on the use of time by urban families in the United States which used the diary procedure found that employed men spent about 42 hours per week on their work-related activities and four hours doing housework. Housewives reported about 34 hours a week of housework. It was also reported that time spent on housework tended to increase with the presence of many young children and to decrease with wives' outside employment. These findings are close to those reported in the text especially if we consider that the latter include rural families as well.[13]

There are some studies that focused on volunteer work done for churches, organizations, and relatives. These studies have shown who does such work, but none has provided an estimate of total hours spent on such activities or participation by age, income, or education.[14]

Few foreign studies have been located. However, in 1962 the Hungarian Central Statistical Office published a study based on a representative sample of married Hungarian families with employed workers between fifteen and fifty-five years old.[15] Sixty-one per cent of the wives in these families worked, and 35 per cent of the husbands of these women helped around

---

[12]J. Roy Leevy, "Leisure Time of the American Housewife," Sociology and Social Research, 35, No. 2 (November-December 1950), 97-105.

[13]Forthcoming study by the Survey Research Center (Part of the United Nations Nine-Nation Project).

[14]David L. Sills, The Volunteers: Means and Ends in a National Organization (Glencoe: The Free Press, 1957). This book has an extensive bibliography on participation in volunteer organizations. See also M. B. Sussman, "The Help Pattern in the Middle Class Family," American Sociological Review, 18 (February 1953), 22-28.

[15]Hungarian Central Statistical Office, Women in Employment and at Home (Budapest, 1962) (Hungarian with English supplement).

the house, compared with 15 per cent of the husbands with nonworking wives. The wife's daily average of hours spent on housework varied from 7 hours, for those employed outside the home, to more than 12 hours, for the rest. Thus, the total hours spent on housework by working wives was about 20 per cent more, on the average, than the time spent by working American wives. It was also reported that the amount of housework increased with the number of children.

The same study reported that most of these Hungarian families with employed wives got some outside help with housework--60 per cent,--compared with 30 per cent of families with nonworking wives. The amount of outside help increased with the size of the family. However, in families of five or six members, about 40 per cent of the families with working wives received help from their mothers or mothers-in-law. Children gave much less assistance.

In 1965, the Hungarian Central Statistical Office published a report based on 12,000 time-budgets.[16] It was reported that hours of housework almost doubled on Sunday and that women do more than three times as much as men on the average day. Employment outside the home, employment in agriculture, sex, and age were the most important variables explaining differences in time budgets. Nonworking wives spent an average of 7 hours per day on their housework, single nonworking women 4.8 hours, and working wives 3.6 hours (6 hours if working in a cooperative); for men, housework time varied between 2.7 and 0.7 hours per day.

---

[16]Hungarian Central Statistical Office, The Twenty-Four Hours of the Day (Budapest, 1965) (English version).

A recent Russian study summarized time budgets of the working day for urban workers in 1924 and 1959. It reported that women's average daily hours of housework declined from 4.8 to 3.9 between 1924 and 1959, while the average daily hours of housework for men remained the same, at 1.7. Hours spent by women on studying, cultural, and leisure activities increased from 1.8 to 2.4 hours per day, while that for men declined slightly, from 3.5 to 3.4 hours per day.[17]

Alain Girard found that in France married urban women, especially those with several children, do more housework than single ones.[18] Jean Warren made a time-use study of 53 selected families in Uruguay in 1957, and in the same year Kathryn E. Walker interviewed a sample of 100 Swedish households about their children.[19]

[17]Vnerabochee vremya, ed. Prudensky (Novosibirsk, 1961), 34.

[18]Alain Girard, "Le budget-temps de la femme mariée dans les agglomérations urbaines," Population, 13 (Octobre-Décembre 1958), 591-618.

[19]Jean Warren, Use of Time by Homeworkers in Uruguay, 1957 (Ithaca: State College of Home Economics, Cornell University, 1957); Kathryn E. Walker, "Homemaker's Use of Time for Care of Children in Sweden, in 1957," Konsument Instituteetat meddelar, No. 11 (Stockholm: Statens Inst. for Konsument Froager, 1964).

CHAPTER 11

TOTAL FAMILY PRODUCTIVE ACTIVITIES

Introduction

In the previous chapters, we analyzed separately the time spent by American families on the various types of productive activities. We found that age, sex, and family size, along with sickness and unemployment set the major bounds on how many hours the family devotes to work for money, regular housework, and home production. In this chapter we examine the total hours of these productive activities for the family. In 1964 families spent, on the average, about 4800 hours on such activities.[1] The complete distribution is as follows:

Total hours of productive activities done by families in 1964	Per cent of cases
Less than 1000	5
1000-1999	8
2000-2999	12
3000-3999	11
4000-4999	17
5000-5999	17
6000-6999	13
7000-7999	8
8000-8999	5
9000-9999	2
10,000 or more	2
Total	100
Number of cases	2214

[1]Included in this definition of total productive activities are

Our analysis of this variable was confined to families where the head of the family was under no severe constraints, that is, the 1426 families where the head worked for money in 1964, was not sick or unemployed for more than three weeks, and was not a student. This analysis of productive effort will be made with a three-stage analysis, rather than the usual two-stage analysis. Only those variables that are clearly basic constraints will be used in the first-stage analysis to explain total hours of productive effort. In the second stage, variables representing costs and opportunities facing the family like education, hourly earnings, and business ownership will be used to explain the residuals from the first analysis (i.e., differences in families' productive behavior unexplained by the variables representing basic constraints). Variables representing motives and desires will be used in the third stage in an attempt to explain the remaining differences in families' productive behavior left unexplained after the second-stage analysis.

Basic Constraints

What determines the amount of time devoted to all kinds of productive activities by American families where heads of families worked in 1964, were not sick or unemployed for a long period, and were not students during 1964?[2] Five predicting characteristics, representing basic constraints on

---

hours of work for money, regular housework, and home production. Excluded are hours of volunteer work, courses and lessons, and journey to work time. If we add the hours spent for the excluded activities, the average increases to about 5100 hours.

[2]For statistical reasons 35 families reporting 10,000 hours or more of productive effort were excluded from the analysis.

187

families' current decisions, were used in a multivariate analysis of hours

of total family productive activities. They are listed below in order of

their importance if used to make a single division of the whole sample:

>*Number of adults in family
> Sex and marital status of head of family
>*Number of children under 18 living at home
> Age of youngest child under 18 living at home
>*Age of head of family
>
> Asterisked variables are those used in Figure 11-1. They
> explained 44 per cent of the variance. The overall standard
> deviation is 1979 hours. Each of the variables could explain
> as much as 0.5 per cent of the total sum of squares by a single
> division of the whole sample.

Figure 11-1 shows the results of the first-stage multivariate

analysis. The expected powerful effects of the number of adults and the

number of young children in the family are shown clearly in the figure.

The total family productive effort varied from 2770 hours for one-adult fami-

lies to 7803 hours for families with at least four adults and young children

living at home. We already accounted for most of the age effect by restrict-

ing the analysis to families where heads worked for money during 1964. How-

ever, Figure 11-1 shows that among families with two adults and no children,

if the head was sixty-five or older, the family reported 1000 hours less of

productive activities on the average. It is interesting, however, to examine

the detailed effect of age on families' total productive activities. Since

age and number of adults are correlated, Figure 11-2 gives this overall age

effect only for the 980 two-adult families taken from the 1426 families

analyzed in Figure 11-1 (unconstrained). Families' productive efforts reach

a maximum of about 6000 hours when people are middle-aged and drop systemati-

cally after the age of fifty-five. This tendency of the middle-aged people

188

FIGURE 11-1

TOTAL HOURS OF PRODUCTIVE ACTIVITIES DONE BY FAMILY IN 1964

(For 1426 families where head of family worked for money in 1964, had between
0 and 120 hours of unemployment, took between 0 and 240 hours of courses
and where total productive hours of the family were less than 10,000)

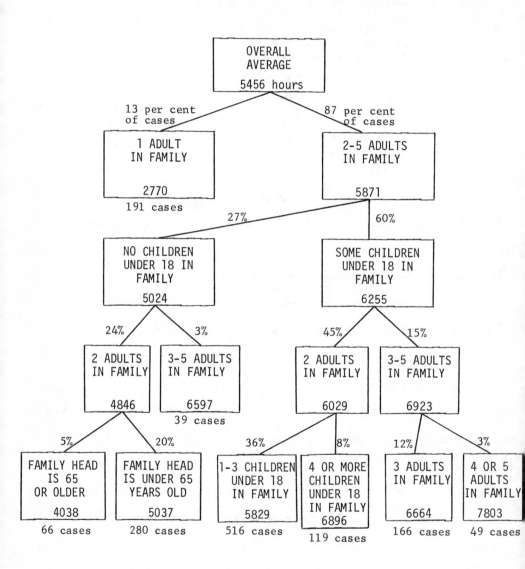

MTR 215

FIGURE 11-2

TOTAL HOURS OF PRODUCTIVE ACTIVITIES DONE BY FAMILIES IN 1964,
BY AGE OF HEAD OF FAMILY
(For all 981 2-adult families in which the head of the family
worked for money in 1964 and was sick or unemployed 120 or
fewer hours and did not take more than 240 hours of
courses and lessons)

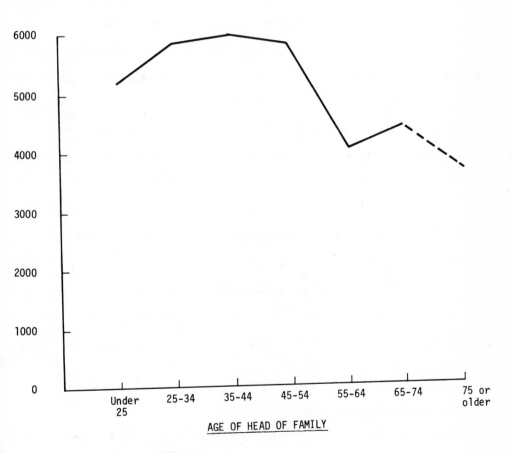

TOTAL HOURS OF
PRODUCTIVE ACTIVITIES

AGE OF HEAD OF FAMILY

– – – Less than 25 cases

MTR 215

to work more was also true for all major groups in Figure 11-1. One explanation is that beyond that age children leave home, and the family moves to a smaller home.

The overall powerful effect of sex and marital status disappeared after the first division of the sample into one and two-or-more-adult families. There was a persistent tendency, however, though not powerful enough to show its way in Figure 11-1, for families headed by women to report doing more hours of productive effort. One explanation, documented by our findings in previous chapters, is that more single women than single men have dependents to support, and their hourly earnings are relatively low so that they have to work longer hours both for money and around the home in order to achieve an acceptable standard of living. Finally, the age of the youngest child living at home showed no appreciable effect in the analysis, though the number of children did.

All the findings of Figure 11-1 were expected; they show the most important combinations of the basic constraints. We can now take the remaining differences from the averages of the final groups of that figure, and examine them further for the effect of other forces. The residuals from the end-group averages of Figure 11-1 can be thought of as mostly a more precise adjustment for family size than merely using hours per adult or per equivalent adult.

Costs and Opportunities

Eight variables representing opportunities open to the family were used in this second stage-analysis. They are listed below in order of their importance if used to make a single division of the whole sample of residuals:

*Hourly earnings of head of family
 Education of head of family
*Whether head of family was self-employed (or in the labor
    force)
*Whether family owns business or farm
 Size of place (town) where family lives
 Housing status (home ownership)

---

*Education of wife
 Race

Asterisked variables are those used in Figure 11-3. They
explained an additional 5 per cent of the variance. The overall
standard deviation of the residual hours is 1484. Variables below
the line could not explain as much as 0.5 per cent of the total
sum of squares by a single division of the whole sample.

Figure 11-3 shows a dramatic "incentive" effect of low hourly earn-

ings. Those families where the head of the family earned less than $3.00

per hour worked 257 hours more than expected (on the basis of family size

and structure), and those making $3.00 or more worked 321 hours less than

expected, a gross difference of 578 hours per year. The difference becomes

still larger when we eliminate a few families where the head of the family

had retired during the year and hence worked less than expected. The other

(nonretired) low-wage people worked 327 hours more than expected, and dif-

fered from the high-wage group by 648 hours per year. It would seem that

$3.00 an hour, or $6000 a year is a kind of standard, below which the family

is driven to extra effort.

Nothing else differentiated the high wage group, but among the low-

wage group still in the labor force, owning a business or farm or making

very low hourly earnings (less than $1.00) led to still longer total produc-

tive hours on the job and off, and by the whole family. Owning a business

or farm means both a freer choice of how long to work, rather than depending

FIGURE 11-3

TOTAL HOURS OF PRODUCTIVE ACTIVITIES DONE BY FAMILY IN 1964: ANALYSIS
OF DIFFERENCES FROM END-GROUP AVERAGES OF FIGURE 11-1

(For 1426 families where head of family worked for money in 1964, had
between 0 and 120 hours of unemployment, took between 0 and 240 hours
of courses and where total productive hours of the family
were less than 10,000)

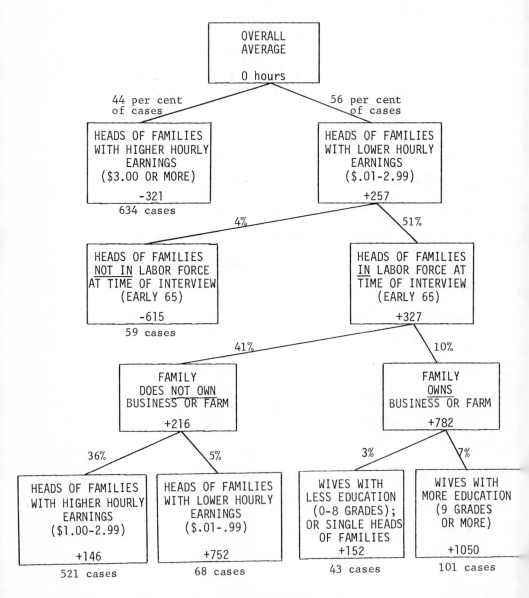

on the head of the family's finding a second job or having the wife work for money outside the home, and also sometimes arbitrary demands of the business and special motivation from being one's own boss. Among families owning a business or farm, the wife's education seemed to matter--the more education she had, the more work the whole family did. Those families having a wife with at least nine grades of education reported total productive hours of 1050 above the average. Whether the educated wife raised family aspirations, or merely was able more easily to find rewarding work, or both, is difficult to say.

Since hourly earnings of the head of the family was the most important variable, Figure 11-4 gives its full effect on the residuals from the end-group averages of Figure 11-1. There is a spread of more than 1400 hours between families where heads earn less than $1.00 an hour and those who earn $7.50 or more. Apparently the impact of rising wages is a reduction in the necessity for very long hours of work allowing somewhat more time for other things.

What seemed to be a strong education effect disappeared from view once the sample was divided on hourly earnings since education of the head of the family and his hourly earnings are so highly correlated.

Looking at the other variables that never managed to get into Figure 11-3, we find that people living in the central cities of the twelve largest metropolitan areas reported fewer total productive hours, and those in rural areas not near a metropolitan area (central city with 50,000 or more population) reported more hours than expected, with the intermediate-sized places falling in between. This is related to home-ownership because homeowners report more work (more opportunities around the house, and perhaps more

FIGURE 11-4

TOTAL HOURS OF PRODUCTIVE ACTIVITIES DONE BY FAMILIES IN 1964: DIFFERENCES
FROM END-GROUP AVERAGES OF FIGURE 11-1, BY HOURLY EARNINGS OF HEAD OF FAMILY
(For all 1426 families in which head of family worked for money in 1964
and was sick or unemployed 120 or fewer hours and did not take more
than 240 hours of courses and lessons)

TOTAL HOURS OF PRODUCTIVE ACTIVITIES

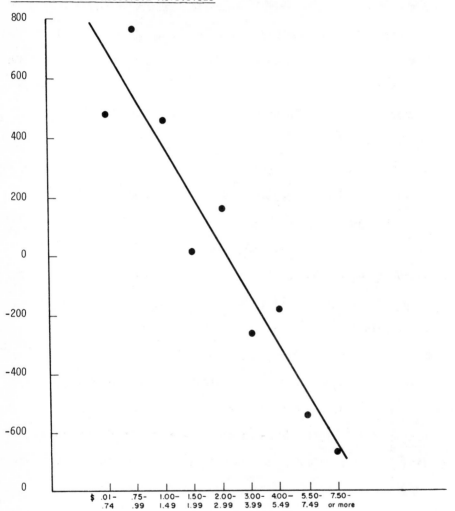

HOURLY EARNINGS OF HEAD OF FAMILY

MTR 215

motivation too), and a larger proportion own their homes in rural areas. Race seemed to have no appreciable relation to total productive hours, over the whole sample of residuals or over any major subgroup.

Our analysis thus far has explained almost 50 per cent of the differences in families' reported hours of total productive effort. However there are still individual variations around the end group averages of Figure 11-3 (left unexplained), and once more we can now take these remaining differences and examine them further for the effect of other forces. This is indeed a very tight test since to the extent that these new variables are correlated with the explanatory variables used in the first two stages, estimates of their effects will be damped.

Motives and Attitudes

The following variables representing motives and attitudes towards productive effort were used in this third stage of the analysis. They are listed below in order of their importance if used to make a single division of the whole sample of residuals:

> Number of responses indicating a sense of personal effectiveness
> Combined index of concern with progress
> Index of caution and risk avoidance
> Attitude toward importance of luck for financial success
> Per cent of adults in county who completed high school
> Hours lost from work by head of family in 1964 from illness or unemployment
> Occupation of head of family
> Whether head of family grew up on a farm
> Region of country
> Index of closeness of family ties
> Index of social participation
> Education of family head's father
> Religious preference
> Index of mobility experience
> Attitude toward mothers' working

None of the variables could explain as much as 0.5 per cent of the total sum of squares by a single division of the whole sample of residuals.

Out of three questions to which the respondent could indicate that he felt a <u>sense of personal effectiveness</u>, there was a rather even distribution into the four frequencies, zero through three, and a systematic tendency for those feeling more effective to be heads of families devoting more hours to some productive activity. But no single division of these classes could reduce the variance of the residual hours by 0.5 per cent.

It was the extremes on the <u>combined index of concern for progress</u> that differed, particularly a small group at the lowest level who worked much less than expected. (See Chapter 20 for the use of this index as a dependent variable.) Cautious people seem to work a little harder but the effect is not systematic. Those who think <u>luck</u> is important for financial success report fewer productive hours for their families than those who think it is not important. Those living in counties where a larger proportion of the adults have graduated from high school, report more productive work, except for a small group in counties where over half the adult population are high school graduates, who do less work.

Families where the head of the family was either a farmer, skilled, or semi-skilled worker reported more hours of productive effort, as did those who grew up on a farm, and those living in the North Central states. Families in the Deep South reported somewhat less work, and a few who are highly active socially reported more work than expected. But these findings are suggestive, since the differences are generally small. It must be kept in mind that the total productive activity of the whole family is being explained on the basis of information from the head of the family, and about his attitudes and motive-related behaviors.

197

Summary

The total productive activity of the American family is of course a function of the size and structure of the family. Allowing for that, the need for income appears after all to be the main determinant of productive effort, aided only by the added freedom and incentive that comes from owning a business or farm, and from having a wife with at least some high school education. Some suggestive results remain supporting the notion that people who feel more effective personally, more able to cope with the world, are working more, as are those generally concerned with progress and not willing to rely much on luck for financial success.

CHAPTER 12

THE CHOICE OF WORK OR LEISURE AT THE MARGIN

The family can be thought of as making its decisions sequentially,
deciding first how much the head of the family will work, and then how much
the wife will work, all in a situation where the amount of regular housework
was predetermined by the family size, structure and standards, and the kind
of dwelling they occupy. Even hours of work for money are under some constraints and limitations. But then the family has marginal decisions it
can make with some freedom. It can add to the family's real control over
goods and services by doing extra things around the house--what we call home
production. Or it can give up some money to have these things done by
others--by hiring people to do things around the house or to take care of
the children, by eating out, or by sending out the laundry. All these decisions involve giving up some of the family's otherwise free time (leisure)
for more goods and services, or giving up money (which could otherwise buy
things) for more free time--the time that would have to be spent doing
things around the house. Since these various choices are so similar, they
may well be substitutes for one another, and it seemed economical to trans-
late them all into a measure, in hours, of the net purchase of leisure.
This measure is positive if more hours of help are received by the family
than the extra hours it puts into home production, and negative if they

spend more time on home production than they receive in help from others.[1]

The distribution of this measure of net purchase or forfeit of leisure--hiring help minus home production--is as follows:

Net purchase or forfeit of hours of leisure by family in 1964	Per cent of cases
+500 or more (net purchase)	11
+400 to 499	2
+300 to 399	3
+200 to 299	5
+100 to 199	7
+1 to 99	13
0 to -99	26
-100 to -199	12
-200 to -299	7
-300 to -399	5
-400 to -499	3
-500 or less (net forfeit)	6
Total	100
Number of cases	2214

A multivariate analysis made use of the following predictors, listed in order of their importance if used to make a single division of the whole sample:

    *Sex and marital status of head of family
    *Age of wife
    Education of wife
    *Hourly earnings of head of family
    *Size of place (town) where family lives
    Number of people in family
    Housing status (home ownership)
    *Age of youngest child under 18 living at home
    Number of rooms in the dwelling
    *Hours of work for money in 1964 by wife

    Hours of work for money in 1964 by head of family

---

[1]This variable is defined as total hours of help received by the family (free or paid for) for work done around the house, eating out, child care, or sending out laundry <u>minus</u> total hours of work done around the house by the family (home production).

Asterisked variables are those actually used in Figure 12-1. They explained 17 per cent of the variance. The overall standard deviation is 559 hours. The variable below the line could not account for as much as 0.5 per cent of the total sum of squares by a single division of the whole sample.

The single men on net balance buy more of their leisure back by having things done for them than they use up doing things beyond their job and the regular housework. (They also spend a great deal less time on regular housework, as we saw in Chapter 8.) If the head of the family makes $7.50 an hour or more, and particularly if he also works more than 2000 hours a year, the family buys back many more hours than it spends on home production. Even if the head earns less than $7.50 an hour, if he has a wife who worked more than half time for money, the family is a net purchaser of leisure, and particularly so if the wife is young and if there are children under eighteen in the family. While it is not shown in the tree, a further division of the group in the lower right (young wives working more than half time with children under 18) would reveal that where there are children under six the family is as big a net buyer of its own time as where the head works more than 2000 hours at $7.50 or more per hour. And the effect is still stronger if the family lives in a central city of 10,000 or more, those families being net buyers on the average of more than 1000 hours of time.

At the other extreme are families where the husband makes less than $7.50 an hour and the wife works 1000 hours or less for money, where the family does more extra hours of home production than they buy back by having things done. This tendency is particularly strong if the family does not live in a city of 50,000 or more but in a smaller city or rural area. Along the way, the analysis separates out the single women who on net balance

FIGURE 12-1

HOURS OF NET PURCHASE OF LEISURE FOR FAMILIES IN 1964
(For 2203 families whose net shift was between -2999 and +2999 hours)

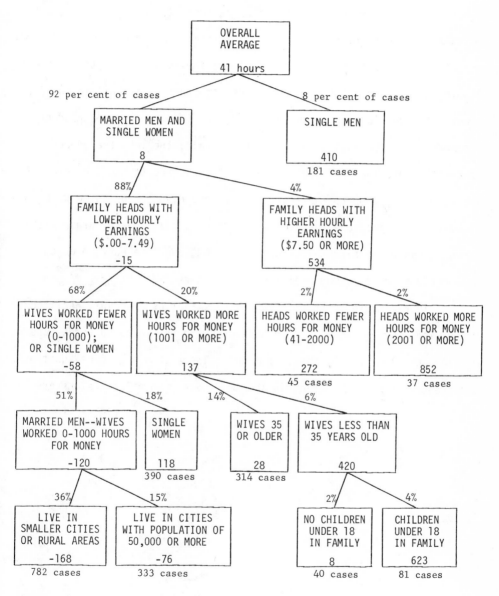

MTR 226

receive more hours of help than they contribute in extra home production.

Summary

Decisions at the margin where the most flexibility exists, between doing more work to increase the family's total command of goods and service or getting others to do it to increase the family's leisure time, form a meaningful pattern. The more one earns, the more he can afford to hire others, and the less he needs the added real income from home production. The more hours the husband or wife work, again, the less they need added income the more they can afford to hire others, and the more precious their leisure time must be to them--since they have given it up to work for money Young children increase the work to be done, and living in larger cities makes it easier to hire things done, eat out, and less easy to engage in home production since many families are renters.

There should be substantial changes in these marginal decisions as wages rise, more wives work, and more ways are developed to reduce one's work around the house by spending money. There should also be substantial differences between countries in the way these marginal decisions are made.

SECTION III

REACTION TO CHANGE

The way people use their time is only one part of a set of behaviors
and attitudes by which we can measure "modernism," and which in general are
thought to be important determinants in a country's rate of economic growth.
Whether the whole set forms a syndrome, that is, whether those who use much
of their time productively are also receptive to change, mobile, ambitious,
and likely to plan, will be examined in Chapter 20. We turn first to an
examination of the component attitudes and behaviors. Some of them have
already been used to help explain time-use, but in this section they are
treated as dependent variables.

The construction of indexes and scales is a ticklish business, to
which much thought has been devoted. We have taken a relatively simple and
straightforward approach, justified by the fact that so long as the components of an index are not negatively correlated with one another, the specific weights by which they are combined do not matter much. Anything strongly
correlated with any of the parts of the index will still be correlated with
the whole index.

Hence, we have built indexes by assigning points to responses considered a priori to represent a particular attitude or behavior, and adding
them. For attitudes or behaviors appropriate to only part of the sample, we
have sometimes avoided spurious relations by assigning weights of 0, 1, and

203

2: 0 for those who could have and didn't, 1 for those for whom the item is irrelevant, and 2 for those who could have and did. For instance, one question was, "When do you think you will retire?" A retired person was scored 1, while a nonretired person who could tell us the age was scored 2, for planning; and a nonretired person who could give no answer was scored 0 for that component of the planning index.

The indexes have been given descriptive titles, such as planning and time horizon, ambition and aspiration, receptivity to change, social participation, mobility behavior, caution and risk avoidance, closeness of family ties, and attitude toward mothers' working.

The findings of Section II were that, in general, these attitudes and behaviors had some modest relationships with the working and time-use behavior of family heads or families. It remains important to know just what accounts for variations within the population in the indexes themselves. In Chapters 13-19 we examine each of these indexes as a dependent variable, often examining also one or more of its principal components; in Chapter 20 we examine whether they can be fitted together to form a "modernism syndrome."

In interpreting the results of the next few chapters, it is
important to remember what behavior patterns relate to the names given
to the indices. The names of the indices should not be taken to imply
that a valid measure of a theoretical construct has been provided, but
should be looked on as mnemonic devices to help the reader recall the
operations by which the measures were developed. The data are, after all,
the answers to questions, suitable categorized and combined. We feel
they reflect a reality, and have tried to emphasize reports of actual
situation, behavior, or plans rather than to de-emphasize self-ratings and
self perceptions.

In any situation where measurement problems exist, the finding of
meaningful and powerful relations allows us to conclude both that there is
likely to be some real relation and that the measures have been adequate
to discover it. There may be differences in interpretation about the
meanings of the measures. On the other hand, where no relation appears,
it may be that the measures were inadequate, so we should be cautious about
rejecting hypotheses.

CHAPTER 13

RECEPTIVITY TO CHANGE

Definition

Resistance to change is a common phenomenon and is generally believed to hamper economic development, even though not all change is for the good. The operational definition of receptivity is clearly different for different cultures and different epochs. For the United States in the 1960's we selected the following four kinds of measures.

First, _use of new products_. For this component, the family received one point for each of the following:

        Use a steam iron
        Use an electric frying pan
        Use a gasoline credit card
        Use coin-operated dry-cleaning machine
        Have seat belts in the car
        Bought car new rather than used

Second, _self perception of receptivity to new products and attitude toward them_. For this component, points were given as follows:

Head of family says he tries new products when they first come out	2 points
Head of family says he sometimes tries new products first, sometimes waits, or does not know what he does	1 point
Head of family thinks that most new products are improvements	2 points
Head of family thinks that some new things are improvements but some are not, or does not know what he thinks	1 point

Third, <u>attraction to new scientific developments</u>. Heads of families
ere given one point for each of the following:

Approve without qualification the addition of fluoride
to the water

At least some of family have had polio vaccine

Think that there is some benefit to trying to land a
man on the moon

Fourth, <u>importance of making changes on the job</u>. The final compo-
ent of the index of receptivity to change was a single zero or one score
epending on whether the respondent liked to make changes on his job. For
he self-employed, the question was, "Do you like to keep things running
moothly or are you more interested in trying new things in your work?" For
he employees, the question was, "How important is it to you to have some
hance to make changes in your work?" The distributions for these four com-
onent indexes, as well as the combined index are given in Table 13-1.

ackground Factors

The average score on the index of receptivity to change is 6.4, and
he two major variables correlated with it are education and age. Figure
3-1 shows, for both the index and its four components, a strong and per-
istent tendency for heads of families with more formal education to show
ore receptivity to change. Figure 13-2 shows a tendency for those heads of
amilies fifty-five or older to be more resistant to change, and even more
o as they grow older.

Age and education are negatively correlated in the population, of
ourse. Most of the older people finished fewer grades of school. Thus, it
ay not even be meaningful to ask whether it is age or education that mat-
ers, since the uneducated among the young, and the highly educated among

TABLE 13-1

DISTRIBUTION OF THE COMPONENTS OF THE INDEX OF RECEPTIVITY TO CHANGE
(For all 2214 heads of families)

Index score	Components of receptivity to change index				Receptiv to chan index
	Use of new products	Self perception of receptivity to new products and atti- tude toward them	Attraction to new scientific developments	Importance of making changes on the job	
Zero	13	8	16	67	1
One	18	17	33	33	2
Two	21	31	34		4
Three	19	20	17		6
Four	17	24			9
Five	10				11
Six	2				12
Seven					13
Eight					14
Nine					28*
Total	100	100	100	100	100

*The top of the receptivity to change index was truncated, calling those sco ing nine or higher exactly nine for mechanical convenience and because the highest scores were possible only for those who owned a car and were not re tired. Since not all components were relevant for everyone, the top tail which was truncated is partly a spurious function of whether the individual was eligible to answer all the questions. The details of the truncated top the combined receptivity index is as follows:

Actual score	Per cent
Nine	12
Ten	7
Eleven	6
Twelve	2
Thirteen	1
Fourteen	0
Total	28

MTR 150

FIGURE 13-1

SCORE ON INDEX OF RECEPTIVITY TO CHANGE AND ITS COMPONENTS,
BY EDUCATION OF HEAD OF FAMILY
(For all 2214 heads of families)*

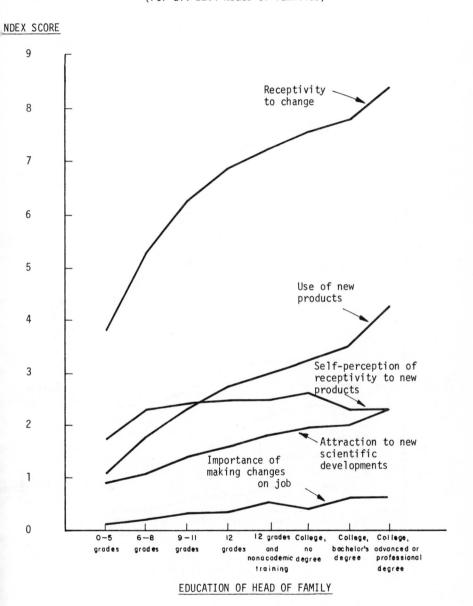

INDEX SCORE

EDUCATION OF HEAD OF FAMILY

MTR 150

*excludes 4 cases in which education of head of family was not ascertained.

FIGURE 13-2

SCORE ON INDEX OF RECEPTIVITY TO CHANGE AND ITS COMPONENTS, BY AGE OF HEAD OF FAMILY
(For all 2214 heads of families)

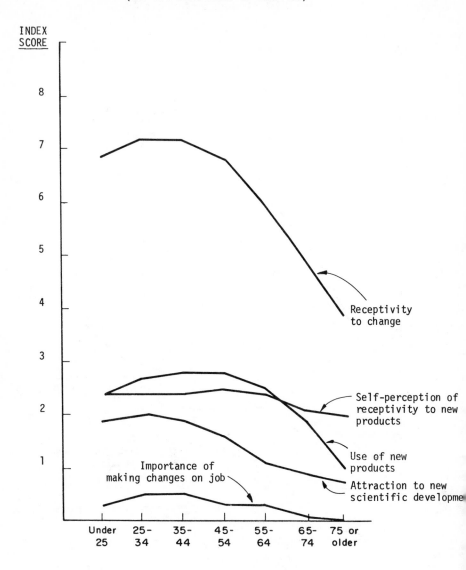

AGE OF HEAD OF FAMILY

MTR 150

he old, are incongruent cases which may be influenced more by that incon-
ruence than by either their age or their education. There is no way to be
ure which is the real "cause," but we can turn to our search process and
ee whether, after a split on the more powerful of the variables, the other
rops from view or still has some influence. Figure 13-3 shows the main
esults. At lower education levels, further division by education is more
owerful than age differences in explaining receptivity to change. Advanced
ge shows up as an important factor in its own right only at higher educa-
ional levels among the single people, and among married white people who
ad completed nine through twelve grades of education. Hence both age and
ducation are important, even though they are correlated, so that their
eparate influences are difficult to untangle.[1]

The important thing to keep in mind is that when two variables are
egatively correlated with each other and have opposite effects on the
ependent variable, the gross relation of each with the dependent variable
ends to exaggerate its effect. What appears to be the effect of more edu-
ation may in part be the effect of youth, and vice versa.

Since the most powerful division is between those with less than
ine grades of formal education and those with nine or more, we can drama-
ize the way the gross age effect exaggerates the true age effect. Figure
3-4 shows that the age effects are smaller for each of the two education
roups than for the whole sample. Younger people tend to be more receptive
nd better educated, while the older ones are less receptive and less educa-
ed. Hence the "all cases" line starts close to the more educated group at

---

[1]See Appendix D for further detail on intercorrelations among the
xplanatory variables.

212

FIGURE 13-3

INDEX OF RECEPTIVITY TO CHANGE
(For all 2214 heads of families)

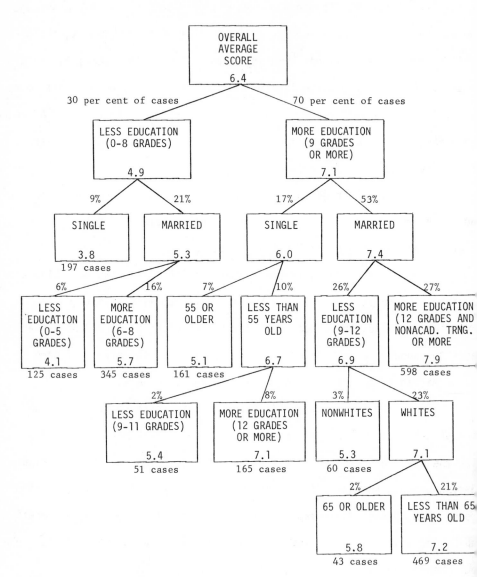

MTR 128

213

FIGURE 13-4

SCORE ON INDEX OF RECEPTIVITY TO CHANGE FOR TWO EDUCATIONAL LEVELS
SEPARATELY, BY AGE OF HEAD OF FAMILY
(For all 2214 heads of families)

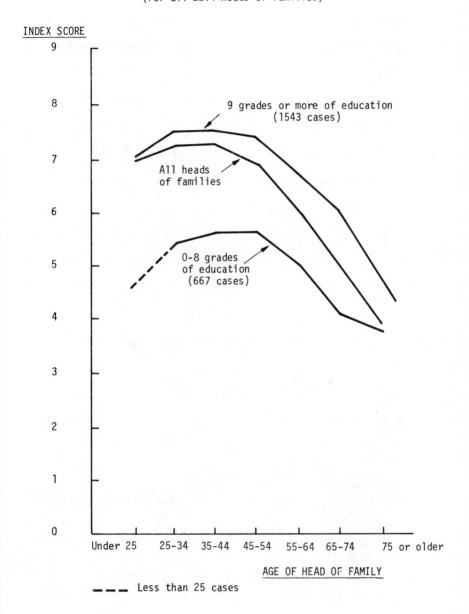

MTR 128

the young ages and ends up closer to the lower line of those with less education.

Returning to Figure 13-3, we find that only two factors other than age and education have come in: marital status and race. The higher score of the married people are not spurious, since most of the components of the index are equally relevant to single and to married people. It is true, of course, that married people are more likely to have need for modern applian ces, and that single people are more likely to be either very young or very old. In any case, the married people at both educational levels seemed more receptive to change.

Race appears as the most important factor for married heads of fami lies who had at least some high school but no education beyond high school --the 60 nonwhites having scores low enough to justify "segregating" them in Figure 13-3. Examination of the data behind the figure shows that the race difference tends to disappear for those with education beyond high school.

The variables used in the analysis, in the order of their importanc if used in making a single division of the whole sample, were:

```
*Education of head of family
*Age of head of family
 Index of achievement orientation
*Sex and marital status of head of family
 Difference in education between head of family and father
 Whether head of family grew up on farm
*Race
 Number of brothers and sisters of head of family
 Religious preference
```

Number of brothers and sisters older than head of family

Asterisked variables are those used in Figure 13-3. They explained 34 per cent of the variance. The overall standard deviation of the score is 2.4. None of the variables below the line could explain as much as 0.5 per cent of the total sum of squares by a single division of the whole sample.

We turn now to the variables that never came into Figure 13-3, dis-
ussing them in order of their importance if used one at a time. Those
coring higher on the index of <u>achievement orientation</u> were also more recep-
ive to change; but, as the figure shows, education, marital status, and
ge were dominant, and once they were taken into account, achievement orien-
ation did not matter much.

When the head of the family had either <u>more or less education than</u>
<u>s father</u>, he appeared more receptive to change. Perhaps it is mobility,
d change, in either direction, that matters. Or perhaps the head's
ther's education affects the head's receptivity to change too, and serves
a substitute for the head's own education where that is inadequate.

Those who <u>grew up on a farm</u> were somewhat less receptive to change,
were those with many brothers and sisters, and the fundamentalist Prot-
tants and Catholics, but the disappearance of these differences after
viding the sample according to education indicates that they may well
rely be the result of correlations between these factors and education.

The absolute level of the family head's father's education is intro-
iced in the analysis of the pooled differences from the final group aver-
es, together with the index of achievement orientation and many other
riables; so these variables do have a second chance.

titudes and Motives: Analysis
Pooled Differences

Most of variables used in the analysis of Figure 13-3 were basic
ckground factors. We turn now to an analysis of a broad range of other
ctors. Some are background factors that may interact with other things,
t most of them are attitudinal or motivational variables that may help

explain receptivity to change. They include such things as past illness or unemployment, and the other measures of modernism such as planning, ambition, social participation, and mobility experience. Before turning to the figure giving the variables that really mattered, we list below the variables, in order of their overall importance in explaining the whole sample of pooled differences from the end-group averages of Figure 13-3:

    *Total family income
    *Index of social participation
    *Interviewer's impression of alertness of respondent
    *Size of place (town) where family lives
     Per cent of adults in county who completed high school
     Age of head of family
    *Index of achievement orientation
     Index of planning and time horizon
     Number of responses indicating a sense of personal
         effectiveness
     Index of ambition and aspiration
     Index of mobility experience
     Education of family head's father
     Housing status (home ownership)
     Difference between education of head of family and wife

---

    *Education of head of family
     Attitude toward importance of luck for financial success
    *Whether head of family had been out of a job for two months
         or more, and when
     Number of brothers and sisters of head of family and his
         birth order
     Attitude toward mothers' working
     Whether head of family had been sick for one month or more,
         and when
     Index of closeness of family ties
     Sex and marital status of head of family
     Whether family owns a business or farm

Asterisked variables are those used in Figure 13-5. They explained an additional 10 per cent of the variance. The overall standard deviation of the residual score is 1.9. None of the variables below the line could explain as much as 0.5 per cent of the total sum of squares by a single division of the whole sample.

The structure of variables that mattered is shown in Figure 13-5. Family income, the most important variable by far, was purposely left to th

217

FIGURE 13-5

INDEX OF RECEPTIVITY TO CHANGE: ANALYSIS OF DIFFERENCES
FROM END-GROUP AVERAGES OF FIGURE 13-3

(For all 2214 heads of families)

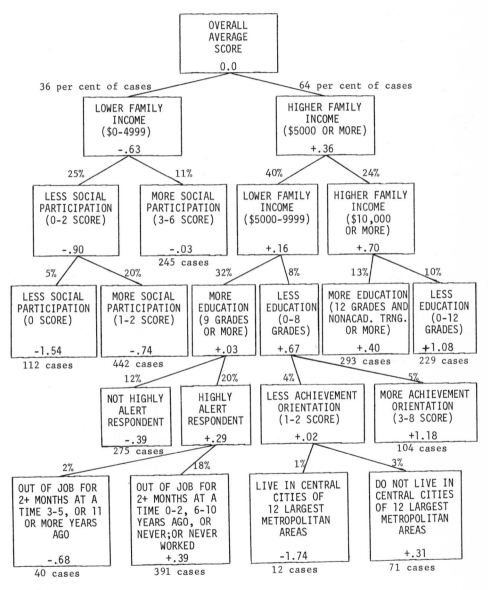

MTR 128

second stage so that we could estimate its effect separately from any that could be attributed to age, education, marital status, and similar background variables that affect both income and receptivity to change. It is well known that using this two-stage approach with variables which are logically at the same stage in the causal process, produces a downward bias in the estimated effectiveness of those used at the second stage.

Another reason for holding income until the second stage is that, in spite of all our efforts to minimize it, there is some tendency for our index of receptivity to change to be more relevant for those with more income. This is particularly true of the component index, use of new products, even though the index is composed of inexpensive products. Even so , income was the first factor to enter Figure 13-5, and it is at least plausible that those who have had unusual financial success are more receptive to change than others of the same age, education, sex, and race. Since the background variables were accounted for in the first stage, the income effect here can be interpreted as showing an effect beyond that of the general income implications of one's age and education group.

The index of social participation, which causes the next two splits for lower-income families, consists of items not automatically correlated with either income or receptivity to change. However, the explanation of the influence is not clear. It may be that social participation makes people more receptive to change, or that both social participation and receptivity to change are associated with some more basic activity level or personality syndrome. It is not likely, however, that there is a spurious correlation through education or income, since both have had most of their effect removed before we get to an effect of social participation. We shall see in Chapter 17 that among people with high incomes, a high score on receptivity to change leads to higher than average scores on social participation.

Interestingly enough, among the two higher-income groups in Figure 13-5, formal education again reappears, in spite of its already having been used four times in Figure 13-3, the pooled residuals from which we are now analyzing. But the direction is reversed.[2]

The interviewer's rating of the respondent's alertness and quickness in replying to questions is again not a clear finding of causation, but only implies that those receptive to change _also_ appear to be alert, quick, and responsive.

The achievement orientation effect, at least in theory, does have a causal or directional implication. If it is true that achievement orientation is developed early in life, and if it is true that our index is a proxy measure of it, then we have some evidence here that it leads to receptivity to change even after one allows for differences resulting from education and income (which may themselves result from achievement orientation).

There is some evidence that those living in the central cities of the twelve largest metropolitan areas are less receptive to change, though part of the reason may be their owning fewer cars. And there is some evidence that past major unemployment reduces receptivity to change.

---

[2]The result looks suspiciously like the sequential adjustments of the sweep-out or stepwise approximation methods of multiple correlation. In other words, one first takes out an education effect, then takes from the residuals an income effect, and then discovers that the residuals are now correlated in a reverse way with education, i.e., that the first process took out too much for education and should be revised. Clearly, in this situation the straightforward processes of simultaneously estimating the effects of income and education, as in multiple regression, are called for. Before turning to that, it may pay to look at the rest of Figure 13-5.

Regression Analysis

In view of the symmetry of Figure 13-3 and the repeated use of the same variables, it seemed appropriate to turn to ordinary multiple regression using "dummy variables." Regression analysis, being simultaneous instead of sequential, imposes upon the results a set of adjusted "effects" of each set of explanatory characteristics, allowing for subgroup differences in the other characteristics. For instance, age and education fight it out for the credit and end up sharing it. The sets of variables used in the dummy variable multiple regression are given in Table 13-2, together with the measures of their importance as the sole set or jointly with the others.

TABLE 13-2

VARIABLES USED TO EXPLAIN INDEX OF RECEPTIVITY TO CHANGE
(For all 2214 heads of families)

Variables used to explain index of receptivity to change	Relative importance	
	Using unadjusted means	Using adjusted means
	(Eta coefficients)*	(Partial beta coefficients)*
Total family income	.568	.331
Education of head of family	.503	.199
Index of social participation	.430	.159
Age of head of family	.410	.123
Index of achievement orientation	.348	.120
Sex and marital status of head of family	.288	.097

*See footnotes to Table 10-2 for a description of the meaning of eta and partial beta coefficient.

MTR 159

Figures 13-6 through 13-11 show the detailed effects of each explanatory variable, both the unadjusted subgroup averages, and the adjusted
averages. The adjusted averages reflect what each subgroup would be like if
it were representative of the population on all the other characteristics.[3]

Components of Receptivity to Change Index: Who Uses an Electric Frying Pan?

One component of the index of receptivity, the use of an electric
frying pan, was selected to represent a product that is new but not so
expensive as to be a measure of affluence rather than receptivity to new
things. The proportion who reported using an electric frying pan did vary
according to family income, from one in ten for those with incomes under
$1000 to more than four in ten for those with incomes of $15,000 or higher.
It varied very little according to age, except that those seventy-five and
older were less likely to use one--many of them also having low incomes.
But the most powerful determinant of use of an electric frying pan was formal education, the proportion varying from 22 per cent among the least educated (none through 5 grades of school completed) to 62 per cent among those
with advanced or professional college degrees. (See Figure 13-12.) There is
a 10 per cent differential between those who did and those who did not
finish high school, every group below that line having fewer than 45 per
cent users and every group with a high school diploma or more having 54 per
cent users or more.

---

[3]The adjusted averages are a simple translation of multiple regression coefficients making them easier to understand. The weighted average of
the adjusted averages for any one characteristic (or of the unadjusted
averages) is equal to the overall average. For an explanation of this use
of multiple regression see Appendix E.

222

FIGURE 13-6

ACTUAL AND ADJUSTED SCORES ON THE INDEX OF RECEPTIVITY TO CHANGE,
BY TOTAL FAMILY INCOME
(For all 2214 heads of families)

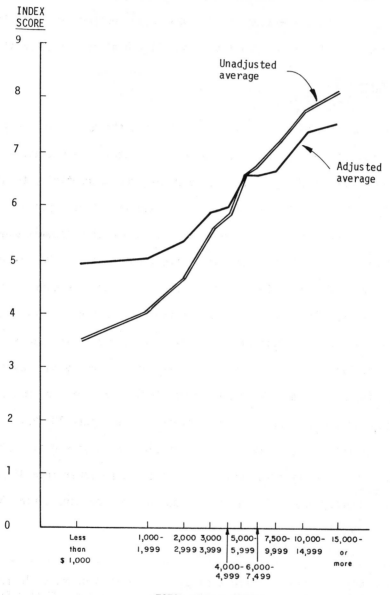

MTR 159

FIGURE 13-7

ACTUAL AND ADJUSTED SCORES ON THE INDEX OF RECEPTIVITY TO CHANGE,
BY EDUCATION OF HEAD OF FAMILY
(For all 2214 heads of families)*

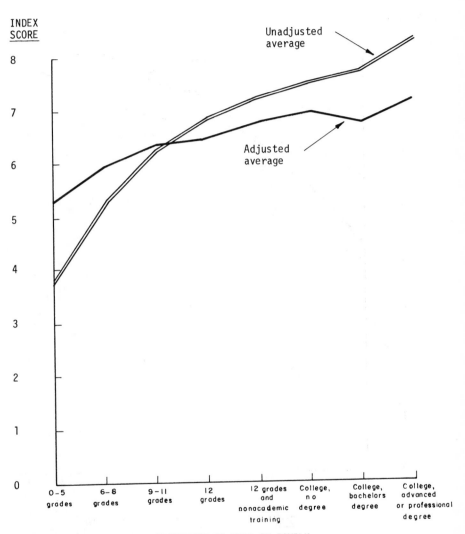

EDUCATION OF HEAD OF FAMILY

MTR 159

*excludes 4 cases in which education of head of family was not ascertained.

224

FIGURE 13-8

ACTUAL AND ADJUSTED SCORES ON THE INDEX OF RECEPTIVITY TO CHANGE,
BY SCORE ON INDEX OF SOCIAL PARTICIPATION
(For all 2214 heads of families)

INDEX SCORE

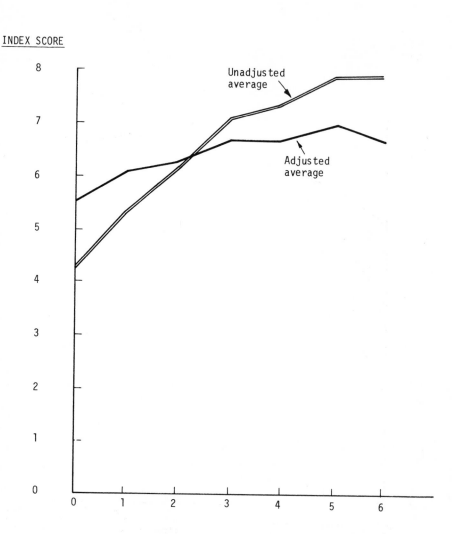

SCORE ON INDEX OF SOCIAL PARTICIPATION

MTR 159

FIGURE 13-9

ACTUAL AND ADJUSTED SCORES ON THE INDEX OF RECEPTIVITY TO CHANGE,
BY AGE OF HEAD OF FAMILY
(For all 2214 heads of families)

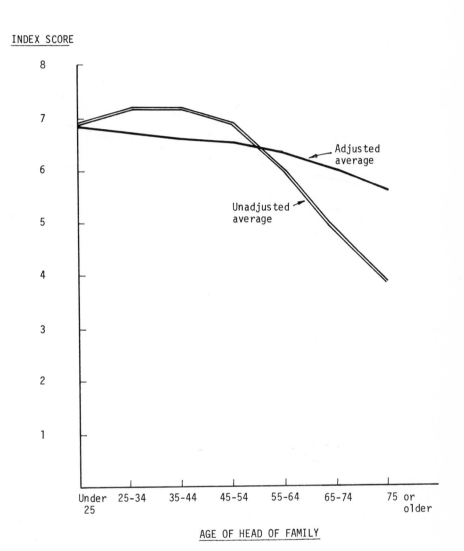

INDEX SCORE

AGE OF HEAD OF FAMILY

MTR 159

FIGURE 13-10

ACTUAL AND ADJUSTED SCORES ON THE INDEX OF RECEPTIVITY TO CHANGE,
BY SCORE ON INDEX OF ACHIEVEMENT ORIENTATION
(For all 2214 heads of families)

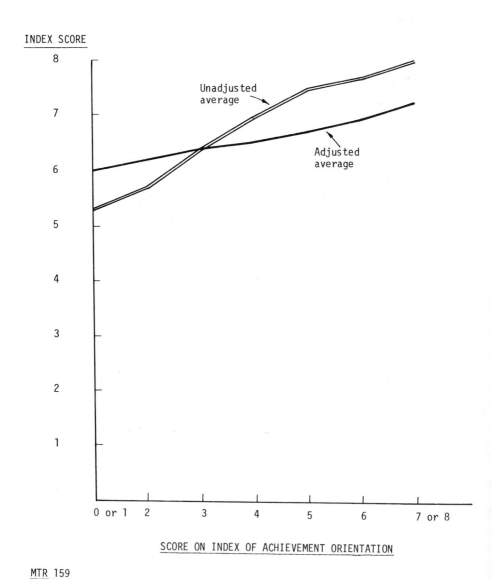

INDEX SCORE

SCORE ON INDEX OF ACHIEVEMENT ORIENTATION

MTR 159

FIGURE 13-11

ACTUAL AND ADJUSTED SCORES ON THE INDEX OF RECEPTIVITY TO CHANGE,
BY SEX AND MARITAL STATUS OF HEAD OF FAMILY
(For all 2214 heads of families)

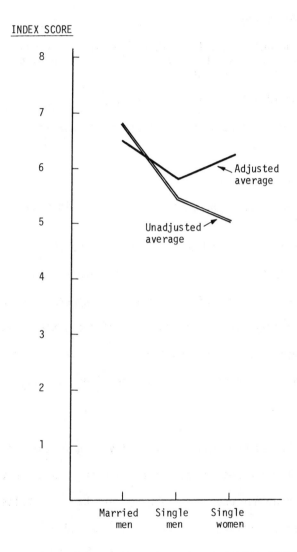

SEX AND MARITAL STATUS OF HEAD OF FAMILY

MTR 159

Who Thinks It Is a Good Idea to Put Fluoride in the Water?

About two-fifths of the heads of families gave answers approving of the addition of fluoride to the water supply. Typical of the answers indicating approval were the following:

"I think it's good because I had fluoride treatments on my son's teeth. The dentist said it should be done. If it was in the water I wouldn't have to pay to have it done."

"I think it's a good idea if it will keep decay away."

Those who were against its addition to the water gave responses like the following:

"I'm against it! It's a poison."

"It's like taking medication; you don't know what it might do to you over a period of time."

The effects of education and income on receptivity to the idea of controlling tooth decay by putting fluoride in the water are even more powerful than their effects on the use of an electric frying pan. The proportion approving wholeheartedly varied from 23 per cent among the least educated to 79 per cent among those with advanced college degrees, and is a more continuous effect than the use of appliances (see Figure 13-12).

Use of Seat Belts

An interesting aspect of modernism not actually used in the index of receptivity (nor in the later indexes of caution or planning) is the actual use of seat belts. Whether or not one of the family cars had seat belts was included in the combined receptivity index. We exclude the 22 per cent who did not own cars; only 34 per cent of the rest had seat belts in their car. The proportion varies little with age, but a great deal--from 17 to 59 per

FIGURE 13-12

APPROVAL OF ADDING FLUORIDE TO WATER AND USE OF ELECTRIC FRYING PAN,
BY EDUCATION OF HEAD OF FAMILY
(For all 2214 heads of families)*

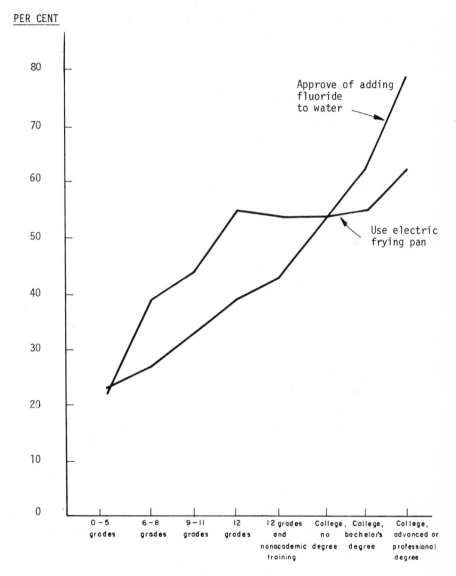

EDUCATION OF HEAD OF FAMILY

MTR 162

*
  excludes 4 cases in which education of head was not ascertained.

cent--with level of formal education. Of those who had seat belts, only one-third used them regularly, the proportion again varying with education.

Figure 13-13 shows for each educational level the proportions who own a car, own a car with seat belts, and actually use seat belts. If it is true that a seat belt actually reduces the severity of injury in accidents, then once again it is the well-educated who are doing things that will minimize the costly disasters.

Other Research

Sociologists and anthropologists have studied reactions to change over many cultures and times, and to summarize all that material here would be impossible. Some of it is concerned with the impact of new things on cultural organizations.[4] Some deals with the process of accepting new ideas and ways of doing things.[5] Two studies focus specifically on aspiration levels and the desire for new things.[6] And a number of studies have dealt

[4] Edward H. Spicer (ed.), Human Problems in Technological Change (New York: Russel Sage Foundation, 1952).

[5] See especially Everett M. Rogers, Diffusion of Innovations (New York: The Free Press, 1962); and for an updating of the bibliography appearing in this book, see Bibliography of Research on the Diffusion of Innovations (East Lansing: Department of Communication, Michigan State University, July 1964).
    See also F. G. Adams and D. S. Brady, "The Diffusion of New Durable Goods and Their Impact on Consumer Expenditures," 1963 Proceedings of the Business and Economic Statistics Section (Washington: American Statistical Association, September 1963), pp. 76-88; C. F. Cannell and J. C. McDonald, "The Impact of Health News on Attitudes and Behavior," Journalism Quarterly, 33 (1956), 315-323; Elihu Katz, Martin Levin, and Herbert Hamilton, "Traditions of Research on the Diffusion of Innovation," American Sociological Review, 28 (April 1963), 237-252; Herbert F. Loinberger and Rex R. Campbell, The Potential of Interpersonal Communicative Networks for Message Transfer from Outside Information Sources, Research Bulletin No. 842 (Columbia, Missouri: University of Missouri Agricultural Experiment Station, September 1963).

[6] Eva Mueller, "The Desire for Innovations in Household Goods,"

FIGURE 13-13

WHETHER CAR HAS SEAT BELTS AND USE OF SEAT BELTS,
BY EDUCATION OF HEAD OF FAMILY
(For all 1736 families that own a car)*

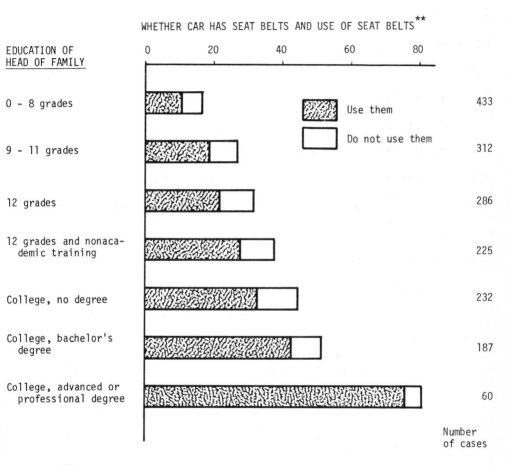

WHETHER CAR HAS SEAT BELTS AND USE OF SEAT BELTS**

MTR 151

*excludes 1 case in which education of head of family was not ascertained.

**"Use them" means all the time or part of the time.

explicitly with resistance or receptivity to the use of fluoride in the water.[7]

In a recent study in Greece, mothers and daughters who had gone to work in a local factory were interviewed, along with a matched sample of mothers and daughters who had not. It was discovered that the main positive incentive of going to work was the possibility of accumulating a bigger dowry and marrying upward.[8]

A study in progress based on a survey in Taiwan shows that the number of "modern" objects owned (mostly small appliances) is associated more strongly with education than with income, though both are important, perhaps because the more educated are also younger and more affluent. The same study shows a strong association between the use of modern objects, and family planning.

Attitudes toward and acceptance of family planning practices have been studied extensively. Family planning is discussed in Chapter 18, as a

---

Consumer Behavior, ed. Lincoln Clark (New York: Harper and Brothers, 1958); Burkhard Strumpel, "Consumption Aspirations: Incentives for Economic Change," Social and Economic Studies, 10 (June 1965), 183-193.

[7]Arnold L. Green, "The Ideology of the Anti-Fluoridation Leaders," Journal of Social Issues, XVII (October 1961), 13-25; John P. Kirscht and Andi L. Knutson, "Science and Fluoridation: An Attitude Study," Journal of Social Issues, XVII (October, 1961); 37-44, and references therein; Donald R. McNeil, The Fight for Fluoridation (New York: Oxford University Press, 1957); F. B. Waisanan, "Change Orientation and the Adoption Process," First Inter-American Research Symposium on the Role of Communications in Agricultural Development, ed. D. T. Myren (Mexico City: October 1964). The data from this study show that a cross section of village people in Guatemala react less favorably to change than a cross section of village people from Costa Rica. And it shows that a cross section of people in Costa Rica react less favorably to change than Costa Rican stockholders in a business enterprise.

[8]Ioanna Lambiri, Social Change in a Greek Country Town (Athens: Center of Planning and Economic Research, 1965).

part of the discussion of caution and risk behavior, though it also involves

acceptance of change.

CHAPTER 14

PLANNING AND TIME HORIZON

Definition

Some people think farther ahead, solve more problems in advance,
than others. Presumably such people encounter fewer emergencies, make fewer
mistakes, and generally are more efficient. A long time horizon is probably
also associated with a lower rate of "time preference," and a willingness to
pay attention to yields and benefits which will not come for some time.

An index was built out of the answers to questions about plans for
vacations, retirement, and children's education. Since each of these three
areas is irrelevant for some people, the index was balanced by assigning
two points for each item when there was evidence of some planning, one point
if the item was inappropriate for that family, and no point if the family
might have shown evidence of planning on that item but did not. Vacation
planning was irrelevant for those who never take vacations; retirement planning was irrelevant for those under thirty-five, those already retired, or
housewives; and saving for children's college education was irrelevant for
those with no children or those who are not planning to send their children
to college.

A head of a family could have an index score of six if he had
planned his last vacation more than one month in advance, knew when he
planned to retire, and had set aside money to help pay for his children's

234

college education. Five per cent of the entire sample fell into this group.
The full distribution of scores is as follows:

Score on planning and time horizon index	Per cent of cases
Zero	1
One	10
Two	23
Three	26
Four	20
Five	14
Six	5
Total	100
Number of cases	2214

Background Factors

Looking first at the background factors related to the index of
propensity to plan ahead, we find it associated with middle-age, more education, and with higher levels of achievement orientation. In Figure 14-1 the
index of achievement orientation almost divided the middle-aged before they
were divided by the difference in educational level between the head of the
family and his father. Even though the variance explained in Figure 14-1
is small, everything is in the expected direction. The very old and very
young do less planning, and this is presumably not just because they are
eligible for fewer of the items, since those eligible for none of the items
still have a score of three (no children planning to go to college, under
thirty-five or retired, do not take vacations). Education has always been
said to increase people's propensity to plan ahead and solve problems in
advance. What is more interesting, however, is that educational mobility--
having more education than one's father--appears more important than the

236

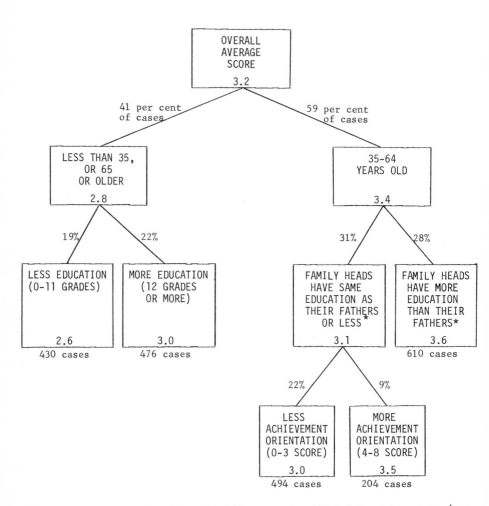

FIGURE 14-1

INDEX OF PLANNING AND TIME HORIZON
(For all 2214 heads of families)

*"Same" means in same bracket. Education was classified into eight groups (see Appendix C, questions E18-E22). "More" means that the head of the family passed into a higher one of the eight classes than his father was in.

MTR 127

family head's absolute educational level in accounting for differences in the propensity to plan ahead. Such mobility presumably implies both higher horizons and more education.

The index of achievement orientation was put in as a background factor because theoretically that is what the achievement motive is. However, the index itself results from a series of questions, some reflecting current outlook (see Appendix D). Hence, a question arises whether the relation is either spurious, or an indication of causation in the other direction. Some of the components of the index of achievement orientation are relevant only to nonretired people, but the group that is divided according to their scores on achievement orientation in Figure 14-1 contains only thirty-five to sixty-four year olds, so that is no problem. What is possible is that there is a dynamic developmental pattern where those who are more achievement oriented plan more, hence are more successful and have their achievement orientation reinforced, hence plan ahead still more, in a mutually reinforcing system. It remains true that with all the crudeness of our measures, both of planning and of achievement orientation, they are related in the expected way. Over the whole sample, the planning scores of persons with high scores on the index of achievement orientation show a highly significant difference from the planning scores of those with low scores on that index.

The predictors allowed in the first-stage analysis are as follows, in order of their importance if used to make one division of the whole sample:

*Age of head of family
*Difference in education between head of family and his father
*Index of achievement orientation

*Education of head of family
 Sex and marital status of head of family
 Number of brothers and sisters of head of family

 Religious preference
 Race
 Whether head of family grew up on a farm
 Number of brothers and sisters older than head of family

Asterisked variables are those used in Figure 14-1. They
explained 7 per cent of the variance. The overall standard deviation of the score is 1.4. None of the variables below the line
could explain as much as 0.5 per cent of the total sum of squares
by a single division of the whole sample.

There were few interesting relations that did not get into Figure

14-1: married people plan more, and those with many brothers and sisters

plan less. However, once the sample was divided on age and the two educa-

tion variables and the score on the index of achievement orientation,

nothing else made much difference.

Attitudes and Motives:
Analysis of Pooled Differences

The pooled differences from the end-group averages of Figure 14-1

were then analyzed using the following twenty-five predictors, again listed

in order of their importance over the whole sample:

 *Index of social participation
 *Total family income
 *Index of receptivity to change
 Index of caution and risk avoidance
 Number of responses indicating a sense of personal
     effectiveness
 Housing status (home ownership)
 *Whether family owns a business or farm
 Interviewer's impression of alertness of respondent

 Age of oldest child under 18 living at home
 *Age of youngest child under 18 living at home
 Whether head of family has been sick for one month or more
     and when

Whether head of family has been out of a job for two months
    or more and when
Index of ambition and aspiration
Index of achievement orientation
Education of family head's father
Sex and marital status of head of family
Difference in education between head of family and wife
Education of head of family (used in first stage)
Number of brothers and sisters of head of family and his
    birth order
Attitude toward importance of luck for financial success
*Race
*Age of head of family (used in first stage)
Index of mobility experience
Attitude toward mothers' working
Index of closeness of family ties

Asterisked variables are those used in Figure 14-2. They
explained an additional 6 per cent of the variance. The overall
standard deviation of the residual score is 1.3. None of the
variables below the line could explain as much as 0.5 per cent of
the total sum of squares by a single division of the whole sample.

The importance of making multivariate and sequential analysis and
not forcing symmetry is dramatized by the scattering of asterisks among
those factors that were unimportant over the whole sample, thus indicating
that for some subgroups the predictor was actually able to account for an
important amount of the total variation.

Figure 14-2 shows the relationships of the more important factors
to the pooled differences from Figure 14-1. Some of the variables, including the most important one, index of social participation, may well represent not causation but interrelation, a syndrome rather than an explanation.
It is clear that high social participation and planning ahead are related.[1]
Similarly, income may allow planning, result from it, or be part of a
general syndrome with it. It is unlikely, however, that income and social

---

[1]See Appendix D for details about the indexes, and Chapter 17 for an
analysis of the index of social participation.

participation are spuriously correlated with planning through their relation to education or age, since the main effects of those two factors on
planning have already been removed.

The lower left part of Figure 14-2 would indicate that among persons
with low incomes and low scores on the index of social participation, those
under sixty-five plan less than those sixty-five or older. Some of the age
effects had been removed at the first stage of the analysis. It would seem
from Figure 14-2 that the effect of age was exaggerated in Figure 14-1,
especially for a particular group of low-income, inactive people.

Among the socially active, those with a youngest child just starting
in school (aged 4 through 8) or just finishing high school (aged 14 through
17) plan more, particularly if they do not own a business or farm. It is
understandable that people with children in high school might be more likely
to be putting money aside for their children's college education, and hence
have a higher score on the planning index. It is not so clear why those
with children four through eight years old should be planning more. And why
should owners of a business or farm plan less? One explanation is that such
people plan their business or farm affairs, and let their vacations come
when they are able to take them. They are also less likely to plan to
retire at all. But given our definition of planning, in the areas we measured they do plan less, even over the whole sample.

Finally, in the center of Figure 14-2 we find that for one group
(with more social participation, and with children under four or nine
through thirteen, or no children at all) those with the highest scores on
receptivity to change also planned ahead more.

Only seven of the twenty-five variables allowed in the analysis of

241

FIGURE 14-2

INDEX OF PLANNING AND TIME HORIZON: ANALYSIS OF DIFFERENCES
FROM END-GROUP AVERAGES OF FIGURE 14-1

(For all 2214 heads of families)

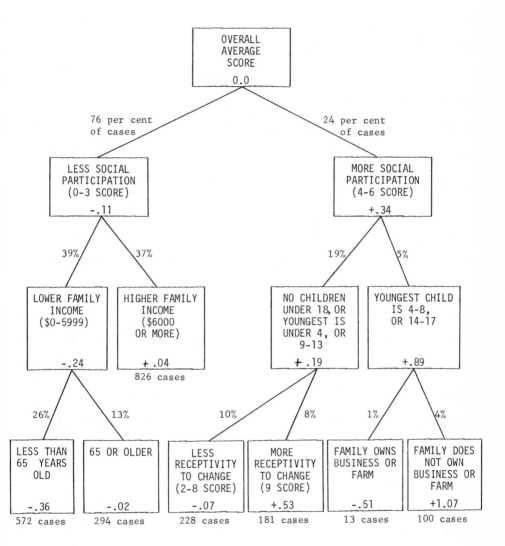

MTR 127

residuals were actually used in Figure 14-2. We have already discussed the fact that several which seemed unimportant over the whole sample acquired importance in certain subgroups and were used. But four variables which could each account for more than 0.5 per cent of the variance over the whole sample--those above the line on the list of predictors--were never used.

Overall it seemed that those who were more cautious also planned ahead more, but the power of that relationship is cut in half by dividing the sample according to their level of social participation, and cut in third or half again by the division by income or the division by age of youngest child.

The same thing happens even more dramatically with the number of responses (of a possible three) expressing a sense of personal effectiveness. Those who feel more effective also report more planning. Again the relationship disappears in the subgroups.

Those who owned their home, and who seemed alert to the interviewer also had higher scores on the index of planning over all the pooled residuals, but the differences faded in the subgroups. The relation with alertness may even be circular, since any respondent seems alert when you ask him things about which he has something immediate to report, such as asking a person about plans for his vacation when he is planning a vacation.

The rest of the variables, all of which had originally persuasive hypotheses justifying their inclusion, do not matter for the whole sample or any part of it. The past frustrations of illness and unemployment did not show up in present shorter horizons or less planning. Pressures from a more educated wife relative to his own education did not lead the husband to do more planning. Believing that luck is important for financial success did

ot reduce planning. Being traditional by maintaining close family ties or
pposing mothers' working did not relate to less planning; nor did a high
core on the index of ambition and aspiration lead to more planning. Whites
id seem to plan ahead more than nonwhites, but racial differences were not
ven close to the importance of some other variables.

omponents of Planning and Time Horizon:
etirement Planning

One planning index component of particular importance in its own
ight has to do with planning for retirement. Evidence has accumulated that
rivate pensions increase people's willingness to make additional provision
or retirement--by saving still more than is provided by the private pension.[2]

The increased aspirations about retirement may also take the form of
arlier planned retirement. However, the tremendous increase in recent
ears in the proportion retiring before they are sixty-five may well be
artly due to poor earnings opportunities, technological obsolescence of
kills, and the appearance for the first time of the possibility of retiring
t age sixty-two with enough retirement income to live on.[3] Hence, it is
articularly important to ask what is happening to people's views about when
hey will retire and about how well off they will be then. Most people
nder thirty-five are so vague about their retirement plans that they can be
mitted from consideration, and most who are sixty-five or older have

---

[2]See George Katona, Private Pensions and Individual Saving (Ann
rbor: Survey Research Center, The University of Michigan, 1965); see also
hilip Cagan, The Effect of Pension Plans on Aggregate Saving (New York:
olumbia University Press, 1965), National Bureau of Economic Research,
ccasional Paper No. 95.

[3]See Lenore A. Epstein, "Early Retirement and Work-Life Experience,"
ocial Security Bulletin (March 1966), pp. 3-10.

already retired. Table 14-1 shows the distribution of expected retirement ages for people of different current ages both from this study and from a study done five years ago. The questions asked were slightly different. For the present study, respondents were asked, "When do you think you will retire, I mean at what age?" In 1960 they were asked, "What about retire- ment, when do you think you will stop working altogether?" And the study done in 1960 was different from the present one in that financially inde- pendent spending units living with relatives were interviewed separately. However, most of those spending units were under thirty-five or sixty-five or older, so that the figures presented in Table 14-1 are not distorted appreciably.

From Table 14-1, it appears that people are not only retiring at an earlier age, but starting at earlier ages to plan on retiring earlier. A recent Harris Poll reported that 22 per cent of those interviewed expected to retire before age sixty, but that 46 per cent would like to retire before that age.[4]

In 1964, half the men who retired under Social Security retired before they were sixty-five, at actuarially reduced benefits. Two-thirds of the women retired before they were sixty-five, some presumably because their (older) husbands were retiring then.[5]

Increasing affluence in general, and increasing coverage under both Social Security and private pension plans, would seem to be starting a

[4]The Detroit Free Press, November 30, 1965.

[5]U.S. Department of Health, Education and Welfare, Social Security Administration, Office of Research and Statistics, Old Age Benefits for Workers Retiring Before Age 65, Research and Statistics Note No. 18, October 14, 1965.

TABLE 14-1

AGE WHEN PLANS TO RETIRE BY PRESENT AGE

(for 1308 nonretired family [1681 spending unit]
heads aged 35-64, data from two surveys)

Age when plans to retire	Present age					
	35-44		45-54		55-64	
	1960*	1965	1960*	1965	1960*	1965
Before 62	13	20	11	13	3	4
62-64	3	9	7	12	10	20
65 or older	49	44	44	45	51	35
Never; or don't know	35	27	38	30	36	41
Total	100	100	100	100	100	100
Number of cases	745	445	560	476	376	387

From Morgan et al., Income and Welfare in the United States.
TRs 161, 167

process of increased aspiration for earlier and better retirement. This may well mean working harder, earning more, and saving more now in order to permit realizing those increasing aspirations.

To look only at the situation in 1965, education had very little effect on retirement plans, but income mattered. Those with the lowest incomes were more likely to say that they never plan to retire, and those with the highest incomes were more likely to say they planned to retire before they were sixty-two. Those with the highest incomes were also less likely to be vague about when they would retire or to say they would "never" retire. Those closer to retirement age seemed more likely to plan to retire between the ages of sixty-two and sixty-four, or not at all.

Self-rating on Planning

The index of planning and time horizon was made up of reported behavior, not of attitudes or self-ratings. We did, however, also ask respondent

"Are you the kind of person that plans his life ahead all the
time, or do you live more from day to day?"

Respondents were divided almost evenly between the two alternatives. It was
the well-educated, the high-income, and the younger respondents who were mos
likely to say they planned ahead, the proportions increasing steadily from
38 to 69 over the educational range, and from 30 to 63 over the income range
The proportions ranged from 62 for the youngest down to 40 for the oldest.
The replies to this question were mildly <u>negatively</u> correlated with planning
for vacations, and mildly positively correlated with planning for retirement
and with two other risk-behavior items, carrying medical insurance and havir
some savings. It was uncorrelated with such things as having set aside mone
for children's college education. It would seem again that self-ratings do
not serve as a substitute for ratings based on reported behavior, though the
may measure something else. This relation with reported behavior was not so
strong as that which we found in 1960, using a different question[6]:

"Some people feel that they can make pretty definite plans for their
lives for the next few years. Others feel that they aren't in a position to plan ahead. How about you? Do you feel able to plan ahead or
not?"

---

[6]For some analysis of this question and a different "index of planning" in the previous study, see Morgan <u>et al</u>., Chapters 30 and 31.
    An identical question asked in Spain recently found a small majorit
claiming that they planned ahead; so if our general impressions are correct
the Spaniards may have been using a different absolute standard for rating
themselves (Strümpel, unpublished data).

The replies to this question were also split nearly evenly, but the variation by education, income, and age was much greater. For that question, when we used a somewhat different income measure which included income other than money but deducted federal income taxes, the proportions varied from 22 per cent to 82 per cent as one went higher up the income scale.

There was also a relation with formal education, the more educated saying more frequently that they planned their lives. Again the relationship in the present study is weaker than that found in 1960.

It was also the young who were more likely to say they planned. In 1960 the percentages fell from 60 per cent, for those under twenty-five to 31 per cent, for those seventy-five or older. In 1964 they fell from 62 to 40. A multivariate analysis of the 1960 data produced groups varying from those with a high school education or more and an income of $5000 or more, of whom 76 per cent felt able to plan, to those with less than nine grades of school and income under $5000 and not self-employed or supervising others on their jobs, of whom 23 per cent felt able to plan. Since income, youth, and education are all positively correlated, the overall relations tend to exaggerate the effects of each of them. It may be that upper-income people plan more partly because they are better educated; or conversely, it may be that the better educated plan more because they have higher incomes. Similarly, the young may plan more because they have more education, and so forth.

Summary

Planning ahead, in the three areas used in the index, appears to be associated as expected, with the background variables of age, education, and income. But it is also associated with higher levels of achievement orientation and higher levels of social participation (activity). On the

other hand, those who are mobile and are ambitious, in the traditional sense

of the word, do not appear to be planning more. Finally, our measurement of

planning shows that farmers and businessmen plan less in the areas about

which they were questioned, though they probably do more planning for their

farm or business.

Planning for early retirement appears to be increasing from one gener-

ation to the next, so the earlier retirement plans of the young reflect at

least in part a real difference from past generations, not just the effects

of youth.

Other Research

It has been known for some time that the length of a man's time

horizon and his willingness to plan ahead were related to his formal educa-

tion and social class.[7] Planning for education of children has been studied

extensively and reported in three studies by the Survey Research Center.[8]

Planning for retirement has been studied with national representa-

tive samples as well.[9] The propensity to plan, and the feeling of ability

[7]See, for example, Orville Brim and Raymond Forer, "A Note on the Relation of Values and Social Structure to Life Planning," Sociometry, XIV (March 1956), 54-60; Walter Firey, "Conditions for the Realization of Value Remote in Time," in Sociological Theory, Values and Sociocultural Change, ed. E. A. Tiryakain (Essays in Honor of Pitirum Sorokin) (Glencoe: The Free Press, 1963); J. E. Hulett, Jr., "The Person's Time Perspective and the Social Role," Social Forces, XXII (December 1944), 155-159; Lawrence L. Leshan, "Time Orientation and Social Class," Journal of Abnormal and Social Psychology, 47 (July 1952), 589-592; James N. Morgan, "Planning for the Future and Living with Risk," American Behavioral Scientist, VI (May 1963), 40, 53-54.

[8]Angus Campbell and William Eckerman, Public Concepts of the Values and Costs of Higher Education (Ann Arbor: Survey Research Center, The University of Michigan, 1964); John Lansing, How People Pay for College (Ann Arbor: Survey Research Center, The University of Michigan, 1960); Morgan et al., Chapters 26-29.

[9]George Katona, Private Pensions and Individual Saving (Ann Arbor:

to plan ahead, were also studied, with findings similar to those of the
present study--those having more education, more income, and more assets
were more likely to plan and to feel able to plan.[10]

Survey Research Center, The University of Michigan, 1965); Morgan et al.,
Chapter 31. See also Chapter 19 of George Katona's Mass Consumption Society,
New York: McGraw Hill, 1964

[10]Morgan et al., Chapter 30.

CHAPTER 15

GEOGRAPHIC AND OCCUPATIONAL MOBILITY

Definition

Another important dimension of behavior that affects an individual's economic situation and a country's flexibility and growth, is mobility. In a changing world, it is necessary for people to change jobs or move to new places willingly, in response to differential opportunities. Unfortunately, we can measure only actual or planned mobility, not willingness to move or how much pressure has caused a reluctant move. Previous analyses of various forms of mobility (geographic, occupational) showed that they were uncorrelated with one another, and raised the implication that a great deal of mobility may have been forced upon unwilling people and hence does not represent purposeful efforts to better one's position.[1]

The index of mobility behavior created for this analysis does not solve this problem, but the analysis may, since the first stage takes account of constraints and pressures, and the second stage takes account of factors which may account for differential willingness to move or desire to find something better. The index allows a point for each of the following:

> Has tried going into business for himself
> Has had a number of different kinds of jobs
> Has thought of changing to another job
> Has lived in more than one state since first regular job
> Has plans to move from present dwelling in less than
> 10 years from the time the family moved in

---

[1]See Morgan et al., Chapter 22.

250

The result is an index with scores ranging from zero to five, but with very few scores of four or five.[2] Some heads of families are ineligible for one or another point, particularly the self-employed and retired. The distribution is as follows:

Score on index of mobility behavior	Per cent of cases
Zero	24
One	31
Two	28
Three	12
Four	4
Five	1
Total	100
Number of cases	2214

Background Factors

The first-stage analysis of the mobility behavior index uses the same variables as were used with the other indexes. Their overall order of importance over the whole sample in accounting for differences in mobility behavior is indicated by the following rank ordering:

*Age of head of family
*Index of achievement orientation
*Sex and marital status
 Education of head of family
 Difference in education between head of family and father
 Whether head of family grew up on a farm

 Number of brothers and sisters of head of family
 Race

---

[2]Another index, including all the components of the mobility behavior index as well as two additional components measuring the family head's distant past mobility, was built. These additional two components were the number of regions lived in over two generations, and the difference in education between family head and his father. This index is called the "index of mobility experience," and it is used mainly as an explanatory variable.

Religious preference
Number of brothers and sisters older than head of family

Asterisked variables are those used in Figure 15-1. They
explained 13 per cent of the variance. The overall standard deviation of the score is 1.1. None of the variables below the line
could explain as much as 0.5 per cent of the total sum of squares
by a single division of the whole sample.

The findings shown in Figure 15-1 seem clear. Older people, particularly women, are less mobile, partly because many of them are retired and
some parts of the index do not apply, but partly in the applicable aspects.
Among the people under fifty-five, those who are either very young or have
a high score on the index of achievement orientation appear more mobile.
And middle-aged women who are heads of families are less mobile.

Some variables had an overall important effect, but were never used
in the division of Figure 15-1. Once the sample was divided, by age, sex,
and achievement orientation, into the first few groups in Figure 15-1, the
importance of education and farm background disappeared. (Those who grew up
on a farm were somewhat less mobile. The education differences were as
expected: those with more education than the average, or with more education
than their fathers, were more mobile.) Since the variables actually used
were clearly logically prior--even the index of achievement orientation was
determined long ago if the theory is correct--we can regard the overall edu
cation "effect" as reflecting age, sex, and achievement orientation in dis-
guise.[3]

---

[3]Achievement motivation is thought to be a stable personality trai
or predisposition developed early in life, largely as a result of the degre
of early training in independence. See John Atkinson, Motives in Fantasy,
Action and Society (Princeton: D. Van Nostrand, 1958). The index of achiev
ment orientation is discussed in Appendix D.

253

FIGURE 15-1

INDEX OF MOBILITY BEHAVIOR
(For all 2214 heads of families)

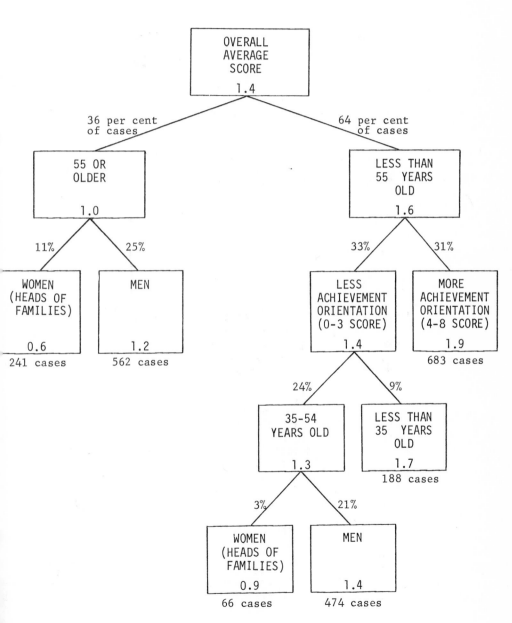

Attitudes and Motives

The differences of individual indexes from the averages of the end groups of Figure 15-1 were subjected to an analysis using twenty-six variables. The variables are attempts to measure various kinds of motives or influences. The direction of causation for some of these factors may be unclear--some may be results of mobility rather than causes.

The variables were:

> *Whether head of family has been out of a job for two months
>   or more, and when
> *Whether head of family has been sick for one month or more,
>   and when (whether <u>ever</u> worked for money)
> *Housing status (home ownership)
> *Index of ambition and aspiration
> *Index of receptivity to change
> *Number of responses indicating a sense of personal effective-
>   ness
> *Age of head of family
> Index of achievement orientation

> Whether family owns a business or farm
> Education of family head's father
> Interviewer's impression of alertness of respondent
> *Age of youngest child under 18 living at home
> Index of planning and time horizon
> *Index of closeness of family ties
> Index of caution and risk avoidance
> *Total family income
> Age of oldest child under 18 living at home
> Education of head of family
> Index of social participation
> Race
> Difference in education between head of family and wife
> Sex and marital status of head of family
> Attitude toward importance of luck for financial success
> Number of disabled people in family
> Number of brothers and sisters of head of family and his
>   birth order
> Attitude toward mothers' working

Asterisked variables are those used in Figure 15-2. They explained an additional 10 per cent of the variance. The overall standard deviation of the residual score is 1.3. None of the variables below the line could explain as much as 0.5 per cent of the tot sum of squares by a single division of the whole sample.

The first two explanatory factors in the above list were the first ones used in Figure 15-2, but they served largely as proxy variables to select those who had never been out of a job two months or more (and a few who were unemployed during 1955-59). From this group, who had never been out of a job, were set aside a group who had never worked (mostly widows). The first group set aside is highly mobile, presumably because of past unemployment. The second group set aside, composed mainly of widows, is very immobile. Nothing accounts for any further differences among those two groups, those never working for money and those suffering extensive unemployment. The figure proceeds to analyze those who have worked for money and have not suffered extensive unemployment (except for a few who did in 1955-59).

Continuing down Figure 15-2 we find that, among those who have worked for money and never had substantial unemployment, homeowners are less mobile, as expected, and there are a few very-high-income renters who are highly mobile. There are also some ambitious homeowners who are more mobile than those with lower scores on the ambition index.

The second part of Figure 15-2 is more difficult to interpret. People who had suffered illnesses, three to ten years ago are split off, and they were more mobile. People reporting a high sense of personal effectiveness were less mobile in two cases where they were split off; this indicates that mobility of the kind we have measured may be more a sign of difficulty, dissatisfaction, or trouble than a characteristic of effective, ambitious, "upwardly mobile" people. There is one split in the upper right of the continuation of Figure 15-2 where those more receptive to change are more mobile, though here the causation may go the other way: those who are more mobile

256

FIGURE 15-2

INDEX OF MOBILITY BEHAVIOR: ANALYSIS OF DIFFERENCES
FROM END-GROUP AVERAGES OF FIGURE 15-1
(For all 2214 heads of families)

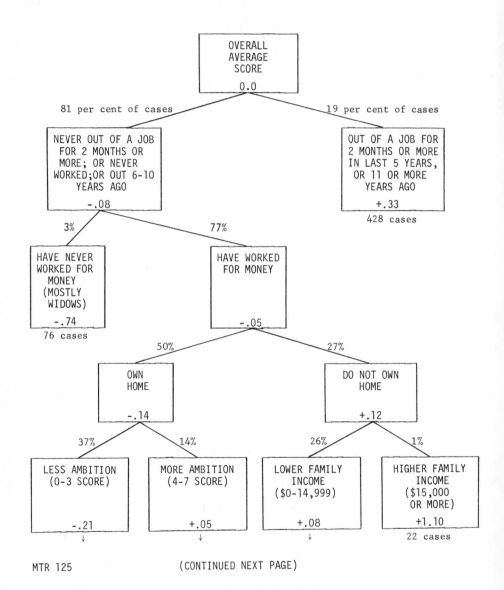

MTR 125   (CONTINUED NEXT PAGE)

257

FIGURE 15-2--(CONTINUED)

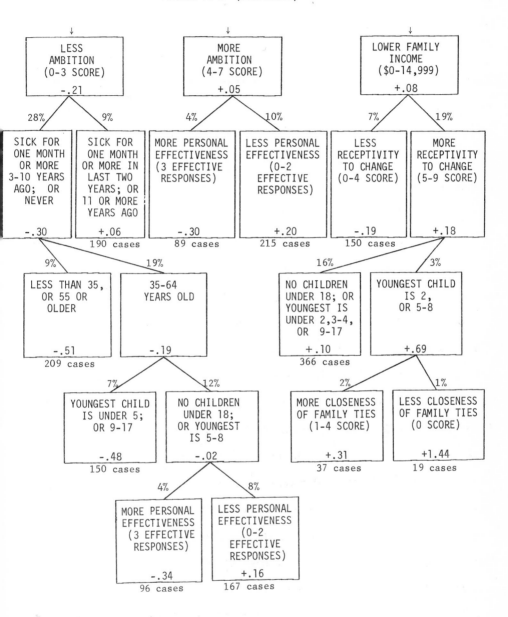

MTR 125

may be exposed to more change and hence more receptive to it. The age of
the youngest child, and whether there are children under eighteen, seem to
have widely differing effects for the renters on the right and the middle-
aged homeowners on the left, although there does seem to be a tendency for
those with children just about to enter school (age five through eight) to
be more mobile. Finally, there is at the lower right a split into two small
groups where higher scores on an index of closeness of family ties seem,
reasonably enough, to be associated with lower mobility.

It must be kept in mind, first that some effects of age, sex, and
the index of achievement orientation have already been removed, and second
that at each stage every predictor has its chance to come in. The figure
shows only what mattered most in this sample.

In view of the impression from our data that geographic and occupational mobility behavior seem to be explained by illness, unemployment, or
the constraints of age or incomplete families or the lack of a sense of personal effectiveness, it is useful to try to discover whether the effects of
the more positive variables, such as the indexes of achievement orientation,
ambition, and receptivity to change, are not being underestimated. The index
of achievement orientation did come in at the first stage, and it nearly did
again at the second stage. The indexes of ambition and receptivity to
change each came in at the second stage. Yet the following four variables
had no important effect over the whole set of residuals nor on any major
subgroup of them: planning index, caution and risk avoidance index, social
participation index, and race. So there is no evidence that those who have
been and promise to be more mobile plan ahead any more than others, or are
less cautious, more active socially, or more likely to be nonwhite.

Geographic Mobility:
Over One Generation

Geographic mobility might be thought to be the most explicit part of any mobility index, and it is of interest in its own right. It has been studied a great deal, though mostly over relatively short periods. Two aspects of it may be commented on here because there are interesting data on them from the present study. The following question was asked of all heads of families who had ever worked:

"Since your first regular job, what states or countries have you lived in (excluding when in military service)?

(If only one state) Since your first regular job, have you ever lived more than 100 miles from here?"

From these questions we were able to determine, at one extreme, whether the respondent had lived in three or more states, or at the other, whether he had lived only in one state and always within 100 miles of his present address.

A multivariate analysis of whether ever lived 100 or more miles from present residence was done. The seven predictors used could account for only 6 per cent of the variance, most of it on the basis of the region where the head of the family now lives, which may well reflect result rather than cause. The percentages, by region, of those who had lived more than 100 miles away from their present residences were as follows:

Northeast	37%
North Central	44
"Deep South"	57
"Other South"	50
West	70

The mobile people who originally lived in the Northeast have presumably moved out, and there has been relatively little immigration into the region.[4] And many have moved to the West, of course. The reason for the high mobility of the people in the Deep South is less obvious. Perhaps it represents movement off the farms and plantations into the cities. It is not the Florida boom, for the "Deep South" includes only Alabama, Georgia, Louisiana, Mississippi, and South Carolina.

Education was the next most important factor, and, as expected, college graduates were more mobile, only 36 per cent of them never having lived more than 100 miles away from their present address. Their talents are, of course, more specialized, and hence they are more likely to find opportunities at a distance. But there is also a tendency for those who did not finish high school to be more mobile. The implication is that they have been forced to move by lack of local opportunity. (Many of them also grew up on a farm where local employment opportunities were poor.) The overall result is that it is those with a high school education, no more and no less, who are the least mobile. Perhaps high school graduates found it possible to find adequate jobs without moving, while those with less education were forced to move to find employment. If so, we have one mobile group among the highly educated, who are attracted to new places where their special skills can be used, and another among the least educated, who are forced to move by lack of local opportunity. The latter group may do their moving mostly during periods of high employment, when labor shortages develop in some areas.

---

[4]Census data also show the phenomenon of lower mobility of those left in the Northeast with the proportions living in the same dwelling or the same county or the same state a year later being highest in the Northeast and lowest in the West.
    See U.S. Bureau of the Census, Current Population Reports, Series P-20, No. 134, Mobility of the Population of the United States, March 1962 to March 1963 (March 25, 1965).

The only other factor that appeared to make any difference at all was religious preference, those outside the Judeo-Christian tradition being the most mobile, and the Lutherans, Catholics, and Jews the least. The last three groups are minorities who have come over in vast migrations, chiefly from Ireland, Germany, and Italy; most Catholics and Jews have stayed in eastern urban areas, and German Lutherans in midwest farming areas.

But the surprising thing about this analysis is that we are able to account for so little of the difference in mobility with the variables at our command. Probably the reason is that mobility results from a myriad of rather special forces, some positive and some negative. It would seem, at least, that theorizing about such mobility is in serious need of better information.

An analysis of whether or not the head of the family had ever lived more than 100 miles from his present residence was also done using the data from a national survey of heads of spending units (including a few economically independent secondary spending units within families) conducted in 1960.[5]

The results of the 1960 analysis are very similar to those of the present study. The lower mobility of those living in the Northeast showed up, as did the higher mobility of those at higher educational levels. Those under twenty-five years old showed less mobility than any other group. This may be due to the fact that some of those spending units in this age group are the economically independent secondary spending units who have not yet left home, mostly children. The results of this analysis also could explain

---

[5]Morgan et al., and unpublished special tabulations.

only 6 per cent of the total variance. We turn now to a measure of two-generation geographic mobility.

Geographic Mobility:
Over Two Generations

The mobility index used earlier in this chapter is based on the recent past and some expectations. A longer-range measure of mobility was also built, though it was not a component of the mobility behavior index, and was included as part of the mobility experience index.

We combined information on the regions where the head of the family, his father, his mother, and his wife grew up, the region where the head of the family lived in early 1965, and any other region the head of the family had lived in since his first regular job. From this we developed a measure of the total number of different regions to which the head of the family, his wife, and his parents had been exposed. The code allowed for five regions in this country, separating the South into the "Deep South" (Alabama Georgia, Louisiana, Mississippi, and South Carolina) and the "Other South," and for all except present residence allowed for two other "regions"-- English-speaking foreign countries and non-English-speaking foreign countries. The other regions were Northeast, North Central, and West. It was thus theoretically possible for seven regions to be involved, but the total number that the family over two generations could be exposed to was only six since only six questions were asked about different people or times. Actually not one head of a family reported more than four, and the distribution was as follows:

Number of regions exposed to over two generations	Per cent of cases
One	45
Two	42
Three	12
Four	1
Total	100
Number of cases	2214

This may seem like surprisingly little geographic movement. It is, however, perfectly consistent with the already known fact that every year about 20 per cent of the people in the United States move. Most of the movement is within the local area, and most of the rest within the state. In creating this index we have excluded both military service and travel and vacations, of course, since the measure attempts to get at the kind of exposure to the culture of another area that probably comes only from living and working there for a period of time. Modern communication may also have recently improved links among regions, but the fact remains that even in one of the most mobile nations in the world (outside the nomadic economies), few Americans have really been directly exposed to the culture of more than one region within this country, even if we include exposure through the parents and wife.

This variable, number of regions over two generations, was subjected to a multivariate analysis using the following variables, listed in order of their importance:

Religious preference
Education of head of family

Age of head of family
Difference between education of head of family and his father
Race
Sex and marital status of head of family

FIGURE 15-3

NUMBER OF REGIONS LIVED IN OVER TWO GENERATIONS, BY EDUCATION OF HEAD OF FAMILY
FOR PROTESTANTS AND NONPROTESTANTS
(For all 2214 heads of families)*

NUMBER OF REGIONS
LIVED IN OVER
TWO GENERATIONS

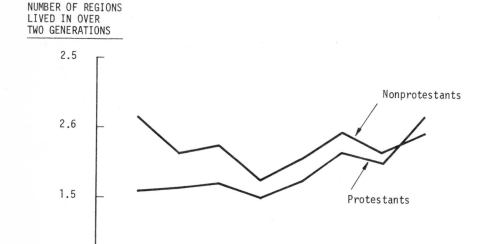

EDUCATION OF HEAD OF FAMILY

MTR 154

*excludes 4 cases in which education of head of family was not ascertained.

Both religious preference and education of family head could account for at least 1 per cent of the total variance, but none of the other four could account for as much as 0.5 per cent of the total variance. The average number of regions was lower for Protestants (1.62) than for the other religious groups (1.83).

This makes sense if we remember that it was the non-Protestants who came to this country most recently, and that minority groups even within a country may find it more necessary, or be more willing, to move for the sake of economic opportunities. Negroes were, if anything, slightly less mobile by this definition. And those with both low and high levels of completed education were more mobile than those with a high school education.

This U-shaped effect of education is accentuated for the non-Protestants, as Figure 15-3 shows. One plausible interpretation is that the non-Protestants are minority groups who may be more likely to have to move to find a job if they are uneducated; that is, their status limits their job opportunities only if they are uneducated. On the other hand, it would seem that higher levels of education are associated with more mobility for everyone, perhaps because of the opportunities advanced education opens up.

Previous Research on Mobility

Mobility is made up of a number of components which have been shown to be uncorrelated with one another.[6] Indeed, the more general concept of social mobility has been shown to be capable of decomposition into at least eight different orthogonal dimensions or "factors."[7]

---

[6]Morgan et al. For a highly critical analysis of mobility studies, see Stephan Thernstrom, Poverty and Progress (Cambridge: Harvard University Press, 1964).

[7]Charles F. Westoff, Marvin Bressler, and Philip C. Sagi, "The

The present chapter has focused on two economically important components: geographical mobility and occupational mobility, the latter only
within the lifetime of the head of the family. Most sociological studies
of occupational mobility have been concerned with intergenerational patterns
References to most of this research may be found in Lipset and Bendix's book
on mobility.[8] Some studies of "occupational mobility" are in reality studies
of occupational achievement or level.[9]

A series of studies have also been made on why workers may be reluctant to change jobs.[10] At least two pieces of research have interpreted
occupational change between generations as a Markov process (son's occupation as a probabilistic function of the father's), but they have ignored the
serious problem that some families have more sons than others, and this
affects the transition probabilities.[11]

When we come to geographic mobility, our findings supplement a large
amount of data on geographic mobility collected by the Survey Research Cente

Concept of Social Mobility: An Empirical Inquiry," American Sociological
Review, 25 (June 1960), 375-385.

[8]Seymour Lipset and Reinhard Bendix, Social Mobility in Industrial
Society (Berkeley: University of California Press, 1959); see also Kaare
Svalastoga, Prestige, Class and Mobility (Copenhagen: Gyldendal, 1959); Otis
Dudley Duncan, "The Trend of Occupational Mobility in the United States,"
American Sociological Review, 30 (August 1965), 491-498.

[9]Bruce K. Eckland, "Academic Ability, Higher Education, and Occupational Mobility," American Sociological Review, 30 (October 1965), 735-746.

[10]Gladys L. Palmer et al., The Reluctant Job Changer: Studies on
Work Attachments and Aspiration (Philadelphia: University of Pennsylvania
Press, 1962).

[11]S. J. Prais, "Measuring Social Mobility," Journal of the Royal
Statistical Society, Series A, 118 (1955), 51-66; see also J. Matras, "Comparison of Intergenerational Occupational Mobility Patterns: An Application
of the Formal Theory of Social Mobility," Population Studies, 14 (November
1960), 163-169.

and the U.S. Bureau of the Census. Census data focused chiefly on showing that the younger people are more mobile, particularly if they do not own a home or have children in school.[12] Other data on geographic mobility vary from the enumerative materials of the Current Population Surveys to detailed studies of the reasons for moving and the costs of moving.[13]

Traveling without moving one's place of residence is also a form of geographic mobility, and John Lansing and others have produced a series of studies based on an on-going program of research on this subject.[14]

---

[12]John B. Lansing et al., The Geographic Mobility of Labor: A First Report (Ann Arbor: Survey Research Center, The University of Michigan, 1963); see also U.S. Bureau of the Census, Current Population Reports, Series P-20, No. 104, Mobility of the Population of the United States, April 1958 to 1959 (September 30, 1960).

[13]Harold C. Brown and Roy C. Buck, Factors Associated with the Migrant Status of Young Adult Males from Rural Pennsylvania, Bulletin No. 676 (State College, Pennsylvania: Agricultural Experiment Station, Pennsylvania State University, January 1961); John Lansing and Eva Mueller, The Geographic Mobility of Labor (Ann Arbor: Survey Research Center, The University of Michigan, 1966); Peter Rossi, Why Families Move: A Study of Social Psychology of Urban Residential Mobility (Glencoe: The Free Press, 1965); Harry K. Schwarzweller, Sociocultural Origins and Migration Patterns of Young Men from Eastern Kentucky, Bulletin No. 685 (Lexington: Kentucky Agricultural Experiment Station, December 1963); Henry S. Shryock, Jr., Population Mobility within the United States (Chicago: Community and Family Studies Center, University of Chicago, 1964); Karl E. Taeuber, "Duration of Residence Analysis of Internal Migration in the United States," Milbank Memorial Fund Quarterly, 39 January 1961); U.S. Bureau of the Census, Current Population Reports, Series P-20, No. 104, Mobility of the Population of the United States, April 1958 to 1959 (September 30, 1960); U.S. Bureau of the Census, Current Population Reports, Series P-20, No. 134, Mobility of the Population of the United States, March 1962 to March 1963 (March 25, 1965); U.S. Department of Commerce, Area Redevelopment Administration, The Geographic Mobility of Labor: A Summary Report (results of a study done at the University of Michigan's Survey Research Center) (1964); Nelson L. LeRay and William W. Reeder, Ex-Farm Operators in a Low-Income Area, Bulletin No. 67-2 (Ithaca: Cornell University Agricultural Experiment Station, November 1965).

[14]John Lansing, The Travel Market, 1964-1965 (Ann Arbor: Survey Research Center, The University of Michigan, October 1965); John Lansing and Dwight Blood, The Changing Travel Market (Ann Arbor: Survey Research Center, The University of Michigan, 1964).

CHAPTER 16

AMBITION AND ASPIRATION LEVELS

Definition

       The desire for possessions has always been assumed an important driving force behind hard work, willingness to adapt to change, and even willingness to take calculated risks. From the results of our interviews we constructed an index using eight different bits of evidence that more income has a high incentive value to the family. A point was given on the index for each one of the following eight items:

> Would like to be earning at least $1000 more five years from now than earning now
>
> Would like to work more hours if paid for it
>
> Ranked "high income" first or second among six job characteristics
>
> Expects to provide financial aid to parents or other relatives within the next twenty years
>
> Currently taking courses that increase economic skills
>
> Family would like to buy some new things or replace some things
>
> Family would like a new home or additions and repairs to present home
>
> Expects to send children to college

The first two components apply only to those working for money, and the last only to those with children under eighteen. The index scores are distributed as follows:

Score on ambition and aspiration index	Per cent of cases
Zero	17
One	19
Two	20
Three	18
Four	14
Five	9
Six	2
Seven	1
Eight	0
Total	100
Number of cases	2214

Background Factors

The most powerful discriminator of which heads of families would have a high level of ambition and aspiration was age, understandably enough. Figure 16-1 shows the relation. Differences according to marital status and sex, race, and the index of achievement orientation were also marked, but in view of the powerful age effects we should turn immediately to the multi-variate analysis.

The variables introduced into the search process, in order of their importance if used to make a single division of the whole sample , were as follows:

        *Age of head of family
        *Index of achievement orientation
        *Sex and marital status of head of family
        Education of head of family
        Difference in education between head of family and his father
        Number of brothers and sisters of head of family
        Whether head of family grew up on a farm

        Race
        Religious preference
        Number of brothers and sisters older than head of family

270

FIGURE 16-1

SCORE ON INDEX OF AMBITION AND ASPIRATION,
BY AGE OF HEAD OF FAMILY
(For all 2214 heads of families)

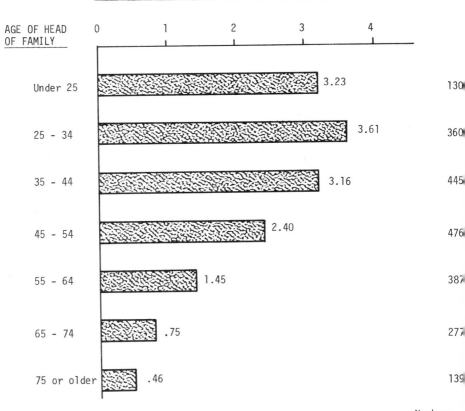

SCORE ON INDEX OF AMBITION AND ASPIRATION

AGE OF HEAD OF FAMILY	Score	Number of cases
Under 25	3.23	130
25 - 34	3.61	360
35 - 44	3.16	445
45 - 54	2.40	476
55 - 64	1.45	387
65 - 74	.75	277
75 or older	.46	139

MTR 126

Asterisked variables are those used in Figure 16-2. They explained 43 per cent of the variance. The overall standard deviation of the score is 1.7. None of the variables below the line could explain as much as 0.5 per cent of the total sum of squares by a single division of the whole sample.

Only the first three variables were actually used, the rest disappearing from view once the sample was divided according to age. Being aged <u>or</u> unmarried is associated with a lower score on the index of ambition and aspiration. Is this an automatic consequence of the way the index was constructed? Older and single people are less likely to have anyone they <u>could</u> plan to send to college, more likely to have a home and the appliances they need, and less likely to be able to look forward to an increase in income. On the other hand, these are real differences.

The only unusual variable was the index of achievement orientation. An examination of its detail with that of the index of ambition and aspiration reveals no automatic correlation; the items are not the same except that the index of ambition and aspiration includes a point for planning to send children to college, whereas the index of achievement orientation assigns a point for a total family income under $10,000 and still having children who will go, are going, or have gone, to college. Indeed, there is a built-in negative correlation between the two, since they both use answers to a question about how the respondent would rank six characteristics of a job. Ranking "high income" first or second adds one point to the ambition and aspiration index, but ranking "chances for advancement are good" or "the work is important, gives a feeling of accomplishment" first or second adds one or two points to the index of achievement orientation.

On the other hand, it is quite possible that what we call the index of achievement orientation is really a tapping of <u>current</u>, rather than

272

FIGURE 16-2

INDEX OF AMBITION AND ASPIRATION
(For all 2214 heads of families)

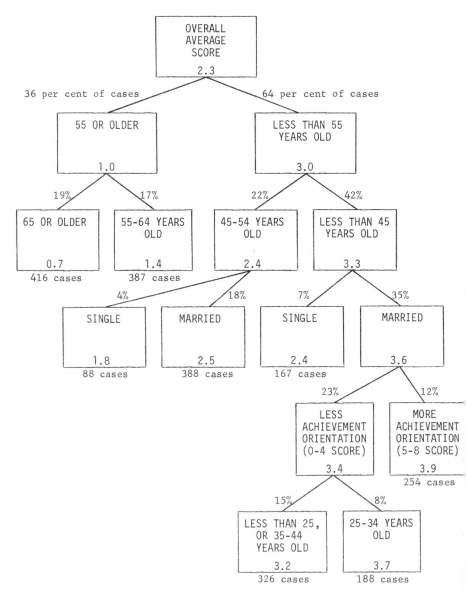

permanent, attitudes and behaviors in the general area of ambition and aspiration. Hence, what we have may be a correlation between two indexes getting at some of the same things, rather than any causal relation. On the other hand, if the index of achievement orientation is tapping a more stable long-since fixed personality characteristic, then that characteristic may be shaping the more current ambitions of the respondent.

Attitudes and Motives

The pooled differences from the end-groups of Figure 16-2 were examined against the following variables, again listed in order of importance:

        *Index of mobility experience
         Index of planning and time horizon
         Index of receptivity to change
        *Index of achievement orientation
         Education of head of family
        *Whether head of family has been out of a job for two months
             or more, and when
         Interviewer's impression of alertness of respondent

         Total family income
        *Attitude toward importance of luck for financial success
         Whether head of family has been sick for one month or more,
             and when
         Attitude toward mothers' working
         Index of social participation
         Age of head of family
         Sex and marital status of head of family
         Difference in education between head of family and wife
         Index of closeness of family ties
         Number of brothers and sisters of head of family and his
             birth order
         Median income of county
         Index of caution and risk avoidance
         Housing status (home ownership)
         Per cent of adults in county who completed high school
         Education of father of family head
         Whether family owns a business or farm
         Number of responses indicating a sense of personal
             effectiveness

Asterisked variables are those used in Figure 16-3. They explained an additional 2 per cent of the variance. The overall standard deviation of the residual score is 1.3. None of the variables below the line explains as much as 0.5 per cent of the total sum of squares by a single division of the whole sample.

The resulting Figure 16-3 used only the indexes of mobility experience, achievement orientation, as well as past unemployment experience, and the head's belief in the importance of luck. Since five final groups in Figure 16-3 account only for 2 per cent more of the original variance, none of the two dozen variables, alone or in combination, were able to explain any substantial part of the interpersonal differences in the index of ambition and aspiration, after we had accounted for the effects of age, sex and marital status, and achievement orientation.

The findings of Figure 16-3 are nevertheless suggestive. Mobility experience is associated with ambitions for the future. Mobile people are more ambitious. Among those who have not been mobile is a small group who never worked (widows mostly) or who have very recently suffered long unemployment, and they have very limited aspirations. Among the mobile, either of two things is associated with still higher aspirations: a high score on the index of achievement orientation, or a belief that luck is important for financial success. Since these are two alternative paths in people's minds, either one making things possible, the finding is sensible.

Why did none of the other twenty variables seem to matter? Some had of course already had their main effect removed in Figure 16-2 and were reintroduced only in case they interacted with some of the second-stage variables. But apparently the income and education levels of the county do not set standards which affect individual's aspirations visibly, nor does being the oldest son or the youngest in a large family, nor does the differential

FIGURE 16-3

INDEX OF AMBITION AND ASPIRATION: ANALYSIS OF DIFFERENCES
FROM END GROUP AVERAGES OF FIGURE 16-2
(For all 2214 heads of families)

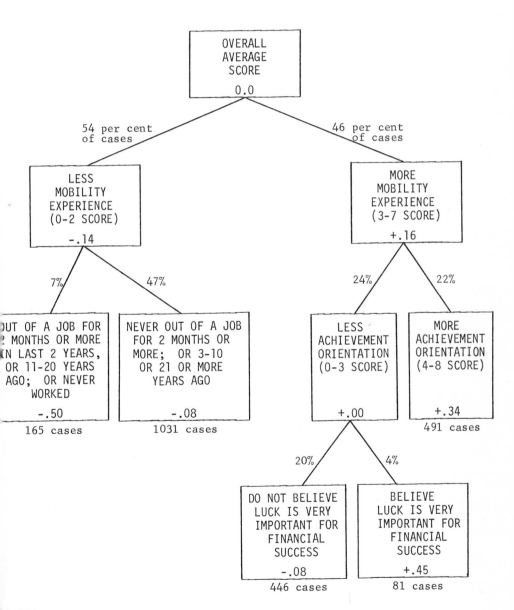

in wife's education from that of her husband, or the family head's <u>father's education</u>, nor indeed the <u>education of the head</u>. Education would seem to affect receptivity to change, but not ambition and aspiration levels, at least on the verbal level of expressed attitudes.

It must be remembered that a measurement of ambition and aspiration tends to measure a gap between achievements and goals. People with past successes find their aspirations rising, and hence there is no <u>a priori</u> theory about whether the successful or the unsuccessful would report the largest gap between their present state and where they would like to be. Indeed, defensive and rationalizing reactions to failure might well leave the unsuccessful with less tendency to express ambitions and aspirations. One could argue that the reason why the index of achievement orientation turned out to be important in explaining the index of ambition and aspiration is that, according to theory, achievement-oriented people should have more elastic aspirations which rise with each success.

Some Components of Ambition and Aspiration: Who Wants More Work?

Indexes have a potential for hiding important relations in a mess of pooled noise, even if the components have been shown in advance to be mildly positively correlated with one another as in all our indexes. Hence, as in earlier chapters, we look at one or two of the more important components individually. Perhaps the most important economic component of the index of ambition and aspiration is the expressed desire for more hours of work. About one-third of the respondents currently in the labor force said that they would like more work. The relationships, however, make such a response look more like desperation than ambition. It is the uneducated and the

blue-collar workers who are most likely to want more work--those who are
making the least amount per hour. More than half the semiskilled workers
said they wanted more work, and only one in ten of them wanted less.

Income has little relation to the desire for more work. Only at the
very highest incomes does the proportion saying they want more work fall off.
It is the young, the uneducated, and the semiskilled who are most likely to
want more work. The percentages fall from 64 per cent, among those under
twenty-five years old, to 20 per cent for those aged fifty-five through
sixty-four. And they fall from 43 per cent, among those who completed less
than six grades of school, to 15 per cent among those with advanced or graduate college degrees. Both these effects are underestimates, since there is
a negative correlation between age and education, so that the generally higher education mix among the young masks the really extensive desire of the
young high-school dropouts for more hours of work, and the smaller proportion of college graduates among older people understates the increasing fit
of work to desires, by adjusting one or the other, among older people.

Who Wants More Income Five Years
from Now?

Another component of the index of ambition and aspiration is the
expression of a desire for an income five years from now at least $1,000
more than the current income of the head of the family. Sixty-three per
cent of those currently working expressed such aspirations. The desire
peaked at the middle of the income range, $6000-7499, and among the college
graduates. But again it was, realistically, the young who were most likely
to hope for higher incomes, 83 per cent among those under twenty-five, and
in the succeeding age groups, 81 per cent, 72 per cent, 59 per cent, and

finally dropping to 39 per cent for those fifty-five to sixty-four years old. In this case, since the young are also more highly educated, the effect of education and that of being young are both exaggerated slightly.

High Income as an Important Criterion in Judging an Occupation

Another component of the index of ambition and aspiration was giving first or second rank to "high income" as one of six characteristics of an occupation. Interestingly enough, expressing such an interest in high income was no more common among those with low or high income, or those with more or less education. There was some tendency for younger people to rank it high. Perhaps people get used to their income as they get older, or else manage to get the income to which they aspired.

Who Says There Are Things He Wants To Buy or Replace?

Another component of the index was an expression of desire for new things. Those with more education were more likely to want more things, and those with more income--who presumably already had more things--were also more likely to want still more, another example of continually rising aspirations. There was some decline at the very highest income, the peak being in the range $5000-7499 where two-thirds said there were some things they would like to buy or replace. There is presumably some basic stock and some potential saturation at the highest income levels.

Even more dramatic is the obvious unfilled desire among the young, the vast majority of whom can think of things they want: three-quarters of those under thirty-five, two-thirds of those thirty-five through forty-four and then consistently fewer, to 59 per cent, 45 per cent, and, for those

ixty-five and older, to less than one-third. The relation of desiring to
uy or replace things to age, and hence of the entire ambition index to
ge,may reflect not so much ambition as the fact that younger people may not
ave accumulated all the "things of this world" that make up the American
tandard of living. On the other hand, since, in fact, even younger people
ften have most of their major appliances, the age effect may reflect a real
ifference in ambition and aspiration levels between the young and the old.

ummary

High ambitions and aspirations are much more common among the young,
he married, and those who give independent evidences of high achievement
rientation. Ambition is also associated with more experience of mobility,
aving had no very recent unemployment experience, and, for those without
 high score on the index of achievement orientation, a belief that luck is
ery important to financial success.

Major components of the index of ambition and aspiration were like-
ise correlated negatively with age, but not strongly with education or in-
ome, except that the uneducated, who have more unemployment experience,
ended to want more work, and those with incomes over $10,000 tended to
ant less work.

A number of variables which have interested psychologists and sociol-
gists for some time seem to have no important relation to our measure of
mbition, namely birth order, wife's education, religious preference, growing
p on a farm, and race.

Related Research

An unpublished study in Spain reveals that about 87 per cent of

Spanish families would like to buy or replace things and 55 per cent would like to work more if they could earn more, much higher proportions than in this country.[1]

---

[1]Burkhard Strümpel, "Spanish Attitudes with Regard to Economic Behavior," unpublished.

CHAPTER 17

SOCIAL PARTICIPATION

Definition

It may seem that our index of social participation is hardly an
economic behavior, and perhaps not anything that would contribute to either
individual or national economic growth. But word of mouth remains the chief
channel for communication of new ideas, and much social activity requires
money and may stimulate earning it. In addition, the index contains two
items of volunteer work, a kind of social participation that is also presumably productive. But even if social activity contributes little to productivity, we analyze it as a possible part of a modernism syndrome, on the
theory that the components of that syndrome may reinforce one another.

The index assigns one point in the score for each of the following:

Head of family attends religious services regularly
     or often

Head of family took a vacation in 1964

Wife of head of family did more than 40 hours of
     volunteer work in 1964

Head of family did more than 40 hours of volunteer
     work in 1964

Family eats at restaurants at least once every other
     week

Head of family participates in sports or hobbies

The resulting index scores range from zero to six and are distributed
as follows:

Score on social participation index	Per cent of cases
Zero	7
One	19
Two	25
Three	25
Four	16
Five	6
Six	2
Total	100
Number of cases	2214

Background Factors

The most important single determinant in explaining level of social participation, nearly twice as effective as its nearest rival, was the level of formal education the head of the family had completed. This variable, of course, serves as a proxy for many things: family background, native ability, energy, initiative, friends and connections, actual learned knowledge and skills, and achievement motivation. Figure 17-1 shows the overall relation of the effect of education.

The background variables introduced simultaneously into the search process were, in order of importance over the whole sample:

> *Education of head of family
> *Index of achievement orientation
> Difference in education between head of family and his father
> Age of head of family
> Whether head of family grew up on a farm
> *Sex and marital status of head of family
> Race
> Religious preference
> Number of brothers and sisters of head of family

Number of brothers and sisters older than head of family

Asterisked variables are those used in Figure 17-2. They explained 20 per cent of the variance. The overall standard

283

FIGURE 17-1

SCORE ON INDEX OF SOCIAL PARTICIPATION,
BY EDUCATION OF HEAD OF FAMILY
(For all 2214 heads of families)*

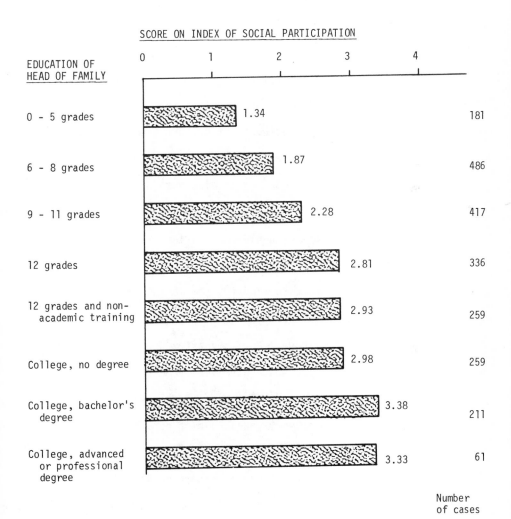

SCORE ON INDEX OF SOCIAL PARTICIPATION

EDUCATION OF HEAD OF FAMILY	Score	Number of cases
0 - 5 grades	1.34	181
6 - 8 grades	1.87	486
9 - 11 grades	2.28	417
12 grades	2.81	336
12 grades and non-academic training	2.93	259
College, no degree	2.98	259
College, bachelor's degree	3.38	211
College, advanced or professional degree	3.33	61

MTR 112

*excludes 4 cases in which education of head of family was not ascertained.

deviation of the score is 1.4. None of the variables below the line could explain as much as 0.5 per cent of the total sum of squares by a single division of the whole sample.

Once the sample is divided according to education of the head of the family, however, only two other factors remain important: the index of achievement orientation and marital status. The details are given in Figure 17-2.

It is interesting to note that the index of achievement orientation is effective with all educational levels except those with college degrees. Those with college degrees are somewhat higher and less varied on the index of achievement orientation, 61 per cent scoring four or higher as against 38 per cent for the whole sample. But it is also possible that college graduates are drawn into more social participation by other social forces, leaving little room for the index of achievement orientation to affect them further.

Many explanations come to mind for the mechanisms by which these three variables affect social participation. The uneducated have such low hourly earnings that, as we have seen, they often work more hours in order to have enough to live on, and hence have less time to devote to social activities. They are also more likely to be older. The single people are more likely to be very old or very young, and if not, to have a household to care for or other problems.

The most interesting relation is that with the index of achievement orientation. Both indexes, social participation and achievement orientation are composite measures, and it is essential to be sure that we are not merely measuring the same thing two ways. This is somewhat less likely in this case than when both measures are attitudinal. The index of social participation

285

FIGURE 17-2

INDEX OF SOCIAL PARTICIPATION
(For all 2214 heads of families)

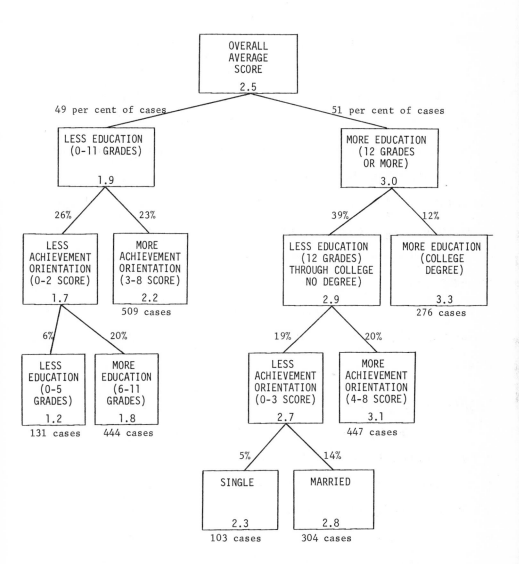

MTR 112

is made up entirely of reported activities. There may be reporting errors, but the range of possible distortion because of the respondents' attitudes is (we hope) small. The index of achievement motivation is partly reported behavior, such as sending children to college even though the family income is below $10,000 or the family head's attending courses, but the index is also partly attitudinal: placing high value on a job where the work is important, or a job that offers chances for advancement, or thinking it is important to make changes on the job, or having aspirations for a high but not unrealistically high income, and feeling that one sometimes falls short and could do better. Whether this mixture of attitudes and behavior really forms a syndrome that could be claimed to be related to the need for achievement as defined and used by psychologists is difficult to say, though it was intended that way (see Appendix D). At least it is related to the index of social participation, indicating that achievement-oriented people by our measures are also active in things not usually thought of as achievement-related.

Attitudes and Motives

We turn now to an examination of the pooled differences from the end groups of Figure 17-2. Most of the important effects of education, marital status, and achievement orientation have presumably been removed, and we can now ask whether any of a large number of other variables matter, without being quite so concerned with spurious correlations. The twenty-eight variables introduced into the simultaneous multivariate search process are listed below in order of their importance if used to make a single division of the whole set of 2214 residuals:

*Total family income
*Index of receptivity to change
*Index of planning and time horizon
 Index of caution and risk avoidance
*Number of responses indicating a sense of personal
    effectiveness
 Housing status (home ownership)
*Index of closeness of family ties
*Age of youngest child under 18 living at home
*Per cent of adults in county who completed high school
*Difference in education between head of family and wife
 Age of head of family
*Size of place (town) where family lives
 Interviewer's impression of alertness of respondent
 Number of people in family
 Whether head of family has been out of a job for two months
    or more, and when
*Whether head of family has been sick for one month or more,
    and when
 Sex and marital status of head of family

Education of head of family
Attitude toward mothers' working
Number of disabled people in family
Index of mobility experience
Education of father of family head
Age of oldest child under 18 living at home
Index of ambition and aspiration
Index of achievement orientation
Number of brothers and sisters of head of family
    and his birth order
Attitude toward importance of luck for financial success
Whether family owns a business or farm

Asterisked variables are those used in Figure 17-3. They
explained an additional 8 per cent of the variance. The overall
standard deviation of the residual score is 1.3. None of the
variables below the line could explain as much as 0.5 per cent of
the total sum of squares by a single division of the whole sample.

As in earlier two-stage analyses, a number of variables used in the
first stage were reintroduced in the analysis of the residuals, in case they
mediated the effects of any of the second-stage variables. The advantage of
this two-stage approach is clear when one considers how an analysis which
simultaneously introduced income and education could have been interpreted.

288

FIGURE 17-3

INDEX OF SOCIAL PARTICIPATION: ANALYSIS OF DIFFERENCES
OF END-GROUP AVERAGES OF FIGURE 17-2
(For all 2214 heads of families)

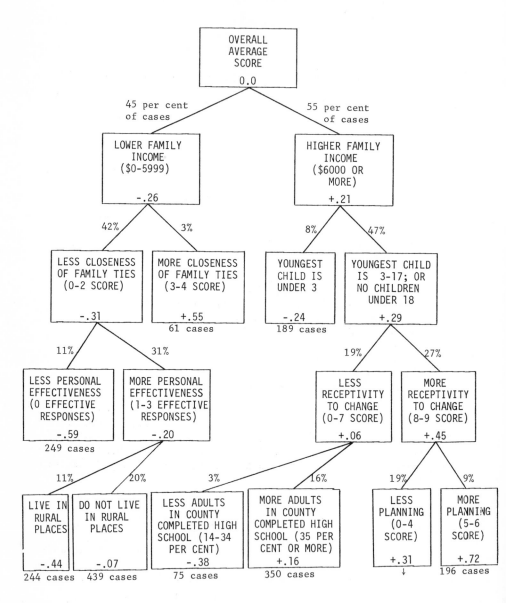

MTR 112

(CONTINUED ON PAGE 289)

FIGURE 17-3--(CONTINUED)

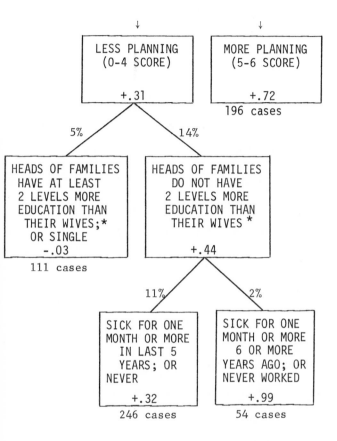

_____

Education was classified into eight groups. "Two levels more" means that the head of the family was in two or more higher classes than his wife. (See Appendix C, Qs. E9-E12 and E18-E21.)

R 112

Using the two-stage approach, we can say that there is surely some income effect, even when we have removed education and with it any "income effect" which could possibly have been attributed to education.

It would seem that there is very little social participation among those with low income, or a child under three in the house, or among those living in rural places, or those with little or no feeling of personal effectiveness. On the other hand, higher income, a high score on the index of family ties, receptivity to change, or a wife with more education than her husband, lead to more social participation.[1] Interestingly enough, the per cent of people in the county who completed high school was effective enough to split one group, even after the first stage analysis had accounted for the family head's own education, and previous divisions in Figure 17-3 had taken some account of family income, the presence of small children, and score on the index of receptivity to change. It would seem reasonable that a county with a higher proportion of educated people in it would also have more activities in which people could participate. If the difference were merely a rural-urban one, the split would have been made into urban and rural residences as it was with the lower-income families.

The wife's education was introduced as a difference from her husband since the latter is highly correlated with it and was used in the first stage and introduced in the second. The result makes sense: where there is no wife or she has much less education than her husband, there is less family social participation.

_____

[1]The positive relation among low-income people between the residuals and the index of closeness of family ties, is at least partly an artifact. Those who reported that head or wife did unpaid work for relatives were given a point on both indexes--on social participation because it was volunteer work, and on closeness of family ties because it was helping relatives.

Again, just in case the components of the index are affected by different forces, we examine some of its main components briefly. They are, in any case, of interest in their own right.

Discussion of Some Components:
Who Takes Vacations?

Well-educated middle- and upper-income people tend to take vacations, provided they are not already retired. As might be expected, income is the most important determinant of who takes vacations. The proportion who took a vacation in 1964 varied from 27 per cent for those with incomes under $1000, to 72 per cent, for those with incomes of $15,000 or more. Every education group with a high school education or higher had at least 60 per cent who took a vacation. The groups least likely to take a vacation were the elderly, the uneducated, and those with very low incomes.

Who Attends Church Regularly?

A previous study by Bernard Lazerwitz combined three Survey Research Center studies and reported that church attendance was more frequent among women, Negroes, people with higher educational levels, and those with high-prestige occupations, but that it did not seem to be associated with age or income.[2]

Data on church attendance were also collected by the Survey Research Center in 1960.[3] A reanalysis of those data with the multivariate technique

---

[2] Bernard Lazerwitz, "Some Factors Associated with Variations in Church Attendance," Social Forces, 39 (May 1961), 301-309.

[3] Morgan et al.; church attendance is used throughout the book as an explanatory factor.

used in the present study provided the basis for part of Table 17-1, which shows for Christians a systematic effect of race and Catholicism on the one hand, and region on the other. Only education actually appeared in the analysis in addition. However, the effects of age, education, and income are still important within the groups of Table 17-1, and are more interesting in terms of explaining and predicting social change.

Our data do show a tendency for people under thirty-five to attend church less frequently, and for the main effect of education to be among college graduates, nearly half of whom claim to attend religious services regularly. On the other hand, those who do not attend church at all tend to be older, to be uneducated, and to have lower incomes.

Who Eats in Restaurants?

Older people eat out less frequently, the uneducated much less frequently. For those with some college education or more, however, education does not seem to matter. It is income which dominates the scene, understandably since eating in restaurants is expensive. The proportions who eat out once every two weeks or more often vary from 18 per cent among those with incomes under $1000 to 71 per cent among those with incomes of $15,000 or more.

Who Does Volunteer Work for Church, Charity, and Relatives?

The middle-aged, better educated, upper-income people, both men and women, are more likely to report spending forty hours or more in 1964 on such unpaid work. It was most frequent among the wives of men with advanced degrees, and with family incomes of $15,000 or more. Hence, not only is a

TABLE 17-1

CHURCH ATTENDANCE BY HEAD OF FAMILY FOR VARIOUS RELIGIOUS PREFERENCES
AND REGIONS
(For all 2214 family [2997 spending unit] heads, data from two studies)

Religious preference and region	Per cent of sample		Per cent who attend church more than once a month	Per cent who attend church regularly or often
	1960*	1965	1960*	1965
Catholics	9			
South	2	2	88	65
Northeast and North Central	15	17	80	79
West	5	3	71	70
Negro Protestants				
South	5	5	72	68
Northeast and North Central	4	2	56	49
West	1	1	60	63**
White Protestants				
South	23	23	58	54
Northeast and North Central	30	29	47	50
West	9	11	30	37
Non-Christian; not ascertained	6	7	0	16
Total	100	100	54	54
Number of cases	2997	2214		

*From Morgan et al. (data presented above from this study).
*Fewer than 25 cases.

Study 678, MTR 778 (AID-2), Deck 36 of Study 678
Study 721, MTR 170, Deck 1, 66/77

great deal of unpaid work being done in this country, but it is being done by people whose time is worth more than average, meaning that the contribution to social welfare would be underestimated if we valued this unpaid work at the national average hourly earnings. One might argue that such work is done inefficiently, or is partly recreation, but unless people are wildly irrational, they are using time very valuable to themselves in such efforts, and presumably receive an equivalent satisfaction from it. They must think it is worth that much.

Since income, age, and education were generally important for most of these five main components of social participation, Figures 17-4, 17-5, and 17-6 provide summaries of their relations to those components. Whether we can extrapolate from these effects to more dynamic implications about the effects of increased education and income on such behavior is uncertain, and will remain so until repeated measurements are made in future years. One hopes, however, that a more educated and affluent population will participate more actively in the kinds of activities measured here. The relative mildness of the decline in activities, even volunteer work, among those sixty-five or older, leads to the hope that as the proportion of older people in the population increases, and their health improves, they will continue to engage in productive, though unpaid, activities.

Other Research

In addition to the earlier Survey Research Center work on church attendance previously cited, there have been a number of studies of partici

FIGURE 17-4

PER CENT OF FAMILIES PARTICIPATING IN VARIOUS ACTIVITIES,
BY TOTAL FAMILY INCOME
(For all 2214 families)

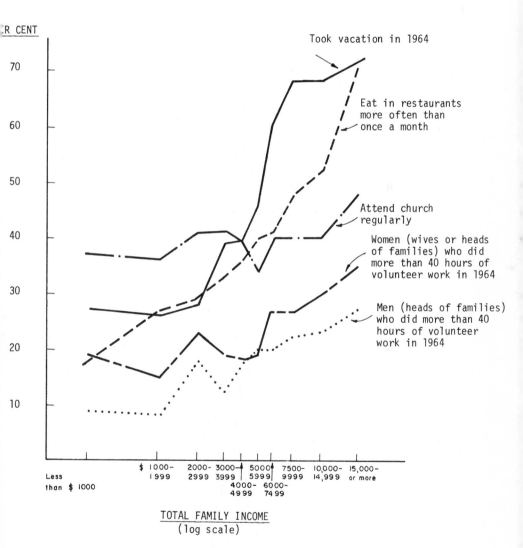

MTR's 161-163

FIGURE 17-5

PER CENT OF FAMILIES PARTICIPATING IN VARIOUS ACTIVITIES,
BY AGE OF HEAD OF FAMILY
(For all 2214 families)

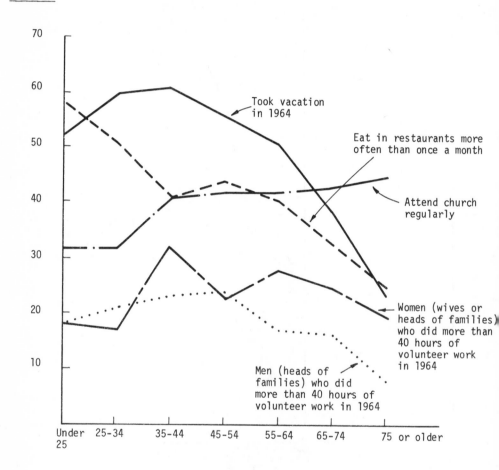

AGE OF HEAD OF FAMILY

MTR's 161-163

297

FIGURE 17-6
PER CENT OF FAMILIES PARTICIPATING IN VARIOUS ACTIVITIES,
BY EDUCATION OF HEAD OF FAMILY
(For all 2214 families)*

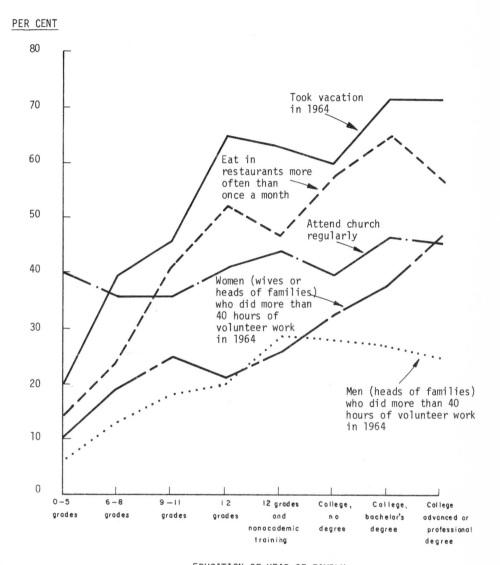

EDUCATION OF HEAD OF FAMILY

MTR's 161-163
*excludes 4 cases in which education of family head was not ascertained.

pation in formal organizations, and the extent of contact with other people.[4]

There are also other studies of church attendance.[5]

Studies of political activity, not measured in this study, show a similar tendency for the more educated, middle-aged, better-off people to be more active as well as more informed.

Morris Axelrod, "Urban Structure and Social Participation, "American Sociological Review, 21 (February 1956), 13-18; W. Bell and M. T. Force, "Urban Neighborhood Types and Participation in Formal Associations," American Sociological Review, 21 (February 1956), 25-34; Floyd Dotson, "Patterns of Voluntary Association," American Sociological Review, 16 (October 1951), 687-693; Albert J. Reiss, Jr., "Rural-Urban and Status Differences in Interpersonal Contacts," American Journal of Sociology, LXV (September 1959), 182-195; Leonard Reissman, "Class, Leisure, and Social Participation," American Sociological Review, 19 (February 1954), 76-84; Judith T. Shuval, "Class and Ethnic Correlates of Casual Neighboring," American Sociological Review, 21 (August 1956), 453-458; David Sills, The Volunteers (Glencoe: The Free Press 1957); B. G. Zimmer and A. H. Hawley, "The Significance of Membership in Associations," American Journal of Sociology, LXV (September 1959), 196-201.

[5]Harold L. Orbach, "Aging and Religion: Religious Attendance in the Detroit Metropolitan Area," Geriatrics, 16 (October 1961), 530-540; B. G. Zimmer and A. H. Hawley, "Suburbanization and Church Participation," Social Forces, 37 (May 1959), 348-354.

CHAPTER 18

CAUTION AND RISK BEHAVIOR

Definition

Allied to planning ahead and having a long time horizon, which we analyzed in Chapter 14, is engaging in activities calculated either to reduce risks or to enable one to handle them. The index was created by allowing points for each of the following:

Head of family has car seat belts fastened all or part of the time when driving	1 point
Head of family says he does not try new products when they first come on the market	1 point
All family members have had polio vaccine	1 point
Family is covered by medical or hospitalization insurance	1 point
Family has liquid reserve funds equal to two months or more of take-home income	1 point
Head of family is married and has used some method to limit the number or plan the spacing of his children	2 points
Head of family is not married (this was done to neutralize those ineligible for family planning)	1 point

The resulting index had the following statistically nice normal distribution:

Score on caution and risk avoidance index	Per cent of cases
Zero	2
One	11
Two	22
Three	26
Four	21
Five	13
Six	4
Seven	1
Total	100
Number of cases	2214

The most powerful single factor affecting risk avoidance appears to be formal education. Figure 18-1 shows its effect.

Background Factors

Since education had such a powerful effect, we turn immediately to our multivariate analysis, introducing the following variables listed in order of their importance if used to make a single division of the whole sample :

> *Education of head of family
> Difference in education between head of family and his father
> Index of achievement orientation
> *Race
> *Age of head of family
> Whether head of family grew up on a farm
> Religious preference
> Number of brothers and sisters of head of family

> Number of brothers and sisters older than head of family
> Sex and marital status of head of family

Asterisked variables are those used in Figure 18-2. They explained 15 per cent of the variance. The overall standard deviation of the score is 1.4. None of the variables below the line could explain as much as 0.5 per cent of the total sum of squares by a single division of the whole sample.

FIGURE 18-1

SCORE ON INDEX OF CAUTION AND RISK AVOIDANCE,
BY EDUCATION OF HEAD OF FAMILY
(For all 2214 heads of families)*

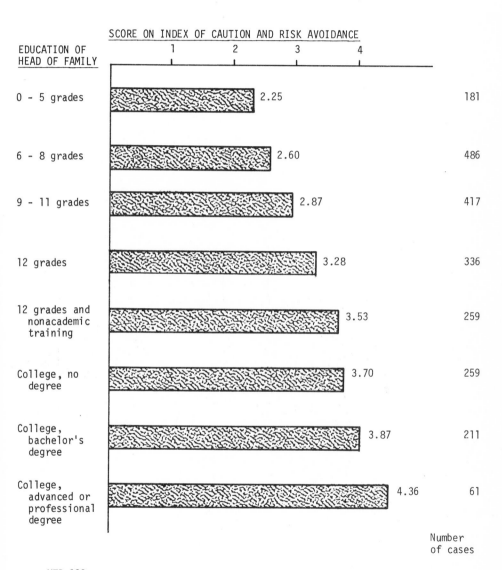

MTR 129

*excludes 4 cases in which education of head of family was not ascertained.

302

FIGURE 18-2

INDEX OF CAUTION AND RISK AVOIDANCE
(For all 2214 heads of families)

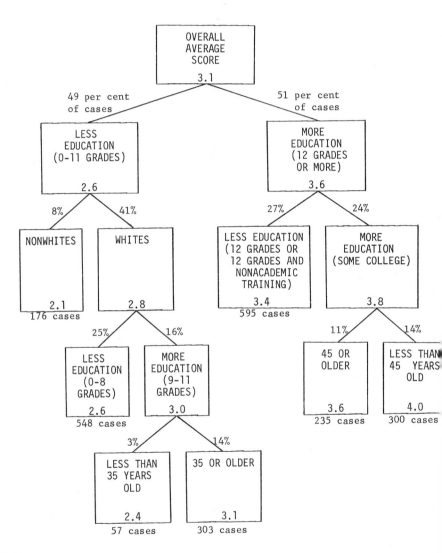

MTR 129

Figure 18-2 shows the results. The average index score varied from
2.1, for nonwhites who did not complete high school, to 4.0, for those under
forty-five with some college education. This is one of the few indexes on
which nonwhites were different enough that, even though they constitute only
one-tenth of the total population, a group of them could still be split off.

The figure shows that it is the educated people who avoid or prepare
for risks, that among the more educated those under forty-five did more such
preparation, and that among the uneducated, the nonwhites did less to avoid
or prepare for risks. It is also clear that none of the other variables in
the list amount to anything once these differences are taken into account.
Their overall effects were all in the expected direction. Heads of families
with more education than their fathers had higher than average scores on the
index of caution and risk avoidance, as did those with higher scores on the
index of achievement orientation, those who did not grow up on a farm
(younger, more educated), the non-Christians and non-fundamentalist Protestants, those with fewer brothers and sisters, those with fewer older brothers
and sisters, and the single men.

Attitudes and Motives

The final groups of Figure 18-2 did account for 15 per cent of the
variance, but we can pool the differences from those group averages, and see
whether they are related to any of a much larger number of variables. The
second-stage analysis makes use of the following variables, listed in order
of their importance over the whole sample:

        *Total family income
        *Index of planning and time horizon
        *Age of youngest child under 18 living at home
        *Index of social participation

Number of responses indicating a sense of personal
  effectiveness
Whether head of family has been out of a job for two months
  or more, and when
Housing status (home ownership)
Whether head of family has been sick for one month or more,
  and when
Age of oldest child under 18 living at home

Index of ambition and aspiration
Age of head of family
Education of head of family
Index of achievement orientation
Interviewer's impression of alertness of respondent
Attitude toward mothers' working
Number of brothers and sisters of head of family and his
  birth order
*Difference in education between head of family and wife
*Sex and marital status of head of family
Education of father of head of family
Attitude toward importance of luck for financial success
Index of mobility experience
Per cent of adults in county who completed high school
Index of closeness of family ties
Whether family owns a business or farm

Asterisked variables are those used in Figure 18-3. They
explained an additional 7 per cent of the variance. The overall
standard deviation of the residual score is 1.3. None of the
variables below the line could explain as much as 0.5 per cent of
the total sum of squares by a single division of the whole sample.

The most powerful variable at this stage was family income, a varia-

ble purposely left out of the first analysis to avoid possible circularity

and because of its high correlation with more basic background factors like

age and education. People with higher incomes might be more likely to have

medical insurance, simply because it takes less effort to buy it. And those

with higher incomes find it easier, as well, to accumulate liquid assets.

But, the ownership of liquid assets was made less income-restricting by

defining it as two months or more of take-home income--a larger amount for

those with higher incomes. The other components of this index are not

heavily income restricted, however.

305

FIGURE 18-3

INDEX OF CAUTION AND RISK AVOIDANCE: ANALYSIS OF DIFFERENCES
FROM END-GROUP AVERAGES OF FIGURE 18-2
(For all 2214 heads of families)

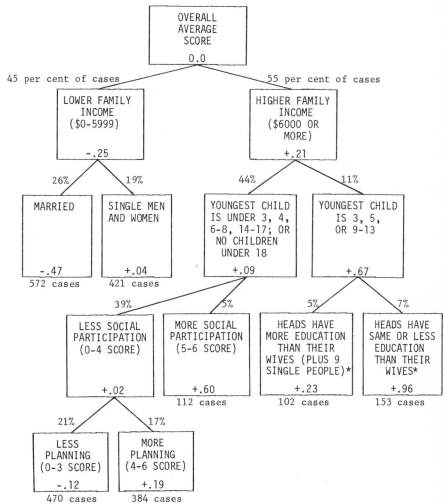

*"Same" means in same bracket. Education was classified into eight groups (see Appendix C, question E18). "More" means that the head of the family is in a higher one of eight classes than his wife is in.

MTR 129

Among lower-income families, it appears to be the married heads of families who are the least cautious, or perhaps we should say it is the les cautious who marry in spite of a low income. This is not a hidden age or education phenomenon. Age and education were both taken into account in the subgroup averages from which we are analyzing differences. They were allowed into the present analysis as possible factors, just in case, but di not come close to getting into Figure 18-3.

A more curious finding is that among the families with higher incomes, the highest caution index is found among those with children, of who the youngest is three, five, or nine through thirteen years old, but the youngest is none of the ages before, between, or after. No other predictor comes close to competing at this stage, and this division reduces the unexplained variance of these pooled deviations by nearly 2 per cent out of the total of 9 per cent for the whole breakdown of Figure 18-3. Since each of the subgroups contain forty cases or more, it is hard to believe that the finding is entirely fortuituous.[1]

The next two divisions were on predictors which were restricted to their scaled order, and both splits make substantive sense. In neither ca does the variable used to split one of the two groups have any appreciable effect on the other. The closest competitor to social participation in splitting the left of the two groups was the index of planning, which inde subsequently divides those with low social participation. The closest competitor to the husband-wife education difference in dividing the right han

---

[1] On the other hand, the IBM machine was scanning over 24 variables and with six of them was selecting the best arrangement (ordering), so tha even at a single step the number of degrees of freedom in a statistical sense is less than one might think.

oup was the number of responses indicating a sense of personal

fectiveness.

The interpretation of the division according to the difference in

lucation between the family head and wife is simple. It is a variable

tended to measure the influence of the wife's education with reasonable

eedom from spurious effects arising from correlation with the husband's

lucation. Having removed most of the effect of the husband's education in

riving the residuals, and using this difference variable, we can be reason-

ly sure that the wife's education had a separate and important positive

fect on the extent to which the family avoids risk or plans to handle it.

parently a family is cautious if either spouse is well educated

The final isolation of one group in which those who do more planning

so avoid more risk shows only a tendency for those who do one to do the

her, not a causal relation.

It is always instructive to ask why so many tempting hypotheses,

plied by the other variables introduced into the analysis, were not borne

t. People who had been out of a job for two months or more within the

st five years, or sick for a month or more within the last two years,

peared somewhat less cautious, but there were not enough of them to come

to Figure 18-3. The number of responses indicating that the head of the

mily felt personally effective was positively related to the index of cau-

on and risk behavior, and came close to entering the figure several times.

re, of course, we have merely a relation, and indeed the causation may go

e other way: the man prepared for emergencies may feel more effective and

 top of things.

A head of a family who had been the only child tended to have a higher index of caution and risk behavior, and the oldest son of a large family tended to have a lower index, but neither tendency was very signifi cant. Homeowners were more cautious, even though they were more likely to be married and married people appeared less cautious (particularly among th low-income people).

Most of the other indexes were positively correlated with caution and risk behavior: social participation, ambition, planning, approval of mothers' working, and achievement orientation. The index of closeness of family ties, is, if anything, negatively related, as is the index of mobil ity experience. But all these relations, except those with planning and social participation, are weak. In view of the extensive and flexible searching of the data, tests of statistical significance cannot be applied

Perhaps the most startling negative finding was that families who own a business or farm did not appear to be significantly more or less cau tious in the areas measured. When we asked how important luck was for fin cial success, those who said it was not at all important were less cautiou but so were those who said luck was important or very important. Apparent the cautious people were also cautious about committing themselves in thei responses to attitudinal questions!

There was some tendency for family heads whose fathers had more ed cation than they had,to be more cautious, even in the residuals where the family head's education had been largely taken into account. Finally, the community influence, crudely measured by the proportion of adults in the county who had finished high school, seemed to have no appreciable or sys- tematic effect on the index of caution.

In general, then, the two-stage analysis explained 22 per cent of the variance, education, age, family income, and marital status doing most of the explaining. A great many other factors appeared to operate in the expected direction, but with little force. Many of the variables examined in the second stage were items thought of not as explanatory, but as related to risk avoidance and it is useful to know that the positive relationships among the various indexes held up even when the possibly spurious relation had been removed by eliminating the effects of age, education, and income from one of them.

Some Components of Caution and Risk Behavior:
Hospital or Medical Insurance

We turn now to an examination of three components of the index of caution and risk behavior and to two other items which were not included as components of the index.[1]

As with the total index, education was the crucial variable in medical insurance, and age was relatively unimportant except for the very aged. The cost of hospital insurance is not beyond the means of many. Such insurance does tend to be carried by fewer than half of those with less than six grades of education, and by fewer than half of those with incomes under $2,000--who are mostly the same people.

Who Has Liquid Assets Amounting to More
than Two Months' Income?

The mixture of desire and ability necessary to accumulate a reserve fund was also found mostly among those with high levels of education, and

---

[1]The use of seat belts was analyzed along with their ownership in Chapter 13 as part of receptivity to new products, even though it is part of the index of caution and risk behavior.

high levels of income. Those under twenty-five, of course, have not had time to accumulate much. Only among those completing high school and among those with family incomes over $7500 a year did more than half report such a reserve fund. It looks as though only the affluent <u>and</u> well educated have the combination of capacity and willingness to save.

Who Has Ever Used Family Planning?

Married respondents were asked:

"Have you and your (husband, wife) used any method to limit the number or plan the spacing of your children?"

Of the 74 per cent of the sample consisting of married couples living together, 41 per cent answered, "yes," 55 per cent answered "no," and the remainder (4 per cent) did not answer the question. As shown in Table 18-1, the proportions who said they had used some kind of family planning were highest among the young and among the highly educated. Both of these effects are exaggerated by the fact that younger people have more education and the well-educated are younger. And it should be noted that there was no way to eliminate from the sample the sterile and subfecund, for whom family planning is, of course, unnecessary and of whom there are a substantial number.

A number of more thorough studies of family planning have been conducted, a few of which are listed below.[2] The Freedman, Whelpton, and

---

[2] See Ronald Freedman, P. K. Whelpton, and A. A. Campbell, <u>Family Planning, Sterility and Population Growth</u> (New York: McGraw-Hill Book Company, Inc., 1959); Bernard Berelson and Ronald Freedman, "A Study in Fertility Control," <u>Scientific American</u>, 210 (May 1964), 29-37; J. Mayone Stycos, "The Potential Role of Turkish Village Opinion Leaders in a Program of Family Planning," <u>Public Opinion Quarterly</u>, XXIX (Spring 1965), 120-130; J. Mayone Stycos and Kurt W. Back, <u>The Control of Human Fertility in Jamaica</u> (Ithaca, New York: Cornell University Press, 1964); Charles F. Westoff,

TABLE 18-1

PER CENT OF MARRIED COUPLES WHO HAVE EVER USED FAMILY PLANNING
BY AGE AND EDUCATION OF HEAD OF FAMILY
(For all 1640 married couples)

	Number of cases	Per cent who have ever used family planning
Age of head of family		
Under 25	89	67
25-34	301	59
35-44	378	52
45-54	388	35
55-64	270	25
65-74	161	17
75 or older	53	2
Education of head of family		
0-5 grades	125	19
6-8 grades	346	28
9-11 grades	302	38
12 grades	272	42
12 grades and nonacademic training	200	50
College, no degree	183	58
College, bachelor's degree	163	53
College, advanced or professional degree	49	49
Total	1640	41

MTR 120

Campbell study used many questions on family planning, including a list of methods, and found about twice as many reporting some use of contraception as we found with one single simple question. Part of the difference in reporting between the two studies may result from the fact that in the present study the husband was usually the respondent, whereas in the Freedman study only wives were interviewed, and by female interviewers.

Multivariate Analysis of Family Planning

These other studies reveal that many couples do not start family planning until they have had the number of children they want, and by that time some discover that because of subfecundity they do not need to use any family planning method. Furthermore, since our question had to do with whether the couple had ever used any method to limit the number or plan the spacing of their children, older couples would have had more opportunity to do so. Finally, though education is clearly a powerful variable, there remains the question whether it is more or less powerful with the younger couples. Figure 18-4 would seem to indicate that there is a rapid increase in acceptance of family planning among young couples, but a persistence of a large differential according to education, even when we omit those under twenty-five (still more of whom are college graduates) and those sixty-five or older.

The positive association between education and family planning was concentrated among Protestants, and as far as we can tell from the small

R. G. Potter, Jr., and P. C. Sagi, The Third Child (Princeton: Princeton University Press, 1963); Charles F. Westoff, R. G. Potter, Jr., P. C. Sagi, and E. G. Mishler, Family Growth in Metropolitan America (Princeton: Princeton University Press, 1961); P. K. Whelpton, A. A. Campbell, J. E. Patterson Fertility and Family Planning in the United States (Princeton: Princeton University Press, 1966).

313

FIGURE 18-4

PER CENT OF MARRIED COUPLES WHO HAVE EVER USED FAMILY PLANNING,
BY AGE AND EDUCATION OF HEAD OF FAMILY
(For all 1336 married couples in which the head of the family
was 25 - 64 years old)

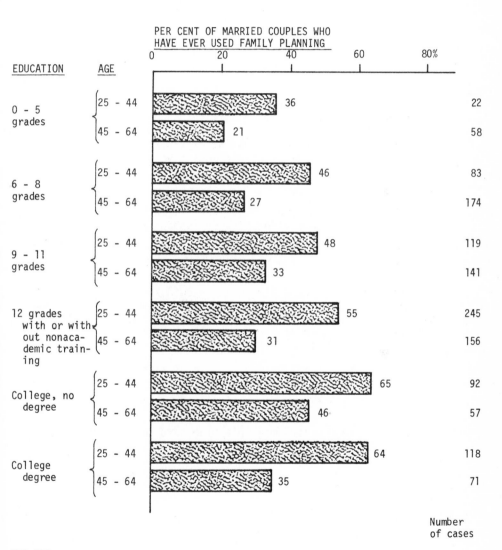

MTR 164

number of Catholics in the sample, this positive association did not exist

for them.   Indeed, even the Catholics with college degrees rarely reported

that they practiced family planning.

In view of the crucial importance of family planning, we have made a

multivariate analysis of the married couples aged thirty-five to sixty-four,

using the following variables, listed in order of importance:

```
*Age of husband
*Religious preference
*Husband's index of receptivity to change
 Education of husband
*Husband's index of achievement orientation
 Liquid savings now or within last five years
 Race
```

```
 Number of brothers and sisters of wife
 Difference in education between husband and wife
*Church attendance of husband
 Number of brothers and sisters of husband
 Whether husband grew up on a farm
```

Asterisked variables are those used in Figure 18-5. They
explained 16 per cent of the variance. The overall standard deviation of the proportion is 0.5 None of the variables below the line
could explain as much as 0.5 per cent of the total sum of squares by
a single division of the whole sample.

Figure 18-5 shows the results. The new findings in Figure 18-5 are

the relation of the husband's score on the index of receptivity to change

(in other areas) to the use of family planning, and the effect on one small

group, of achievement orientation. The powerful effects of religious affil-

iation are made even more dramatic by the finding that among the more

liberal Protestants, it is the regular church attenders who are the most

likely to report using family planning. And it is clear that the increasing

acceptance of family planning among the young is what is important. Actual-

ly, education nearly came into the figure in several places.

315

FIGURE 18-5

PROPORTION OF MARRIED COUPLES WHO HAVE EVER USED FAMILY PLANNING
(For all 1036 married couples in which the husbands are 35-64 years old)

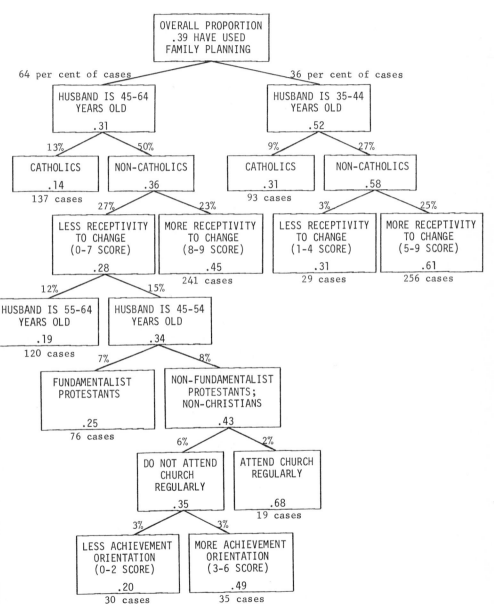

MTR 120

Studies currently being analyzed of data from Taiwan are showing a similar association between family planning and acceptance of other new things, even though the other new things, such as an electric rice cooker, are appropriately different.[3] A fascinating study of the adoption of family planning in Korea has been made by John Ross and Sook Bang, using reinterviews, as well as the same multivariate analysis program as the present study, but with a more appropriate set of explanatory variables.[4]

Increasing acceptance in this country of other forms of risk avoidance is shown in the changes in the percentages of women who report seeing a doctor in the first three months of pregnancy. Table 18-2 combines data from three national studies to show a rapid increase in prenatal care among the less educated, and a consequent narrowing of educational differences. Increased affluence and better insurance coverage during this period must have helped make the change.

TABLE 18-2

PER CENT OF WOMEN HAVING LIVE BIRTHS WHO SAW A DOCTOR
IN THE FIRST THREE MONTHS OF PREGNANCY
BY EDUCATION OF WIFE
(data from three national studies)[*]

Education of wife	1953	1958	1963
0-8 grades	42%	57%	68%
9-11 grades	58	75	88
12 grades	72	79	80
Some college	90	88	88

*Three NORC studies reported in Progress in Health Services, 15 (March-April 1966), 3.

[3]Deborah Freedman (unpublished Ph.D. dissertation, The University of Michigan, forthcoming).

[4]John Ross and Sook Bang, "Predicting the Adoption of Family Planning," Studies in Family Planning, 9 (January 1965), 8-12.

High Ranking of Secure Jobs
or Steady Income

Two other variables not used in the index of caution and risk behavior were giving a high preference rank to an occupation in which there was no danger of being fired, and giving it to an occupation with a steady income. It is well that they were not included as components of the index, for they were negatively related to education, the less educated being more concerned with job security and a steady income. Giving a high preference rank to steady income was not more frequent in any one age or income group, but favoring occupations with no danger of being fired was more common among the older people and among those with lower incomes. In other words, these two items would seem to represent a desire or felt need for security rather than a careful set of activities devoted to eliminating or providing for risks.

Summary

Activity in avoiding risks or preparing to handle them appeared to be encouraged by formal education, and facilitated by a high income, and correlated with other kinds of "modernism," such as planning ahead, ambition, achievement orientation, social participation, receptivity to change, and approval of mothers' working. But it was not correlated with expressed desires for security; hence one must be careful to separate attitudes, often expressing unfulfilled desires, from behavior, which results from a combination of the desire and the ability to fulfill it.

CHAPTER 19

RESISTANCE TO CHANGE

Closeness of Family Ties

We turn now from measures of receptivity to change to some measures of resistance to change. It has been a general thesis of sociology and anthropology that when the family is the center of everything a person does, other broader social forces are more likely to be resisted or will be less influential. The closeness of family ties, often dubbed "familism," has been arbitrarily measured here as the sum of the following four components, one point given for each:

> Head of family says it is important for him or any other family member to live near relatives

> Head of family feels that people should be able to count on financial support from relatives if needed

> Head of family did some volunteer work for relatives (not living in the same dwelling) in 1964

> Wife of head of family did some volunteer work for relatives (not living in same dwelling) in 1964

This index has less variability than some of the other indexes because of the restricted number of items. The distribution is as follows:

Score on index of closeness of family ties	Per cent of cases
Zero	31
One	42
Two	22
Three	4
Four	1
Total	100
Number of cases	2214

The index is higher for those at both ends of the age scale than for the middle-aged, as shown in Figure 19-1. The very old and the very young are, of course, more likely to feel both an emotional and an economic need for family support.

319

FIGURE 19-1

SCORE ON INDEX OF CLOSENESS OF FAMILY TIES,
BY AGE OF HEAD OF FAMILY
(For all 2214 heads of families)

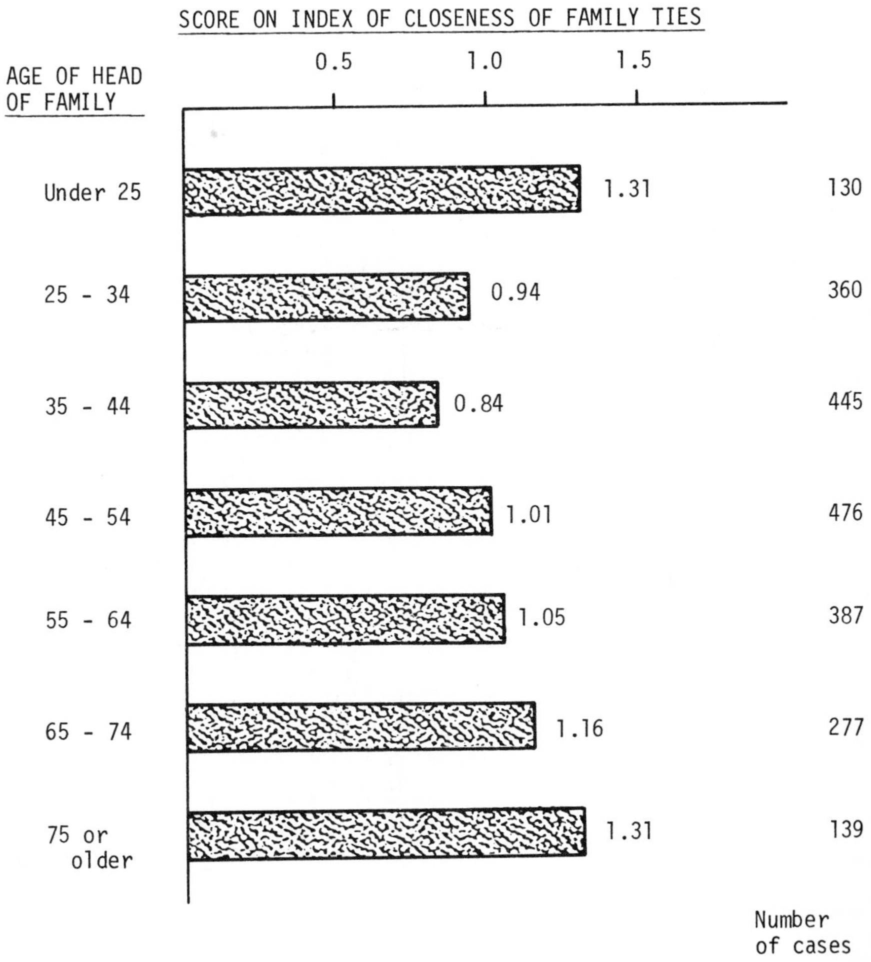

SCORE ON INDEX OF CLOSENESS OF FAMILY TIES

AGE OF HEAD OF FAMILY	Score	Number of cases
Under 25	1.31	130
25 - 34	0.94	360
35 - 44	0.84	445
45 - 54	1.01	476
55 - 64	1.05	387
65 - 74	1.16	277
75 or older	1.31	139

MTR 113

Background factors

The usual multivariate procedure used only two of the ten variables tried. The variables used, in order of their importance if taken singly over the whole sample, were:

* Age of head of family
* Whether head of family grew up on a farm
  Education of head of family
  Sex and marital status of head of family

Difference in education between head of family and
  his father
Number of brothers and sisters of head of family
Number of brothers and sisters older than head of family
Index of achievement orientation
Race

Asterisked variables are those used in Figure 19-2. They explained 3 per cent of the variance. The overall standard deviation of the score is 0.9. None of the variables below the line could explain as much as 0.5 per cent of the total sum of squares by a single division of the whole sample.

Once the sample was divided according to age of the head of the family and whether he had grown up on a farm, nothing else made any difference. Figure 19-2 shows the results. A high index score means more concern with the family, and presumably more resistance to moving away from them, participation in organizations outside the family, or even accepting change.

The results are as expected, that the very old and the very young are more family-oriented. The surprising thing is the weakness of the relation and the absence of any important effects of education, sex and marital status, religious preference, or race. As can be seen in Appendix D, the components of the index were positively related to one another as well as appearing to be measuring similar things. Hence, the index is clearly measuring something independent of the demographic or the other attitudinal factors.

FIGURE 19-2

INDEX OF CLOSENESS OF FAMILY TIES
(For all 2214 heads of families)

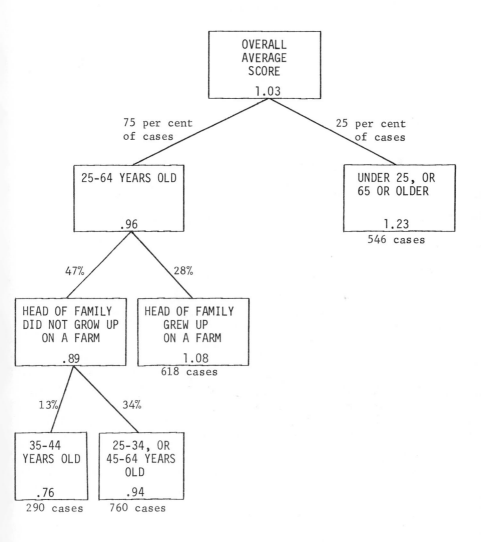

In that case, then, the index of closeness of family ties might be a new and independent variable which would help explain behavior or other attitudes. But the findings reported earlier in this book suggest that it does not explain any of the forms of time use and work behavior, nor even the index of receptivity to change. It _is_ related to social participation. Those reporting low incomes tend to participate more in organizations if they also report close family ties (see Chapter 17). And it appears in the analysis of mobility behavior, though it is unclear whether close family ties restrict mobility, or mobility loosens family ties (see Chapter 15).

Attitudes and Motives

We can, however, proceed to examine the differences from the final group averages of Figure 19-2, to see whether they are related to any of a much larger number of other variables. The variables introduced are listed below, in order of their individual importance in explaining these residuals if taken one at a time:

* Whether head of family has been sick for one month or
    more, and when (and whether ever worked for money)
* Index of social participation
* Total family income
* Index of mobility experience

Index of ambition and aspiration
Attitude toward importance of luck for financial success
Whether head of family had been out of a job for two months
    or more, and when
Sex and marital status of head of family
* Number of brothers and sisters of head of family, and his
    birth order
Age of youngest child under 18 living at home
Education of head of family
Age of head of family
Index of caution and risk avoidance
Number of disabled people in family
Number of people in family
Interviewer's impression of alertness of respondent
Whether family owns a business or farm
Index of planning and time horizon
Age of oldest child under 18 living at home

Difference in education between head of family and wife
Index of achievement orientation
Education of father of head of family
Index of receptivity to change
Housing status (home ownership)
Number of responses indicating a sense of personal
  effectiveness
Attitude toward mothers' working

Asterisked variables are those used in Figure 19-3. They explained an
additional 3 per cent of the variance. The overall standard deviation of
the residual score is 0.9. None of the variables below the line could
explain as much as 0.5 per cent of the total sum of squares by a single
division of the whole sample.

Figure 19-3 gives the results. The weak relations lead to some

fortuitous results, but in general having had a major illness (or being

a widow) seems to be associated with closer family ties, as does a lower

income. The associations with less past mobility may reflect the

influence of family ties in reducing mobility, or of past mobility in

loosening family ties. One earlier study shows that family ties inhibit

migrating, but another that moving does not eliminate people's close

feelings toward their extended family.[1] The association of family ties

with current social participation may be partly circular, for the index

of social participation includes doing volunteer work, some of which

may be work for relatives living in another dwelling. The last division,

which again may not be reliable, seems to indicate that for high income,

low-mobility people, heads of families who come from larger families

retain closer family ties unless they are the youngest child in a large

family.

[1]Eugene Litwak, "Geographic Mobility and Extended Family Cohesion,"
American Sociological Review, 25 (June, 1960), pp. 285-394;
Harry K. Schwarzweller, Family Ties, Migration, and Transitional Adjustment
of Young Men from Eastern Kentucky, Bulletin No. 691 (Lexington, Kentucky:
Kentucky Agricultural Experiment Station, May, 1964).

324

FIGURE 19-3

INDEX OF CLOSENESS OF FAMILY TIES: ANALYSIS OF DIFFERENCES
FROM END-GROUP AVERAGES OF FIGURE 19-2
(For all 2214 heads of families)

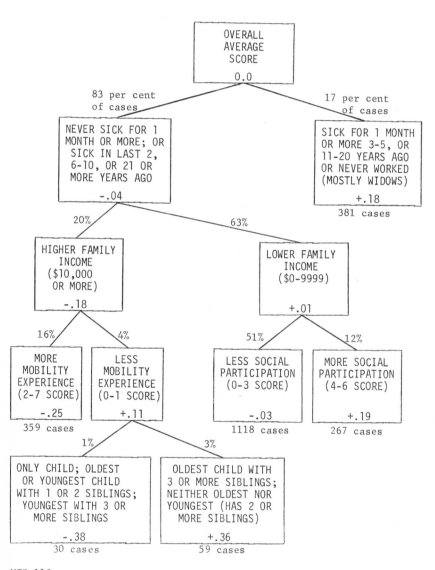

MTR 113

It is reassuring that the associations between the index of closeness of family ties on the one hand, and mobility and social participation on the other, appear regardless of which one the unexplained residuals of the other are analyzed against. Perhaps the most interesting finding is that even after the effects of age and education (and in one case income) are removed, social participation seems not to compete with strong family ties but to be positively associated with it. True, some of the association may be spurious through volunteer work for the extended family, but certainly there is no strong negative relation between participation in organizations and strong family ties.

An examination of the two major components of the index attitudes about the importance of living near relatives and about whether one should be able to count on financial support from relatives when needed - indicates that they are each associated with the extremes of age, with lower income, and with less formal education, with one exception. The least educated are the most likely to say it is important to live near relatives, but they are also the least likely to say that one should count on financial support from relatives. The actual question was:

> "Do you think a person should be able to count on financial
> support from his family if he needs it?"

Respondents with the least education may have been reflecting their own and their families' lower education and hence limited financial capacity, and answering only in terms of their own expectations. Some of the responses to this question given by middle-aged married men were as follows:

> "No, I think one should make provision on his own. Only
> health emergencies would change this."

> "Depends on how close you are."

> "No, a person must learn to be self-supporting."

"Yes -- should help childredn while they are getting
started, although, we wouldn't ask it from them."

The following are indicative of the answers given by those who were either
very old or very young:

"Yes, if he cannot support himself."

"Yes, if the family has it."

"Up to other person if he helps you. You shouldn't expect or
ask for it."

"Yes, but not too much."

Attitude toward mothers' working:

Definition:

Another dimension of resistance to change not included in the index
of closeness of family ties is the attitude of heads of families toward
mothers' working. A question asked in an earlier study about whether it
was a good idea for wives to work had led to many replies like "It
depends on whether there are children."[2] Data from the same study showed
that the differences between racial groups in actual frequency of working
wives were large only when there were children all of whom were in school.[3]
Hence we designed a question that seemed to take account of this fact:

"Suppose a family has children but they are all in school --
would you say it is a good thing for the wife to take a job
or a bad thing, or what?"

The question did indeed divide the population, the answers being
distributed as follows:

---

[2]James Morgan et al., Chapter 9.

[3]James Morgan, "Time, Work and Welfare," Patterns of Market Behavior,
Essays in Honor of Philip Taft, ed. Michael J. Brennan (Providence: Brown
University Press, 1965).

Attitude toward mothers' working	Per cent of cases
Favorable	15
Favorable with qualifications	17
Pro-con or depends	17
Unfavorable with qualifications	14
Unfavorable	35
Not ascertained; don't know	2
Total	100
Number of cases	2214

This distribution includes single people who were also asked the question, but they are not so large a portion of the total population that they affect the distribution much. Among husbands, the proportion who approved mothers' working when the children were all in school varied from 44 per cent among those under twenty-five to 19 per cent for those sixty-five or older. The less educated husbands were more likely to disapprove of mothers' working; the well educated were more likely to refuse to make value judgments, preferring to say it was all right for some but not for others, in spite of our restriction of the question to a relatively well defined situation.

Typical of the attitudes expressed by heads of families with low levels of education were the following:

"Nowadays, women hire a babysitter -- that's wrong. They take away a young girl's job. If her husband is working then she shouldn't be working -- that's what I think."

"Bad thing -- she can keep busy and happy doing things at home. My daughter keeps busy keeping up with hers (her children) that are in school."

"Well if they are in school it's OK. The way it is now they almost have to. One salary just won't supply the necessities for a large family nowadays."

"I don't think a wife should neglect a home and family. If she can run the two then it is all right."

Responses of those with higher levels of education were similar to the following:

> "Good thing -- she can hardly stay at home."

> "I think it's all right to. Up to individual themselves -- if not get too wrapped up in it. A change of scene does them good."

> "Mother should be in the home until children reach 5th grade -- if it is necessary for her to work at all."

> "Well -- unless it's an absolute necessity for the mother to work, I'd say she should be at home. Maybe it's OK if the kids are up in high school."

Multivariate analysis

To determine whether or not there were multivariate effects, we introduced nine of the same explanatory variables used with the other indexes (Excluded were sex and marital status, since the analysis was done only for married family heads.) They are listed below in their order of importance if used to make a single division over the whole sample in explaining the proportion who <u>favored</u> mothers' working:

* Age of husband
* Race

      Religious preference
      Number of brothers and sisters of husband
      Difference in education between husband and his father
      Number of brothers and sisters older than husband
      Education of husband
      Whether husband grew up on a farm
      Husband's index of achievement orientation

Asterisked variables are those used in Figure 19-4. They explained 4 per cent of the variance. The overall standard deviation of the proportion is 0.5. None of the variables below the line could explain as much as 0.5 per cent of the total sum of squares by a single division of the whole sample.

Figure 19-4 gives the results, and although the proportions differ markedly between the older whites, of whom only about one-fifth favor mothers' working, and the younger nonwhites, over half of whom favor it, the four groups account for only 4 per cent of the variance. This is mainly because the nonwhites are not a very large proportion of the population. The younger whites were almost divided by the computer according to religious preference, with the Non-Christians more favorable to mothers' working -- nearly half of them in favor. Dividing the same group according to age would have done nearly as much good -- among those under 55, the younger people are still more favorable; but neither of these additional details would have reduced the unexplained variance by as much as 0.5 per cent of the original total.

There is always a question whether we are explaining an attitude, or relating it to a behavior which it rationalizes. The racial relation, in particular, may reflect merely the acceptance of a necessity. Presumably the forces keeping the mother at home are weaker when the children are in school, so that the lower and unsteadier income of the nonwhite husbands made it necessary for their wives to work, and thereby more acceptable.

On the other hand, the age differences may well reflect more than just an intercorrelation or a rationalization. There is no particular reason why older mothers would find it more difficult to work than younger ones, except perhaps for their somewhat lower average levels of education. A simpler interpretation is that acceptance of the idea of wives' working is increasing with each succeeding generation, and that when the present young people get older, they will remain favorable to the idea. This is certainly

330

FIGURE 19-4

PROPORTION OF HUSBANDS APPROVING OF MOTHERS' WORKING
(For all 1640 married heads of families)

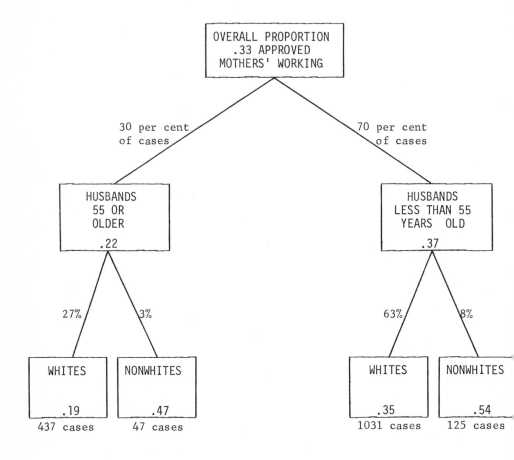

consonant with the historical trend for more and more wives to work, even though it is also true that the increases in the proportions working have been, if anything, more dramatic among the older wives.

Among the variables which never came into Figure 19-4 were education, religious preference, and the number of brothers and sisters the head of the family had. There was some tendency for those with the least education to oppose mothers' working, but actually this reflects mostly their greater willingness to take sides. There were more qualified answers among the better educated. This may well reflect what happens when any new thing is really part of a culture: attitudes toward it become differentiated and qualified rather than polarized. There is some evidence that attitudes toward installment credit in this country are becoming more discriminating too, fewer people being for or against it in general. Had we analyzed opposition to mothers' working, education would almost certainly have come into play.

The head of the family was more likely to favor mothers' working if he had been an only child, and among religious groups it was the Non-Christians and the Fundamentalist Protestants who were more likely to favor it. Nothing else mattered.

Dr. Burkhard Strümpel recently asked a sample in Spain,

> "Suppose a family has children but they are all grown up --
> would you say it is a good thing for the wife to take a job
> or a bad thing?"

The question is different, implying the children are past school age, which should produce more favorable replies, but actually there were 72 per cent who disapproved and only 12 per cent who approved, as against 49 per cent and 32 per cent here [4] Hence we may expect real differences between countries in their acceptance of the notion of women working outside the home.

---

[4] Unpublished data.

332

A 1960 Survey Research Center study asked a national sample of heads
of families;

> "There are many wives who have jobs these days. Do you think
> it is a good thing for a wife to work, or a bad thing, or
> what?
>
> Why do you say so?
>
> (If children mentioned) What if there are no children at
> home to be cared for?"

A multivariate analysis of the percentage who approved wives' working,
using a slightly different set of variables and for husbands only, found
similar results: nonwhites were more likely to approve, particularly those
living in small towns. Whites were less likely to approve, particularly
if they had children. But with the less structured question it was the
very young (under 25) who were most favorable, rather than everyone under
55 as in Figure 19-4. What appeared to be a regional difference disappeared
once race was taken into account. [5]

Conclusions

The young and the old and those who grew up on a farm put more emphasis
on close family ties. And taking that into account, past illness or low
income seem to lead to closer family ties, while less mobility and more
social participation are at least associated with closer family ties. And
where the head of the family was the oldest child or not the youngest and
came from a large family, he seems to desire closer family ties himself.
But we were not able to explain much of the variability in closeness of

---

[5] The husband's attitude toward wives' working was used in the original
study only as an explanatory variable in analyzing the wives' labor force
participation. See Morgan et al.,pp. 112-113, 120.

amily ties, perhaps because there is less variability, and fewer people
ith very strong ties, than in other countries. When something varies
ittle, it is difficult to explain those small differences.

Respondents' attitudes toward mothers' working when there are school-
ge children   proved to be more favorable for younger and nonwhite res-
ondents than for older or white respondents.

The striking thing with both indicators is the failure of such enticing
ariables as education, religious preference, sex and marital status, to
ake any important difference. When we remember also that neither of these
ndicators explained much of the other behavior of these families, we must
onclude that strength of family ties is not an important explanatory variable
n America today, however crucial it may be in explaining differences between
merica and other countries, or in explaining differences within other
ountries.

CHAPTER 20

IS THERE A MODERNISM SYNDROME?

The work effort of families has been related in part to various indicators of progressive attitudes and behaviors. Then each of these indicators in turn has been treated as something to be explained. At the second-stage analyses in these explanations, the indexes seemed to be explaining one another, and the question arises whether they are all aspects of a general set of progressive, modern attitudes and ancillary behaviors.

The same principle that was used to build the original indexes out of component reports of behavior, plans, expectations, and attitudes, is used in this chapter to build a combined index which we shall call "concern with progress." That principle was to apply a theoretical test to show whether the items have some conceptual, a priori similarity or cohesion, and then a practical test to be sure that they are at least mildly positively correlated. Adding two negatively correlated items would cancel out each of their separate movements, and hence their possible contributions to explanation.

It should be clear that these indexes are operationally defined measures, not theoretical constructs, even though they are, we hope, related to the concepts by which we have named them. We have made no great investment in scaling procedures, since the history of investigations into the weighting of index numbers makes it clear that substantial differences in the weights assigned to components make very little difference. If any one component has a strong relationship with some behavior, the whole index will also be related to it, except in the rare instances where another correlated component has an opposite effect.

334

If a whole index is related to some behavior, one could then systematically search for which components of the index were really responsible, and we have done some of this in the analysis so far. The procedure is efficient in the same way as the solution to the riddle about how to find the counterfeit (off-weight) coin with a minimum number of weight comparisons. If the intercorrelation of the components is high enough, it may even be unnecessary or impossible to decide which "subpart" really accounted for the effect of the combined index of some economic behavior.

The intercorrelations among the components of the eight indexes we have examined are given in Appendix D, along with the details of the construction of the indexes. In practice, few of the indexes were powerful enough in explaining work behavior to make it worthwhile to break them down into subparts to see which component was doing the work.

Turning now to the possibility of combining these indexes, and some others not so fully used before, we must see how they are correlated with one another. Table 20-1 shows the rank correlations (Kendall's Tau-B) among the major indexes, including three (achievement orientation, sense of personal effectiveness, and use of new products) which have not been treated as dependent variables, and of which one (use of new products) is really a component of receptivity to change.[1]

---

[1]See Chapter 13 and Appendix D for a discussion of the component indexes from which the index of receptivity to change was built. It is shown there that the use of new products is most highly correlated with the rest of the receptivity index, and that a self-rating on use and on attitudes toward new products was the least correlated.

TABLE 20-1

RANK CORRELATIONS AMONG INDEXES THAT MAY COMPRISE A MODERNISM SYNDROME
(For all 2214 heads of families)

Variable number

Index	Variable number	(1)	(2)	(3)	(4)	(5)	(6)	(7)	(8)	(9)	(10)	(11)
Achievement orientation	(1)											
Receptivity to change	(2)	.26										
Caution and risk avoidance	(3)	.17	.19									
Ambition and aspiration	(4)	.27	.26	.11								
Social participation	(5)	.24	.33	.24	.14							
Planning and time horizon	(6)	.10	.15	.14	.08	.17						
Mobility behavior	(7)	.21	.15	[.00]	.24	.07	[.03]					
Attitude toward mothers' working	(8)	[-.01]	[.02]	[.03]	.11	-.05	[-.02]	[.00]				
Closeness of family ties	(9)	[-.02]	-.06	[-.03]	[-.05]	[.02]	[-.02]	-.08	[.00]			
Use of new products	(10)	.18	*	.27	.14	.34	.16	.09	[-.02]	-.08		
Sense of personal effectiveness	(11)	.11	.18	.16	[.01]	.20	.11	[-.02]	[-.01]	[-.01]	.19	
Mobility experience	(12)	.21	.18	.04	.22	.10	[.04]	**	[-.01]	-.09	.13	[.00]

[ ] Not significantly different from .00 (at P=.05)when Kendall's Tau-B is used.
 * Use of new products is a component of the receptivity index.
 ** correlation is an artifact.

MTR 66-183

It is clear from Table 20-1 that there are important intercorrelations among a subset of the indexes: receptivity to change, achievement orientation, ambition and aspiration, planning and time horizon, caution and risk avoidance, and social participation. The mobility behavior index might also be considered part of the composite, although it is not correlated with caution and risk avoidance, or with planning and time horizon.[2]

The highest correlation among the major indexes is that between social participation and receptivity to change (see Table 20-2). An inspection of the components of the two reveals no identical components that could have made the relation an artifact. Actually social participation correlates significantly with each of the four components of receptivity, but most highly with the index of the use of new products, its most explicit and behavioral component. Table 20-3 shows the relation, which produced a rank correlation in Table 20-1 of 0.33. The correlations of social participation with the other components of the receptivity to change index were

Attraction to new scientific developments	.22
Importance of making changes on the job	.19
Self perception of receptivity to new products and attitude toward them	.09

The relation may be a reflection of a general activity level or of a constellation of behaviors. The fact that both indexes are correlated with higher education and income and with middle age does not weaken the

---

[2]A different index of mobility (mobility experience) was used as an explanatory variable because it contained some past mobility components which could not be considered the result of decisions made by the respondent. Since the two mobility indexes are highly correlated (0.80), they have the same pattern of intercorrelations with the other indexes.

TABLE 20-2

INDEX OF SOCIAL PARTICIPATION BY INDEX OF RECEPTIVITY TO CHANGE
(For all 2214 heads of families)

Score on index of social participation	All cases	Score on index of receptivity to change					
		Zero one, two	Three or four	Five or six	Seven	Eight	Nine
Zero	7	27	13	8	4	3	2
One	19	34	31	23	18	13	7
Two	25	23	30	28	29	27	18
Three	25	13	15	23	25	31	33
Four	16	3	9	13	14	18	25
Five or six	8	0	2	5	10	8	15
Total	100	100	100	100	100	100	100
Number of cases	2214	172	331	500	294	297	620

MTR 183

TABLE 20-3

INDEX OF SOCIAL PARTICIPATION BY INDEX OF USE OF NEW PRODUCTS
(For all 2214 heads of families)

Score on index of social participation	All cases	Score on index of use of new products					
		Zero	One	Two	Three	Four	Five or six
Zero	7	22	11	7	4	3	1
One	19	33	31	21	14	8	7
Two	25	31	26	27	28	22	15
Three	25	10	21	27	23	31	38
Four	16	4	9	13	20	25	20
Five	6	0	2	4	8	10	15
Six	2	0	0	1	3	1	4
Total	100	100	100	100	100	100	100
Number of cases	2214	276	398	463	428	370	279

importance of the association, but only tells something about the forces that affect both components. Indeed, if one looks at the residuals of the social participation index (Chapter 17), it can be seen that after the effects of age, education, and marital status are removed, the residuals are still highly correlated with receptivity. Indeed, in Figure 17-3 it appears that among families with incomes of $6000 or more and without a young child under three years old, receptivity to change is the most important variable in explaining differences on the index of social participation.

Looking at the reverse, the residuals of the index of receptivity to change, discussed in Chapter 13 (Figure 13-5), social participation was the most important variable for those with family incomes under $5000. An examination of the data shows that after age, education, marital status, and family income are taken into account, the residuals of each of the two indexes are related to the level of the other index. Hence, the correlation is not merely the result of correlations of both indexes with education and other background variables.

Similar examination of the relations among other major indexes, show that the deviations of each index from the end group means that take account of background variables, are related to the level of the other index. This indicates that the relationships among the indexes cannot be accounted for by the fact that almost all of the indexes are correlated with education, age, sex, and marital status. This interrelation among the first seven items of Table 20-1 does not, however, extend to the other two indexes we have analyzed: attitude toward mothers' working, and closeness of family ties.

340

It seems clear that close family ties, often mentioned as sources of resistance to modernization, are not negatively correlated with most of the other components. This index does have a weak negative correlation with mobility and receptivity to change. People who believe that it is important to live near their relatives, or that they should be able to count on them for financial help if needed, might be expected to move about less in order to stay closer to relatives. Of course, those who have not moved and are closer would find it easier to favor staying close to their extended family, and those who had moved might rationalize their own situation. Hence, we cannot determine the direction of causation.

Favorable attitudes toward mothers' working for money when their children were all school-aged or older were related positively to ambition and negatively to social participation. Presumably, many of these respondents had working wives because they had ambitions for more things, and with both of them working there was less time for social participation. But the correlations were weak, and attitude toward mothers' working was not correlated with the other indexes, and not even with the index of closeness of family ties.

Thus the whole notion of "familism", insofar as the two measures succeed in quantifying its meaning, seems to have little relation to economic decisions or even to the other attitudes that affect economic decisions. Perhaps in our society we have found ways to keep the family close without constraining economic choices.

The earlier analyses of the indexes seem to bear this out. The index of closeness of family ties never showed itself important in analyzing the other indexes, except for a negative effect on the mobility residuals fairly

341

far down in Figure 15-2 and a negative effect on social participation residuals in Figure 17-3. The latter seems to suggest that even though there is no overall relation between closeness of family ties and social participation, there is a tendency, after education, marital status, and achievement orientation are taken into account, for low-income people with close family ties to score higher on social participation. But this relation may be partly spurious, because doing unpaid work for relatives adds a point to each of these indexes.

We have added at the bottom of Table 20-1 the most important component of the receptivity to change index, an indicator of the use of new products. It correlates with the other indexes about as well as the total receptivity index, its correlation with caution and risk avoidance being somewhat higher, and that with achievement orientation, ambition and aspiration, and mobility behavior being somewhat lower, than the correlations of receptivity with the same indexes.

The second line from the bottom in Table 20-1 shows the relations to another index, the number of times out of a possible three when the respondent indicated a sense of his own personal effectiveness. This index correlates well with the others except, strangely enough, ambition and mobility.

An important part of Atkinson's theory of motivation is an interaction between motives like achievement orientation, incentive value of the possible rewards, and the expectancy that a particular course of action may lead to success.[3] The product of the three forces is seen as producing the resultant

---

[3]John W. Atkinson, "Motivational Determinants of Risk-Taking Behavior," *Psychological Review*, 64 (1957), pp. 359-372.

motivation, hence all three need to be measured. Family size was thought

of as a measure of the incentive value of financial success. The third

factor, expectancy, was tapped by asking:

> "How important do you think luck is for a person's financial
> success?"

The replies were completely uncorrelated with any of the indexes being

discussed here. There was a weak nonsignificant negative relationship

with the index of achievement orientation.

Such independence is helpful in looking for interaction effects, but

substantively it means that there appears to be not only no direct relation

between such a belief in luck and the behavior we have measured, but no

indirect connection through relevant attitudes as measured by the indexes.

For those who like data less highly manufactured than rank correlation

coefficients, Table 20-4 finds an arbitrary way to cut each index so that

those scoring "high" on it make up a substantial number but are fewer

than a third of the total sample, and then asks what proportion of that

third are high on each of the other indexes. Thus, reading across the

first row of Table 20-4, for those who scored high on achievement orientat-

ion, 44 per cent scored high on the index of receptivity to change, 28 per

cent scored high on the index of caution and risk avoidance, and so forth.

From the studies of the individual indexes we already have some

evidence that, after background factors have been taken into account,

past and current situations may also have been affecting the indexes. For

instance, after the effects of age, education, race, and marital status were

removed, income still had a powerful effect on the residual variations in

the index of receptivity to change. Income was the most important variable

explaining the residuals in receptivity to change, social participation, and

TABLE 20-4

PER CENT OF HEADS OF FAMILIES HIGH ON EACH INDEX AMONG THOSE HIGH ON EACH OF THE OTHERS
(For all 2214 heads of families)

Among those heads of families high on:	Variable number	Per cent who are also high on: Variable number								
		(1)	(2)	(3)	(4)	(5)	(6)	(7)	(8)	(9)
Achievement orientation	(1)		44	28	45	37	24	29	35	25
Receptivity to change	(2)	32		29	37	40	31	20	33	23
Caution and risk avoidance	(3)	30	44		37	38	28	18	40	22
Ambition and aspiration	(4)	36	40	27		29	25	30	38	27
Social participation	(5)	32	47	30	32		33	20	28	32
Planning and time horizon	(6)	26	47	27	35	41		17	26	26
Mobility behavior	(7)	36	35	20	47	29	21		37	26
Attitude toward mothers' working	(8)	22	29	23	30	21	18	19		27
Closeness of family ties	(9)	19	23	15	25	27	18	16	32	
All cases		20	28	18	25	24	19	16	32	27

MTR 66,182

caution and risk avoidance. It was the second most important variable
explaining the residuals in the planning and time horizon index. It
appeared farther down in the analysis of residuals on mobility behavior,
and not at all in the residual analysis of ambition and aspiration.
However, past unemployment did seem to be associated with a lower score
on the ambition index in Figure 16-3.

If failure or success affects these attitudes and ancillary behaviors,
and they in turn affect a man's economic success, then there may well be
a cumulative process by which success breeds success through fostering
attitudes and behavior of the right sorts.

Such a notion has a bearing on possible comparative studies with
other countries. Not only might we find that family ties were more varied
and more effective elsewhere, but we might find more variety in people's
past economic experience, and hence in the extent to which they had
developed success-oriented attitudes and behavior patterns. Even within
countries, among groups who have been in difficult economic circumstances,
the hypothesis that past success may change attitudes and then these
changed attitudes lead to the kinds of behavior that bring success, may
have a bearing on strategy for dealing with poverty problems.

A combined index of concern with progress

For any one person, any one item in an index can be inappropriate.
A man with no hobbies cannot be interested in getting better at his hobbies
A man who is not currently employed cannot be asked about whether he likes
to be able to make changes in his work. In each of the indexes, however,
we have attempted to combine enough items to give each person several chanc

to reveal his particular composite attitude or behavior pattern. But
it may well pay to go further and combine the indexes themselves into a
summary index, particularly since some of them are intercorrelated anyway.

Four of the indexes we analyzed not only are highly correlated but
substantively seem to form a meaningful composite reflecting individual
motivation that should be reflected in economic behavior. These are

> Ambition and aspiration (eight items)
> Planning and time horizon (three items each, scored 2-1-0
>   to allow for eligibility)
> Achievement orientation (nine items)
> Receptivity to change, itself a sum of four sub-indexes:
>> Use of new products (six items)
>> Attraction to new scientific developments (three items)
>> Attitude toward new products (two items, each scored 2-1-0
>>   depending on strength of attitude)
>> Attitude toward making changes on the job (one item, based
>>   on separate questions for employed and self-employed)

Hence, we proceed to build a composite index, which we call "combined
index of concern with progress," by simply adding, for each individual
in the sample, his score on the various four indexes. The four components
of receptivity were added without the truncation used for the index of
receptivity to change. The sum could potentially vary from 0 through 37,
but actually it varied only from 3 through 30, and it was nicely normally
distributed as follows with a mean of 15.3:

Score on combined index of concern with progress	Per cent of cases
3-6	3
7-9	11
10-11	11
12-13	12
14-16	21
17-18	14
19-20	12
21-24	13
25-30	3
Total	100
Number of cases	2214

With this new index we redo two analyses, perhaps in improved form because of our experience: One treats concern with progress as a dependent variable, asking first its relation to background factors like age, education race, sex, and then whether the residual variation is associated with experiences of success or failure as indicated by past illness, unemployment, income changes, present earnings rate, current savings, occupation etc. The other asks whether concern with progress affects working behavior.

Why did we use just these four indexes and not the indexes of social participation, mobility behavior, caution and risk avoidance, concern with family ties, or attitude toward mothers' working? The decision was based partly on their intercorrelations and on the smallness of their ability to explain behavior, particularly for the last two, and partly on theoretical considerations. The included items were all considered to be relatively direct evidence of concern with progress -- the kinds of things that should drive a man to work hard, and help him get ahead in the world. On the other hand, social participation would only seem to be vaguely linked with this, through general activity or ability levels of the individual, or social forces. Mobility behavior could be high for reasons other than ambition and seemed to be of little use in explaining economic behavior. And caution and risk avoidance, although it might avoid disasters, seems less directly to be a part of progressive, ambitious behavior.

At any rate, assuming for the time that the combined index of concern with progress is a meaningful composite -- and it is certainly an important set of attitudes and behaviors -- we turn now to examine it. First we shall see what "explains" it, that is, what background factors are correlated with it. Then we shall look to see whether it can improve our explanation of the total productive hours the family works.

347

hat is related to the combined index of concern with progress?

To what extent is enterprise stimulated by success and dampened by 'ailure? One way to tell is first to remove the influence of such clearly xogenous background factors as age, education, sex, and race, and then ee whether evidences of success or failure are correlated with the residuals. f they are, we may still be a little uncertain of the direction of causation, ut we can at least be tempted to argue that modernism feeds on itself, hat success and affluence, which result partly from ambition and hard work nd receptivity to change, lead to increased ambition and more work and more eceptivity to change.

As a first step then, we use our multivariate search-process to find he most important background factors affecting the combined index of oncern with progress. The factors used are listed below in order of their mportance if used to make a single divison of the whole sample:

* Age of head of family
* Education of head of family
  Difference in education between head of family and his father
* Sex of head of family
  Number of brothers and sisters of head of family and
    his birth order
  Race
  Religious preference

Asterisked variables are those actually used in Figure 20-1. They xplained 43 per cent of the variance. The overall standard deviation s 5.0. Each of the variables could account for at least 1 per cent of he total sum of squares by a single divison of the whole sample.

The results fit with our common stereotypes. The old and less well ducated have low scores, and the young, well educated men have high ones. ow much of this is an artifact of the relevance of the questions to ifferent groups? Some of the questions deal with job attitudes and some ith expectations about income and family responsibilities, but in general

348

FIGURE 20-1

COMBINED INDEX OF CONCERN WITH PROGRESS
(For all 2214 heads of families)

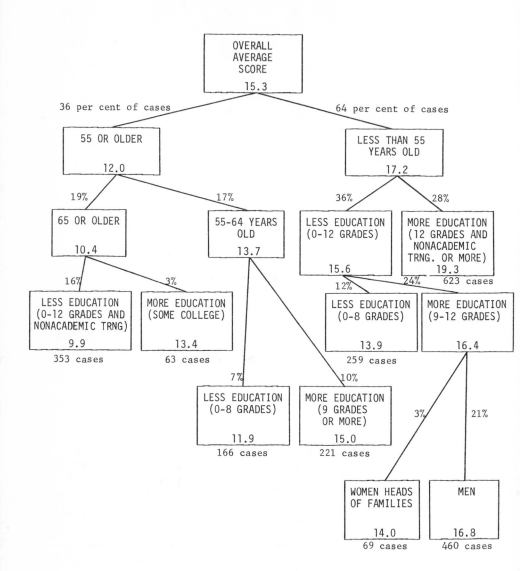

MTR 190

it hardly seems possible that differential relevance could account for more than a point or two.

Figure 20-2 gives the full range of age differences in the index, and since age and education are correlated, Figure 20-3 gives the education effects separately for those under fifty-five and those fifty-five or older. It is clear that the education differences within each age group are smaller than the overall differences, because the latter compounds the effects of youth and more education, which occur together and work in the same direction. There seems, however, to be no reinforcing effect or interaction effect, merely two additive influences.

Among heads of families, there is a persistent tendency in all groups for men's scores on the index of concern with progress to be higher than women's, though in only one category were there enough women to justify a separate group in Figure 20-1. There were even larger racial differences among those under fifty-five, the whites having higher scores, but there were not enough nonwhites to account for enough of the overall variance to make a division possible. Religious differences were too small to matter, but were in the expected direction with the Fundamentalist Protestants scoring the lowest on the index, and the other Protestants scoring the highest on the index.

The combination of the head's number of siblings and his order among them shows an effect almost entirely attributable to the size of the family in which he grew up, and not of whether he was the oldest, youngest, or in the middle. Heads of families who reported being an only child, or the oldest child in a family of two or three children, or the youngest of two of three children, had the highest scores. Children from smaller families generally have better educated and more affluent parents, get more education, and presumably get more attention from their parents.[4]

---

[4]For additional evidence see Morgan et al.

FIGURE 20-2

SCORE ON COMBINED INDEX OF CONCERN WITH PROGRESS,
BY AGE OF HEAD OF FAMILY
(For all 2214 heads of families)

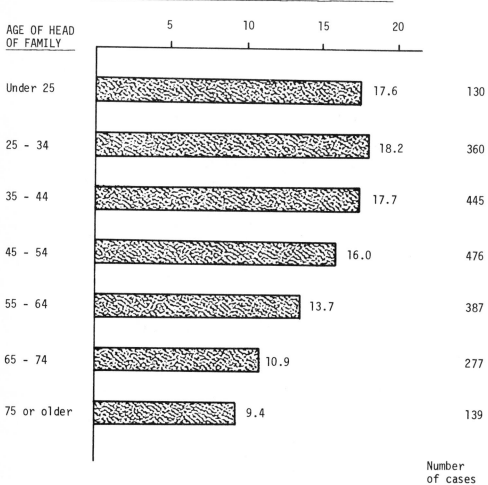

SCORE ON COMBINED INDEX OF CONCERN WITH PROGRESS

AGE OF HEAD OF FAMILY		Number of cases
Under 25	17.6	130
25 - 34	18.2	360
35 - 44	17.7	445
45 - 54	16.0	476
55 - 64	13.7	387
65 - 74	10.9	277
75 or older	9.4	139

MTR 190

FIGURE 20-3

SCORE ON COMBINED INDEX OF CONCERN WITH PROGRESS,
BY EDUCATION OF HEAD OF FAMILY
(For all 2214 heads of families)*

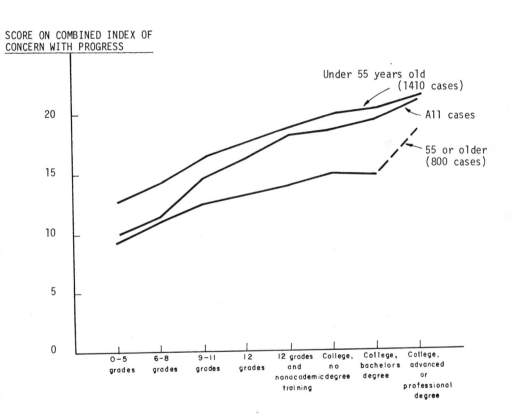

SCORE ON COMBINED INDEX OF
CONCERN WITH PROGRESS

EDUCATION OF HEAD OF FAMILY

MTR 190
*excludes 4 cases in which education of head of family was not ascertained.

Analysis of residuals

The variables used in Figure 20-1 were clearly predetermined long ago and have had effects on the individuals' attitudes, capacity to plan, and their success; but within any group categorized by such background factors, there are differences in the extent to which the individuals have experienced success or failure, good luck or bad. We therefore take the differences from the end-group average of Figure 20-1 to see whether or not they are related to evidences of past difficulties or successes. Successes are indicated chiefly by present status or recent changes in income or rates of pay. Difficulties are indicated by reports of major illnesses or long periods of unemployment.

In the multivariate analysis of the residuals, we used the following variables, listed in order of their importance if used to make a single division of the whole pooled set of residuals:

* Hourly earnings of head of family
* Whether head of family was self-employed (or whether in the labor force)
* Liquid savings now or within the last five years
  Whether head of family has overtime or short work weeks
* Difference in education between head of family and wife
  Marital status of head of family
* Prestige level of family head's occupation
  Reasons why family income was higher in 1964 than in 1963 (for those for whom it was higher)
  Change in family income from 1963 to 1964
  Housing status (home ownership)
* Whether head of family had been out of a job for two months or more, and when

---

Whether head of family had been sick for one month or more, and when
Whether there were any children under five in family
Whether family owns a business or a farm

Asterisked variables are those used in Figure 20-4. They explained an additional 6 per cent of the variance. The overall standard deviation of the residual score is 3.8. None of the variables below the line could explain as much as 0.5 per cent of the total sum of squares by a single division of the whole sample.

Figure 20-4 shows a number of clear effects of past success or of present prosperity on the index of concern with progress. The most powerful is current earning rate.[5] Farther down it appears that those who have managed to save a few liquid assets, or have not been out of a job for two months or more at a time within the last twenty years, or who have a high-status occupation, have higher scores on the index of concern with progress, after the effects of age, education, sex, and current earnings rate have been allowed for. Although the effects were not powerful enough to appear in the tree, similar findings for the positive effects of success appeared in the form of relations with home ownership, recent income increases, and an increased rate of pay as a reason for a recent income increase.

The overall pattern of relations between the individual indicators of past success or difficulty and the pooled unexplained residuals of the index of concern for progress is shown in summary form in Table 20-5, though many of the groups described there overlap with one another.

The consistent pattern of relations by which success is associated with present concern with progress, and past failure or difficulty with less such concern, is impressive. The detailed effect of current hourly earning rate is given in Figure 20-5.

---

[5]It is always possible that causal directions are the reverse of our interpretation, that earnings are high because the man is actually striving. The main implication is however that the attitudes, behavior, and success or failure, reinforce one another.

For a summary of other evidence of the effects of success and failure on aspiration level, see Sidney Siegel, "Level of Aspiration and Decision Making," Psychological Review, 64 (July, 1957), pp. 253-261.

FIGURE 20-4

COMBINED INDEX OF CONCERN WITH PROGRESS: ANALYSIS OF DIFFERENCES
FROM END-GROUP AVERAGES OF FIGURE 20-1
(For all 2214 heads of families)

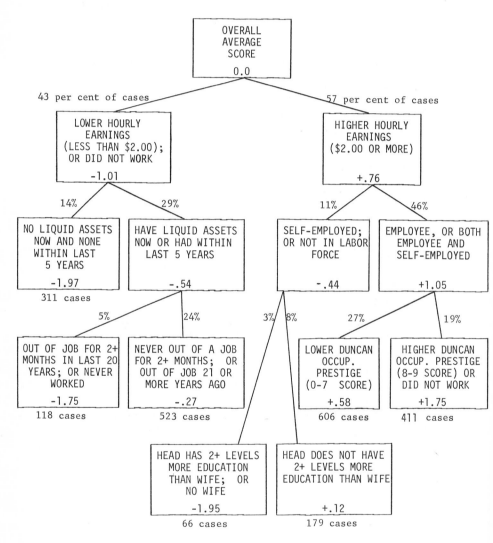

MTR 190

TABLE 20-5

COMBINED INDEX OF CONCERN WITH PROGRESS: DIFFERENCES FROM END-GROUP AVERAGES OF
FIGURE 20-1 ACCORDING TO VARIOUS INDICATORS OF PAST SUCCESS OR DIFFICULTY
(For all 2214 heads of families)

Past Difficulties	Average Residual	Number of Cases	Past Success	Average Residual	Number of Cases
Unemployed or on strike for two months or more at one time within the last two years	-1.11	136	Never unemployed or on strike for two months or more at a time	0.17	1608
Ill for a month or more at a time in the last two years	-1.11	194	Never ill for a month or more at a time	-0.02	1375
No liquid savings now and none in last five years	-1.40	458	Has two months take home pay or more in liquid savings	0.44	1203
Family income decreased from 1963 to 1964:			Family income increased from 1963 to 1964:		
a little	-0.32	178	a little	0.80	337
a lot	-0.27	186	a lot	0.45	674
Earn less than $.75 an hour	-1.12	85	Earn $7.50 an hour or more	0.97	90
Occupation is in lowest prestige decile	-2.06	98	Occupation is in highest prestige decile	1.47	321
Neither own nor rent home	-1.52	115	Own home	0.37	1445

FIGURE 20-5

COMBINED INDEX OF CONCERN WITH PROGRESS: DIFFERENCES FROM END-GROUP AVERAGES
OF FIGURE 20-1, BY HOURLY EARNINGS OF HEAD OF FAMILY
(For all 2214 heads of families)

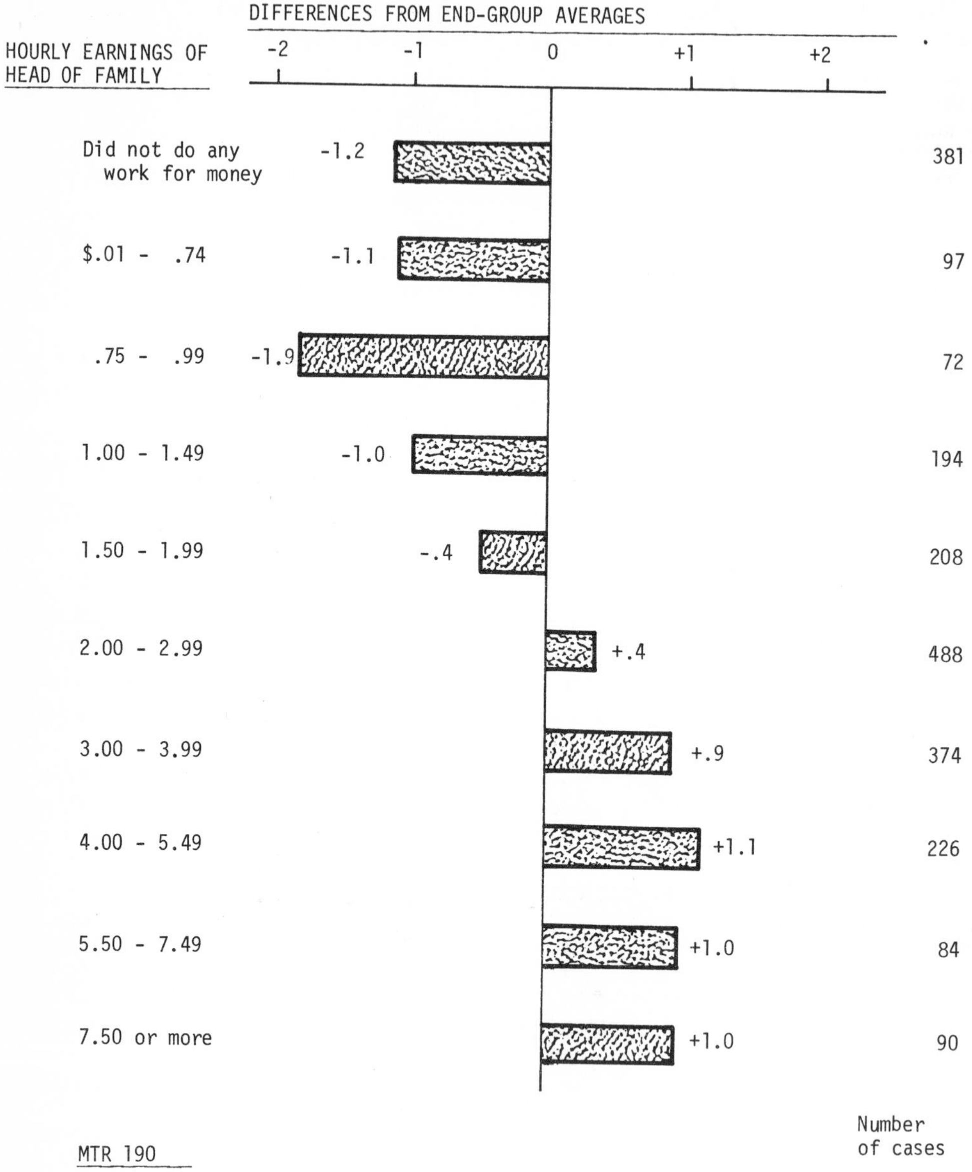

DIFFERENCES FROM END-GROUP AVERAGES

HOURLY EARNINGS OF HEAD OF FAMILY	Difference	Number of cases
Did not do any work for money	-1.2	381
$.01 - .74	-1.1	97
.75 - .99	-1.9	72
1.00 - 1.49	-1.0	194
1.50 - 1.99	-.4	208
2.00 - 2.99	+.4	488
3.00 - 3.99	+.9	374
4.00 - 5.49	+1.1	226
5.50 - 7.49	+1.0	84
7.50 or more	+1.0	90

MTR 190

What effect does past unemployment or illness have if we look separately at those with low hourly earnings and those making $2.00 per hour or more? Figure 20-6 shows that whether unemployment is followed by a period of discouragement and lower concern with progress depends on the kind of earnings the individual manages to make afterwards. The discouraging effects of two months or more of unemployment are more persistent for low-earning people, more likely to be temporary for the others.

Illness, however, seems to have no significant effect on people's concern with progress, regardless of their hourly earnings, perhaps because an illness may be seen as an event occurring only once, whereas unemployment may increase the threat of further unemployment, especially at low hourly earnings.

Two other interesting divisions appear in Figure 20-4. One, unexpected, shows that the self-employed and those not in the labor force tend to be lower on the index than those who work for others. Is this partly an artifact resulting from the fact that one item, liking to make changes on the job, gives a score of two to the employed and a score of one to the self-employed, or is it really true that self-employed people, businessmen and farmers, are actually more resistant to change (conservative)?

The other division, which appears once in Figure 20-4 and almost appreared in some other places in that analysis, indicates that those with no wife, or a wife with considerably less education than her husband, had lower scores on the index. Sociologists have argued for years that the wife tends to set the consumption standards of the family, based on her own family background and education -- a theory consistent with these findings.

FIGURE 20-6

COMBINED INDEX OF CONCERN WITH PROGRESS: DIFFERENCES FROM END-GROUP AVERAGES OF
FIGURE 20-1, BY WHETHER HEAD OF FAMILY WAS OUT OF A JOB FOR TWO MONTHS OR MORE
-- FOR THOSE WITH LOW AND HIGH HOURLY EARNINGS SEPARATELY
(For all 2214 heads of families)

SCORE OF COMBINED INDEX
OF CONCERN WITH PROGRESS

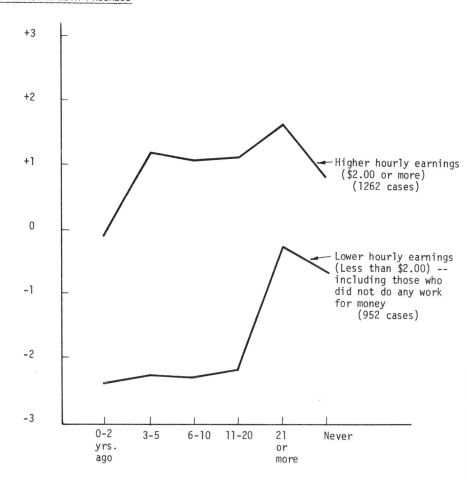

WHETHER HEAD OF FAMILY WAS OUT OF A JOB FOR TWO MONTHS OR MORE AND WHEN

MTR 190

Summary

Aside from such basic background matters as age, sex, and education, concern with progress is associated with the individual's experience of success or failure, particularly recent experiences. Though a man's drive may be a more basic result of his personality, or his level of serum uric acid, which then make both for more concern with progress and for more progress, some of the experiences we have shown to be related to current concern with progress, such as illness and unemployment, are not completely under the individual's control, and yet they appear to have effects, of varying duration, on his concern with progress.

If past events thus affect a man's view of the world and the extent to which he aspires for better things, does that view in turn affect his explicit economic behavior?

To complete such a model showing that success leads to concern with progress and receptivity to change, which then lead to hard work and further success , we need to ask whether present concern with progress is associated with hard work. Hence we return to our analysis of hours of work for money in Chapter 2 and our summary measure of total productive effort in Chapter 11 to ascertain the effect of the index of concern with progress on these two variables. In Chapter 2 we found that the index of concern with progress had a positive relationship with hours of work for money, especially for those who worked in spite of being under severe constraints. And we found in Chapter 11 that this index was an important variable in explaining total productive effort, even after allowing for basic constraints and opportunity factors. There does appear to be a cumulative dynamics, by which economic progress generates and reinforces the very attitudes and behaviors which contribute to further economic progress.

APPENDIX A

SAMPLING METHODS AND SAMPLING VARIABILITY[*]

Sample design

The data for this study were obtained through personal interviews, with
2214 adults, conducted by the Survey Research Center during January and
February, 1965. Eligible respondents were a national cross-section sample
of family heads living in households.[1]

The sample design is that used by the Survey Research Center to select
national probability samples of dwellings.[2] The sample for the present study,
in 74 sample points, differed from the design commonly used only with respect
to some reduction in the clustering of neighboring dwellings from approx-
imately four per cluster to two or three on the average. It was anticipated
that the reduced clustering would lead to some moderate reduction in sampling
variability.[3]

---

[1]In this appendix, the term "national" refers to the conterminous United
States.
    The Survey Research Center uses the dwelling unit concept defined by the
U.S. Bureau of the Census. See U.S. Bureau of the Census, 1950 Census of
Housing, Vol. I, Part I (Washington, D.C.: U.S. Government Printing Office,
1953), p. XVI. Dwelling units on military reservations are excluded from the
study universe. Also excluded are persons living in nondwelling unit quarters;
examples of these are large rooming houses, residential clubs, hospitals,
penal institutions, and dormitories.
    Persons living in a dwelling unit comprise a household, which may include
one or more family groups. A family may be one individual living alone, or two
or more household members related by blood, marriage or adoption. The primary
family includes the head of the household; household members not related to the
household head may compose one or more secondary families.

[2]Leslie Kish and Irene Hess, The Survey Research Center's National Sample
of Dwellings (Ann Arbor: Institute for Social Research, The University of
Michigan, 1965).

[3]The reduction in cluster size from four dwellings to two or three occurred
because segments of an expected four dwellings were shared by two different
personal interview studies conducted simultaneously by the Center. Thus with
no increase in survey cost, each study benefited from reduced sampling variability
and increased precision of sample estimates.

[*]This appendix was written by Irene Hess and Thomas Tharakan, of the Sampling
Section, The Institute for Social Research, University of Michigan.

360

At an over-all selection rate of 1 in 21,540, about 2650 family heads
2575 occupied dwellings were selected for interviewing.[4] Where more
an one family occupied a dwelling, an interview was attempted with each
mily head. If the head of the family was not at home on the first call,
veral additional calls were made.[5] If after repeated calls the designated
spondent was not at home or refused to be interviewed, no substitution
s made except in the few instances when information was obtained from the
fe of a married head of family who would be unavailable during the entire
terviewing period. The over-all response rate was about 84 per cent. No
justment was made for nonresponse.

mpling Variability

Sample statistics, such as means (ratios, proportion), medians, indices
d scales, calculated from survey data are subject to errors arising from
veral sources. Among these are sampling errors, noncoverage, response and
porting errors, nonresponse and processing errors. In this study,
ocessing errors are thought to be negligible because of careful checks
ilt into the analysis. In general, response and reporting errors are reason-
ly small as indicated by various validity checks. A part of the findings

---

[4]Our estimate of 55.5 million households,obtained by multiplying the
mber of occupied sample dwellings by the reciprocal of the sampling fraction,
not directly comparable with the Census Bureau's estimate of 57.3 million
useholds reported for March, 1965. See U.S. Bureau of the Census, Current
pulation Reports, Series P-20, No. 144 (November 1965).
The Bureau's estimate includes Alaska and Hawaii while we exclude these
ates. Furthermore, comparatability is diminished because of differences in
e time period and in household definition. Clearly some discrepancy can be
tributed to sampling variability. Also, it is possible that the Center's
rveys are subject to a small undercoverage of households occurring because
me dwellings are overlooked by our interviewers.
[5]In the case of a married couple, the husband is always considered to be
e head of the family.

reported in this study, namely, hours of unpaid work, were calculated for the first time in the United States, and therefore a validity check cannot be made from independent sources. The distributions, however, are not badly skewed and do fit well with expectations.

In the case of probability designs, sampling errors can be estimated from the sample. Sample statistics reflect the random variations arising from the fact that the individuals interviewed for the study form only a fraction of the population. With respect to many characteristics, the distribution of respondents generally differs from that of the populations by an unknown amount. The sampling error gives a measure of the deviation of a sample statistic from the corresponding population value, but it does not measure the actual error in a sample estimate. The sampling error allows the construction around a sample statistic of a region or intervals -- such as confidence intervals, fiducial intervals, or credible intervals -- which will cover the population value with a specified probability. In this report the standard error is taken as a measure of the sampling variability.

Table A-1 presents some important sample statistics for major groups of the sample and estimates of their standard errors, computed by taking into consideration the complexity of the sample design.[6] Sampling errors in this study are frequently higher than simple random sampling errors because clusters of dwellings were sampled, a procedure which may increase the sampli error if the characteristic being sampled also occurs in clusters. However, the technique of cluster sampling usually results in the reduction of field

---

[6]The sampling errors of means or proportions and their differences were calculated by using estimation formulas described in Kish and Hess, op.cit., p. 46.

costs. The last column of Table A-1 gives the ratio of the sampling variance to the variance obtained on assumption of simple random sampling. These ratios (k_i) -- sometimes referred to as the design effect -- vary with the number of sample cases (n_i) in the base of the sample statistic.[7]

Figure A-1 results from having plotted the k_i values for the estimated statistics against the corresponding n_i values (size of base). For most of the estimated statistics the k_i values are found to be between 1 and 1.4 + 0.0007 n_i. Thus the lines k = 1 and k = 1.4 + 0.0007 n are presented as "safe lower" and "safe upper" bounds for the k values of the sample statistics for the present study. If the researcher wishes to choose an average value of k_i in order to estimate the standard error of a sample statistic not presented in Table A-1, then for the appropriate n_i (size of base) he may choose a value of k_i midway between the upper and lower bounds.

For means and proportions of some major groups whose standard errors are not given in Table A-1, estimates of the population standard deviations are presented with the means and proportions where they appear in the text. If one is interested in estimating the population standard deviations for subgroups of a major group, (i) estimates of the population standard deviations or means could be the corresponding values for that major group (notice that for homogeneous subgroups this might be an overestimate); (ii) an estimate of the population standard deviation for a proportion, P could be p (1 - p), where p is the sample estimate of P. Therefore, the interested reader can approximate the standard errors for those statistics whose standard

---

[7]Leslie Kish, Survey Sampling (New York: John Wiley and Sons, Inc., 1965).

errors are not given in Table A-1 in the following manner:

1. Determine the size of base (n_i) for the desired statistic (r_i).

2. Obtain the estimated population standard deviation (SD) for the statistic r_i.

3. Calculate the simple random variance of r_i as srv = $(SD)^2/n_i$.

4. For this n_i, choose a value of k_i from Figure A-1 (one may choose an average value of k_i, as explained in the preceding paragraph).

5. The sampling variance of r_i is

$$var\ (r_i) = k_i\ \frac{(SD)^2}{n_i}$$

6. The standard error of r_i is the square root of var (r_i).

To find the standard error of the difference of two statistics r_1 and r_2, an approximate value is SE($r_1 - r_2$) = $\sqrt{var\ (r_i) + var\ (r_2)}$. The approximation is justifiable if there is only very low correlation between the two subgroups. This is true for most of the statistics for which we have calculated standard errors.[8]

The reader is warned that the procedure described to approximate samplin variances of statistics not given in Table A-1 applies only to characteristi of subpopulations at the national level. That is, the procedure is not applicable to regional estimates, or for statistics on special groups such as Negroes, farmers, or foreign-born populations.

Confidence limits for the means or proportions, or for the differences between means or proportions can be obtained by taking, on either side of th sample statistics, a range two or three times the standard errors, according to the probability desired.

---

[8]Kish and Hess, op. cit., pp. 48-53.

TABLE A-1

SAMPLING VARIABILITY OF ESTIMATES FOR MAJOR SUBGROUPS OF THE SAMPLE

Definition of sub-groups	Number of sample cases (n_i)	Esti-mated mean, propor-tion	Estimated standard errors[*]	Ratio of sample variance to variance of simple random sample[**] (k_i)

A. Hours of work for money by heads of families in 1964 (for all 1833 heads of families who worked for money; see Chapter 2)

Age of head of family	Number of cases	Hours	Hours	Ratio
65 or older	141	1436	102	1.3
Less than 65	1692	2212	24	1.8
Difference	--	775	107	1.4
Less than 35	479	2147	51	2.1
35 - 64 years old	1213	2237	24	1.2
Difference	--	91	52	1.6

Education of head of family				
Less than 12 grades	797	2082	28	.9
12 grades but no college degree	785	2199	34	1.5
Difference	--	117	42	1.1
No college degree	1582	2140	23	1.3
College degree	251	2230	59	1.4
Difference	--	90	58	1.2

Marital status of head of family				
Married	1474	2260	26	1.7
Single	359	1709	54	1.3
Difference	--	551	64	1.6

Score on index of achievement orientation				
Low (0-4 score)	1395	2135	23	1.1
High (5-8 score)	438	2206	43	1.5
Difference	--	71	43	1.1

[*] The standard error of the statistic, calculated by taking into consideration the complexity of the sample design.

[**] The variance of the statistic that would be obtained if a simple random sampling design had been used, rather than the design actually used.

TABLE A-1 (continued)

B. Whether wife worked for money in 1964
(For all 1640 wives; see Chapter 3)

Age of wife	Number of cases	Propor- tion	Propor- tion	Ratio
65 or older	139	.12	.03	1.20
Less than 65	1501	.49	.02	1.45
Difference	--	.36	.03	1.26
Less than 35	514	.47	.02	1.12
35-64 years old	987	.49	.02	1.50
Difference	--	.02	.03	1.17

Education of wife

Less than 12 grades	702	.39	.02	1.14
12 grades but no college degree	814	.49	.02	1.23
Difference	--	.10	.02	.96
No college degree	1516	.44	.02	1.39
College degree	124	.60	.05	1.27
Difference	--	.15	.05	1.25

Husband's score on
index of achievement
orientation

Low (0-4 score)	1294	.45	.02	1.51
High (5-8 score)	346	.49	.03	1.23
Difference	--	.05	.03	1.32

C. Hours of work for money by wives in 1964
(For all 747 wives who worked for money;
see Chapter 4)

Age of wife	Number of cases	Hours	Hours	Ratio
65 or older	17	705	190	.95
Less than 65	730	1268	31	1.03
Difference	--	564	190	.94
Less than 35	243	1093	53	1.06
35-64 years old	487	1356	39	1.09
Difference	--	263	66	1.10

TABLE A-1 (continued)

Education of wife	Number of cases	Hours	Hours	Ratio
Less than 12 grades	273	1252	273	1.32
12 grades but no college degree	400	1268	37	.82
Difference	--	16	69	1.09
No college degree	673	1261	673	1.05
College degree	74	1203	74	1.12
Difference	--	58	100	1.14

Husband's score on
index of achievement
orientation

Low (0-4 score)	576	1314	36	1.08
High (5-8 score)	171	1058	171	.84
Difference	--	256	66	.94

Total family income

Less than $7500	539	1291	40	1.25
$7500 or more	208	1164	55	.96
Difference	--	127	59	1.12

D. Hours of regular housework done by heads of
   families and wives in 1964
   (For all 2214 cases; see Chapter 8)

Age of head of family	Number of cases	Hours	Hours	Ratio
65 or older	416	1590	61	1.43
Less than 65	1798	2010	42	1.97
Difference	--	420	69	1.35
Less than 35	490	2139	86	1.96
35-64 years old	1308	1962	43	1.61
Difference	--	177	91	1.65

Education of head
of family

Less than 12 grades	1084	1961	54	2.07
12 grades but no college degree	854	1966	48	1.04
Difference	--	5	68	1.39
No college degree	1938	1963	39	1.91
College degree	276	1703	75	1.09
Difference	--	260	76	.98

TABLE A-1 (continued)

Marital status of head of family	Number of cases	Hours	Hours	Ratio
Married	1640	2243	38	1.70
Single	574	1040	43	1.08
Difference	--	1203	46	.83

Score on index of achievement orientation				
Low (0-4 score)	1765	1921	37	1.62
High (5-8 score)	449	1969	78	1.51
Difference	--	48	72	1.08

Total family income				
Less than $7500	1297	1881	52	2.26
$7500 or more	917	2002	39	.91
Difference	--	122	55	1.06

E. Total hours of unpaid productive hours done by heads of families and wives in 1964 (For all 2214 cases; see Chapter 9)

Age of head of family	Number of cases	Hours	Hours	Ratio
65 or older	416	233	18	.84
Less than 65	1798	373	18	2.18
Difference	--	139	22	.87
Less than 35	490	424	49	3.02
35-64 years old	1308	353	15	1.31
Difference	--	71	50	2.57

Education of head of family				
Less than 12 grades	1084	279	17	1.49
12 grades but no college degree	854	394	29	2.52
Difference	--	114	33	2.17
No college degree	1938	330	16	2.08
College degree	276	464	38	1.15
Difference	--	134	38	1.01

369

TABLE A-1 (continued)

Marital status of head of family	Number of cases	Hours	Hours	Ratio
Married	1640	393	18	2.00
Single	574	214	32	2.95
Difference	--	179	36	2.58
Score on index of achievement orientation				
Low (0-4 score)	1765	317	16	1.83
High (5-8 score)	449	462	29	1.29
Difference	--	145	27	.90
Total family income				
Less than $7500	1297	327	24	2.65
$7500 or more	917	374	17	1.26
Difference	--	48	29	1.81

F. Index of receptivity to change
(For all 2214 heads of families; see Chapter 13

Age of head of family	Number of cases	Score	Score	Ratio
65 or older	416	4.62	.18	2.04
Less than 65	1798	6.83	.07	1.65
Difference	--	2.22	.16	1.53
Less than 35	490	7.14	.09	1.20
35-64 years old	1308	6.72	.08	1.48
Difference	--	.43	.11	1.01
Education of head of family				
Less than 12 grades	1084	5.40	.10	1.93
12 grades but no college degree	854	7.23	.07	1.06
Difference	--	1.83	.12	1.37
No college degree	1938	6.21	.08	2.03
College degree	276	7.86	.12	1.34
Difference	--	1.65	.13	1.25

TABLE A-1 (continued)

Marital status of head of family	Number of cases	Score	Score	Ratio
Married	1640	6.82	.07	1.59
Single	574	5.26	.13	1.68
Difference	--	1.55	.13	1.32
Score on index of achievement orientation				
Low (0-4 score)	1765	6.11	.09	2.23
High (5-8 score)	449	7.62	.09	1.36
Difference	--	1.51	.12	1.55
Total family income				
Less than $7500	1297	5.57	.10	2.05
$7500 or more	917	7.62	.06	.96
Difference	--	2.05	.10	1.33

G. Index of planning and time horizon
(For all 2214 heads of families; see Chapter

Age of head of family	Number of cases	Score	Score	Ratio
65 or older	416	2.74	.06	1.53
Less than 65	1798	3.25	.04	1.42
Difference	--	.51	.07	1.41
Less than 35	490	2.93	.07	1.43
35-64 years old	1308	3.37	.05	1.34
Difference	--	.44	.08	1.35
Education of head of family				
Less than 12 grades	1084	2.97	.05	1.43
12 grades but no college degree	854	3.29	.05	1.03
Difference	--	.32	.07	1.25
No college degree	1938	3.11	.03	1.17
College degree	276	3.48	.10	1.12
Difference	--	.37	.10	1.03

TABLE A-1 (continued)

arital status of ead of family	Number of cases	Score	Score	Ratio
arried	1640	3.23	.04	1.33
ingle	574	2.95	.05	.90
Difference	--	.28	.06	.94
core on index of chievement rientation				
ow (0-4 score)	1765	3.11	.04	1.32
igh (5-8 score)	449	3.35	.07	1.02
Difference	--	.25	.08	1.00
tal family income				
ess than $7500	1297	2.90	.04	1.07
7500 or more	917	3.52	.05	.97
Difference	--	.63	.06	.85

H. Index of mobility experience
(For all 2214 heads of families' used in
various chapters as an explanatory variable;
see Chapter 15 for a related index, that of
mobility behavior)

je of head of family	Number of cases	Score	Score	Ratio
or older	416	1.77	.10	2.62
ess than 65	1798	2.59	.05	2.20
Difference	--	.82	.08	1.49
ess than 35	490	2.94	.08	1.44
-64 years old	1308	2.45	.05	2.02
Difference	--	.49	.09	1.25
ucation of head family				
ss than 12 grades	1084	2.16	.07	2.78
grades but no college degree	854	2.63	.06	1.53
Difference	--	.47	.07	1.19
college degree	1938	2.37	.06	3.14
llege degree	276	2.90	.10	1.50
Difference	--	.54	.12	1.72

TABLE A-1 (continued)

Marital status of head of family	Number of cases	Score	Score	Ratio
Married	1640	2.57	.05	2.49
Single	574	2.05	.08	1.63
Difference	--	.52	.08	1.16

Score on index of achievement oritentation

Low (0-4 score)	1765	2.27	.06	3.53
High(5-8 score)	449	3.06	.07	1.15
Difference	--	.78	.09	1.53

Total family income

Less than $7500	1297	2.28	.07	3.04
$7500 or more	917	2.65	.05	1.36
Difference	--	.37	.07	1.54

I. Index of ambition and aspiration
(For all 2214 heads of families; see Chapter 16)

Age of head of family	Number of cases	Score	Score	Ratio
65 or older	416	.66	.04	1.11
Less than 65	1798	2.68	.04	1.01
Difference	--	2.03	.06	1.10
Less than 35	490	3.51	.08	1.52
35-64 years old	1308	2.37	.04	.88
Difference	--	1.14	.09	1.22

Education of head of family

Less than 12 grades	1084	1.86	.05	1.00
12 grades but no college degree	854	2.69	.05	.91
Difference	--	.82	.07	.81
No college degree	1938	2.23	.04	1.13
College degree	276	2.84	.11	1.03
Difference	--	.62	.11	.93

TABLE A-1 (continued)

Marital status of head of family	Number of cases	Score	Score	Ratio
Married	1640	2.61	.04	1.00
Single	574	1.43	.06	1.10
Difference	--	1.17	.07	.86
Score on index of achievement orientation				
Low (0-4 score)	1765	2.06	.04	1.30
High (5-8 score)	449	3.25	.09	1.26
Difference	--	1.19	.09	1.20
Total family income				
Less than $7500	1297	2.03	.06	1.46
$7500 or more	917	2.69	.06	1.07
Difference	--	.66	.08	1.41

J. Index of social participation
(For all 2214 heads of families; see Chapter 17)

Age of head of family	Number of cases	Score	Score	Ratio
65 or older	416	1.92	.09	2.09
Less than 65	1798	2.62	.04	1.41
Difference	--	.70	.08	1.29
Less than 35	490	2.70	.07	1.35
35-64 years old	1308	2.58	.04	1.22
Difference	--	.12	.08	1.15
Education of head of family				
Less than 12 grades	1084	1.94	.05	2.03
12 grades but no college degree	854	2.90	.05	1.41
Difference	--	.96	.07	1.49
No college degree	1938	2.36	.05	2.16
College degree	276	3.34	.08	.98
Difference	--	.98	.09	1.21

TABLE A-1 (continued)

Marital status of head of family	Number of cases	Score	Score	Ratio
Married	1640	2.59	.04	1.57
Single	574	2.17	.07	1.64
Difference	--	.42	.07	1.17

Score on index of achievement oritentation	Number of cases	Score	Score	Ratio
Low (0-4 score)	1765	2.34	.05	2.12
High (5-8 score)	449	3.06	.07	1.13
Difference	--	.72	.08	1.22

Total family income				
Less than $7500	1297	2.12	.06	2.42
$7500 or more	917	3.00	.03	.62
Difference	--	.88	.06	1.17

K. Index of caution and risk avoidance
(For all 2214 heads of families; see Chapter 1)

Age of head of family	Number of cases	Score	Score	Ratio
65 or older	416	2.77	.07	1.51
Less than 65	1798	3.21	.05	1.98
Difference	--	.44	.07	1.13
Less than 35	490	3.33	.08	1.45
35-64 years old	1308	3.17	.05	1.48
Difference	--	.16	.08	.98

Education of head of family				
Less than 12 grades	1084	2.65	.07	2.65
12 grades but no college degree	854	3.48	.06	1.39
Difference	--	.84	.08	1.79
No college degree	1938	3.01	.05	2.23
College degree	276	3.95	.10	1.33
Difference	--	.93	.12	1.65

TABLE A-1 (continued)

arital status of ead of family	Number of cases	Score	Score	Ratio
arried	1640	3.12	.05	1.76
ingle	574	3.17	.06	1.67
Difference	--	.06	.07	1.12
core on index of chievement rientation				
ow (0-4 score)	1765	3.01	.05	1.97
igh (5-8 score)	449	3.59	.07	1.18
Difference	--	.58	.07	.99
tal family income				
ss than $7500	1297	2.77	.06	2.53
7500 or more	917	3.64	.05	1.17
Difference	--	.87	.07	1.46

L.   Index of closeness of family ties
(For all 2214 heads of families; see Chapter 19)

e of head of family	Number of cases	Score	Score	Ratio
or older	416	1.21	.05	1.45
ss than 65	1798	.98	.02	1.18
Difference	--	.22	.05	1.30
ss than 35	490	1.03	.04	1.00
-64 years old	1308	.96	.02	1.03
Difference	--	.07	.04	.85
cation of head family				
s than 12 grades	1084	1.10	.03	1.23
grades but no college egree	854	.99	.03	1.10
Difference	--	.11	.05	1.23
college degree	1938	1.05	.02	1.10
lege degree	276	.87	.05	.98
Difference	--	.18	.04	.72

TABLE A-1 (continued)

Marital status of head of family	Number of cases	Score	Score	Ratio
Married	1640	.99	.02	1.10
Single	574	1.13	.04	1.19
Difference	--	.14	.04	1.10

Score on index of achievement orientation				
Low (0-4 score)	1765	1.03	.03	1.44
High (5-8 score)	449	.99	.05	1.15
Difference	--	.04	.05	1.23

Total family income				
Less than $7500	1297	1.13	.03	1.38
$7500 or more	917	.87	.03	.93
Difference	--	.26	.04	.99

M. Attitude toward mothers' working
(For all 1640 married heads of families;
see Chapter 19)

Age of head of family	Number of cases	Score	Score	Ratio
65 or older	214	.19	.03	1.07
Less than 65	1426	.35	.01	1.37
Difference	--	.16	.03	1.23
Less than 35	390	.42	.03	1.06
35-64 years old	1036	.32	.02	1.31
Difference	--	.10	.03	.98

Education of head of family				
Less than 12 grades	771	.31	.02	1.32
12 grades but no college degree	654	.35	.02	1.13
Difference	--	.04	.03	1.16
No college degree	1425	.33	.01	1.29
College degree	215	.32	.03	1.09
Difference	--	.01	.04	1.06

TABLE A-1 (continued)

Score on index of achievement orientation	Number of cases	Score	Score	Ratio
Low (0-4 score)	1294	.32	.01	1.33
High (5-8 score)	346	.35	.02	.88
Difference	--	.03	.03	.89
Total family income				
Less than $7500	1071	.34	.02	1.30
$7500 or more	569	.31	.02	1.22
Difference	--	.03	.03	1.20

N. Index of achievement orientation
(For all 2214 heads of families; used in
various chapters as an explanatory variable;
see Appendix D for a description of this variable)

Age of head of family	Number of cases	Score	Score	Ratio
65 or older	416	2.35	.06	1.15
Less than 65	1798	3.36	.05	1.62
Difference	--	1.01	.07	1.77
Less than 35	490	4.07	.08	1.27
35-64 years old	1308	3.09	.06	1.92
Difference	--	.98	.10	1.40
Education of head of family				
Less than 12 grades	1084	2.59	.05	1.73
12 grades but no college degree	854	3.62	.06	1.19
Difference	--	1.04	.07	1.18
No college degree	1938	3.04	.04	1.64
College degree	276	4.04	.10	1.01
Difference	--	1.00	.11	1.06
Marital status of head of family				
Married	1640	3.21	.05	1.45
Single	594	3.04	.08	1.40
Difference	--	.17	.08	1.13

378

TABLE A-1 (continued)

Total family income	Number of cases	Score	Score	Ratio
Less than $7500	1297	3.01	.05	1.64
$7500 or more	917	3.39	.06	1.10
Difference	--	.38	.07	1.07

0. Attitude toward man who tries difficult things
    but does not always succeed
    (For all 2013 cases where attitude was ascertained

Age of head of family	Number of cases	Score	Score	Ratio
65 or older	353	2.22	.07	1.27
Less than 65	1660	2.02	.03	1.06
Difference	--	.19	.07	1.08
Less than 35	457	2.00	.05	1.11
35-64 years old	1203	2.03	.03	1.02
Difference	--	.03	.06	1.07

Education of head
of family

	Number of cases	Score	Score	Ratio
Less than 12 grades	939	2.27	.05	1.61
12 grades but no college degree	813	1.92	.03	.61
Difference	--	.35	.06	1.23
No college degree	1752	2.10	.03	1.19
College degree	261	1.76	.05	.89
Difference	--	.34	.06	.86

Marital status of
head of family

	Number of cases	Score	Score	Ratio
Married	1500	2.04	.03	1.13
Single	513	2.10	.05	1.17
Difference	--	.06	.06	1.04

Score on index of
achievement
orientation

	Number of cases	Score	Score	Ratio
Low (0-4 score)	1577	2.19	.03	1.37
High (5-8 score)	436	1.59	.05	1.16
Difference	--	.59	.06	1.29

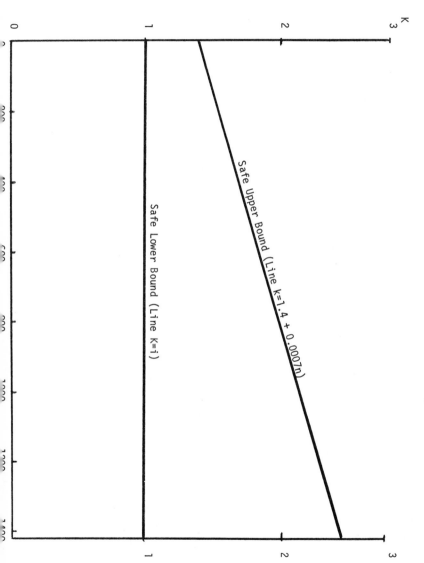

FIGURE A-1

APPROXIMATE RANGE OF THE K VALUES FOR VARYING VALUES OF BASE (N) OF MEANS AND PROPORTIONS (K is the ratio of the sampling variance var (r) to the simple random variance srv (r) of a statistic having the same magnitude and base as the sample statistic)

APPENDIX B

EDITING AND CODING

Editing

The use of an elaborate worksheet was required in this study
in order to assemble the facts on how family members spend their time.
An editing procedure was required as well, since many of the numbers from
the questionnaire could not be entered directly on the worksheet. For
example, respondents were questioned generally in terms of "a usual week"
or "usual day," while hours of time on the worksheet were in terms of
hours per year. Most of the questionnaire-to-worksheet entries were
simple conversions, but, for some items, it was difficult for respondents
to give precise numbers of hours. The worksheet used to calculate hours
is reproduced on the next page. Another worksheet used to calculate
income is not reproduced.

The study staff, therefore, found it necessary to apply consistent
rules for handling such imprecise statements about amounts, as well as
assign missing data, and interpret complex situations. Assignments were
seldom made for more than 2 per cent of the cases for any one item. The
adding together of bits of information to form totals necessitated the
assignment of missing parts, so as to avoid having totals being coded
"not ascertained" merely because one of the parts was not ascertained. The
remainder of this section on editing describes the procedures used,
variable by variable.

380

TIME WORKSHEET   STUDY NUMBER   CARD NUMBER   INTERVIEW NUMBER

SB# _____ Ed. by _____ CKd. by _____

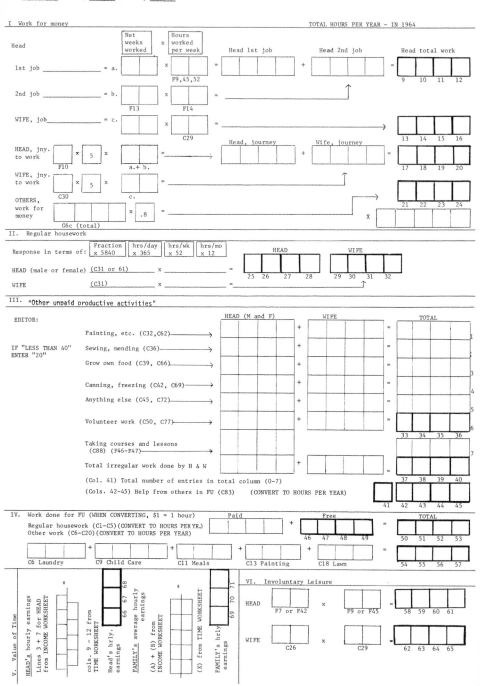

I Work for money

TOTAL HOURS PER YEAR - IN 1964

Head

	Net weeks worked	x	Hours worked per week	Head 1st job	Head 2nd job	Head total work

1st job _____ = a.   x   =   +   =
F9,45,52

2nd job _____ = b.   x   =
F13   F14   9 10 11 12

WIFE, job _____ = c.   x
C29   13 14 15 16

HEAD, jny. to work   x 5 x   =   Head, journey   Wife, journey
F10   a.+ b.   +   =
     17 18 19 20

WIFE, jny. to work   x 5 x   =
C30   c.
     21 22 23 24

OTHERS, work for money   x .8 =   X
G6c (total)

II. Regular housework

	Fraction x 5840	hrs/day x 365	hrs/wk x 52	hrs/mo x 12	HEAD	WIFE

Response in terms of:

HEAD (male or female) (C31 or 61) __ x _____ =   25 26 27 28   29 30 31 32

WIFE   (C31) __ x _____ =

III. "Other unpaid productive activities"

EDITOR:

HEAD (M and F)   WIFE   TOTAL

Painting, etc. (C32,C62) →   +   =   1

IF "LESS THAN 40" ENTER "20"

Sewing, mending (C36) →   +   =

Grow own food (C39, C66) →   +   =   3

Canning, freezing (C42, C69) →   +   =   4

Anything else (C45, C72) →   +   =   5

Volunteer work (C50, C77) →   +   6
     33 34 35 36

Taking courses and lessons (C88) (F46-F47) →   7

Total irregular work done by H & W   +   37 38 39 40

(Col. 41) Total number of entries in total column (0-7)

(Cols. 42-45) Help from others in FU (C83)   (CONVERT TO HOURS PER YEAR)
     41 42 43 44 45

IV. Work done for FU (WHEN CONVERTING, $1 = 1 hour)

Paid   Free   TOTAL

Regular housework (C1-C5)(CONVERT TO HOURS PER YR.)   +   =
Other work (C6-C20)(CONVERT TO HOURS PER YEAR)
     46 47 48 49   50 51 52 53

  +   +   +   +   =
C6 Laundry   C9 Child Care   C11 Meals   C13 Painting   C18 Lawn   54 55 56 57

V. Value of Time

HEAD's hourly earnings Lines 3 + 7 for HEAD from INCOME WORKSHEET

cols. 9 - 12 from TIME WORKSHEET

Head's hrly. earnings   66 67 68

FAMILY's average hourly earnings

(A) + (B) from INCOME WORKSHEET

(X) from TIME WORKSHEET   69 70 71

FAMILY's hrly earnings

VI. Involuntary Leisure

HEAD   F7 or F42   x   F9 or F45   =   58 59 60 61

WIFE   C26   x   C29   =   62 63 64 65

Hours of Work for Money by Head of Family

After first asking about illness, unemployment, and vacations for
those currently in the labor force, these two questions were used to
estimate the head of the family's total hours of work for money:

"Then how many weeks did you actually work last year?

On the average, about how many hours a week did you work
(when you were working)?"

Those who were not currently in the labor force were asked:

"How many weeks did you work last year?

About how many hours a week did you work (when you worked)?"

Those who were students at the time of the interview were asked:

"About how many weeks last year did you work at this job?

How many hours a week did you work when you worked?"

Hence, every head of a family was asked if and how many hours he worked
for money during 1964 even though he may not have been working at the
time of the interview. For most individuals, these questions on hours
of work were easy to answer -- the majority had a regular work schedule
or did not work at all.

Wherever the hours worked per week was unavailable, 40 hours were
assigned unless there was evidence otherwise. Many salesmen could not
tell us the number of hours they worked per week. Farmers, however,
presented a different problem. Often no better response than, "when the
weather is good, from sunrise to sunset," was given. In such cases,
farmers were assumed to work 60 hours per week. Some were able to give
estimates that revolved around the different stages of their crops like,
"60 hours a week when harvesting and otherwise about 40 hours a week."
Such responses enabled us to make fairly good estimates.

For some individuals where there were few clues as to the number of hours worked but where earned income was known, a wage rate was calculated from the multivariate analysis of head's hourly earnings in Income and Welfare in the United States.[1] By knowing the average wage rate for individuals in conditions similar to the respondent's and the respondent's total earnings, his hours of work could then be estimated by dividing total earnings by this "wage rate."

Those who stated that they "had lots of overtime" had 5 hours added to their average work week, while those stating that they had "some overtime" had 2 hours added to their average work week.

Those currently in the labor force were asked the following questions about their second job (if they had one):

"How much time did you spend on that job last year?

How many hours a week is that?"

Some individuals were making money from an activity not ordinarily considered a "job," such as racing cars, raising horses for show, etc. The total earnings given in the income section of the questionnaire were used to assign the number of hours worked on this second job by assuming the same hourly earnings as for the first job. There appeared in some cases, for those with second jobs, to be a possible upward bias in the reported number of hours worked. It seemed likely that those who reported working 60 or more hours per week on their first job and who also had a second job were counting the hours of their second jobs with the hours of their first job. Each such case was handled individually. If the series of questions about the second job was omitted, and there was no indication of a second job from the income section of the questionnaire, the individual was assumed not to have a second job.

---

[1] James Morgan, et.al. Income and Welfare in the United States (New York: The McGraw-Hill Book Company, Inc., 1962), Appendix E, pp. 508-511.

Those who worked during the year but were retired or housewives at the time of the interview were often quite vague about the number of hours they worked. Female domestics who worked only now and then were very vague. A $1.00 per hour wage rate was used in these cases to estimate hours. Retired farmers who were unclear about their hours of work were assumed to work about 35 hours per week unless they were very aged or disabled. Some retired individuals who owned rental property which they managed as well, often neglected to report the number of hours they spent keeping up the property. Again, estimates were made from data in Income and Welfare in the United States.[2] Those making things and selling them (usually female heads of families) were vague. A wage rate of $1.00 or $1.25 was used to determine the number of hours in such cases. Wherever necessary for those making and selling things, the hours worked were reduced so that no wage rate for such activities fell below $.30 with the remaining hours included in the category, "other unpaid productive activities."

Hours of Work for Money by Wife

The following questions were asked of wives who were working for money at the time of the interview:

"How many weeks did you (WIFE) work last year?

How many hours a week did you (WIFE) work (when working)?"
Problems here were similar to those for the head of the family. In cases where the wife worked "around the clock" as a housekeeper, baby-sitter, nurse, etc., we allowed no more than 16 hours of work, 7 days a week, even if she stated, "I am on call 24 hours a day." In a few cases, it was necessary to impute an amount to include free food and housing, in addition to money earnings, so as not to understate the real wage rate.

---

[2] Ibid.

Journey to Work of Head of Family and Wife

Heads of families and wives who worked were asked:

"How much time does it take you to get to work and back each day?"
Journey to work was calculated on the basis of a five-day workweek unless
there was indication otherwise. A 72 hour workweek was assumed to be a
six-day workweek, for instance. In the case of the normal 40-hour workweek,
it was assumed that there was one round trip for every 8 hours worked. For
second jobs, it was assumed that there was one round trip for every 4 hours
worked. The length of time of each journey to work for second jobs was
assumed to be equal to that for the first job. When the respondent stated
that his journey to work varied and gave a range, the midpoint was used in
the calculation. One-half hour was used for responses such as "depends on
where the work is." Most salesmen indicated that travelling was part of
their work time, and hence a zero journey to work was assumed for them.
This assumption was also used for others whose jobs involved extensive
day-to-day travelling.

Work for Money by Others in Family

Detailed information on hours of work for money was secured only for
the head of the family and his wife. The source of income was the only
information obtained that enabled us to estimate hours worked for money by
others in the family, such as minor children or extra adults. If the source
of income for these individuals was wages or salaries, they were assumed to
have worked for money, and the further assumption of an hourly earning rate
of $1.25 was made. However, in instances where the total income from wages
and salaries was higher than $2500, meaning that the assumption of $1.25
wage rate made for hours of work in excess of 2000, 2000 was assigned. In
instances where the source of the other person's income was unknown, it was
assumed to be from wages and salaries if he was both under sixty-five and
not disabled.

Hours of Regular Housework of Head of Family

These hours were calculated from separate questions for a female head and for a male head. They were as follows:

> "We'd like to know about how much of your (FEMALE HEAD) time is spent on work around the house, such as preparing meals, cleaning, and straightening up. On the average, about how much of your (FEMALE HEAD) time is spent working around the house?"

> "Now about your (MALE HEAD) work around the house, do you do any regular things such as doing dishes, cleaning, and straightening up? (IF YES) On the average how much of your time do you spend on these things?"

The questions used for female heads of families were used to determine hours of regular housework for the wife, as well. A response such as "all the time" was assumed to be 16 hours a day, 365 days a year, and was also used as an upper limit on the time spent by an individual on his total productive activities. Responses such as "now and then," "in emergencies," "only when my wife is sick," "very little," "occasionally," or "a small amount," were assigned 26 hours for the year, that is, one-half hour per week. And the response, "don't know," was assumed to be 60 hours per year. But if the question was omitted by mistake, 40 hours were assigned for the year. This assignment of 40 hours per year was parallel with that made for each of the other unpaid productive activities.

Hours of Regular Housework of Wives

For wives, essentially the same assumptions were used as for male and female heads of families. A response such as, "5 per cent of my time," was assumed to mean 5 per cent of 5840 (total awake hours during the year).

For wives who worked for money and stated that they did regular housework,
"from the time I get off from work to the time I get back," her hours of
regular housework were calculated as follows: 5840 (total awake hours)
minus hours spent working for money, minus her journey to work time, and
minus the hours spent on other unpaid productive activities. If she
answered, "about 8 hours a day, but resting, eating, and everything else
is included," it was assumed to be 6 hours per day. A response from a
wife such as "as little as possible," was assumed to be one hour per day.
"Many hours" was assumed to be 12 hours per day. A statement such as "I
prepare the meals" was assumed to mean that she did only that, and 3 hours
per day were assigned.

Hours of Other Unpaid Productive Activities of Head of Family and Wife

Unpaid work other than regular housework included (1) painting,
redecorating, or major housecleaning, (2) sewing and mending, (3) growing
own food, (4) canning or freezing, (5) volunteer work without pay for
friends or relatives, or charity, and (6) anything else that could be
considered economically productive (See worksheet Section III). Only
heads of families and wives were asked about this type of productive work.

In determining the number of hours spent on such activities, respondents
were asked merely if they spent more than 40 hours doing it, and if so, how
many hours it did take during the year. If they stated that the job did not
take as many as 40 hours, they were not asked how many hours it did take;
20 hours for the year was assigned in such instances. But if they did not
know whether or not it did take more or less than 40 hours, 40 hours were
assigned. A response such as "all week" to any of these other unpaid items
was assumed to be 40 hours. For wives and female heads of families, if thes

questions on irregular things were omitted by mistake, she was assumed to
have done 20 hours of painting, redecorating, or major housecleaning,
and 20 hours of something that would have fitted into the "anything else"
catchall category, based on the most usual responses for wives. Where
these questions were omitted by mistake in the case of male heads of
families, all categories were assumed to be zero. Again, this estimate
was made on the basis of the most common response. These questions on
hours of regular housework and other unpaid work were asked directly, in
most cases, of the person for whom the question was relevant. (The
interviewer had a provision in the questionnaire for returning to the
household a second time in cases where the husband was unable to answer
for the wife and wife was not present at the time.)

Hours of Courses and Lessons for Head of Family

This information was secured only for heads of families. A student
head of a family who said that he was in school for two semesters, was
assumed to have attended two 16-week semesters. And if a student replied
that he was in school "all year," it was assumed to mean three 16-week
semesters. Time spent studying was also included under this category.

Help around the House from Other Members in the Family

The questions used for this information were as follows:

"Does anyone else (OTHER THAN HEAD OR WIFE) in the family living
here help with any of the work around the house? (IF YES) Who
is it?

In an ordinary week, about how many hours, does he (she, they)
spend doing these things?"

In general, it proved to be somewhat difficult for heads of families or
wives to answer the above with very much precision; they were being asked
about another person as well as about things commonly done on an irregular
basis. This question was sometimes skipped by interviewers in cases where

the children in the family were all 5 or under. In such cases zero hours
were assumed. Otherwise, in cases where this question was mistakenly not
asked, the number of hours was assigned on the basis of the number of
"others" living with the family and their ages. For instance, if the
family had one ten-year old child and there was no indication anywhere in
the interview of how much time he spent working around the house, one-half
hour per week was assigned for him. If there were three children in the
family and the head of the family answered, "hard to say, but they
straighten up some," they were assigned a total of one hour per week.
Eight children in a family ranging from ages four through twenty-two were
assigned a total of three hours per week. When the other person in the
family was a sister, brother, or some other adult relation to the head of
the family, sex was taken into consideration, as well, in assigning the
amount of work done around the house. For instance if a single man had a
sixty-six year old sister living with him, the sister was assigned 4.5
hours of work around the house per day.

Help Received by the Family

The questions used to determine the number of hours of help received
from outside the family were as follows:

> "We're interested in how people get the things done that have to
> be done around the house, such as preparing meals, cleaning and
> making repairs. Do you (and your wife) have some help from
> outside the household, or do you do all your own regular house-
> work?
>
> (IF HAVE SOME HELP) For what kind of housework do you have help?
> ordinarily how many hours a week would that be? Is any of it
> done without pay by relatives or friends from outside the house-
> hold? (IF YES) About how many hours a week is that?"

Responses such as "now and then," "once in awhile," and other similar
nonquantitative phrases were assumed to be one-half hour per week. If the
family had a full-time housekeeper who lived in the dwelling, she was assumed

o work for the family 16 hours per day, 6 days a week. (The hours of
work for money reported by a housekeeper who lived in the dwelling, of
course, had to equal the hours of help received by the primary family
from this individual.) A housekeeper who did not live with the family
for whom she worked was assumed to work 40 hours per week for them.
Remember, all the above estimates were made only when the respondent was
not able to answer how many hours were involved.

The amount of time saved by having someone else do the laundry was
ascertained by the following two questions:

> "Do you people send out any of your family's laundry, or pay
> to have any of it done?
>
> (IF YES) About how much does that cost each week?"

It was assumed that for each dollar the family spent on laundry, one hour
of time was saved. For those who had laundry sent out, but did not know
its weekly cost, the calculation of the number of hours was made on the
basis of the size and composition of the family. For example, one-half
hour per week was assigned for a young single man and an elderly woman,
while 2 hours per week were assigned for a family of four persons. These
estimates are surely conservative.

Whether the family had child care from outside the family was determined
for families with children under 12 years old by the following questions:

> "Do you have someone else from outside the household just to
> care for the children?
>
> (IF YES) About how many hours a week is that?"

Responses such as "occasionally" and "once in a while" were assigned one-
half hour per week. Families who had child care and who had a wife working
outside the home were assigned hours of babysitting equal to the hours worked
by the wife plus her journey to work.

Hours of work saved by eating meals outside the home were determined

by the following question:

> "What about meals, about how often do you (people) eat at
> restaurants or drive-ins?"

Those who ate out very little were the most likely to give the interviewer

a vague response such as "hardly ever," "not often," "almost never," or

"very very seldom." Such responses were assumed to be 6 times a year,

or 6 hours saved per year, assuming that a meal eaten out saved a total of

one hour of the wife's time of preparation and clean-up. If there was

indication that eating out only meant that the wife ate lunches out when

she went shopping, or that the children ate their lunches at school, these

hours were excluded. If the head of the family (usually husband) ate his

lunches out, however, these hours were included as time saved in preparing

meals. Hours spent by a head of a family eating his meals at a restaurant

where he worked were considered a part of working time; hence these hours

were not included as time saved by eating out.

Respondents were also asked the following about help from outside the

family:

> "What about painting, redecorating, or spring cleaning, did you
> have any outside help to do these things in the last year?
>
> (IF YES) How many hours of work did it take? (IF DON'T KNOW)
> How much did it cost to have it done? What part of this was
> labor cost?"

The fraction of the cost that was labor cost was assumed to be related,

1-for-1, to the number of hours saved by hiring outside help. In cases

where the individual did not know how many hours the job took, two-thirds

of the total cost was assumed to be labor cost, again related 1-for-1,

in cases where the individual knew neither the number of hours the job took nor what part of its total cost was labor cost.

Respondents were also asked the following about lawn work:

"Did you pay to have some of the lawn work done last year?

(IF YES) How many hours of work were involved? (IF DON'T KNOW) How much did this lawn work cost you?"

Responses such as "I have the lawn work done once a week" were assigned hours on the basis of the climate of the area. It was assumed that lawns needed mowing for a six-month period in such places as Detroit, New York, and the Chicago areas,while a nine-month period was assumed for climates like Los Angeles. Again one dollar spent was assumed to be one hour saved.

For all of the above items for which the family had help, anything that increased the value of something, that is an investment, was omitted as were any business expenses that may have been reported.

Hourly Value of Time for Head of Family and for Total Family

The head of the family's earned and mixed-labor capital income were divided by his total number of hours of work for money to obtain his hourly earnings. The family's hourly earnings were calculated by adding all earned and mixed labor capital income for each family member, and then dividing this income figure by hours of work for money.

The distribution of family hourly earnings is as follows:

Hourly earnings for entire family	Per cent of cases
No one in family worked	13
$.01 - .49	2
$.50 - .99	7
$1.00 - 1.49	13
$1.50 - 1.99	14
$2.00 - 2.49	15
$2.50 - 2.99	12
$3.00 - 3.99	13
$4.00 - 4.99	5
$5.00 - 6.99	3
$7.00 or more	3
Total	100
Number of cases	2214

The average hourly earnings for the entire family were $2.60 while the average was $3.07 for all heads of families who worked. The average for the entire family was generally lower than that for the head of the family, since heads of families usually earn more per hour than any other family member. And the figure for the entire family includes the journey to work time of the head of the family and the wife as well.

Both of these calculations had in their numerators   earned income plus mixed labor capital income for the appropriate individuals. However, in some cases amounts had to be imputed when it was evident that large fractions of the income received were in nonmoney form, such as free housing in the case of farm laborers or apartment-house managers, or free food, as in the case of someone who worked in a restaurant. Where the wife, son, daughter, or some other member of the family other than the head worked without pay in the family business, these hours were added to the total hours of work for money by the family, so as to calculate a more realistic hourly earnings for the family.

Hours lost from Work by Unemployment of Heads of Families and Wives

Hours lost from work were calculated from the following question:

"How many weeks were there last year when you were unable to to work because of illness or unemployment?"

The number of hours that an individual was unemployed or ill was calculated by multiplying the number of weeks ill or unemployed by the average number of hours that the individual worked on his first job. If an individual worked an average of 60 hours or more, the estimate made of involuntary leisure may be somewhat high. However, we could not assume from his attitude toward his working hours whether he would have preferred forty or fifty hour of work. Hence in all cases we used the number of hours worked per week to lculate hours of illness or unemployment. For heads of families who

re unemployed during the entire year, 2000 hours of involuntary leisure

re assigned for them. If the reason for unemployment was pregnancy,

was omitted.

ding: Number of Not Ascertained Answers

Before coders were allowed to production-code interviews, they were

ven training as a group, conducted by those in charge of the study. Also,

ey were required to code a "practice" interview and were allowed to code

ly after they satisfactorily coded this practice interview. However,

nce the questionnaire was long and contained a number of attitude questions,

was decided to record the number of items coded "not ascertained" per

terview. It was thought that perhaps some coders might be more rigid than

ners in deciding whether to code a response "not ascertained" while others

ght be more liberal in their interpretation of what they thought the

spondent was saying. Hence, an analysis of variance was made to determine

ether or not there was any systematic difference among coders in the

ber of items coded "not ascertained". The R^2 obtained was .0063, indicating

t practically none of the variance in number of not-ascertained answers

ld be accounted for by differences between the coders.

Since so little of the variance could be accounted for by the coders, it

decided to look at the difference in the number of items coded "not ascert-

ed" according to education of the head of the family. The distribution

ow indicates that there is some difference in the number of items coded

t ascertained" according to education of the head of the family.

Education of head of family	Average number of answers coded "not ascertained"
0 - 5 grades	5.9
6 - 8 grades	4.6
9 - 11 grades	4.6
12 grades	3.9
12 grades and nonacademic training	4.1
College, no degree	4.1
College, bachelor's degree	3.8
College, advanced or professional degree	4.0
Total	4.4

The averages given above indicate that respondents with low levels of education may have had some slight difficulty in either understanding the questions or communicating verbally their ideas to the interviewer.

Our usual multivariate procedure was applied to the number of not ascertained codes per interview. The following variables were used listed in order of their importance if used to make a single division over the entire sample:

* Race
* Education of head of family
  Total family income

_____

Age of head of family
Marital status of head of family
Sex of head of family

The first three variables listed could explain as much as 0.5 per cent of the variance, but none of the variables below the line could explain that much of the variance by a single division of the whole sample. All of these variables together could explain only 3.4 per cent of the total variance. Race and education of head of family were the only variables actually used. Whites gave codable replies to a larger proportion of the questions.

Coding: Reliability

Since the analyses yielded so little in helping to explain the variance in the number of replies coded "not ascertained" it was decided to look at specific questions to see whether or not there were any differences in the reliability of coding certain questions. Reliability in coding was determined by "check-coding" every one in ten interviews. This means merely that the entire interview is coded again by an experienced and accurate coder and then checked item-for-item. The average number of differences per interview was 3.01, which is about a 1.25 per cent error rate. The coding of factual questions such as age of children, simple yes-no responses, and dollar amounts was very reliable and involved very few disagreements among coders. It was found that most of the discrepancies which did arise involved questions where interpretation and scaling had to be done by the coder.

This percentage error rate is based on the number of items coded, not the number of columns of information coded, since some items like dollar amounts were coded in fields of maybe three or four columns in length. This error rate based on per item coded may be slightly understated, however, since the coder did not, for every item in the questionnaire, have to make a new and independent decision as to what to code, since not all items were relevant for every respondent. For instance, if the head of the family was already retired, he was not asked a series of questions about his plans for the time when he is retired. In such instances, all that the coder was required to do was to put a string of zeros in the appropriate columns. Errors in the coding of these zeros were, of course, very infrequent, as well as being very easy to detect. One question selected for this reliability check was: "What do you think of a man who tries difficult things but doesn't always succeed? Why is that?" The categories into which the coder had to fit the respondent's answer were as follows: (1) admires such a man for his initiative and desire to take on tought tasks, (2) admires such a man for his persistence and ability to do hard work, (3) excuses his failure, (4) disapproves of such a man, thinks he is foolish to do things so much beyond his ability, or (5) not ascertained. The answers given by respondents did not necessarily have to parallel the language used in the code categories; the response just had to fit in one place better than any of the other four possible categories. For instance, the response: "He's all right, he's always trying to make progress. He's not self-satisfied," should obviously not be coded into categories 3,4, or 5 listed above. But a case could be made for coding it either into category 1 or 2. The idea of "trying" indicates persistence and hard work which are the notions of category 2. But the idea of "progress" is very similar to initiative and taking on tough tasks in order to get ahead. These notions are appropriate to category 1 above. Another example of an equivocal response is "If he tries, that is one thing in his favor. He may have himself overrated however." The idea of "trying" is appropriate to category 2, while that of "overrating himself" expresses disapproval. Of course, not all the responses to this question were so difficult. For this particular question there was disagreement between coders in 25 per cent of the cases as to the appropriate coding of responses to this question.

"How important do you think luck is for a person's financial success?" was another question where the coder had to make a decision in coding a response on a five-point scale from "very important" to "not at all important. A response such as "It's small in importance," required the coder to decide whether to code it in the "somewhat important" category or the "not very important" category. For this question, in 16 per cent of the cases there was disagreement between the coders as to how to code this question. In the few other attitude questions in the questionnaire the disagreement among coders was less. Most disagreements even in these two cases with substantial numbers of differences, were between adjacent codes in the scale, or between some code and "not ascertained", so the reliability is not so bad as it may seem.

Hence, since there was consistency among coders in the decision whether or not to code something not ascertained and since the reliability in the coding of attitude questions was acceptable, considering the nature of the responses to be coded, errors in the data due to coding seemed to be unbiased so far as one can tell from this brief overview. Nor were coding errors frequent enough to cause concern with the amount of "noise" introduced into the data by the coding procedures.

APPENDIX C

SUMMARY OF REPLIES TO QUESTIONS

The distribution of answers to all the questions asked of
respondents is given in this appendix, in the order in which the
questions were asked.

Some questions were asked only of an appropriate subgroup, but
the percentages given are always of the total sample. Where the
appropriate subgroup is less than one-half of the total sample,
that is 1107 cases or less, percentages are carried to one-tenth
of a per cent. And where the subgroup is more than one-half of
the entire sample, percentages are rounded to the nearest whole per
cent.

In cases where two or more replies to a question were coded, the
tabulated per cents will add to more than the total per cent who were
asked the question.

INFORMATION CODED FROM FIRST PAGE OF QUESTIONNAIRE	Per cent of entire sample

Questions 1 - 4 not coded

WHETHER FAMILY IS THE PRIMARY FAMILY LIVING IN THE DWELLING UNIT, THAT IS THE OWNER OF THE DWELLING OR THE MAIN RENTER

Primary family with no other family in dwelling	96
Primary family with another family living in dwelling	2
Secondary family (roomer, roommate, servant, etc.)	2
Total	100

5. LIST ALL PERSONS 18 YEARS OF AGE OR OVER LIVING IN THE DWELLING UNIT, AND ANY DU HEAD OR MARRIED PERSON REGARDLESS OF AGE. (ALL INFORMATION BELOW IS ON A FAMILY BASIS.)

FROM QUESTION 5. AGE OF FAMILY HEAD

Under 25	6
25 - 34	16
35 - 44	20
45 - 54	22
55 - 64	17
65 - 74	13
75 or older	6
Total	100

FROM QUESTION 5. AGE OF WIFE OF FAMILY HEAD

Under 25	8
25 - 34	15
35 - 44	18
45 - 54	16
55 - 64	11
65 - 74	5
75 or older	1
Family head is not married (574 cases)	26
Total	100

FROM QUESTION 5. NUMBER OF ADULTS IN FAMILY UNIT

One	20
Two	64
Three	12
Four or more	4
Total	100

FROM QUESTION 5. NUMBER OF ADULTS AGED 65 OR OLDER IN FAMILY UNIT

None	78
One	15
Two or more	7
Total	100

	Per cent of entire sample
6, 6a. DO YOU (FAMILY COVERED BY THIS INTERVIEW) HAVE ANY CHILDREN UNDER 18 LIVING HERE? HOW MANY?	

One	14.9
Two	15.4
Three	8.8
Four	4.2
Five	2.3
Six	1.2
Seven	.5
Eight or more	.4
Have no children under 18 (1159 cases)	52.3
Total	100.0

FROM QUESTION 6b. HOW OLD ARE THEY? AGE OF YOUNGEST CHILD UNDER EIGHTEEN	

Under 2	9.9
2	4.6
3	3.6
4	2.9
5	2.7
6 - 8	6.6
9 - 13	9.7
14 - 17	7.5
Not ascertained	.2
No children under 18 (1159 cases)	52.3
Total	100.0

FROM QUESTION 6b. HOW OLD ARE THEY? AGE OF OLDEST CHILD UNDER EIGHTEEN	

Under 6	10.4
6 - 9	7.6
10 - 12	7.2
13	3.0
14	3.3
15	4.1
16	5.6
17	6.1
Not ascertained	.4
No children under 18 (1159 cases)	52.3
Total	100.0

7, 7a. DO YOU HAVE ANY OTHER CHILDREN WHO DON'T LIVE HERE, THAT IS, INCLUDING GROWN SONS AND DAUGHTERS? HOW MANY UNDER 18?	

One	1.8
Two	.7
Three or more	.6
No children under 18 who do not live with the family (2145 cases)	96.9
Total	100.0

7b. HOW MANY 18 OR OVER?	Per cent of entire sample
One	13.8
Two	12.4
Three	6.0
Four	2.7
Five	2.3
Six	.8
Seven	.5
Eight or more	.6
Not ascertained	.3
No children 18 or older not living with the family; or no children 18 or older (1342 cases)	60.6
Total	100.0

FROM QUESTIONS 5, 6, 6a, 6b, 7, 7a, 7b.
TOTAL NUMBER OF LIVING CHILDREN OF FAMILY HEAD

None	20
One	17
Two	25
Three	16
Four	10
Five	5
Six	4
Seven	1
Eight or more	2
Total	100

FROM QUESTIONS 5, 6, 6a, 6b, 7, 7a, 7b.
NUMBER OF CHILDREN OF FAMILY HEAD LIVING IN THE
FAMILY UNIT

None	46
One	17
Two	18
Three	10
Four	5
Five	2
Six	1
Seven	0
Eight or more	1
Total	100

FROM QUESTIONS 5, 6, 6a, 6b, 7, 7a, 7b. NUMBER OF PEOPLE IN FAMILY UNIT (ADULTS + CHILDREN)	Per cent of entire sample
One	17
Two	29
Three	17
Four	17
Five	10
Six	5
Seven	2
Eight or more	3
Total	100

SECTION A: EDUCATION

A2, A3. WE ARE INTERESTED IN YOUR CHILDREN'S EDUCATION. DO YOU HAVE ANY CHILDREN IN COLLEGE NOW? DO YOU EXPECT ANY OF THEM TO GET A DEGREE FROM A FOUR-YEAR COLLEGE?

Have children in college now and expect them to get a degree from a four-year college	6
Have children in college now but do not expect them to get a degree from a four-year college	1
Do not have children in college now	72
Not ascertained whether children in college now	1
Family head does not have any children (445 cases)	20
Total	100

A5, A7. DO YOU HAVE ANY CHILDREN WHO WILL GO TO COLLEGE? WILL ANY OF THEM GET DEGREES FROM A FOUR-YEAR COLLEGE?

Have children who will go to college and expect them to get a degree from a four-year college	31.5
Have children who will go to college, but do not expect them to get a degree from a four-year college	1.8
Have children who will go to college, but don't know whether they will get a degree	5.1
Children will not go to college	7.5
Not ascertained whether children will go to college	3.2
Family head does not have any children under 18 (1127 cases)	50.9
Total	100.0

	Per cent of entire sample

6. HAVE YOU SET ASIDE ANY MONEY ESPECIALLY TO HELP PAY FOR THEIR COLLEGE EDUCATION?

Yes	18.1
No	20.0
Not ascertained whether money set aside for college	.3
Family head does not have any children under 18 or none who will go to college (1364 cases)	61.6
Total	100.0

A9, A10. DO YOU HAVE ANY CHILDREN WHO HAVE ALREADY GONE TO COLLEGE? DID ANY OF THEM GET DEGREES FROM A FOUR-YEAR COLLEGE?

Have children who have already gone to college and got degree from four-year college	9.5
Have children who have already gone to college but did not get degree from four-year college	7.2
Children did not go to college	27.4
Not ascertained whether children already went to college	.8
Family head does not have any children 18 or older (1219 cases)	55.1
Total	100.0

SECTION B: HOUSING

B1. HOW MANY ROOMS DO YOU HAVE FOR YOUR OWN FAMILY, NOT COUNTING BATHROOMS?

One	2
Two	2
Three	11
Four	17
Five	26
Six	22
Seven	12
Eight or more	7
Not ascertained	1
Total	100

B2. DO YOU (FAMILY UNIT) OWN THIS HOME, OR PAY RENT OR WHAT?

Own or is buying	65
Rent	30
Neither own nor rent	5
Total	100

	Per cent of entire sample

B3. COULD YOU TELL ME WHAT THE PRESENT VALUE OF THIS HOUSE (FARM) IS? I MEAN, ABOUT WHAT WOULD IT BRING IF YOU SOLD IT TODAY?

Less than $5000	5
$5000 - $9999	12
$10,000 - 14,999	17
$15,000 - 19,999	13
$20,000 - 24,999	7
$25,000 or more	11
Do not own (769 cases)	35
Total	100

B4. ABOUT HOW MUCH RENT DO YOU PAY A MONTH?

Less than $50	8.5
$50 - 74	18.6
$75 - 99	6.5
$100 - 149	3.4
$150 or more	1.8
Not ascertained	.7
Do not rent (1560 cases)	70.5
Total	100.0

B5. DO YOU RENT THIS PLACE FURNISHED OR UNFURNISHED?

Furnished	5.4
Unfurnished	22.5
Not ascertained	1.6
Do not rent (1560 cases)	70.5
Total	100.0

B6. HOW IS THAT (IF NEITHER OWNS NOR RENTS)?

Farm laborers	1.4
Other persons for whom housing is part of compensation (janitors, gardeners, nurses, etc.)	1.6
Persons for whom housing is a gift; housing owned by a relative	1.5
Other	.5
Own or rent (2099 cases)	95.0
Total	100.0

B7. HOW LONG HAVE YOU LIVED IN THIS HOUSE (APARTMENT)?

Less than 1 year	17.6
1 year	8.1
2 - 3 years	14.5
4 - 8 years	21.9
9 - 13 years	12.1
14 - 18 years	8.9
19 - 23 years	5.5
24 years or more	10.9
Not ascertained	.5
Total	100.0

	Per cent of entire sample

38. DO YOU THINK YOU MIGHT SOMEDAY MOVE TO ANOTHER PLACE?

Yes	52
No	47
Not ascertained	1
Total	100

39. WHY MIGHT YOU MOVE?

Involuntary reasons (company might move me, dwelling being torn down, expressway coming through, etc.)	6
Space related reasons (dwelling too big or too small, move when family gets larger, not enough storage space.)	16
Location reasons (too far from work, better wages elsewhere, changing neighborhood, too far from schools, shopping area, churches, climate is bad, too much traffic, etc.)	14
Combination of space and location related reasons	1
Want to own a home, don't like paying rent	6
Other (will move when retire, etc.)	6
Not ascertained	3
Do not plan to move (1062 cases)	48
Total	100

39. FRAME OF REFERENCE FOR MOVING (CODED FROM ABOVE QUESTION)

Mention advantages of new place or attraction to new place	19
Mention advantages of new place and disadvantages of present place	3
Mention disadvantages of present place	14
Not ascertained frame of reference	16
Do not plan to move (1062 cases)	48
Total	100

40. WHEN DO YOU THINK THAT MIGHT BE?

This year, very soon	12
1 - 2 years	8
3 - 4 years	4
5 years or more	6
When children are all gone or when I retire	1
Sometime in the future	3
Not ascertained	18
Do not plan to move (1062 cases)	48
Total	100

	Per cent of entire sample

B11. HOW IMPORTANT IS IT TO YOU TO LIVE NEAR YOUR RELATIVES (OR YOUR WIFE'S RELATIVES)?

Very important	14
Important	17
Somewhat important	5
Not very important	17
Not at all important	43
Not ascertained	4
Total	100

SECTION C: HOUSEWORK

C1, C2. WE'RE INTERESTED IN HOW PEOPLE GET THE THINGS DONE THAT HAVE TO BE DONE AROUND THE HOUSE, SUCH AS PREPARING MEALS, CLEANING, AND MAKING REPAIRS. DO YOU (AND YOUR WIFE) HAVE SOME HELP FROM OUTSIDE THE HOUSEHOLD, OR DO YOU DO ALL YOUR OWN REGULAR HOUSEWORK? FOR WHAT KIND OF HOUSEWORK DO YOU HAVE HELP?

Have help for regular housework only	10
Have help for things other than regular housework	3
Have help for regular housework and things other than regular housework	1
Do not have any help	86
Total	100

C3. ORDINARILY, HOW MANY HOURS A WEEK WOULD THAT BE?

Less than 2	2.6
2 - 4	3.3
5 - 9	3.4
10 - 19	1.2
20 - 29	.6
30 - 39	.5
40 or more	.9
Not ascertained	1.4
Do not have any help (1906 cases)	86.1
Total	100.0

C4, C5. IS ANY OF IT DONE WITHOUT PAY BY RELATIVES OR FRIENDS FROM OUTSIDE THE HOUSEHOLD? ABOUT HOW MANY HOURS A WEEK IS THAT?

Some done without pay by friends or relatives:

Less than 2	1.5
2 - 4	.7
5 - 9	.3
10 - 19	.3
20 - 29	.2
30 - 39	.1
40 or more	.3
Not ascertained how much	1.2
None done without pay	9.3
Do not have any help (1906 cases)	86.1
Total	100.0

Per cent of
entire sample

C6, C7. DO YOU PEOPLE SEND OUT ANY OF YOUR FAMILY'S LAUNDRY,
OR PAY TO HAVE ANY OF IT DONE? ABOUT HOW MUCH DOES THAT COST
EACH WEEK?

Send out laundry:

Less than $2.00 per week	13
$2.00 - 4.99 per week	12
$5.00 or more per week	4
Not ascertained how much per week	1
Do not send out laundry	70
Total	100

C9, C10. DO YOU HAVE SOMEONE ELSE FROM OUTSIDE THE HOUSEHOLD
JUST TO CARE FOR THE CHILDREN? ABOUT HOW MANY HOURS A WEEK
IS THAT?

Have someone to care for children:

Less than 2	2.1
2 - 4	2.3
5 - 9	.9
10 - 19	.7
29 - 29	.7
30 - 39	.3
40 or more	1.7
Not ascertained how many hours	.5
Do not have someone to care for children	28.0
Not ascertained	.2
Do not have children twelve or under (1385 cases)	62.6
Total	100.0

C11. WHAT ABOUT MEALS, ABOUT HOW OFTEN DO YOU (PEOPLE)
EAT AT RESTAURANTS OR DRIVE-INS?

Once a day or more frequently	6
Four or five times a week	2
Two or three times a week	8
Once a week or once every other week	26
Once a month or less	38
Never	20
Total	100

408

	Per cent of entire sample

C12, C13, C14, C15. WHAT ABOUT PAINTING, REDECORATING, OR SPRING CLEANING, DID YOU HAVE ANY OUTSIDE HELP TO DO THESE THINGS IN THE LAST YEAR? HOW MANY HOURS OF WORK DID IT TAKE? HOW MUCH DID IT COST TO HAVE IT DONE? WHAT PART OF THIS WAS LABOR COST?

Did have help doing these things:

40 hours or less	9
41 - 120 hours	2
121 - 240 hours	1
241 or more hours	1
Not ascertained how many hours	1
Did not have help doing these things	86
Total	100

C16. HOW MUCH OF THIS WORK COULD YOU (PEOPLE) HAVE DONE YOURSELVES?

All	5.0
Some	2.6
None	6.2
Not ascertained	.3
Did not have help doing painting, redecorating, or spring cleaning (1901 cases)	85.9
Total	100.0

C17. WOULD IT HAVE TAKEN YOU LONGER TO DO IT THAN THE PERSON(S) YOU HIRED?

Would have taken me longer	5.9
Would have taken me about the same time	1.3
Would have taken me less time	.2
Not ascertained	.5
Did not have help doing painting, redecorating, or spring cleaning (2039 cases)	92.1
Total	100.0

C18, C19, C20. DID YOU PAY TO HAVE SOME OF THE LAWN WORK DONE LAST YEAR? HOW MANY HOURS OF WORK WERE INVOLVED? (IF DON'T KNOW) HOW MUCH DID THIS LAWN WORK COST YOU?

Did pay to have lawn work done last year:

40 hours or less	10
41 - 120 hours	4
121 - 240 hours	1
241 or more hours	0
Not ascertained how many hours	1
Did not pay to have lawn work done last year	84
Total	100

C22. DID YOU (WIFE) DO ANY WORK FOR MONEY LAST YEAR?	Per cent of entire sample
Yes	34
No	40
No wife (574 cases)	26
Total	100

C23. WHAT DID YOU (WIFE) DO? (OCCUPATION OF WIFE)

Professional and technical workers	4.3
Managers and nonself-employed officials	.9
Self-employed businesswomen	1.4
Clerical and sales workers	11.2
Craftsmen and foremen	.5
Operatives and kindred	5.6
Unskilled laborers and service workers	8.6
Not ascertained	1.2
Wife did not work for money in 1964; or no wife (1467 cases)	66.3
Total	100.0

C24. WHAT KIND OF BUSINESS IS THAT IN?

Agriculture	1.0
Mining	.1
Manufacturing	6.5
Construction	.3
Transportation, communication, utilities	.6
Retail and wholesale trade	7.0
Finance, insurance, real estate	1.9
Services (including professional services)	8.6
Government medical, health, and educational services; all federal employees	6.8
Not ascertained	.9
Wife did not work for money in 1964; or no wife (1467 cases)	66.3
Total	100.0

C25. HOW MANY WEEKS DID YOU (WIFE) WORK LAST YEAR?

13 or less	7.1
14 - 26	4.2
27 - 39	3.9
40 - 47	3.6
48 - 49	3.3
50 - 51	7.6
52	3.3
Not ascertained	.7
Wife did not work for money in 1964; or no wife (1467 cases)	66.3
Total	100.0

C26. HOW MANY WEEKS WERE THERE LAST YEAR WHEN YOU (WIFE) WERE UNABLE TO WORK BECAUSE OF ILLNESS OR UNEMPLOYMENT?

	Per cent of entire sample
None	25.2
One	.8
Two	1.0
Three	.3
Four	.7
Five or more	3.9
Not ascertained	1.8
Wife did not work for money in 1964; or no wife (1467 cases)	66.3
Total	100.0

C29. HOW MANY HOURS A WEEK DID YOU (WIFE) WORK (WHEN WORKING)?

1 - 19	4.4
20 - 34	5.1
35 - 40	16.1
41 - 48	4.4
49 - 59	1.2
60 or more	1.1
Not ascertained	1.4
Wife did not work for money in 1964; or no wife (1467 cases)	66.3
Total	100.0

C30. HOW MUCH TIME DOES IT TAKE YOU (WIFE) TO GET TO WORK AND BACK EACH DAY?

None (work where lives)	2.9
One-quarter of an hour	11.9
One-half hour	5.8
Three-quarters of an hour	3.9
One hour	5.2
One and one-half hours	1.5
Two or more hours	1.4
Not ascertained	1.1
Wife did not work for money in 1964; or no wife (1467 cases)	66.3
Total	100.0

Questions C31 through C56 are for women, both wives and female heads.

C31. WE'D LIKE TO KNOW ABOUT HOW MUCH OF YOUR TIME IS SPENT ON WORK AROUND THE HOUSE, SUCH AS PREPARING MEALS, CLEANING, AND STRAIGHTENING UP. ON THE AVERAGE ABOUT HOW MUCH OF YOUR TIME IS SPENT WORKING AROUND THE HOUSE? (HOURS PER YEAR)

See Chapter 8 for distributions of this variable.

	Per cent of entire sample

C32, C34, C35. DID YOU DO ANY PAINTING, REDECORATING, OR MAJOR HOUSECLEANING IN THE LAST YEAR? ALTOGETHER DID THIS TAKE YOU MORE THAN 40 HOURS LAST YEAR? ABOUT HOW MANY HOURS DID IT TAKE YOU?

Did painting, redecorating, or major housecleaning:

40 hours or less	26
41 - 120 hours	14
121 - 240 hours	2
241 or more hours	1
Not ascertained how many hours	1
Did no painting, redecorating, or major housecleaning	48
Single male family head (183 cases)	8
Total	100

C33. WHAT DID YOU DO?

Painting and redecorating, including repairs	28.9
Major housecleaning	14.1
Other things	1.2
Did no painting, redecorating, or major housecleaning; single male family head (1238 cases)	55.8
Total	100.0

C36, C37, C38. WHAT ABOUT SEWING OR MENDING -- DID YOU DO ANY OF THAT IN THE LAST YEAR? ALTOGETHER, DID THIS TAKE YOU MORE THAN 40 HOURS LAST YEAR? ABOUT HOW MANY HOURS DID IT TAKE YOU?

Did sewing and mending:

40 hours or less	45
41 - 120 hours	18
121 - 240 hours	4
241 or more hours	4
Not ascertained how many hours	1
Did not do sewing and mending	20
Single male family head (183 cases)	8
Total	100

C39, C40, C41. DID YOU GROW ANY OF YOUR OWN FOOD LAST YEAR? ALTOGETHER, DID THIS TAKE YOU MORE THAN 40 HOURS LAST YEAR? ABOUT HOW MANY HOURS DID IT TAKE YOU?

Did grow own food:

40 hours or less	15
41 - 120 hours	6
121 - 240 hours	1
241 or more hours	1
Not ascertained how many hours	0
Did not grow own food	69
Single male family head (183 cases)	8
Total	100

412

Per cent of
entire sample

C42, C43, C44. DID YOU DO ANY CANNING OR FREEZING
LAST YEAR? ALTOGETHER, DID THIS TAKE YOU MORE THAN 40
HOURS LAST YEAR? ABOUT HOW MANY HOURS DID IT TAKE YOU?

Did canning or freezing:

40 hours or less	24
41 - 120 hours	8
121 - 240 hours	1
241 or more hours	0
Not ascertained how many hours	1
Did no canning or freezing	58
Single male family head (183 cases)	8
Total	100

C45, C48, C49. DID YOU DO ANYTHING ELSE THAT SAVED YOU
(OR YOUR FAMILY) FROM HAVING TO HIRE SOMEONE ELSE TO DO IT?
ALTOGETHER, DID THIS TAKE YOU MORE THAN 40 HOURS LAST YEAR?
ABOUT HOW MANY HOURS DID THIS TAKE YOU?

Did something else that saved money:

40 hours or less	6
41 - 120 hours	4
121 - 240 hours	1
241 or more hours	2
Not ascertained how many hours	0
Did nothing else that saved money	79
Single male family head (183 cases)	8
Total	100

C46, C47. WHAT DID YOU DO? ANYTHING ELSE?

Repairs to things (cars, appliances, furniture, etc.)	2.5
Built things (furniture, trailer, boat, etc.)	0.2
Services (home haircuts, lawn work, etc.)	8.3
Other	2.0
Did nothing else that saved money; or single male family head (1924 cases)	87.0
Total	100.0

C50, C52, C53. DID YOU DO ANY VOLUNTEER WORK WITHOUT PAY SUCH
AS WORK FOR CHURCH OR CHARITY, OR HELPING RELATIVES? ALTOGETHER
DID THIS TAKE YOU MORE THAN 40 HOURS LAST YEAR?

Did volunteer work:

40 hours or less	23
41 - 120 hours	12
121 - 240 hours	6
241 or more hours	5
Not ascertained how many hours	1
Did no volunteer work	45
Single male family head (183 cases)	8
Total	100

C51. WHAT DID YOU DO? (ORGANIZATION OR INDIVIDUALS)

Per cent of
entire sample

Did volunteer work for:

Church or charitable organizations	33.5
Other organizations (political parties, Chamber of Commerce, etc.)	5.9
Relatives	13.0
Other individuals	4.1
Did no volunteer work; or single male family head (1193 cases)	53.9
Total	*

C55. WHEN WERE YOU MARRIED?

1964	2
1963	2
1961 - 1962	5
1955 - 1960	12
1950 - 1954	9
1945 - 1949	11
1940 - 1944	10
1939 or earlier	23
Single family head (574 cases)	26
Total	100

C56. HAVE YOU AND YOUR (HUSBAND, WIFE) USED ANY METHOD TO LIMIT THE NUMBER OR PLAN THE SPACING OF YOUR CHILDREN?

Yes	30
No	41
Not ascertained	3
Not married (574 cases)	26
Total	100

Questions C60 through C81 are for men, both single and married.

C60. NOW ABOUT YOUR WORK AROUND THE HOUSE, DO YOU DO ANY REGULAR THINGS SUCH AS DOING DISHES, CLEANING, AND STRAIGHTENING UP? ON THE AVERAGE HOW MUCH OF YOUR TIME DO YOU SPEND ON THESE THINGS?

See Chapter 8 for distributions of this variable.

---

*Adds to more than 100 per cent because some respondents mentioned more than one thing.

C62, C64, C65. DID YOU DO ANY PAINTING, REDECORATING,
OR MAJOR HOUSECLEANING IN THE LAST YEAR? ALTOGETHER DID THIS
TAKE YOU MORE THAN 40 HOURS LAST YEAR? ABOUT HOW MANY
HOURS DID IT TAKE YOU?

Per cent of entire sample

Did painting, redecorating, or major housecleaning:

40 hours or less	22
41 - 120 hours	14
121 - 240 hours	4
241 or more hours	3
Not ascertained how many hours	1
Did no painting, redecorating, or major housecleaning	38
Single female family head (391 cases)	18
Total	100

C63. WHAT DID YOU DO?

Painting and redecorating, including repairs	40.7
Major housecleaning	2.3
Other things	.8
Did no painting, redecorating, or major housecleaning; single female family head (1245 cases)	56.2
Total	100.0

C66, C67, C68. DID YOU GROW ANY OF YOUR OWN FOOD LAST YEAR?
ALTOGETHER DID THIS TAKE YOU MORE THAN 40 HOURS LAST YEAR?
ABOUT HOW MANY HOURS DID IT TAKE YOU?

Did grow own food:

40 hours or less	12
41 - 120 hours	7
121 - 240 hours	1
241 or more hours	1
Not ascertained how many hours	1
Did not grow own food	60
Single female family head (391 cases)	18
Total	100

C69, C70, C71. DID YOU DO ANY CANNING OR FREEZING LAST YEAR?
ALTOGETHER DID THIS TAKE YOU MORE THAN 40 HOURS LAST YEAR?
ABOUT HOW MANY HOURS DID IT TAKE YOU?

Did canning or freezing:

40 hours or less	8
41 - 120 hours	1
121 - 240 hours	0
241 or more hours	0
Did no canning or freezing	73
Single female family head (391 cases)	18
Total	100

Per cent of
entire sample

C72, C75, C76. DID YOU DO ANYTHING ELSE LAST YEAR THAT
SAVED YOU FROM HAVING TO HIRE SOMEONE ELSE TO DO IT IN THE
LAST YEAR? ALTOGETHER DID THIS TAKE YOU MORE THAN 40 HOURS
LAST YEAR? ABOUT HOW MANY HOURS DID IT TAKE YOU?

Did something else that saved money:

40 hours or less	16
41 - 120 hours	10
121 - 240 hours	2
241 or more hours	2
Did nothing else that saved money	52
Single female family head (391 cases)	18
Total	100

C73, C74. WHAT DID YOU DO? ANYTHING ELSE?

Repairs to things (cars, appliances, furniture, etc.)	15.9
Built things (furniture, trailer, boat, etc.)	2.4
Services (home haircuts, lawn work, etc.)	15.4
Other	1.7
Did nothing else that saved money; or single female family head (1567 cases)	70.8
Total	*

C77, C80, C81. DID YOU DO ANY VOLUNTEER WORK WITHOUT PAY SUCH
AS WORK FOR CHURCH OR CHARITY, OR HELPING RELATIVES IN THE LAST
YEAR: ALTOGETHER, DID THIS TAKE YOU MORE THAN 40 HOURS LAST YEAR?
ABOUT HOW MANY HOURS DID IT TAKE YOU?

Did volunteer work:

40 hours or less	16
41 - 120 hours	9
121 - 240 hours	4
241 or more hours	3
Not ascertained how many hours	1
Did no volunteer work	49
Single female family head (391 cases)	18
Total	100

C78, C79. WHAT DID YOU DO? ANYTHING ELSE? (ORGANIZATION OR
INDIVIDUALS)

Did volunteer work for:

Church or charitable organizations	19.5
Other organizations (political parties, Chamber of Commerce, etc.)	5.8
Relatives	9.2
Other individuals	3.7
Did no volunteer work; or single female family head (1474 cases)	66.6
Total	*

---

*
  Adds to more than 100 per cent because some respondents mentioned
more than one thing.

Per cent of entire sample

C83, C84. DOES ANYONE ELSE (OTHER THAN HEAD OR WIFE) IN THE FAMILY LIVING HERE HELP WITH ANY OF THE WORK AROUND THE HOUSE? WHO IS IT?

Others help around the house:

Children 17 or younger	20
Children 18 or older	6
Children, but age not ascertained	2
Other adults	5
Combination of above	2
No others help around the house	18
Not ascertained	6
No others in family unit (896 cases)	41
Total	100

C85. IN AN ORDINARY WEEK, ABOUT HOW MANY HOURS DOES HE (SHE, THEY) SPEND DOING THESE THINGS?

Less than 2	2.4
2 - 3	7.6
5 - 9	9.5
10 - 19	8.1
20 - 29	3.7
30 - 39	1.5
40 or more	1.6
Not ascertained	1.4
No others in family helped around the house; or no others in family (1421 cases)	64.2
Total	100.0

C86, C87. THINKING OF THE THINGS YOU (PEOPLE) NOW DO AROUND THE HOUSE, WOULD IT BE EASY OR DIFFICULT TO FIND SOMEONE TO DO THESE THINGS FOR YOU? HAVE YOU THOUGHT OF HIRING SOMEONE TO DO SOME OF THESE THINGS FOR YOU?

Easy to hire someone:

Have thought of hiring someone	9
Have not thought of hiring someone	26
Not ascertained whether thought of hiring someone	1
Difficult to hire someone	53
Don't know whether easy or difficult	10
Not ascertained	1
Total	100

417

	Per cent of entire sample

C88, C90, C91. DID YOU ATTEND ANY COURSES OR TAKE
LESSONS OF ANY KIND IN THE LAST YEAR? ALTOGETHER DID THIS
TAKE YOU MORE THAN 40 HOURS LAST YEAR? ABOUT HOW MANY HOURS
DID IT TAKE ALTOGETHER?

Did attend courses or take lessons:

40 hours or less	6
41 - 120 hours	5
121 - 240 hours	2
241 or more hours	4
Did not attend courses or take lessons	83
Total	100

C89. WHAT DID YOU DO?

Type of course:

Something that increased head's economic skills	11.6
No evidence that course increased economic skills	4.7
Not ascertained	.2
Did not take any courses or lessons (1848 cases)	83.5
Total	100.0

C92. WHAT HOBBIES, GAMES, OR SPORTS DO YOU TAKE PART IN?

Sports or other athletic events	34
Games and nonathletic events	3
Hobbies and spectator sports	17
Combination of two or more	18
Do not take part in any hobbies, games, or sports	28
Total	100

C93. WHAT DO YOU ENJOY ABOUT THEM?

Enjoy hobbies for the following reasons:

Getting better at them	3
Winning or competing	6
Sociability reasons	11
Fun, excitement, thrills	19
Relaxation, good for my health	34
Being creative	5
Keep me busy, wouldn't know what to do with my time otherwise	3
Other	7
Not ascertained	6
Does not take part in any hobbies, games, or sports	28
Total	*

*Adds to more than 100 per cent because some respondents mentioned
more than one thing.

C94. HOW IMPORTANT IS IT TO YOU TO KEEP GETTING BETTER AT IT (THEM)?

	Per cent of entire sample
Very important	12
Important	12
Somewhat important	2
Not very important	11
Not at all important	22
Takes part only as a spectator	13
Do not take part in any hobbies, games, or sports	28
Total	100

C95. DO YOU (PEOPLE) HAVE AN AUTOMATIC WASHER?

Yes, including located in apartment building in which respondent lives	53
No	47
Total	100

C96. DO YOU (PEOPLE) HAVE AN AUTOMATIC CLOTHES DRYER?

Yes, including located in apartment building in which respondent lives	31
No	69
Total	100

C97. DO YOU (PEOPLE) HAVE AN AUTOMATIC DISHWASHER?

Yes	10
No	90
Total	100

NUMBER OF APPLIANCES FAMILY HAS (AUTOMATIC WASHER, CLOTHES DRYER, DISHWASHER)

None	43
One	27
Two	23
Three	7
Total	100

C98. DO YOU USE EACH OF THE FOLLOWING PRODUCTS OFTEN, SOMETIMES, OR NOT AT ALL?

(1) FREQUENCY OF USE OF INSTANT COFFEE

Often	39
Sometimes	27
Not at all	34
Total	100

C98 CONTINUED

Per cent of
entire sample

(2) FREQUENCY OF USE OF STEAM IRON

Often	59
Sometimes	14
Not at all	27
Total	100

(3) FREQUENCY OF USE OF ELECTRIC FRYING PAN

Often	28
Sometimes	19
Not at all	53
Total	100

(4) FREQUENCY OF USE OF GASOLINE CREDIT CARD

Often	22
Sometimes	7
Never	71
Total	100

C99, C100. HAVE YOU HEARD ABOUT THE NEW COIN-OPERATED
DRY-CLEANING MACHINE? DO YOU (PEOPLE) EVER USE ONE?

Have heard about dry-cleaning machine:

Have used one	37
Have not used one	49
Have not heard about dry-cleaning machine	14
Total	100

C101, C102. HAVE YOU HEARD ABOUT ADDING FLUORIDE TO THE
WATER TO REDUCE TOOTH DECAY AND CAVITIES? WHAT DO YOU
THINK OF THE IDEA?

Have heard about adding fluoride to water:

Unqualified approval of idea	39
Qualified approval or disapproval	14
Unqualified disapproval of idea	12
Does not know what to think of idea	15
Have not heard about adding fluoride to water	20
Total	100

C103. HAVE (ANY OF) YOU HAD POLIO VACCINE, EITHER THE SHOTS
OR ANY OTHER WAY?

Yes	72
No	28
Total	100

420

	Per cent of entire sample

C104, C105. WHAT DO YOU THINK OF THE PROGRAM OUR
COUNTRY HAS TO TRY TO LAND A MAN ON THE MOON? WHY IS THAT?

Good	31
Good, qualified	9
Depends	7
Bad, qualified	4
Bad	41
Don't know	8
Total	100

C104, C105. ATTITUDE TOWARD MAN ON MOON PROJECT

Reasons why good:

Scientific value	12
Military or political value	14
Exciting, adventurous, thrilling	3
Other	14

Reasons why bad:

Should spend money on other scientific endeavors	3
Should spend money for humanitarian purposes (schools, better housing, recreation)	11
Too much money being spent on project	17
Anti-science reasons (God put man on earth, etc.)	27
Other	3
Don't know enough about it, don't take any interest in that sort of thing	18
Total	*

C106. ARE THERE SOME THINGS YOU (PEOPLE) WOULD LIKE TO BUY
OR REPLACE OR DO YOU (PEOPLE) HAVE MOST OF THE THINGS YOU WANT?

Things we would like to buy or replace	57
Have most things we want	43
Total	100

*Adds to more than 100 per cent because some respondents mentioned more than one thing.

	Per cent of entire sample
C107. WHAT THINGS DO YOU HAVE IN MIND?	
House	6
Additions or repairs to present home	8
Car	14
Appliances	25
Furniture	26
Furnishings for the home (curtains, lamps, rugs, etc.)	7
Hobby items	2
"Everything", want a higher standard of living	2
Other	4
Have most things we want (953 cases)	43
Total	*

C108. WOULD YOU SAY YOU TRY NEW PRODUCTS WHEN THEY FIRST COME OUT, OR DO YOU WAIT UNTIL OTHERS HAVE TRIED THEM FIRST, OR WHAT?

Try things when first come out	36
Depends	16
Wait until others have tried things first	44
Not ascertained	4
Total	100

C109. SOME PEOPLE SAY THAT MOST NEW THINGS ARE JUST A WAY TO GET US TO SPEND MORE MONEY, OTHERS FEEL THAT MOST NEW THINGS ARE REALLY IMPROVEMENTS. HOW DO YOU FEEL?

Most new things are improvements	56
Some new things are improvements, some are a way to get us to spend money	27
Most new things are a way to get us to spend money	12
Not ascertained	5
Total	100

SECTION D: CARS

D1. NOW WE WOULD LIKE TO TALK ABOUT CARS. DO YOU, (YOUR WIFE) OR ANYONE ELSE IN THE FAMILY HERE OWN A CAR?

Own car	78
Do not own car	22
Total	100

D2. HOW MANY CARS DO YOU AND YOUR FAMILY LIVING HERE OWN? * *

None	22
One	54
Two	22
Three or more	2
Total	100

* *For further information on car ownership (Questions D3-D25 of questionnaire) see the 1965 Survey of Consumer Finances (Ann Arbor: Survey Research Center, The University of Michigan, 1966).

*Adds to more than 100 per cent because some respondents mentioned more than one thing.

Some questions are omitted in this section because they were used for another study.

Per cent of
entire sample

D8. DID YOU BUY THIS CAR NEW OR USED?

New	38
Used	40
Do not own a car (478 cases)	22
Total	100

D26, D27. DOES THE CAR YOU DRIVE HAVE SEAT BELTS? DO YOU HAVE THEM FASTENED ALL THE TIME WHILE YOU ARE DRIVING, PART OF THE TIME, OR PRACTICALLY NONE OF THE TIME?

Car has seat belts and they are fastened:

All the time	8
Part of the time	12
Practically none of the time	6
Car does not have seat belts	52
Do not own a car (478 cases)	22
Total	100

SECTION E: FAMILY HISTORY

E1. NOW I HAVE SOME QUESTIONS ABOUT YOUR FAMILY AND PAST EXPERIENCES. WHERE DID YOUR FATHER AND MOTHER GROW UP?

Region where father grew up:

Northeast	14
North Central	26
Deep South	9
Other South	26
West	4
English-speaking foreign country	4
Non-English-speaking foreign country	16
Not ascertained	1
Total	100

Region where mother grew up:

Northeast	15
North Central	26
Deep South	9
Other South	26
West	5
English-speaking foreign country	4
Non-English-speaking foreign country	14
Not ascertained	1
Total	100

	Per cent of entire sample

E2, E3, E4, E5. HOW MANY GRADES OF SCHOOL DID YOUR FATHER FINISH? COULD HE READ AND WRITE? DID HE GO TO COLLEGE? DID HE GET A COLLEGE DEGREE?

0 - 5 grades; or could not read and write	16
6 - 8 grades; or could read and write	60
9 - 11 grades	5
12 grades	9
12 grades and nonacademic training	0
College, no degree	3
College, Bachelor's degree	4
College, advanced or professional degree	1
Not ascertained	2
Total	100

E7. NOW ABOUT YOUR WIFE, WHERE DID SHE GROW UP?

Region where wife grew up:

Northeast	16
North Central	24
Deep South	5
Other South	18
West	7
English-speaking foreign country	1
Non-English-speaking foreign country	3
No wife (574 cases)	26
Total	100

E8. HOW MANY BROTHERS AND SISTERS DID SHE HAVE? (WIFE)

None	5
One	11
Two	11
Three	10
Four	8
Five	7
Six	5
Seven	5
Eight or more	11
No wife (574 cases)	26
Total	100

E9, E10, E11, E12. HOW MANY GRADES OF SCHOOL DID SHE FINISH? DID SHE HAVE ANY OTHER SCHOOLING? WHAT OTHER SCHOOLING DID SHE HAVE? DID SHE GET A COLLEGE DEGREE?

0 - 5 grades	3
6 - 8 grades	12
9 - 11 grades	17
12 grades	21
12 grades and nonacademic training	8
College, no degree	8
College, Bachelor's degree	5
College, advanced or professional degree	0
No wife (574 cases)	26
Total	100

E13. WHAT COLLEGE WAS IT?

Per cent of entire sample

College rated on basis of its selectivity:*

Very highly selective	.6
Highly selective	.9
Selective	1.0
Nonselective but accredited	2.5
Clearly inferior (nonaccredited)	.2
Wife did not get a college degree; or no wife (2098 cases)	94.8
Total	100.0

E14. WHERE DID YOU (HEAD) GROW UP?

Region where head grew up:

Northeast	21
North Central	30
Deep South	8
Other South	26
West	9
English-speaking foreign country	1
Non-English-speaking foreign country	5
Total	100

E15. WAS THAT ON A FARM, OR IN A CITY, OR WHAT?

Farm	40
City	58
Many different places	2
Total	100

E16. HOW MANY BROTHERS AND SISTERS DID YOU HAVE?

None	7
One	14
Two	15
Three	13
Four	10
Five	10
Six	8
Seven	6
Eight or more	16
Not ascertained	1
Total	100

*The measure of selectivity was derived from James Cass and Max Birnbaum, Comparative Guide to American Colleges (New York: Harper and Row, 1964), with additional advice from Professor Benno Fricke of The University of Michigan.

	Per cent of entire sample
E17. HOW MANY WERE OLDER THAN YOU?	
None	23
One	22
Two	17
Three	10
Four	6
Five	5
Six	3
Seven	2
Eight or more	4
Did not have any brothers or sisters	7
Not ascertained	1
Total	100

E18, E19, E20, E21. HOW MANY GRADES OF SCHOOL DID YOU FINISH? HAVE YOU HAD ANY OTHER SCHOOLING? WHAT OTHER SCHOOLING HAVE YOU HAD? DID YOU GET A COLLEGE DEGREE?

0 - 5 grades	8
6 - 8 grades	22
9 - 11 grades	19
12 grades	15
12 grades and nonacademic training	12
College, no degree	12
College, Bachelor's degree	9
College, advanced or professional degree	3
Total	100

E22. WHAT COLLEGE WAS IT?

College rated on basis of selectivity:*

Very highly selective	1.3
Highly selective	2.8
Selective	2.5
Nonselective but accredited	4.4
Clearly inferior (nonaccredited)	.6
Not ascertained	.7
Did not get a college degree (1942 cases)	87.7
Total	100.0

*The measure of selectivity was derived from James Cass and Max Birnbaum, Comparative Guide to American Colleges (New York: Harper and Row, 1964).

426

	Per cent of entire sample

E23. THINKING OF YOUR FIRST FULL-TIME REGULAR JOB, WHAT DID YOU DO?

Professional and technical workers	10
Managers and nonself-employed officials	1
Self-employed businessmen	1
Clerical and sales workers	16
Craftsmen and foremen	8
Operatives and kindred	17
Unskilled laborers and service workers	24
Farmers	8
Government protective workers, members of the armed forces	2
Not ascertained	10
Never worked (61 cases)	3
Total	100

E24. HAVE YOU HAD A NUMBER OF DIFFERENT KINDS OF JOBS, OR HAVE YOU MOSTLY WORKED IN THE SAME OCCUPATION YOU STARTED IN, OR WHAT?

Have had a number of different kinds of jobs	35
Have had a number of different kinds of jobs, but mostly the same occupation	14
Mostly the same occupation	47
Not ascertained	1
Never worked (61 cases)	3
Total	100

E25, E26. SINCE YOUR FIRST REGULAR JOB, WHAT STATES OR COUNTRIES HAVE YOU LIVED IN (EXCLUDING WHEN IN MILITARY SERVICE)? SINCE YOUR FIRST REGULAR JOB, HAVE YOU EVER LIVED MORE THAN 100 MILES FROM HERE?

Region first mentioned by family head:

Northeast	22
North Central	30
Deep South	8
Other South	21
West	12
English-speaking foreign country	1
Non-English-speaking foreign country	2
Not ascertained	1
Never worked (61 cases)	3
Total	100

25, E26. CONTINUED:

umber of above regions family head has lived in:

ne	68
wo	21
hree	4
our or more	2
ot ascertained	2
ever worked (61 cases)	3
otal	100

umber of states family head has lived in:

ne but less than 100 miles from where lives now	49
ne but more than 100 miles from where lives now	8
wo	23
hree	8
our or more	7
ot ascertained	2
ever worked (61 cases)	3
otal	100

27, E28. HAVE YOU EVER BEEN OUT OF A JOB OR ON STRIKE
OR TWO MONTHS OR MORE AT ONE TIME? WHEN WAS THE LAST TIME
HAT HAPPENED?

ave been out of job or on strike:

963 - 1965	6
960 - 1962	3
955 - 1959	4
945 - 1954	4
944 or earlier	5
ot ascertained when	1
ave never been out of job or on strike	73
ot ascertained	1
ever worked (61 cases)	3
otal	100

29, E30. HAVE YOU EVER HAD A MAJOR ILLNESS THAT LAID YOU UP
OR A MONTH OR MORE? WHEN WAS THAT?

ave had major illness:

963 - 1965	9
960 - 1962	7
955 - 1959	6
945 - 1954	6
944 or earlier	5
ot ascertained when	1
ave not had major illness	62
ot ascertained	1
ever worked (61 cases)	3
otal	100

SECTION F: OCCUPATION

F1. NOW, WE WOULD LIKE TO ASK YOU ABOUT YOUR PRESENT JOB.
ARE YOU WORKING NOW, UNEMPLOYED, RETIRED, OR WHAT?

Working now	74
Unemployed or laid off; disabled, not working	4
Retired	14
Student	2
Housewife	6
Total	100

F2. WHAT IS YOUR MAIN OCCUPATION?

Professional and technical workers	10
Managers and nonself-employed officials	6
Self-employed businessmen and artisans	7
Clerical and sales workers	10
Craftsmen and foremen	14
Operatives and kindred	12
Unskilled laborers and service workers	8
Farmers and farm managers	4
Miscellaneous	3
Not in labor force (575 cases)	26
Total	100

F3. WHAT KIND OF BUSINESS IS THAT IN?

Agriculture, forestry and fishing	7
Mining and extracting	1
Manufacturing	19
Construction	6
Transportation, communications, and utilities	5
Retail and wholesale trade	12
Finance, insurance, and real estate	2
Services (including professional services)	10
Government medical, health, and educational services, all federal employees	10
Not ascertained	2
Not in labor force (575 cases)	26
Total	100

F4. DO YOU WORK FOR YOURSELF, OR SOMEONE ELSE, OR WHAT?

Self	13
Someone else	61
Both self and someone else	0
Not in labor force (575 cases)	26
Total	100

Per cent of
entire sample

5. DO YOU SOMETIMES HAVE OVERTIME WORK, OR
HORT WORK WEEKS?

es	47
o	25
ot ascertained	2
ot in labor force (575 cases)	26
otal	100

6. HOW MANY WEEKS OF VACATION DID YOU TAKE LAST YEAR?

one	23
ne	9
wo	21
hree	12
our	5
ive or more	3
ot ascertained	1
ot in labor force (575 cases)	26
otal	100

7. HOW MANY WEEKS WERE THERE LAST YEAR WHEN YOU WEREN'T
ORKING BECAUSE OF ILLNESS OR UNEMPLOYMENT?

one	55
ne	3
wo	3
hree	2
our	2
ive or more	8
ot ascertained	1
ot in labor force (575 cases)	26
otal	100

8. THEN, HOW MANY WEEKS DID YOU ACTUALLY WORK LAST YEAR?

3 or less	0
4 - 26	1
7 - 39	4
0 - 47	11
8 - 49	19
0 - 51	26
2	13
ot in labor force (575 cases)	26
otal	100

Per cent of
entire sampl

F9. ON THE AVERAGE, ABOUT HOW MANY HOURS A WEEK
DID YOU WORK WHEN YOU WERE WORKING?

1 - 19	1
20 - 34	3
35 - 40	31
41 - 48	15
49 - 59	13
60 or more hours	10
Not ascertained	1
Not in labor force (575 cases)	26
Total	100

F10. HOW MUCH TIME DO YOU SPEND GETTING TO WORK AND HOME
AGAIN EACH DAY?

None (work where I live)	7
1 - 22 minutes	18
23 - 38 minutes	14
39 - 52 minutes	9
53 - 75 minutes	14
76 - 119 minutes	4
120 or more minutes	6
Not ascertained	2
Not in labor force (575 cases)	26
Total	100

F11. DO YOU HAVE A SECOND JOB, OR DO YOU DO ANY WORK FOR
PAY IN ADDITION TO YOUR MAIN JOB?

Yes	11
No	63
Not in labor force (575 cases)	26
Total	100

F12. ON THIS JOB, DO YOU WORK FOR YOURSELF, OR SOMEONE
ELSE, OR WHAT?

Self	4.0
Someone else	7.1
Both self and someone else	.2
Does not have second job, or not in labor force (1964 cases)	88.7
Total	100.0

F13, F14. HOW MUCH TIME DID YOU SPEND ON THAT JOB LAST YEAR?
HOW MANY HOURS A WEEK IS THAT?

Information not separated from total hours that family head
worked for money. Not coded separately.

Per cent of
entire sample

15. SOME PEOPLE WOULD LIKE TO WORK MORE HOURS A
EK IF THEY COULD BE PAID FOR IT. OTHERS WOULD PREFER TO
)RK FEWER HOURS A WEEK EVEN IF THEY EARNED LESS. HOW DO YOU
EL ABOUT THIS?

)uld strongly prefer more work and more pay	4
)uld prefer more work and more pay	22
itisfied with present situation	27
)uld prefer less work and less pay	10
)uld strongly prefer less work and less pay	0
)t ascertained	11
)t in labor force (575 cases)	26
)tal	100

6. WHAT WOULD YOU SAY ARE YOUR CHANCES FOR PROMOTION OR
TTING AHEAD IN THE KIND OF WORK YOU ARE DOING NOW?

cellent	7
od	16
pends	2
ir	11
or	25
ready at the top; own the business	6
an to retire soon	1
t ascertained	6
t in labor force (575 cases)	26
tal	100

7, F18. DOES GETTING AHEAD IN YOUR LINE OF WORK DEPEND ON
E AND EXPERIENCE, OR ON HARD WORK, OR WHAT? (IF MENTIONS
VERAL THINGS) WHICH DO YOU THINK IS MOST IMPORTANT?

king on tough tasks, aggressiveness, taking initiative, enterprising	1
rd work and persistence	18
ucation, ability, intelligence, or knowledge about job	9
e, seniority, or experience	32
rsonality (no mention of above factors)	1
cial status, race, or religion	0
ck, help from friends, or "being in the right place at the right time"	3
her things	2
t ascertained	8
t in labor force (575 cases)	26
tal	100

F19. HOW MUCH EDUCATION DOES YOUR JOB REQUIRE?

None,"anyone can do it"	16
Vocational or on the job training only	4
1 - 8 grades of schooling	6
Some high school (9 - 12 grades)	21
Business school or more than high school but not college	3
Some college	10
Advanced or professional college degree	3
Not ascertained	11
Not in labor force (575 cases)	26
Total	100

F20. OF COURSE THE FUTURE IS UNCERTAIN, BUT HOW MUCH
WOULD YOU LIKE TO BE MAKING FIVE YEARS FROM NOW?

$3000 more than making now	30
$1000 - 2999 more than making now	17
$1 - 999 more than making now	5
Same or less than making now; or plan to retire shortly	10
Not ascertained	12
Not in labor force (575 cases)	26
Total	100

F21. IF YOU WERE EXTREMELY SUCCESSFUL, WHAT IS THE LARGEST
AMOUNT YOU MIGHT BE MAKING FIVE YEARS FROM NOW?

Largest amount possible is greater than the amount would like in 5 years by $1000 or more	20
Largest amount possible is greater than the amount would like in 5 years by $1 - 999	3
Largest amount possible in 5 years and amount would like in 5 years are the same	18
Largest amount possible is smaller than the amount would like in 5 years by $1 - 999	2
Largest amount possible is smaller than the amount would like in 5 years by $1000 or more	9
Will retire shortly	4
Not ascertained	18
Not in labor force (575 cases)	26
Total	100

F22 is only a contingency check box for the interviewer.
Questions F23-F25 are for those who are self employed and in
the labor force.

F23. DO YOU LIKE TO KEEP THINGS RUNNING SMOOTHLY OR ARE YOU
MORE INTERESTED IN TRYING NEW THINGS IN YOUR WORK?

Like to keep things running smoothly	7.1
Like to keep things running smoothly and try new things	2.6
Like to try new things	2.1
Not ascertained	1.5
Not self-employed; or not in the labor force (1920 cases)	86.7
Total	100.0

433

	Per cent of entire sample

24. HAVE YOU EVER THOUGHT OF CHANGING TO ANOTHER
JOB OR ANOTHER TYPE OF WORK?

...es	3.0
...o	10.1
...t ascertained	.2
...t self-employed; or not in the labor force (1920 cases)	86.7
...tal	100.0

25. WHY IS THAT (REASON FOR JOB CHANGE)?

...hievement reasons (make better use of my skills, make a success of myself, find something more challenging)	.3
...onomic incentives	.6
...her incentives	.5
...her attractions to another job	.2
...onomic disincentives of present job	.5
...her disincentives of present job	.5
...t ascertained	.4
...ver thought of changing to another job; not self-employed; not in the labor force (1920 cases)	97.0
...tal	100.0

...estions F26 - F30 are for those who are nonself-employed.

26. IS YOUR PRESENT JOB RATHER ROUTINE, OR ARE THERE CHANGES
YOU HAVE TO MAKE AND NEW PROBLEMS YOU HAVE TO SOLVE FREQUENTLY?

...utine	23
...th routine and changes to be made and problems solved	4
...anges to be made and problems solved	32
...t ascertained	2
...lf employed; or not in labor force (869 cases)	39
...tal	100

27. HOW IMPORTANT IS IT TO YOU TO HAVE SOME CHANCE TO MAKE
CHANGES IN YOUR WORK?

...ry important	17
...portant	14
...mewhat important	1
...t very important	6
...t at all important	14
...t ascertained including "like to make changes on job"	9
...lf-employed; or not in labor force (869 cases)	39
...tal	100

F28. HAVE YOU EVER THOUGHT OF CHANGING TO ANOTHER JOB
OR ANOTHER TYPE OF WORK?

Yes	23
No	37
Not ascertained	1
Self-employed; or not in labor force (869 cases)	39
Total	100

F29. WHY IS THAT (REASON FOR JOB CHANGE)?

Achievement reasons (make better use of my skills, make a success of myself, find something more challenging)	4.5
Economic incentives	7.3
Other incentives (something more interesting, something I would like more)	1.9
Other attractions to another job	1.4
No chance for promotion on present occupation	.6
Economic disincentives of present job	.6
Other disincentives of present job	4.0
Not ascertained	2.9
Never thought of changing to another job; not nonself-employed; not in labor force (1700 cases)	76.8
Total	100.0

F30. HAVE YOU EVER TRIED GOING INTO BUSINESS FOR YOURSELF?

Yes	11
No	48
Not ascertained	2
Not nonself-employed; not in labor force (869 cases)	39
Total	100

F31. WHAT KIND OF WORK DO YOU DO WHEN YOU WORK? (FOR THOSE
UNEMPLOYED AT THE TIME OF INTERVIEW)

Professional and technical workers	.2
Managers and nonself-employed officials	.0
Self-employed businessmen and artisans	.1
Clerical and sales workers	.4
Craftsmen and foremen	1.0
Operatives and kindred	1.1
Unskilled laborers and service workers	1.0
Farmers and farm managers	.1
Miscellaneous	.3
Not unemployed (2120 cases)	95.8
Total	100.0

	Per cent of entire sample
32. WHAT KIND OF BUSINESS IS THAT IN?	
griculture, forestry, and fishing	.5
ining and extracting	.1
anufacturing	1.0
onstruction	1.0
ransportation, communications, and utilities	.1
etail and wholesale trade	.6
inance, insurance, and real estate	.1
ervices (including professional services)	.5
overnment medical, health, and educational services; all federal employees	.1
ot ascertained	.2
ot unemployed (2120 cases)	95.8
otal	100.0

33. DID YOU WORK AT ALL LAST YEAR? (FOR THOSE UNEMPLOYED T THE TIME OF THE INTERVIEW)	
es	3.3
o	.9
ot unemployed at the time of the interview (2120 cases)	95.8
otal	100.0

34. WHAT KIND OF WORK DID YOU DO WHEN YOU WORKED (FOR THOSE ETIRED AT THE TIME OF INTERVIEW)	
rofessional and technical workers	1.4
anagers and nonself-employed officials	.6
elf-employed businessmen and artisans	1.0
lerical and sales workers	1.7
raftsmen and foremen	2.3
peratives and kindred	1.6
nskilled laborers and service workers	2.4
armers and farm managers	1.9
iscellaneous	.7
ot retired at time of interview (1912 cases)	86.4
otal	100.0

35. WHAT KIND OF BUSINESS WAS THAT IN? (FOR THOSE RETIRED THE TIME OF INTERVIEW)	
griculture, forestry and fishing	2.6
ining and extracting	.3
anufacturing	2.8
onstruction	.9
ransportation, communications, and utilities	1.0
etail and wholesale trade	1.8
inance, insurance, and real estate	.3
ervices (including professional services)	1.5
overnment medical, health, and educational services; all federal employees	2.2
ot ascertained	.2
t retired at time of interview (1912 cases)	86.4
otal	100.0

	Per cent of entire sampl

F36. WHEN DID YOU RETIRE?

1964 or 1965	1.6
1963	1.3
1961 - 1962	2.3
1956 - 1960	4.2
1951 - 1955	2.3
1946 - 1950	1.1
1941 - 1945	.4
1940 or before	.3
Not ascertained	.1
Not retired (1912 cases)	86.4
Total	100.0

F37. DURING THE LAST YEAR (1964) DID YOU DO ANY WORK FOR MONEY (FOR THOSE RETIRED AT THE TIME OF INTERVIEW)?

Yes	3.0
No	10.6
Not retired (1912 cases)	86.4
Total	100.0

F38. DURING THE LAST YEAR (1964) DID YOU DO ANY WORK FOR MONEY (FOR THOSE WHO WERE HOUSEWIVES AT THE TIME OF INTERVIEW)

Yes	1.0
No	5.5
Not housewives (2071 cases)	93.5
Total	100.0

F39. WHAT KIND OF WORK DID YOU DO (FOR HOUSEWIVES WHO WORKED)?

Too few cases to percentagize

F40. WHAT KIND OF BUSINESS IS THAT IN? (FOR HOUSEWIVES WHO WORKED)

Too few cases to percentagize

F41, F51. HOW MANY WEEKS DID YOU WORK LAST YEAR (FOR UNEMPLOYED, RETIRED, HOUSEWIVES, STUDENTS WHO WORKED FOR MONEY IN 1964)

13 weeks or less	2.0
14 - 26 weeks	1.7
27 - 39 weeks	1.4
40 - 47 weeks	1.3
48 - 49 weeks	.4
50 - 51 weeks	.3
52 weeks	.8
Not ascertained	.8
Not unemployed, retired, housewives, or students who worked for money last year (2022 cases)	91.3
Total	100.0

	Per cent of entire sample

uestions F42 - F44 were used to calculate total
ours of work only.

45, F52. ABOUT HOW MANY HOURS A WEEK DID YOU WORK
WHEN YOU WORKED)? (FOR UNEMPLOYED, RETIRED, HOUSEWIVES,
TUDENTS WHO WORKED FOR MONEY IN 1964)

- 19	1.0
0 - 34	1.1
5 - 40	3.4
1 - 48	1.1
9 - 59	.8
0 or more hours	.5
ot ascertained	.8
ot unemployed, retired, housewives, or students who worked for money last year (2022 cases)	91.3
otal	100.0

46. HOW MUCH OF 1964 WERE YOU IN SCHOOL? (FOR THOSE WHO
ERE STUDENTS AT THE TIME OF INTERVIEW)

weeks or less	.2
- 39 weeks	.8
- 47 weeks	.2
- 49 weeks	.3
- 52 weeks	.1
ot a student (2179 cases)	98.4
otal	100.0

7. IN AN AVERAGE SCHOOL WEEK, HOW MANY HOURS DO YOU SPEND
UDYING AND IN CLASS? (FOR THOSE WHO WERE STUDENTS AT THE
ME OF INTERVIEW)

wer than 35	.3
- 40	.7
- 48	.0
- 59	.2
or more	.4
t a student (2179 cases)	98.4
tal	100.0

8. DID YOU DO ANY WORK FOR PAY IN 1964?(FOR THOSE WHO
RE STUDENTS AT THE TIME OF INTERVIEW)

s	1.3
	.3
t a student (2179 cases)	98.4
tal	100.0

9. WHAT DID YOU DO?(FOR THOSE WHO WERE STUDENTS AT THE
ME OF INTERVIEW)

o few cases to percentagize

Per cent of
entire samp

F50. WHAT KIND OF BUSINESS WAS THAT IN?
(FOR THOSE WHO WERE STUDENTS AT THE TIME OF INTERVIEW)

Too few cases to percentagize

F53, F54. WHAT DO YOU THINK OF A MAN WHO TRIES DIFFICULT
THINGS BUT DOESN'T ALWAYS SUCCEED? WHY IS THAT?

Admires such a man for his initiative	27
Admires such a man for his persistence	50
Excuses him if he fails	5
Disapproves of such a man	9
Not ascertained	9
Total	100

F55, F56. SOMETIMES TWO PEOPLE SEEM TO HAVE THE SAME SKILL
AND TRAINING, BUT ONE IS MORE SUCCESSFUL THAN THE OTHER. WHY
DO YOU THINK THIS HAPPENS? (IF MENTIONS 2 OR MORE REASONS)
WHICH OF THESE DO YOU THINK IS MOST IMPORTANT?

More imaginative, enterprising, ingenious, ability to make decisions, more ambitious	19
Hard work, persistence	23
Education, age, experience, intelligence	18
Personality, self-confidence	18
Social status, race, religion, family background	1
Knowing the right people, luck, help from friends, being in the right place at the right time	7
God's will, fate	1
Other	5
Not ascertained	8
Total	100

F57. HOW IMPORTANT DO YOU THINK LUCK IS FOR A PERSON'S
FINANCIAL SUCCESS?

Very important	14
Important	13
Somewhat important	11
Not very important	20
Not at all important	34
Not ascertained	8
Total	100

	Per cent of entire sample

58. SUPPOSE A FAMILY HAS CHILDREN BUT THEY ARE ALL IN SCHOOL -- WOULD YOU SAY IT IS A GOOD THING FOR THE WIFE TO TAKE A JOB, OR A BAD THING, OR WHAT?

Good	15
Good, qualified	17
Depends, Pro-con responses	17
Bad, qualified	14
Bad	35
Not ascertained	2
Total	100

SECTION G: INCOME

G1, G1a, G1b, G1c. FOR FARMERS. WHAT WERE YOUR TOTAL RECEIPTS FROM FARMING IN 1964, INCLUDING SOIL BANK PAYMENTS AND COMMODITY CREDIT LOANS? WHAT WERE YOUR TOTAL OPERATING EXPENSES, NOT COUNTING LIVING EXPENSES? THAT LEFT YOU A NET INCOME FROM FARMING OF........

Net farm income for farmers

$1 - 499; negative income	.4
$500 - 999	.5
$1000 - 1999	.9
$2000 - 2999	.5
$3000 - 4999	1.3
$5000 - 7499	.8
$7500 - 9999	.3
$10,000 or more	.3
Not a farmer; or no income from this source (2103 cases)	95.0
Total	100.0

G2, G2a. DID YOU (R AND FAMILY) OWN A BUSINESS AT ANY TIME IN 1964, OR HAVE A FINANCIAL INTEREST IN ANY BUSINESS ENTERPRISE? IS IT A CORPORATION OR AN UNINCORPORATED BUSINESS, OR DO YOU HAVE AN INTEREST IN BOTH KINDS?

Own a corporation	2.1
Own an unincorporated business	7.8
Own both a corporation and unincorporated business	.4
Own, but not ascertained whether corporation or unincorporated business	.4
Not ascertained whether owns business	.1
Do not own business (1974 cases)	89.2
Total	100.0

G2b. IN 1964, HOW MUCH WAS YOUR FAMILY'S SHARE OF THE
TOTAL INCOME FROM THE BUSINESS, THAT IS, WHAT YOU TOOK OUT
PLUS ANY PROFITS YOU LEFT IN?

Unincorporated business income for entire family:

$1 - 499; negative income	.5
$500 - 999	.4
$1000 - 1999	.7
$2000 - 2999	.7
$3000 - 4999	1.4
$5000 - 7499	1.7
$7500 - 9999	1.1
$10,000 or more	1.6
Zero unincorporated business income; or does not own an unincorporated business (2035 cases)	91.9
Total	100.0

G3, G3a, G3b, G4a. HOW MUCH DID YOU (HEAD) RECEIVE FROM WAGES
AND SALARIES IN 1964, THAT IS BEFORE DEDUCTIONS FOR TAXES OR
ANYTHING? IN ADDITION TO THIS, DID YOU HAVE ANY INCOME FROM
BONUSES, OVERTIME, OR COMMISSIONS? HOW MUCH WAS THAT? DID
(HEAD) RECEIVE ANY OTHER INCOME IN 1964 FROM (a) PROFESSIONAL
PRACTICE OR A TRADE?

Family head's earned income:

$1 - 499	3
$500 - 999	3
$1000 - 1999	5
$2000 - 2999	5
$3000 - 4999	13
$5000 - 7499	24
$7500 - 9999	12
$10,000 or more	10
No income from this source (558 cases)	25
Total	100

Earned income for entire family:

$1 - 499	4
$500 - 999	3
$1000 - 1999	6
$2000 - 2999	5
$3000 - 4999	12
$5000 - 7499	19
$7500 - 9999	15
$10,000 or more	18
No income from this source (417 cases)	19
Total	100

441

	Per cent of entire sample

G4b.   DID (HEAD) RECEIVE ANY OTHER INCOME IN 1964 FROM:
(b) FARMING OR MARKET GARDENING, ROOMERS OR BOARDERS?

Data from above question not coded separately. Information
below is mixed labor capital income for entire family. Includes
farm income for farmers and nonfarmers, unincorporated business
income where some member in family worked in business, and
income from roomers or boarders:

$1 - 499; negative income	2.2
$500 - 999	1.7
$1000 - 1999	2.1
$2000 - 2999	1.3
$3000 - 4999	2.7
$5000 - 7499	2.6
$7500 - 9999	1.5
$10,000 or more	1.9
No income from this source (1859 cases)	84.0
Total	100.0

G4c. ......RENT, INTEREST, DIVIDENDS, TRUST FUNDS,
OR ROYALTIES?

Capital income for entire family:

$1 - 499	13.8
$500 - 999	5.3
$1000 - 1999	4.8
$2000 - 2999	1.9
$3000 - 4999	1.2
$5000 - 7499	.9
$7500 - 9999	.2
$10,000 or more	1.0
No income from this source (1570 cases)	70.9
Total	100.0

G4d, G4e.......SOCIAL SECURITY, OTHER RETIREMENT PAY,
PENSIONS OR ANNUITIES? (e) ANY OTHER SOURCES, LIKE ALIMONY,
UNEMPLOYMENT COMPENSATION, WELFARE, HELP FROM RELATIVES?
(ANYTHING ELSE?)

Transfer income for entire family:

$1 - 499	6.2
$500 - 999	7.7
$1000 - 1999	10.4
$2000 - 2999	4.4
$3000 - 4999	2.6
$5000 - 7499	.6
$7500 - 9999	.2
$10,000 or more	.1
No income from this source (1500 cases)	67.8
Total	100.0

G5, G5a, G5b. DID YOUR WIFE HAVE ANY INCOME DURING
1964? WAS IT INCOME FROM WAGES, SALARY, A BUSINESS, OR WHAT?

Per cent of
entire sample

Wages or salaries	31.9
Self-employment income (from a business or farm)	1.8
Transfer income	3.2
Capital income	1.3
Wife had no income; or no wife (1338 cases)	60.4
Total	*

G5c. HOW MUCH WAS IT BEFORE DEDUCTIONS? (INCOME OF WIFE)

Included below is earned income of wife only (Other forms under
questions G4b, G4c, G4d, G4e for entire family)

$1 - 499	7.7
$500 - 999	3.1
$1000 - 1999	6.3
$2000 - 2999	4.8
$3000 - 4999	7.3
$5000 - 7499	2.7
$7500 - 9999	.4
$10,000 or more	.0
Wife had no earned income; or no wife (1498 cases)	67.7
Total	100.0

G6, G6a, G6b. DID (MENTION MEMBER) HAVE ANY INCOME DURING 1964?
WAS IT FROM WAGES, INTEREST, A BUSINESS, OR WHAT? (FOR FAMILY
MEMBERS 14 YEARS OF AGE OR OLDER OTHER THAN FAMILY HEAD OR WIFE)

Wages or salaries	18.9
Self-employment income (from a business or farm)	.5
Transfer income	3.1
Capital income	.5
Others in family had no income; or no others in family (1733 cases)	78.3
Total	**

---

* Adds to more than 100 per cent because some wives had income from
more than one source.
** Adds to more than 100 per cent because some family members had more
than one "other source of income".

Per cent of
entire sample

G6c. HOW MUCH WAS IT? (INCOME OF OTHERS IN FU)

Not coded separately. Included among the various types
of income for total family unit.

TOTAL FAMILY INCOME:

Under $1000	5
$1000 - 1999	9
$2000 - 2999	7
$3000 - 3999	8
$4000 - 4999	7
$5000 - 5999	9
$6000 - 7499	14
$7500 - 9999	18
$10,000 - 14,999	15
$15,000 or more	8
Total	100

DISPOSABLE INCOME FOR FAMILY (TOTAL FAMILY INCOME MINUS
FEDERAL INCOME TAXES FOR FAMILY)

Under $1000	5
$1000 - 1999	9
$2000 - 2999	8
$3000 - 3999	9
$4000 - 4999	9
$5000 - 5999	10
$6000 - 7499	16
$7500 - 9999	17
$10,000 - 14,999	12
$15,000 or more	5
Total	100

G7. WAS THERE SOMEONE ELSE IN THE FAMILY WHO EARNED MONEY
BEFORE LAST YEAR, BUT NOT LAST YEAR?

Yes	6
No	92
Not ascertained	2
Total	100

G8, G9, G11. WAS YOUR FAMILY'S TOTAL INCOME HIGHER IN 1964 THAN
IT WAS THE YEAR BEFORE THAT, OR LOWER, OR WHAT? (IF HIGHER)
WAS IT A LOT HIGHER OR JUST A LITTLE HIGHER? (IF LOWER) WAS IT A
LOT LOWER, OR JUST A LITTLE LOWER?

A lot higher	15
A little higher	31
Same	37
A little lower	8
A lot lower	8
Not ascertained	1
Total	100

G10. WHY WAS THAT? (REASONS WHY FAMILY INCOME HIGHER)	Per cent of entire samp
Higher rate of pay for family head	23.8
Higher earned income for family head because worked longer hours; more business or farm income	14.4
Others in family started to earn at a higher rate, or work more hours	9.4
Higher capital income	1.6
Higher transfer income	1.2
Other	.5
Not ascertained	2.3
No change in income; or no reason why income higher (1179 cases)	53.3
Total	*

G12. WHY WAS THAT? (REASONS WHY FAMILY INCOME LOWER)	
Lower rate of pay for family head	1.6
Lower earned income for family head because worked shorter hours; less business or farm income	10.4
Others in family stopped working, or earned at a lower rate of pay or worked shorter hours	3.0
Lower capital income	.5
Lower transfer income	.4
Other	.9
Not ascertained	1.5
No change in income; or no reason why income lower (1823 cases)	82.3
Total	**

G13. ARE THERE ANY PEOPLE THAT DO NOT LIVE WITH YOU WHO ARE DEPENDENT ON YOU FOR MORE THAN HALF OF THEIR SUPPORT?	
No, none	96
One person	3
Two or more persons	1
Total	100

*Adds to more than 100 per cent because some respondents gave more than one reason why income was higher in 1964 than in 1963.
**Adds to more than 100 per cent because some respondents gave more than one reason why income lower in 1964 than in 1963.

445

Per cent of
entire sample

14, G15. HAVE YOU HAD AN ILLNESS, PHYSICAL CONDITION
R NERVOUS CONDITION WHICH LIMITS THE TYPE OF WORK OR THE
MOUNT OF WORK YOU CAN DO? HOW MUCH DOES IT LIMIT YOUR WORK?

ave a disability:

ork is completely limited	4
ork is severely limited	4
ork is somewhat limited	8
ork is not limited at all	1
ot ascertained limitation on work	1
o not have a disability	82
otal	100

17. IS THERE ANYONE ELSE LIVING HERE WHOSE WORK OR SCHOOLING
S LIMITED BY SOME ILLNESS, PHYSICAL CONDITION, OR NERVOUS
ONDITION?

es	9
o	74
ot ascertained	1
ne-person family (349 cases)	16
otal	100

18. WHO IS THAT? (DISABLED PERSON OTHER THAN FAMILY HEAD)

no disabled members of family are:

disabled person:

ife	4.7
hild 17 or younger	1.7
ther adult in family	2.7
or more disabled persons:	.3
o other disabled person in family (2005 cases)	90.6
otal	100.0

19. HOW DOES IT LIMIT HIS (HER) WORK (SCHOOLING)?

isability of other person (Wife, if wife disabled):

ompletely limited	2.4
everely limited	2.0
omewhat limited	4.0
ot at all limited	.4
imitation not ascertained	.6
o other person disabled (2005 cases)	90.6
otal	100.0

FROM G17, G18. TOTAL NUMBER OF DISABLED PERSONS IN FAMILY UNIT	Per cent of entire sampl
None	76
One	20
Two or more	4
Total	100

SECTION H: FUTURE PLANNING

H1. WE'RE INTERESTED IN WHAT KIND OF PLANS PEOPLE HAVE. HOW FAR IN ADVANCE DO YOU USUALLY PLAN YOUR VACATIONS?

Not at all	21
1 week	5
1 month	12
2 through 6 months	23
7 through 12 months	10
More than 1 year	0
Depends	1
Not ascertained	10
Don't take vacations (388 cases)	18
Total	100

H2. WHEN DID YOU LAST TAKE A VACATION?

6 months ago or more recently	18
7 - 12 months ago	34
2 - 3 years ago	15
4 - 5 years ago	5
6 or more years ago	8
Not ascertained	2
Don't take vacations (388 cases)	18
Total	100

H3. HOW LONG BEFORE HAD YOU PLANNED THIS VACATION?

Not at all	11
1 week	10
1 month	17
2 - 6 months	28
7 - 12 months	9
More than 1 year	1
Not ascertained	6
Don't take vacations (388 cases)	18
Total	100

H4. PEOPLE OFTEN HAVE TO MAKE PROVISIONS FOR EMERGENCIES. ARE YOU (YOUR FAMILY) COVERED BY BLUE CROSS OR SOME OTHER HOSPITAL OR MEDICAL INSURANCE?

Yes	79
No	21
Total	100

Per cent of
entire sample

H5. DO YOU THINK A PERSON SHOULD BE ABLE TO COUNT ON
FINANCIAL SUPPORT FROM HIS FAMILY IF HE NEEDS IT?

Yes	32
Yes, qualified	17
Depends	2
No, qualified	4
No	43
Not ascertained	2
Total	100

H6, H7. WHAT ABOUT FUTURE FAMILY OBLIGATIONS, DO YOU
EXPECT TO HAVE TO PROVIDE FINANCIAL AID TO YOUR PARENTS OR
OTHER RELATIVES SOMETIME IN THE FUTURE? WHEN DO YOU THINK
THAT WILL BE?

Expect to provide financial aid:

Within next 2 years	8.4
3 - 5 years	2.7
6 - 10 years	1.5
11 - 15 years	.8
16 - 20 years	.8
21 or more years	.3
Not ascertained when	7.0
Do not expect to provide financial aid (1700 cases)	76.8
Not ascertained whether expects to provide financial aid	1.7
Total	100.0

H8, H9, H10. DO YOU (PEOPLE) HAVE ANY RESERVE FUNDS, SAY IN A
CHECKING OR SAVINGS ACCOUNT, OR GOVERNMENT BONDS? WOULD THEY
AMOUNT TO AS MUCH AS TWO MONTHS OF TAKE HOME INCOME OR MORE?
WAS THERE A TIME IN THE LAST FIVE YEARS WHEN YOU HAD AS MUCH AS
TWO MONTHS OF TAKE HOME INCOME SAVED UP?

Have reserve funds:

Equal to two months of take home income or more	54
Equal to less than two months of take home income	15

Do not have reserve funds:

Had reserve fund equal to two months of take home income or more within last 5 years	9
Have not had reserve funds equal to two months of take home income or more within last 5 years	21
Not ascertained whether reserve funds	1
Total	100

Questions H12 through H17 were asked only of those
who were thirty-five or older and not yet retired.

Per cent of
entire sample

H12. NOW I HAVE A FEW QUESTIONS ABOUT RETIREMENT.
WHEN DO YOU THINK YOU WILL RETIRE, I MEAN AT WHAT AGE?

Age at which plans to retire:

54 or younger	1.0
55 - 59	2.4
60 - 61	4.0
62 - 64	7.9
65 - 69	23.3
70 or older	2.1
"Within a few years"	.4
"Not for a long time"	.2
Not ascertained at what age will retire	5.5
Will not retire; not ascertained whether will retire; retired; or under age 35 (1178 cases)	53.2
Total	100.0

FROM H12. (FOR THOSE WHO WILL NOT RETIRE)

Frame of reference for stating will not retire:

Work as long as possible	7.0
Cannot afford to retire	.4
Occupation from which no one retires (photographer, artist, etc.)	.3
Not ascertained frame of reference	2.7
Not ascertained whether will retire	5.2
Will retire; or retired; or under age 35 (1868 cases)	84.4
Total	100.0

H13. HOW DO YOU FEEL ABOUT RETIREMENT, IS IT SOMETHING
TO BE LOOKED FORWARD TO, OR IS IT TO BE DREADED, OR WHAT?

Looks forward to retirement	28
Looks forward to retirement with qualifications	4
Pro-con response	3
Does not look forward to retirement, dreads it	13
Neither looks forward to it nor dreads it, will take it in stride	2
Not any difference from present situation	0
Not yet thinking about retirement	5
Not ascertained	3
Retired; or under age 35 (932 cases)	42
Total	100

	Per cent of entire sample

4, H15. DO YOU HAVE ANY PLANS FOR THE TIME WHEN
)U ARE RETIRED? WHAT ARE YOUR PLANS?

ve plans:

11 go into business for myself; start a farm	3
11 get another job (no mention of self-employment)	2
11 work on hobbies; do unpaid community or volunteer work	4
11 travel	4
11 move to another location	3
:her	1
ntions plans only in preparation for retirement	0

ve no plans   40

t ascertained whether any plans   1
tired; or under age 35 (932 cases)   42

tal   100

6, H17. DO YOU OR YOUR WIFE EXPECT TO EARN MONEY
' WORKING AFTER YOUR RETIREMENT? WHAT WILL YOU DO?

ad and/or wife will go into business for self; or start a farm	6
ad and/or wife will get another job (no mention of self-employment)	8
pect to earn money but not ascertained what will do	9
plans to earn money after retirement	29
t ascertained	6
tired; or under age 35 (932 cases)	42

tal   100

8. WOULD YOU PLEASE LOOK AT THIS CARD AND TELL ME WHICH
ING ON THIS LIST ABOUT A JOB (OCCUPATION) YOU WOULD MOST
REFER; WHICH COMES NEXT, WHICH IS THIRD, AND SO FORTH?

e card showed to the respondents had the following six
aracteristics of an occupation to rank from first
eference to last preference:

come is steady
come is high
ere's no danger of being fired or unemployed
rking hours are short, lots of free time
ances for advancement are good
e Work is important, gives a feeling of accomplishment

Rank of A. INCOME IS STEADY

Highest preference among the six characteristics	45
Second	21
Third	15
Fourth	10
Fifth	4
Lowest preference	2
Not ascertained	3
Total	100

Rank of B. INCOME IS HIGH

Highest preference among the six characteristics	9
Second	13
Third	16
Fourth	20
Fifth	26
Lowest preference	11
Not ascertained	5
Total	100

Rank of C. THERE'S NO DANGER OF BEING FIRED OR UNEMPLOYED

Highest preference among the six characteristics	10
Second	21
Third	17
Fourth	16
Fifth	19
Lowest preference	12
Not ascertained	5
Total	100

Rank of D. WORKING HOURS ARE SHORT, LOTS OF FREE TIME

Highest preference among the six characteristics	2
Second	4
Third	6
Fourth	11
Fifth	18
Lowest preference	54
Not ascertained	5
Total	100

Rank of E. CHANCES FOR ADVANCEMENT ARE GOOD

Highest preference among the six characteristics	10
Second	22
Third	23
Fourth	20
Fifth	14
Lowest preference	6
Not ascertained	5
Total	100

	Per cent of entire sample
Rank of F. THE WORK IS IMPORTANT, GIVES A FEELING OF ACCOMPLISHMENT	
Highest preference among the six characteristics	20
Second	16
Third	18
Fourth	18
Fifth	14
Lowest preference	10
Not ascertained	4
Total	100

H19. HAVE YOU USUALLY FELT PRETTY SURE YOUR LIFE WOULD WORK OUT THE WAY YOU WANT IT TO, OR HAVE THERE BEEN MORE TIMES WHEN YOU HAVEN'T BEEN VERY SURE ABOUT IT?	
Pretty sure	56
Haven't been very sure	41
Not ascertained	3
Total	100

H20. ARE YOU THE KIND OF PERSON THAT PLANS HIS LIFE AHEAD ALL THE TIME OR DO YOU LIVE MORE FROM DAY TO DAY	
Plans ahead	51
Lives from day to day	47
Not ascertained	2
Total	100

H21. WHEN YOU MAKE PLANS AHEAD, DO YOU USUALLY GET TO CARRY OUT THINGS THE WAY YOU EXPECTED, OR DO THINGS USUALLY COME UP TO MAKE YOU CHANGE YOUR PLANS?	
Things work out as expected	54
Have to change plans	41
Not ascertained	5
Total	100

H22. WOULD YOU SAY THAT YOU OFTEN FALL SHORT OF WHAT YOU COULD DO AND THAT YOU COULD DO THINGS BETTER?	
Yes	47
Yes, qualified	9
Pro-con response	3
No, qualified	4
No	29
Not ascertained including references to getting older ·	8
Total	100

H23, H24. IS YOUR RELIGIOUS PREFERENCE PROTESTANT, CATHOLIC, OR JEWISH? (IF PROTESTANT) WHAT DENOMINATION IS THAT?

Protestant:

Baptists	21
Methodists	14
Episcopalians	2
Presbyterians	6
Lutherans	7
Congregationalists; Christian Scientists; Dutch Reformed; Quakers; Latter Day Saints; Mormons; Unitarians; Bahai; Evangelical and Reformed	9
Other Protestants	11
Catholic	23
Jewish	3
Other; or none	4
Total	100

H25. WOULD YOU SAY YOU ATTEND RELIGIOUS SERVICES REGULARLY, OFTEN, SELDOM, OR NEVER?

Regularly	39
Often	14
Seldom	34
Never	12
Not ascertained	1
Total	100

H26, H27, H28, H29. GENERALLY SPEAKING, DO YOU USUALLY THINK OF YOURSELF AS A REPUBLICAN, A DEMOCRAT, AN INDEPENDENT, OR WHAT? (IF REPUBLICAN) WOULD YOU CALL YOURSELF A STRONG REPUBLICAN OR A NOT VERY STRONG REPUBLICAN? (IF DEMOCRAT) WOULD YOU CALL YOURSELF A STRONG DEMOCRAT OR A NOT VERY STRONG DEMOCRAT? (IF INDEPENDENT OR OTHER) DO YOU THINK OF YOURSELF AS CLOSER TO REPUBLICAN OR DEMOCRATIC PARTY?

Strong Republican	12
Not very strong Republican	13
Independent closer to Republican	4
Independent closer to neither party	9
Independent closer to Democrat	8
Not very strong Democrat	24
Strong Democrat	25
Not a citizen; not old enough to vote; no voting residence	1
Neither; minor party; refused to answer question	2
Not ascertained	2
Total	100

	Per cent of entire sample
H30. ARE YOU SINGLE, WIDOWED, DIVORCED, OR SEPARATED?	

Single	7.0
Widowed	11.3
Divorced	3.1
Separated	2.6
Not ascertained, but not married	1.9
Married (1640 cases)	74.1
Total	100.0

SECTION J: BY OBSERVATION ONLY (FILLED OUT BY INTERVIEWER)

J1. SEX OF HEAD OF FAMILY UNIT

Married man	74
Single man	8
Single woman	18
Total	100

J2. SEX OF RESPONDENT

Man	73
Woman	26
Both - two respondents	1
Total	100

J3. RACE OF FAMILY HEAD

White	89
Negro	9
Other	1
Not ascertained	1
Total	100

J4. NUMBER OF CALLS REQUIRED TO SECURE INTERVIEW

One	31
Two	32
Three	16
Four	8
Five	4
Six	3
Seven or more	3
Not ascertained	3
Total	100

454

J5. WHO WAS PRESENT DURING INTERVIEW?	Per cent of entire sample
Family head only	26
Wife only	4
Family head and wife	35
Family head and someone else (not wife)	11
Wife and someone else (not family head)	3
Family head and wife and someone else	20
Not ascertained	1
Total	100

J6. DID THE RESPONDENT UNDERSTAND THE QUESTIONS AND ANSWER READILY OR DID HE HAVE SOME DIFFICULTY UNDERSTANDING AND ANSWERING? (NOT COUNTING LANGUAGE DIFFICULTY)

Respondent was alert and quick to answer	50
Respondent could understand and answer questions satisfactorily	37
Respondent was slow to understand and had difficulty answering questions	10
Not ascertained	3
Total	100

J7. TYPE OF STRUCTURE IN WHICH FAMILY LIVES

Detached single family house	73
2 - 4 family house, duplex, or row house	15
Apartment house (5 or more units) 3 stories or less	5
Apartment house (5 or more units) 4 stories or more	3
Apartment in partly commercial structure	2
Other	2
Total	100

J8. NEIGHBORHOOD: LOOK AT 3 STRUCTURES ON EACH SIDE OF THE DU BUT NOT MORE THAN 100 YARDS OR SO IN EITHER DIRECTION, AND CHECK AS MANY BOXES AS ARE APPROPRIATE.

Per cent of times each item below checked:

Detached single family house	72
2 - 4 family house, duplex, or row house	17
Apartment house (5 or more units), 3 stories or less	6
Apartment house (5 or more units), 4 stories or more	3
Mixed commercial and residential structure	6
Wholly commercial or industrial structure	3
Trailers	2
Other	2
Vacant land only around dwelling unit (mutually exclusive category)	9
Total	*

*
Adds to more than 100 per cent because more than one item was checked for some dwelling units.

The following are demographic items coded for
each completed interview.

Per cent of
entire sample

LOCATION OF RESIDENCE RELATIVE TO NEAREST LARGE CITY[*]

In central cities of 12 largest Standard Metropolitan Areas	13
In suburbs of 12 largest Standard Metropolitan Areas	14
In central cities of other Standard Metropolitan Areas	17
In suburbs of other Standard Metropolitan Areas	15
In areas adjacent to Standard Metropolitan Areas	18
In areas outlying Standard Metropolitan Areas	23
Total	100

SIZE OF PLACE WHERE LIVES (1960 CENSUS CLASSIFICATION)

In central cities of the 12 largest Standard Metropolitan Areas	13
In cities of 50,000 and over population (exclusive of the central cities of the 12 largest Standard Metropolitan areas)	21
Urban places with 10,000 - 49,999 population	17
Urban places with 2500 - 9999 population	20
Rural areas, near a metropolitan area	6
Rural areas not near a metropolitan area	23
Total	100

DISTANCE FROM CENTER OF THE CENTRAL CITY

Less than 1 mile	1
1 mile	6
2 - 3 miles	7
4 - 5 miles	3
6 - 7 miles	5
8 - 9 miles	4
10 - 14 miles	10
15 - 24 miles	6
25 or more miles	8
Address is inside the central cities of the 12 largest Standard Metropolitan areas; or no metropolitan area nearby	50
Total	100

---

[*] A Standard Metropolitan area is a county or group of contiguous counties which contain at least one city of 50,000 inhabitants or more, or "twin cities" with a combined population of at least 50,000. In addition, contiguous counties are included in an SMA if, according to certain criteria, they are essentially metropolitan in character and are socially and economically integrated with the central city. An area adjacent to the Standard Metropolitan area includes all territory beyond the outer boundary of the suburban area but within 50 miles of the central business district of a central-city-residential belt. "Outlying" areas include territory more than 50 miles from the central business district.

1959 MEDIAN INCOME OF ALL FAMILIES IN COUNTY (COUNTIES WHERE INTERVIEWS WERE TAKEN)*	Per cent of entire sample
$2065 - 2999	7
$3000 - 3999	13
$4000 - 4999	10
$5000 - 5999	32
$6000 - 7499	33
$7500 - 9317	5
Total	100

WHETHER COUNTY (IN ITS ENTIRETY OR IN PART) WAS A DEPRESSED AREA IN 1963 *	
Depressed area	18
Not a depressed area	82
Total	100

PERCENTAGE INCREASE IN MEDIAN COUNTY INCOME BETWEEN 1949 AND 1959*	
21 - 40	19
41 - 60	59
61 - 80	16
81 - 100	2
101 - 120	3
121 or greater	1
Total	100

REGION OF COUNTRY WHERE INTERVIEW TAKEN**	
Northeast	22
North Central states	31
Deep South	6
Other South	25
West	16
Total	100

---

*Data from Claude C. Haren and Robert B. Glasgow, Median Family Income and Related Data, by Counties, Including Rural Farm Income, Statistical Bulletin # 339 (Washington: Resource Development Economics Division, Economic Research Service, U.S. Department of Agriculture, February, 1964).

**The above definition is that used by the U.S. Bureau of the Census with the exception of the separation of the South into "Deep South" and "Other South." Northeast includes Conn., Maine, Mass., N.H., N.J., N.Y., Penn., R.I., and Vt. The North Central states include Ill., Ind., Iowa, Kan., Mich., Minn., Mo., Neb., N.D., Ohio, S.D., and Wis. The "Deep South" includes Ala., Ga., La., Miss., and S.C. The "Other South" includes Ark., Del., Fla., Ky., Md., N.C., Okla., Tenn., Texas, Va., Wash. D.C., and W. Va. The West includes Ariz., Calif., Colo., Id., Mont., N.M., Nev., Oreg., Utah., Wash., and Wyo.

PER CENT OF THOSE IN COUNTY 25 OR OLDER WHO COMPLETED HIGH SCHOOL*	Per cent of entire sample
14 - 24	8
25 - 34	13
35 - 44	36
45 - 54	37
55 - 72	6
Total	100

*Data from U.S. Bureau of the Census, County and City Data Book, 1962 (Washington: U.S. Government Printing Office, 1962).

APPENDIX D

A CONCEPTUAL FRAMEWORK AND INTERCORRELATIONS AMONG THE EXPLANATORY VARIABLES

Introduction

The major portion of the analysis presented in this book has been concerned with people's attitudes and ancillary behavior and how these may relate to economically productive activities. Basic throughout the analysis has been the assumption that economically productive activities lead to further prosperity for the individual and to economic growth of the nation. And, in Chapter 20, the dynamic circle was completed by showing that individual success itself (or lack of difficulty) reinforced the very attitudes and behaviors that led to economic activity and more success. Progressive attitudes lead to a greater desire for more success, expressed in better resource allocation (longer work hours, second jobs), or in an accumulation of assets (and home ownership), or moving to a better job, investing in education for self or children, or making provision for emergencies. See Figure D-1 for the schematic presentation of this model.

If past success and lack of disaster lead to more progressive attitudes and over a longer run, more formal education seems to have the same result, then economic progress and stability feed on themselves. Rising incomes, better public and private provisions for risk avoidance and medical care, avoidance of unemployment and injury, have dynamic effects on people's attitudes and behavior that are above and beyond their immediate and obvious payoffs.

459
FIGURE D-1

A MODEL OF INDIVIDUAL BEHAVIOR: A SCHEMATIC PRESENTATION

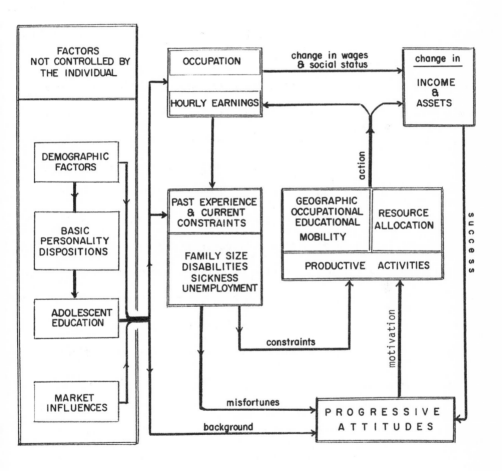

But any neat formal model restricts us from looking at some side issues. One of these is that some of the variables we have used as explanatory and basically predetermined in the model, can themselves be examined, both in terms of their interrelationships with one another, and in terms of what more basic factors in turn affect them.

Intercorrelation among explanatory variables

Hence, we turn to some of the more important intermediate variables, namely education of head of family, total family income, hourly earnings of head of family, housing status (home ownership), score on index of achievement orientation, region of country, and occupation of head of family. Each of these seven variables has been cross-tabulated by age, race, and sex and marital status in the tables which follow.

Table D-1 shows a negative relationship between education and age. Note that none of those under twenty-five were in either of the two extreme education brackets. The table also suggests that those in this age group who intend to acquire a college or an advanced degree sometime in the future have not yet completed it (30 per cent of them have some college but with no degree). Table D-2 shows that there is no significant difference in the completed education of married versus single men, while female heads of families, on the other hand, seem to be less likely to have completed high school -- 58 per cent versus 47 per cent for men. The disproportionate per cent of single men in the college, no degree category are mostly students living outside college dormitories in private apartments, thus making them eligible respondents. Most women of this age group in college, however, would be more likely to live in college-owned dormitories making them part of the institutional population

TABLE D-1

EDUCATION OF HEAD OF FAMILY BY AGE OF HEAD OF FAMILY

(For all 2214 heads of families)

Education of head of family	All cases	Age of head of family						
		Under 25	25-34	35-44	45-54	55-64	65-74	75 or older
0 - 5 grades	8	0	2	4	7	10	19	22
6 - 8 grades	22	3	11	13	21	33	37	42
9 - 11 grades	19	20	15	20	20	24	14	12
12 grades	15	27	18	20	16	11	7	10
12 grades and non-academic training	12	13	19	15	14	5	6	4
College, no degree	12	30	12	14	10	9	8	4
College, bachelor's degree	9	7	18	11	8	6	8	5
College, advanced or professional degree	3	0	5	3	4	2	1	1
Total	100	100	100	100	100	100	100	100
Number of cases	2214	130	360	445	476	387	277	139

TABLE D-2

EDUCATION OF HEAD OF FAMILY BY SEX AND MARITAL STATUS OF HEAD OF FAMI

(For all 2214 heads of families)

| | | Sex and marital status of head of family | | |
| | | Married | Single | |
Education of head of family	All cases	Male	Male	Female
0 - 5 grades	8	8	9	10
6 - 8 grades	22	21	21	26
9 - 11 grades	19	18	17	22
12 grades	15	17	7	13
12 grades and non-academic training	12	12	12	10
College, no degree	12	11	20	10
College, bachelor's degree	9	10	11	7
College, advanced or professional degree	3	3	3	2
Total	100	100	100	100
Number of cases	2214	1640	183	391

463

and hence ineligible for interviewing. Table D-3 indicates that there
is a very pronounced education difference between white and Negro heads
of families. Seventy-three per cent of Negro heads of families did not
complete high school while the comparable figure for whites is 49 per
cent. in none of the brackets at the level of completed high school or
higher did Negroes have a higher percentage of heads of families than did
whites.

Table D-4 indicates that there is a general overall negative
correlation of age with income. For the income groups under $2000, there
is a U-shaped effect; 21 per cent of those under twenty-five have incomes
of less than $2000, dropping to 3 per cent for those thirty-five to forty-
four years old, and then rising sharply to 48 per cent for those seventy-
five or older. The high percentage for those under twenty-five with
incomes under $2000 indicates the presence of students and those who have
just recently entered the labor force who therefore may not have worked
for the entire year. The percentage of those with incomes of $10,000 or
more is low for both extreme age groups, but rises to 39 per cent for
those with heads of families aged forty-five through fifty-four. Table
D-5 indicates that married men are likely to have a higher level of income
on the average than do families headed by single men or women. Many of
the single female heads of families are relatively old, and hence this
may reflect a hidden age difference. Overall, 14 per cent of families had
incomes of less than $2000, while in families headed by married men only
6 per cent had incomes of less than $2000. And finally, Table D-6 indicates
that Negroes have relatively lower family incomes than whites. It should

TABLE D-3

EDUCATION OF HEAD OF FAMILY BY RACE OF HEAD OF FAMILY

(For all 2214 heads of families)

Education of head of family	All cases	Race of head of family		
		White	Negro	Other; not ascertained
0 - 5 grades	8	7	24	9
6 - 8 grades	22	22	25	29
9 - 11 grades	19	18	24	16
12 grades	15	16	10	11
12 grades and non-academic training	12	12	6	11
College, no degree	12	12	8	9
College, bachelor's degree	9	10	2	11
College, advanced or professional degree	3	3	1	4
Total	100	100	100	100
Number of cases	2214	1961	208	45

465

TABLE D-4

TOTAL FAMILY INCOME BY AGE OF HEAD OF FAMILY

(For all 2214 heads of families)

		Age of head of family						
Total family income	All cases	Under 25	25-34	35-44	45-54	55-64	65-74	75 or older
Under $1000	5	5	2	0	2	6	9	22
1000 - 1999	9	16	3	3	4	9	24	26
2000 - 2999	7	10	3	4	4	8	17	16
3000 - 3999	8	16	5	5	5	11	13	11
4000 - 4999	7	11	9	6	6	7	7	5
5000 - 5999	9	7	14	9	8	8	7	5
6000 - 7499	14	15	21	15	15	12	6	6
7500 - 9999	18	12	26	28	17	16	4	4
10,000 - 14,999	15	6	14	21	24	13	7	2
15,000 or more	8	2	3	9	15	10	6	3
Total	100	100	100	100	100	100	100	100
Number of cases	2214	130	360	445	476	387	277	139

466

TABLE D-5

TOTAL FAMILY INCOME BY SEX AND MARITAL STATUS OF HEAD OF FAMILY

(For all 2214 heads of families)

Total family income	All cases	Sex and marital status of head of family Married Male	Single Male	Female
Under $1000	5	1	8	17
$1000 - 1999	9	5	15	22
$2000 - 2999	7	5	12	14
$3000 - 3999	8	7	9	12
$4000 - 4999	7	7	11	7
$5000 - 5999	9	10	8	6
$6000 - 7499	14	15	6	10
$7500 - 9999	18	21	15	7
$10,000 - 14,999	15	19	11	3
$15,000 or more	8	10	5	2
Total	100	100	100	100
Number of cases	2214	1640	183	391

TABLE D-6

TOTAL FAMILY INCOME BY RACE OF HEAD OF FAMILY

(For all 2214 heads of families)

| Total family income | All cases | Race of head of family | | |
		White	Negro	Other; not ascertained
Under $1000	5	4	10	11
$1000 - 1999	9	8	18	11
$2000 - 2999	7	6	17	11
$3000 - 3999	8	8	10	13
$4000 - 4999	7	7	8	9
$5000 - 5999	9	8	12	6
$6000 - 7499	14	15	10	2
$7500 - 9999	18	19	7	22
$10,000 - 14,999	15	16	7	13
$15,000 or more	8	9	1	2
Total	100	100	100	100
Number of cases	2214	1961	208	45

be noted that a larger fraction of Negro heads of families are female, which may account for some of this difference in income as well as the general lower level of education of Negroes compared with whites.

Hourly earnings of the head of the family generally show a non-linear relationship with age of head of family. (See Table D-7.) A peak in hourly earnings occurs in the age bracket of forty-five to fifty-four. Our data suggest, however, that the effect of age on hourly earnings is different within educational groups. For people with college degree or more, hourly earnings increase sytematically with age. Table D-8 indicates that relatively more married heads of families have hourly earnings of $3.00 or more, 41 per cent, compared with 31 per cent for single men and 10 per cent for women heads of families. Table D-9 shows that about six in ten of the Negro heads of families who worked had hourly earnings of less than $2.00, while only about three in ten of the whites who worked did. And almost three times as many whites who worked had hourly earnings of $3.00 or higher as did Negroes. Some of this difference may be a reflection of an education difference, however.

Table D-10 indicates that the percentage of families owning their home increases systematically from about one-quarter for those under twenty-five to three-quarters for those seventy-five or older. Most of that increase, however, occurs in the three youngest age brackets. Married couples are far more likely to own their homes than are single heads of families -- 71 per cent for married couples versus 43 per cent for single men and 51 per cent for single women. (See Table D-11.) Relatively more whites own their homes than do Negroes. And a larger per cent of Negroes neither own nor rent the place where they live -- 11 versus 4 per cent for white families. However, there are very vew Negroes in the sample. (See Table D-12.)

TABLE D-7

HOURLY EARNINGS OF HEAD OF FAMILY BY AGE OF HEAD OF FAMILY

(For all 2214 heads of families)

Hourly earnings of head of family	All cases	Under 25	25-34	35-44	45-54	55-64	65-74	75 or older
Did not work for money in 1964 ($0.00)	17	6	1	2	6	15	58	81
.01 - .74	4	5	2	3	4	7	8	4
.75 - .99	3	5	1	2	5	4	2	3
1.00 - 1.49	9	16	8	7	9	11	8	5
1.50 - 1.99	10	21	13	11	8	8	5	1
2.00 - 2.99	22	30	36	27	21	20	7	1
3.00 - 3.99	17	11	24	23	20	17	4	1
4.00 - 5.49	10	4	12	16	14	8	3	1
5.50 - 7.49	4	1	1	6	7	4	1	0
7.50 or more	4	1	2	3	6	6	4	3
Total	100	100	100	100	100	100	100	100
Number of cases	2214	130	360	445	476	387	277	139

TABLE D-8

HOURLY EARNINGS OF HEAD OF FAMILY BY SEX AND MARITAL STATUS OF HEAD OF FAMILY

(For all 2214 heads of families)

| | | Sex and marital status of head of family | | |
| | | Married | Single | |
Hourly earnings of head of family	All cases	Male	Male	Female
Did not work for money in 1964 ($0.00)	17	10	19	46
$.01 - .74	4	3	7	8
$.75 - .99	3	3	6	3
$1.00 - 1.49	9	8	9	12
$1.50 - 1.99	10	10	9	9
$2.00 - 2.99	22	25	19	12
$3.00 - 3.99	17	20	14	6
$4.00 - 5.49	10	12	8	3
$5.50 - 7.49	4	4	5	1
$7.50 or more	4	5	4	0
Total	100	100	100	100
Number of cases	2214	1640	183	391

TABLE D-9

HOURLY EARNINGS OF HEAD OF FAMILY BY RACE OF HEAD OF FAMILY

(For all 2214 heads of families)

Hourly earnings of head of family	All cases	White	Negro	Other; not ascertained
Did not work for money in 1964 ($0.00)	17	17	19	13
$.01 - .74	4	4	9	6
$.75 - .99	3	3	7	11
$1.00 - 1.49	9	8	18	7
$1.50 - 1.99	10	9	14	7
$2.00 - 2.99	22	22	19	27
$3.00 - 3.99	17	18	10	18
$4.00 - 5.49	10	11	3	7
$5.50 - 7.49	4	4	0	2
$7.50 or more	4	4	1	2
Total	100	100	100	100
Number of cases	2214	1961	208	45

Race of head of family

472

TABLE D-10

HOUSING STATUS BY AGE OF HEAD OF FAMILY
(For all 2214 heads of families)

Housing status of family	All cases	Age of head of family						
		Under 25	25-34	35-44	45-54	55-64	65-74	75 old
Own	65	24	47	71	74	73	69	70
Rent	30	71	49	24	18	23	27	10
Neither own nor rent	5	5	4	5	8	4	4	8
Total	100	100	100	100	100	100	100	100
Number of cases	2214	130	360	445	476	387	277	139

TABLE D-11

HOUSING STATUS BY SEX AND MARITAL STATUS OF HEAD OF FAMILY
(For all 2214 heads of families)

Housing status of family	All cases	Sex and marital status of head of family		
		Married	Single	
		Male	Male	Female
Own	65	71	43	51
Rent	30	24	48	43
Neither own nor rent	5	5	9	6
Total	100	100	100	100
Number of cases	2214	1640	183	391

TABLE D-12

HOUSING STATUS BY RACE OF HEAD OF FAMILY
(For all 2214 heads of families)

Race of head of family

Housing status of family	All cases	White	Negro	Other; not ascertained
Own	65	69	37	47
Rent	30	27	52	42
Neither own nor rent	5	4	11	11
Total	100	100	100	100
Number of cases	2214	1961	208	45

A high negative correlation exists between head of family's score on the index of need for achievement and his age. (See Table D-13.) Forty-six per cent of those under twenty-five scored five or higher on the index, while only 2 per cent of those seventy-five or older did. Some of this relationship is an artifact, since there are, in the index, two work-related attitudes, which are not relevant for those currently not in the labor force. However, the strength of the relationship is far greater than that which could be accounted for by an artifact alone. There is no significant relationship between score on the index of need for achievement and sex and marital status of the head of the family, although the scores of female heads of families were generally lower, reflecting in part, an age difference. (See Table D-14.) Table D-15 indicates that there are differences in the head's score on the index of need for achievement according to race, but only at the two extremes of value of the index. The per cent scoring three or four on the index was about the same for both whites and Negroes. However the percentage of Negroes scoring zero through two on the index was 48, while

TABLE D-13

HEAD'S SCORE ON INDEX OF NEED FOR ACHIEVEMENT BY AGE OF HEAD OF FAMILY

(For all 2214 heads of families)

Head's score on index of need for achievement	All cases	Under 25	25-34	35-44	45-54	55-64	65-74	75 olde
			Age of head of family					
Zero or one	13	3	5	9	13	18	25	20
Two	25	9	12	21	28	30	35	44
Three	24	15	26	20	25	26	25	22
Four	18	27	19	22	18	16	11	12
Five	12	24	22	16	12	6	3	1
Six	5	15	10	8	3	3	1	1
Seven or eight	3	7	6	4	1	1	0	0
Total	100	100	100	100	100	100	100	100
Number of cases	2214	130	360	445	476	387	277	139

TABLE D-14

HEAD'S SCORE ON INDEX OF NEED FOR ACHIEVEMENT BY SEX AND

MARITAL STATUS OF HEAD OF FAMILY

(For all 2214 heads of families)

Head's score on index of need for achievement	All cases	Sex and marital status of head of family		
		Married	Single	
		Male	Male	Female
Zero or one	13	13	11	18
Two	25	24	20	30
Three	24	23	21	26
Four	18	19	16	14
Five	12	13	16	7
Six	5	5	12	4
Seven or eight	3	3	4	1
Total	100	100	100	100
Number of cases	2214	1640	183	391

TABLE D-15

HEAD'S SCORE ON INDEX OF NEED FOR ACHIEVEMENT BY RACE OF HEAD OF FAMILY

(For all 2214 heads of families)

Head's score on index of need for achievement	All cases	White	Negro	Other; not ascertained
Zero or one	13	12	20	20
Two	25	25	28	25
Three	24	24	23	20
Four	18	18	16	13
Five	12	12	12	11
Six	5	6	1	9
Seven or eight	3	3	0	2
Total	100	100	100	100
Number of cases	2214	1961	208	45

Race of head of family

477

that for whites was 37; and the percentage of Negroes scoring six through
eight was 1, while that for whites was 9.

There is no significant relation of region of country with either age
of head of family or sex and marital status of head of family. (See Tables
D-16 and D-17.) However, Table D-18 indicates that, as expected, there
are significantly more Negroes living in the "Deep South" and the "Other
South" than whites -- 59 per cent for Negroes versus 28 per cent for whites.

Table D-19 indicates that there is practically no correlation of age
with occupation, except for the increase in per cent of farmers among the
older working population. Relatively few female heads of families work
for money compared with men. Fifty-six per cent of female heads of families
were in the labor force while the comparable percentages for single men
and married men were 77 and 88 respectively. None of the female heads of a
family in this sample were farmers or self-employed businesswomen. (See
Table D-20). Table D-21 shows that there is very little difference in the
percentage of whites in the labor force compared with Negroes. However
there is considerable difference in the type of occupation held by whites
compared with Negroes. Eleven per cent of white heads of families had jobs
in professional or technical occupations, while only 4 per cent of the
Negroes did. And a much higher percentage of Negroes held unskilled jobs
than did whites. Some of these Negro unskilled workers are female heads
of families working as domestics, while very few white female heads of
families work for money outside the home. However, of course, many of
these unskilled Negro workers are men. It is also noteworthy that there
are practically no Negroes in the managerial or self-employed businessman
category.

TABLE D-16

REGION OF COUNTRY BY AGE OF HEAD OF FAMILY
(For all 2214 heads of families)

Age of head of family

Region of country	All cases	Under 25	25-34	35-44	45-54	55-64	65-74	75 old
Northeast	22	14	22	23	22	24	23	19
North Central	31	37	28	31	32	32	27	29
Deep South	6	5	6	6	6	5	5	4
Other South	25	24	26	22	24	26	30	31
West	16	20	18	18	16	13	15	17
Total	100	100	100	100	100	100	100	100
Number of cases	2214	130	360	445	476	387	277	139

TABLE D-17

REGION OF COUNTRY BY SEX AND MARITAL STATUS OF HEAD OF FAMILY
(For all 2214 heads of families)

Sex and marital status of head of family

Region of country	All cases	Married Male	Single Male	Single Female
Northeast	22	22	20	24
North Central	31	32	31	27
Deep South	6	5	7	6
Other South	25	25	23	29
West	16	16	19	14
Total	100	100	100	100
Number of cases	2214	1640	183	391

TABLE D-18

REGION OF COUNTRY BY RACE OF HEAD OF FAMILY

(For all 2214 heads of families)

Region of country	All cases	White	Negro	Other; not ascertained
		Race of head of family		
Northeast	22	23	13	18
North Central	31	32	18	22
Deep South	6	5	13	4
Other South	25	23	46	25
West	16	17	10	31
Total	100	100	100	100
Number of cases	2214	1961	208	45

Intercorrelation among five explanatory variables

Table D-22 gives the rank correlations (Kendall's Tau-B) for each of the five main explanatory variables used in the analyses.[1] It is interesting to note that the relationship of the index of achievement orientation with education is stronger than that of the index of achievement with income or hourly earnings. Home ownership appears to be mostly an income phenomenon.

_____

[1]M.G. Kendall and A. Stuart, The Advanced Theory of Statistics, Vol. II, 5th ed. (London: Griffin Co., 1961), pp. 538-542.

TABLE D-19

OCCUPATION OF HEAD OF FAMILY BY AGE OF HEAD OF FAMILY

(For all 2214 heads of families)

Occupation of head of family	All cases	Age of head of family						
		Under 25	25-34	35-44	45-54	55-64	65-74	75 o olde
Professionals or technical workers	10	8	18	13	12	7	3	0
Managers and nonself-employed officials	6	2	8	9	7	6	1	1
Self-employed businessmen	7	1	4	9	12	8	5	2
Clerical and sales workers	10	8	15	15	10	9	3	0
Craftsmen and foremen	15	16	17	20	20	17	1	1
Operatives and kindred	13	24	20	16	15	11	2	0
Unskilled laborers and service workers	10	11	9	9	11	15	4	1
Farmers	4	2	2	4	6	7	5	2
Miscellaneous (includes government protective workers, students, housewives under 55)	6	28	7	5	6	2	0	0
Retired (includes housewives 55 or older)	19	0	0	0	1	18	76	93
Total	100	100	100	100	100	100	100	100
Number of cases	2214	130	360	445	476	387	277	139

TABLE D-20

OCCUPATION OF HEAD OF FAMILY BY SEX AND MARITAL STATUS OF HEAD OF FAMILY

(For all 2214 heads of families)

		Sex and marital status of head of family		
		Married	Single	
Occupation of head of family	All cases	Male	Male	Female
Professionals or technical workers	10	11	9	8
Managers and nonself-employed officials	6	7	8	3
Self-employed businessmen	7	9	5	0
Clerical and sales workers	10	9	9	13
Craftsmen and foremen	15	19	12	1
Operatives and kindred	13	15	8	8
Unskilled laborers and service workers	10	9	12	13
Farmers	4	5	4	0
Miscellaneous (includes government protective workers, students, housewives under 55)	6	4	10	10
Retired (includes housewives 55 or older)	19	12	23	44
Total	100	100	100	100
Number of cases	2214	1640	183	391

TABLE D-21

OCCUPATION OF HEAD OF FAMILY BY RACE OF HEAD OF FAMILY

(For all 2214 heads of families)

Race of head of family

Occupation of head of family	All cases	White	Negro	Other; not ascertained
Professionals or technical workers	10	11	4	7
Managers and nonself-employed officials	6	7	1	4
Self-employed busi-nessmen	7	8	1	2
Clerical and sales workers	10	10	6	7
Craftsmen and foremen	15	16	9	13
Operatives and kindred	13	13	19	16
Unskilled laborers and service workers	10	6	37	27
Farmers	4	5	2	4
Miscellaneous (includes government protective workers, students, housewives under 55)	6	5	6	9
Retired (includes housewives 55 or older)	19	19	15	11
Total	100	100	100	100
Number of cases	2214	1961	208	45

TABLE D-22

INTERCORRELATION AMONG THE FOLLOWING VARIABLES: EDUCATION OF HEAD OF
FAMILY, TOTAL FAMILY INCOME, HOURLY EARNINGS OF HEAD OF FAMILY,
HOME OWNERSHIP, HEAD'S SCORE ON INDEX OF NEED FOR ACHIEVEMENT
(For all 2214 heads of families)

Variables	Variable number	Variable number (1)	(2)	(3)	(4)	(5)
Education of head of family*	(1)		.34	.35	(.04)	.34
Total family income	(2)			.65	.21	.14
Hourly earnings of head of family	(3)				.13	.17
Home ownership**	(4)					.09
Score on index of need for achievement	(5)					

( ) not significantly different from .00 (at three standard deviations)

*   Intercorrelations exclude four cases in which education of head of family
      was not ascertained

**   Intercorrelations exclude those who neither own nor rent.

484

Construction of the indexes and intercorrelations among them

All of the indexes were constructed with some theoretical relationship in mind; however before accepting the construction on this basis
alone, we examined the actual relationships between the variables proposed
for each index and omitted those variables that were negatively correlated
with the others. Table D-23 through D-32 give our findings for the various
indexes. Each table presents a summary of the interrelationships among
the proposed components of an index. Instead of giving correlation
coefficients, however, for each pair of variables we present the actual
per cent of people who were eligible to score on that index for both
components and expressed that per cent as a ratio of the per cent expected
to score on both components of the index.[2] A ratio of 1.00 indicates no
correlation, while a ratio greater than 1.00 indicates positive correlation
and a ratio of less than 1.00 indicates negative correlation.

For example, taking two components from the use of new products index,
use of a steam iron and use of an electric frying pan, we derive the relevant
two-by-two table as follows:

	Use an electric frying pan	Do not use an electric frying pan	Total
Use a steam iron	39.9	32.9	72.8
Do not use a steam iron	6.7	20.5	27.2
Total	46.6	53.4	100.0

---

[2]Expected proportion is the product of the marginal proportions. What
we did, essentially, was to reduce large contingency tables into simple two-
by-two tables, thus enabling us to give simple statements of association.
See, for example, G.U. Yule and M.G. Kendall, Introduction to the Theory
of Statistics, 14th edition (New York: Hafner Publishers, 1950), p. 51

The actual per cent of those getting scores on the index for both of
the above components is 39.9, which is shown in Table D-23, while the
expected per cent is the product of the two marginals, that is 46.6 x
72.8, or 33.9 per cent. And the ratio of the actual per cent to the expected
per cent is 1.18 indicating positive correlation. This ratio and the marginal
percentages are also given in the tables.

Index of Receptivity to Change

The index of receptivity to change was actually built from four sub-
indexes -- use of new products, self-perception of receptivity to new products
and attitude toward them, attraction to new scientific developments, and
whether important to make changes on the job. Chapter 13 analyzes this index
as a dependent variable.

Looking at Table D-23, it is obvious that none of the six variables
making up the use of new products sub-index is negatively related to the
others, while the majority are significantly positively related to one another.
There is an especially high positive relationship of use of steam iron with
use of a coin-operated dry-cleaning machine. Both of these items represent
a new way of doing a particular household task, both of which may be adopted
at the same time. Use of a gasoline credit card, having seat belts in one's
car, and whether bought car new or used all show a significant positive
relationship with one another. Again, these items represent new things, but
three things which are likely to be adopted all at once. One point was
given for each of these six components. This index did have in it two items
which were dependent upon the ownership of a car -- whether seat belts in
car, and whether bought car new. Hence, the 78 per cent of families who own
a car have a chance to score six points, while the maximum number of points
that could be scored by the remaining 22 per cent was four.

TABLE D-23

ASSOCIATION BETWEEN COMPONENTS OF INDEX OF USE OF NEW PRODUCTS [a]

(For all 2214 cases)

Component variables	Variable number	Variable number (1)	(2)	(3)	(4)	(5)	(6)	All cases
Use a steam iron	(1)		1.18	1.20	2.01	1.17	1.13	72.8
Use an electric frying pan	(2)	39.9		1.35	1.19	1.28	1.24	46.0
Use a gasoline credit card	(3)	25.1	18.2		1.28	1.75	1.54	28.9
Have used a coin-operated dry-cleaning machine	(4)	53.5	20.4	13.6		1.23	1.07	36.8
Have seat belts in the car	(5)	22.6	15.7	13.5	12.1		1.76	26.5
Bought car new rather than used	(6)	31.7	22.2	17.1	35.4	18.0		38.5
All cases		72.8	46.6	28.9	36.8	26.5	38.5	

[a] Upper right: Ratio of actual to expected percentage.
Lower left: Actual percentages doing both.
Right column and bottom row: Percent doing each thing.

Table D-24 shows the intercorrelations of the three component parts of the attraction to new scientific developments part of the receptivity to change index. Two of the component variables are attitudinal, and are based on the following two sets of questions:

> "What do you think of the program our country has to try to land a man on the moon? Why is that?"

> "Have you heard about adding fluoride to the water to reduce tooth decay and cavities? What do you think of the idea?"

Those approving of the addition of fluoride to water supplies with no qualifications were given one point on this index, while those who thought the program to try to land a man on the moon was a good idea, with or without qualifications, were given one point. The third component of this index, whether some member of the family has had polio vaccine, represents an activity; again, one point was given if any member of the family had had polio vaccine, for a possible total of three points for any one head of a family. There may be some slight age difference in this component index, since it is sometimes recommended that older people not get polio vaccine. The correlation between the above-two attitude variables of this index is significant and positive, while the activity variable, whether or not at least some member of the family has had polio vaccine, is only mildly positively related to the two attitude variables.

The third part of the index of receptivity to change, self-perception of receptivity to new products and attitude toward them, is based on two attitude questions as follows:

> "Would you say you try new products when they first come out, or do you wait until others have tried them first, or what?"

> "Some people say that most new things are just a way to get us to spend more money. Others feel that most new things are really improvements. How do you feel?"

TABLE D-24

ASSOCIATION BETWEEN COMPONENTS OF INDEX OF ATTRACTION TO NEW SCIENTIFIC DEVELOPMENTS [a]

(For all 2214 cases)

		Variable number			
Component variables	Variable number	(1)	(2)	(3)	All cases
Head of family approves without qualification the addition of fluoride to water	(1)		1.14	1.23	39.2
At least some of family have had polio vaccine	(2)	32.5		1.12	72.4
Heads think that the program to try to land a man on the moon is good	(3)	19.5	32.6		40.4
All cases		39.2	72.4	40.4	

[a]Upper right: Ratio of actual to expected percentage.
Lower left: Actual percentages doing both.
Right column and bottom row: Percent doing each thing.

The scores given in response to these two questions were scaled according to the strength of the attitude. Two points were given if the individual stated that he tried new products when they first came out and likewise for believing that most new things were improvements. And respondents were given one point if they sometimes tried new products when they first came out and one point if they thought some new things were improvements but that some others were a way to get people to spend money. Zero points were given for stating that they waited for others to try new products first and if they thought most new things were a way to get people to spend money.

A "don't know" response to either of these two questions was also given a score of one. Table D-25 indicates that the relationship is positive between those who try new products when they first come out and those who think most new things are improvements. Likewise there is a positive relationship between those who sometimes try new products when they first come out and sometimes wait and who also believe that some new things are improvements but that others are merely just a way to get us to spend our money.

The last Sub-index of receptivity to change is a zero-one measure of whether or not the head of the family thought it was important for him to make changes on his job. The two questions used for this index were as follows, the first one for the self-employed and second one for those employed by someone else:

> "Do you like to keep things running smoothly or are you more interested in trying new things in your work?"

> "How important is it to you to have some chance to make changes in your work?"

TABLE D-25

ASSOCIATION BETWEEN COMPONENTS OF INDEX OF SELF-PERCEPTION OF
RECEPTIVITY TO NEW PRODUCTS AND ATTITUDE TOWARD THEM[a]

(For all 2214 cases)

Component variables	Variable number	Variable number (1)	(2)	(3)	(4)	All cases
Head of family says he tries new products when they first come out	(1)		*	1.20	.84	36.5
Head of family says he sometimes tries new products first, sometimes waits; or does not know what he does	(2)	*		.90	1.21	19.8
Head of family thinks that most new products are improvements	(3)	24.5	10.0		*	56.1
Head of family thinks that some new things are improvements, but that some are not; or does not know what he thinks	(4)	9.7	7.5	*		31.5
All cases		36.5	19.8	56.1	31.5	

---

*Inapplicable, since variables 1 and 2 are based on responses to the same question; therefore the giving of a particular response automatically precludes the giving of a different response. The same is true for variables 3 and 4 as well.

[a]Upper right: Ratio of actual to expected percentage.
Lower left: Actual percentages doing both.
Right column and bottom row: Percent doing each thing.

The self-employed were given one point if they stated that they liked to try new things in their businesses, and those employed by someone else were given a point if they said it was "very important" or "important" for them to have some chance to make changes in their work. Both of these questions, however, were relevant only for those currently in the labor force.

None of the Sub-indexes was negatively related to the other Sub-indexes. Hence, all four sub-indexes were combined into the receptivity to change index. Two points of the index were contingent upon the family's owning a car, while one point was contingent upon the head of the family's being in the labor force. A score of fourteen was possible on the index, but the index was truncated with a maximum of nine being allowed for analysis purposes. For the distribution of scores on this index of receptivity to change and its component parts, see Table 13-1.

Planning and Time Horizon

This index was built from questions about education plans for children, vacation plans, and retirement plans as shown in Table D-26. This index did have to take account of fairly substantial percentages of cases which were ineligible to give a response for various components of this index: 62 per cent were ineligible for the question of whether or not they had savings set aside for their children's education (no children under 18, or no children who will go to college); 18 per cent of families never took vacations, so they were ineligible for any questions about their vacations; and 42 per cent of heads of families were either under thirty-five years old or already retired, and therefore were not eligible for the question on when they planned to retire.

TABLE D-26

ASSOCIATION BETWEEN COMPONENTS OF INDEX OF PLANNING AND TIME HORIZON

(For all 2214 cases)

Component variables	Variable number	Variable number (1)	(2)	(3)	(4)	(5)	(6)	All Cases
Head of family has money set aside to pay for his children's college education	(1)		*	1.42	.41	.77	1.32	18.2
Head of family has no children under 18, or has children who will not go to college	(2)	*		.87	1.22	1.05	1.05	61.6
Family planned its most recent vacation more than one month in advance	(3)	9.8	20.3		*	.95	1.10	38.0
Family never takes vacations	(4)	1.3	13.2	*		1.26	.52	17.5
Head of family is retired, or less than 35 years old	(5)	5.9	27.3	15.2	9.3		*	42.1
Head of family knows when he will retire	(6)	9.9	26.6	17.1	4.3	*		41.1
All cases		18.2	61.6	38.0	17.5	42.1	41.1	

*Inapplicable, since variables 1 and 2 are based on a response to the same question; therefore, the giving of a particular response automatically precludes the giving of a different response. The same is true of variables 3 and 4, and variables 5 and 6.

[a]Upper right: Ratio of actual to expected percentage.
Lower left: Actual percentages doing both.
Right column and bottom row: Percent doing each thing.

For each question that the head of the family was eligible to answer, two points were given, that is, if he had money set aside to pay for his children's college education, planned his most recent vacation more than one month in advance, and knew when he would retire. Each of these three variables was positively related to each of the others, with having set aside money to pay for children's education being significantly and positively related to the other two. And the balancing values indicating ineligibility were positively related to one another. This index is used as a dependent variable in Chapter 14, and its distribution is given there.

Mobility indexes

Two indexes of mobility were constructed, one representing the mobility behavior of the head of the family, and the other representing his total mobility experience, both geographical and occupational. For the mobility behavior index, one point for each of the following was given:

> Head of family has lived in more than one state since his
> first regular job
> Head of family has had a number of different kinds of jobs
> Head of family has thought of changing to another job
> Head of family has tried going into business for himself

In addition to the above five variables, the index of mobility experience included, the following two things, both of which had elements of predeterminance in them, hence do not represent entirely the behavior of the head of the family:

> Head of family has more education than his father
> Family has lived in more than one region of the country
> over two generations

The first two component variables listed above were relevant only for those who have ever had a regular full-time job, including 97 per cent of the population, however. The next two were relevant only for those currently in the labor force or 74 per cent of the total population. The index of mobility behavior was used as a dependent variable in Chapter 15, and its overall distribution is given there. The index of mobility experience has been used throughout the book as an explanatory variable. Its distribution is as follows:

Score on index of mobility experience	Per cent of cases
Zero	8
One	20
Two	26
Three	23
Four	15
Five	6
Six	2
Seven	0
Total	100
Number of cases	2214

The remainder of the discussion on the mobility index will be for all of the components, including those used in the mobility experience index. There was a positive relation, 1.49, between families who have lived in their present residence for four years or less and who are planning to move within the next five years. (See Table D-27.) It should be noted, however, that both conditions must hold before the individual is given a point on the index. There was also a positive relation between the head's having thought of going into business for himself and his already having had a number of different types of jobs, living in more than one state since his first regular job, his planning to move within the next five years, and his thinking of changing to another job. And, whether or not the head of

TABLE D-27

ASSOCIATION BETWEEN COMPONENTS OF INDEX OF MOBILITY EXPERIENCE

(For all 2214 cases)

Component variables	Variable number	Variable number (1)	(2)	(3)	(4)	(5)	(6)	(7)	(8)	(9)	All cases
Head of family has more education than his father	(1)		1.02	.98	.94	1.08	1.18	1.27	1.19	1.11	48.7
Head of family has had a number of different kinds of jobs	(2)	24.4		1.16	1.03	1.05	1.09	1.13	1.24	1.36	49.1
Head of family has lived in more than one state since his first regular job	(3)	18.3	21.9		1.41	1.15	1.18	1.08	1.06	1.39	38.5
Family has lived in more than 1 region of the country over two generations	(4)	25.3	27.7	30.0		1.04	1.13	1.00	.99	1.13	55.0
Family has lived less than 4 years in present residence	(5)	21.2	20.6	17.9	23.0		1.49	1.00	1.37	.72	40.2

TABLE D-27 (Continued)

Component variables	Variable number	Variable number (1)	(2)	(3)	(4)	(5)	(6)	(7)	(8)	(9)	All cases
Family plans to move within next five years	(6)	13.3	12.4	10.6	14.5	13.9		*	1.54	1.30	23.3
Self-employed head of family has thought of changing to another job	(7)	1.9	1.7	1.3	1.7	1.2	*		**	⊥	3.0
Employee head of family has thought of changing to another job	(8)	13.4	1.5	9.4	12.7	12.7	8.3	**		1.96	23.2
Head of family has tried going into business for himself	(9)	6.2	14.1	6.1	7.1	3.3	3.5	⊥	5.3		11.5
All cases		48.7	49.1	38.5	55.0	40.2	23.3	3.0	23.2	11.5	

* Too few cases for which to provide data

** Self-employed respondents were eligible to score a point on variable 7, while employees were eligible for variable 8, but no one was eligible for both

⊥ Only those heads of families who were not self-employed were eligible to score on this variable.

the family had thought of changing to another job was significantly
positively related to the other three occupational mobility variables.
On the whole, there was either a positive or no relation among the various
components. However, there is only one correlation which is significantly
negative: that of families who have lived in their present residence
less than four years and having tried going into business for one's self.
However, it is quite unlikely that this played havoc with the index, since
before being eligible to score a point one had to both have lived in their
present residence less than four years and be planning to move within the
next five years.

Ambition and Aspiration

One point was given for each of the components listed in Table D-28
of the ambition and aspiration index. Two of the components of this index,
head of family would like to work more if paid for it and head of family
would like to be earning at least $1000 more five years from now than
earning now, were relevant only for that 74 per cent of the population
currently in the labor force. And the variable, head of family expects to
send his children to college, was applicable only for the 48 per cent of the
population having children under eighteen. The distribution of the scores
on this index is given in Chapter 16. Out of a possible twenty-eight
relations between components, twenty-two were both positive and powerful.
But there was an apparent negative relationship between taking courses to
increase one's economic skills and desiring a new home or desiring to make
additions and repairs to one's present home. This is not a disturbing
relationship, however, since many of those who are taking courses to increase
their economic skills are young and hence most of them have not yet made plans
to buy a home.

TABLE D-28

ASSOCIATION BETWEEN COMPONENTS OF INDEX OF AMBITION AND ASPIRATION

(For all 2214 cases)

Component variables	Variable number	Variable number								All cases
		(1)	(2)	(3)	(4)	(5)	(6)	(7)	(8)	
Head of family expects to send children to college	(1)		1.21	1.19	1.42	1.26	1.51	1.54	1.50	38.4
Head of family expects to provide financial aid to parents or other relatives within next 20 years	(2)	5.4			.97	1.25	1.07	1.35	1.48	13.2
Head of family ranks high income first or second among 6 job characteristics	(3)	10.0	2.8		.88	1.10	1.25	1.37	1.23	22.0
Head of family took courses to increase his economic skills	(4)	6.4	2.4	2.3		1.24	.75	1.33	1.37	11.6

(Continued on page 499)

499

TABLE D-28 (Continued)

ASSOCIATION BETWEEN COMPONENTS OF INDEX OF AMBITION AND ASPIRATION

Component variables	Variable number	Variable number (1)	(2)	(3)	(4)	(5)	(6)	(7)	(8)	All cases
Family would like to buy some new things or replace some things	(5)	27.6	9.4	13.8	8.2		1.75	1.28	1.21	56.9
Family would like a new home or would like to make additions or repairs to present home	(6)	6.2	1.5	3.0	.9	10.7		1.44	1.28	10.7
Head of family would like to work more hours if paid for it	(7)	15.2	4.6	7.8	4.0	18.7	3.9		1.57	25.7
Head of family would like to be earning at least $1000 more five years from now than earning now	(8)	26.9	9.2	12.7	7.4	32.0	6.4	18.8		
All cases		38.4	13.2	22.0	11.6	56.9	10.7	25.7		

MTR 43

Social Participation

Table D-29 indicates the intercorrelations among variables used in the index of social participation. The distribution of this index is given in Chapter 17. Only one component of the index was not relevant for the entire sample, the wife's doing more than forty hours of volunteer work during the year, which was relevant for the 74 per cent of married couples in the population. The expressed political preference of the head of the family was not included in the final index since, if anything, there is a somewhat negative relationship between it and the other seven variables. Political preference is, of course, an attitude, while the other variables represent behavior.

Caution and Risk-Avoidance

Table D-30 indicates the intercorrelations among variables used in the caution and risk-avoidance index. Its distribution is given in Chapter 18. Included in the index is a diverse set of behaviors each done presumably for the purpose of attenuating disasters. Since the use of a method to limit or plan the spacing of children was relevant only for families consisting of married couples, one point was given to the 26 per cent of the population where heads of families were single, and two points were given where the head of the family was married and he had used some method to limit the number or plan the spacing of his children. The use of seat belts all or part of the time when driving was relevant only for the 78 per cent of the population owning cars. However, no adjustment was made for the irrelevant subpopulation in the case of this variable. Two attitude variables considered for inclusion in this index, the giving of a high rank to steady income or no danger of being fired as characteristics of a job (variables 7 and 8) were

TABLE D-29

ASSOCIATION BETWEEN COMPONENTS OF INDEX OF SOCIAL PARTICIPATION

(For all 2214 cases)

Component variables	Variable number	(1)	(2)	(3)	(4)	(5)	(6)	(7)	All cases
Head of family took a vacation in 1964	(1)		1.03	1.21	1.13	1.18	1.17	.97	52.4
Head of family attends religious services regularly or often	(2)	29.0		.98	1.17	1.15	.98	1.08	53.9
Family eats at restaurants at least once every 2 weeks	(3)	26.9	22.3		1.13	1.17	1.18	.94	42.3
Wife did more than 40 hours of volunteer work in 1964	(4)	13.8	14.6	11.1		2.10	1.14	.95	23.2
Head of family did more than 40 hours of volunteer work in 1964	(5)	10.5	10.6	8.4	8.2		1.18	.87	17.0
Head of family participates in sports or hobbies	(6)	36.7	31.6	29.9	15.9	14.0		.92	59.7
Head of family is strong Republican or strong Democrat	(7)	18.8	21.4	14.8	8.2	5.5	20.3		37.0
All cases		52.4	53.9	42.3	23.2	17.0	59.7	37.0	

MTR 43

TABLE D-30

ASSOCIATION BETWEEN COMPONENTS OF INDEX OF CAUTION AND RISK-AVOIDANCE

(For all 2214 cases)

Component variables	Variable number	Variable number (1)	(2)	(3)	(4)	(5)	(6)	(7)	(8)	All cases
Family is covered by hospital or medical insurance	(1)		1.11	1.07	.94	1.17	1.10	1.00	.97	78.5
Family has reserve funds equal to 2 months or more of take-home income	(2)	47.2		1.05	1.00	1.31	.99	.99	.88	54.3
All members of family have had polio vaccine	(3)	25.6	17.3		.92	1.35	1.12	.92	.85	30.4
Families do not try new products when they first come out	(4)	32.6	23.7	12.2		.83	.89	1.02	1.04	43.9

(continued next page)

TABLE D-30 (continued)

Variable number

Component variables	Variable number	(1)	(2)	(3)	(4)	(5)	(6)	(7)	(8)	All cases
Head of family has car seat belts fastened all or part of the time when driving	(5)	18.2	14.2	8.1	7.2		1.37	.90	.68	19.9
Head of family is married and has used a method to limit or plan the spacing of his children	(6)	25.9	16.1	10.3	11.7	8.2		.96	.82	30.1
Head of family ranked steady income first or second of 6 job characteristics	(7)	52.2	35.7	18.4	29.7	11.9	19.1		1.08	66.2
Head of family ranked no danger of being fired first or second of 6 job characteristics	(8)	23.5	14.8	8.0	14.1	4.2	7.6	22.2		31.0
All cases		78.5	54.3	30.4	43.9	19.9	30.1	66.2	31.0	31.0

found to be, if anything, slightly negatively related to most of the other variables. It seems that these two attitudes represented an expression of a desire for security rather than actual risk avoidance behavior, and therefore it was decided to omit these two attitude variables from the index. The head of the family's having his seat belt fastened when driving was positively related to having reserve funds equal to two months or more of take-home income, all members of the family having had polio vaccine, and having used a method to limit the number or plan the spacing of his children. None of the other variables used in the index showed any strong relationship with any of the other variables.

Index of Closeness of Family Ties

Closeness of family ties was built to represent a measure of the individual's resistance to change including a point for the following four components: an expressed importance of living near relatives, the belief that one should count on financial support from relatives if needed, the head of the family's doing some volunteer work for relatives, and finally the wife's doing some volunteer work for relatives. The score values ranged from zero to four and the distribution of these scores is given in Chapter 19. Table D-31 indicates that there is a very powerful positive relation between the wife's doing volunteer work for relatives with the head of the family's also doing volunteer work for relatives. The wife's doing some volunteer work for relatives was significantly and positively correlated with an expression of the desire to live near relatives. This may indicate that it is important to live near some family member's relative because of the volunteer work done for them, such as care for an aged parent or support for other indigent relatives.

TABLE D-31

ASSOCIATION BETWEEN COMPONENTS OF INDEX OF
CLOSENESS OF FAMILY TIES

(For all 2214 cases)

Component variables	Variable number	Variable number				All cases
		(1)	(2)	(3)	(4)	
Important for any family member to live near relatives	(1)		1.12	1.24	1.10	31.7
Head of family feels that people should be able to count on financial support from relatives if needed	(2)	17.3		.95	.93	48.7
Wife of head of family did some volunteer work for relatives	(3)	5.1	6.0		3.17	13.0
Head of family did some volunteer work for relatives	(4)	3.2	4.2	3.8		9.2
All cases		31.7	48.7	13.0	9.2	

MTR 43

Attitude toward Mothers' Working

This index was a simple zero or one score based on the response to
the following question:

> "Suppose a family has children but they are all in school --
> would you say it is a good thing for the wife to take a job
> or a bad thing, or what?"

Those who believed that it was a good idea for mothers to work were given

one point, 32 per cent of the sample, while those who gave a pro-con or

depends, or an unfavorable response were given a score of zero.   The

question used had a specific situation structured into it, because an earlier

study used a less-structured situation and elicited a large percentage of

pro-con and ambivalent responses.[3]   Chapter 19 gives a distribution of the

responses, which were coded into a five-point scale depending on the strength

of attitude.

Index of Achievement Orientation

The measure of achievement orientation used in this study builds upon

years of research and empirical testing.   Professor Atkinson defines the

achievement motive as the "propensity to strive for success in situations

involving an evaluation of one's performance in relation to some standard

of excellence," which underlies a "capacity for taking pride in accomplish-

ment where success at one or another activity is achieved."[4]   It is generally

theorized that this motive is developed during the early stages of life and

is a relatively stable personality disposition which does not change over

various situations for the same person.   The following behavioral and

attitudinal attributes were thought to be a composite measure of people with

high levels of achievement motivation:

---

[3] Morgan, et al.

[4] John W. Atkinson, An Introduction to Motivation (Princeton:
D. Van Nostrand, 1964), p. 242.

1. Derives satisfaction from overcoming obstacles
    by their own effort

2. Focus on goals and take calculated risks (i.e., do not
    play long shots or attempt only things where the outcome
    is certain)

3. Is associated with upward mobility in general

4. Put strong distinctions between easy and difficult tasks.

Accordingly, such an index should give point values to various scores on

these attributes; thus, one point was given for each of the following:

> Head of family has sent, is sending, or will send children
> to a four-year college and expects them to get a degree
> (only for families where total family income is under $10,000)

> Head of family ranked chances for advancement are good first
> or second among six job characteristics

> Head of family ranked the work is important, gives a feeling
> of accomplishment first or second among six job character-
> istics

> Head of family believes that he falls short of what he could do

> Head of family took more than forty hours of courses in 1964

> Head of family desires to get better at his sports or hobbies

> Head of family's income aspirations are realistic but positive

> Nonself-employed head of family thinks it is important to make
> changes in his work

> Head of family admires those who try difficult things for their
> initiative

Hence it was possible to score between zero and nine on the index with

the actual scores ranging from zero through eight. The distribution is as

follows:

Score on index of achievement orientation	Per cent of cases
Zero	1
One	12
Two	25

Three	24
Four	18
Five	12
Six	6
Seven	2
Eight	0
Total	100
Number of cases	2214

Each component of the index had some theoretical justification, though, of course, some were relevant only to a subfraction of the population. The above-listed variables focus on actions and attitudes which indicate an appreciation of the importance of initiative and undertaking difficult tasks, and setting goals that are neither easy nor unrealistically high.

There are several problems with such an index. One is that it may be reflecting something more mundane, like level of completed formal education or a set of attitudes. And whatever predictive power the index may have, it may be because of only one or two of its components, while some of the other components may even have reverse effects. However, since the components are all positively correlated with one another, and some significantly so, if any of the components has the hypothesized effect, the index should show it, at least in an attenuated form. (See Table D-32.) The following questions were asked regarding education of children of the head of the family:

> "Do you have any children in college? Do you expect any of them to get a degree from a four-year college?"

> "Do you have any children who will go to college? Will any of them get degrees from a four-year college?"

> "Do you have any children who have already gone to college? Did any of them get degrees from a four-year college?"

It is postulated that people who send their children to college (or are planning to) are setting and focusing on goals for themselves (and their families). However, the goal as such may or may not imply achievement motivation, depending upon whether or not a high value is placed on succeeding where it is difficult. Sending children to college was regarded as trying something that would be difficult only in cases where family incomes were under $10,000. For those with incomes of $10,000 or more, sending children to college was regarded not as a reflection of an incentive to achieve, but as an indication of fulfillment of role expectations. Thus, one point for these series of questions was given only for those with family incomes under $10,000, who had sent, were sending, or planned to send their children to college.

Even though other studies have shown that direct questions about the importance of achievement are uncorrelated with the indirect measures which predicted behavior, the following question was formulated to reduce the bias in connection with the respondent's own occupation:

"Would you say that you often fall short of what you could do and that you could do things better?"

Those satisfied all the time with the outcome of what they do presumably are setting low standards of excellence for their performance or are choosing only easy tasks. And however successful the highly achievement oriented person has been, he is expected to keep raising his standards of excellence. Hence, those who answered that they thought they fell short of what they could do, with or without qualification, were given one point on the index. A positive response to this question was mildly positively correlated with the other variables used in the index, as is shown in Table D-32.

It was postulated that heads of families who were taking courses were actually trying to implement the goals on which they had focused. And such activity is associated with upward mobility in general, and one point on the index was given for heads of families who had taken more than forty hours

TABLE D-32

ASSOCIATION BETWEEN COMPONENTS OF INDEX OF ACHIEVEMENT ORIENTATION

(For all 2214 cases)

Component variables	Variable number	Variable number (1)	(2)	(3)	(4)	(5)	(6)	(7)	(8)	(9)	All cases
Head of family ranked chances for advancement are good first or second of 6 job characteristics	(1)		1.05	1.06	1.63	1.18	1.26	1.35	1.13	.48	32.2
Head of family ranked the work is important, gives a feeling of accomplishment first or second of 6 job characteristics	(2)	12.2		1.02	1.44	1.12	1.13	1.29	1.28	.35	36.0
Head of family believes that he falls short of what he could do	(3)	19.2	20.8		1.10	1.11	1.04	1.03	1.07	.97	56.3
Head of family took more than 40 hours of courses in 1964	(4)	5.7	5.6	6.7		1.81	1.64	1.82	1.34	.92	10.8
Head of family desires to get better at his sports or hobbies	(5)	9.3	9.9	15.2	4.7		1.33	1.44	1.11	1.06	24.4

(Continued on page 511)

510

TABLE D-32 (Continued)

ASSOCIATION BETWEEN COMPONENTS OF INDEX OF ACHIEVEMENT ORIENTATION

(For all 2214 cases)

Component variables	Variable number	Variable number (1)	(2)	(3)	(4)	(5)	(6)	(7)	(8)	(9)	All cases
Head of family's income aspirations are realistic but positive	(6)	9.2	9.3	13.3	4.1	7.3		1.53	1.11	1.12	22.7
Nonself-employed head of family thinks it is important to make changes in his work	(7)	13.4	14.3	17.9	6.0	10.8	10.7		1.28	.97	30.9
Head of family admires those who try difficult things for their initiative	(8)	9.7	12.3	16.2	3.9	7.2	6.8	10.6		1.00	26.8
Head of family ranks high income first or second of 6 job characteristics	(9)	3.4	2.8	12.0	2.2	5.7	5.6	6.6	5.9		22.0
All cases		32.2	36.0	56.3	10.8	24.4	22.7	30.9	26.8	22.0	

of courses during 1964. Of all the variables used in this index, it was
the one that was most highly positively correlated with the other variables
used in this index, its correlation being nonsignificant only with believing
that he falls short of what he could do.

Asking the head of the family whether or not it was important for him
to get better at his hobbies was a direct question meant to examine the extent
to which the individual was setting standards of excellence for himself.
It therefore measures the intensity of his achievement motive. It was
thought that this might be particularly relevant for those whose jobs did
not provide any opportunity for the setting of internal goals of achievement
or accomplishment, that is, those whose jobs were by nature structured and
routine. This component was especially highly correlated with the taking
of more than forty hours of courses and lessons, another variable indicating
the striving for success outside of one's occupation. And desiring to get
better at sports or hobbies had a high significant positive correlation with
thinking it is important to make changes on the job, which may indicate a
sense of frustration with one's present job for those who are highly achievement oriented but are unable to satisfy this motivation on their jobs. One
point was thus given for those desiring to get better at their hobbies. Of
course the 28 per cent of the heads of families who had no hobbies were not
eligible to score a point on this variable.

Those heads of families who were currently in the labor force were
asked how much income they thought they would be making in five years by the
following questions:

> "If you were extremely successful, what is the largest amount
> you might be making five years from now?"

> "Of course the future is uncertain, but how much would you like
> to be making five years from now?"

he difference of the amounts answered for these two questions was coded
s a measure of the individual's realism in the setting of his expectations.
he amount the individual might make if extremely successful in five years
as taken to be a measure of realistic expectations, while the amount the
ndividual said he would like to be making in five years was taken to be
 measure of desires and wishes. If the amount that the individual reported
e might make if he were extremely successful were more than the amount he
ould like to be making, this was believed to be a standard of excellence
igh enough so that its achievement was difficult but not so high that it
ould, in itself, be an excuse for failure. This measure is based on an
tudy done by Mahone where the "unrealism' in aspiration took the form of
veraspiration."[5] This variable was positively correlated with all of the
ther variables used in the index, but significantly so with ranking
hances for advancement high as a characteristic of a job, taking more than
orty hours of courses during 1964, and desiring to get better at hobbies
r sports.

All heads of families were asked:

"What do you think of a man who tries difficult things but
doesn't always succeed? Why is that?"

his set of questions is about as close to an indirect measure of achievement
rientation that we had, without making direct reference to the respondent's
wn situations.Those who stated that they admired such a man for his initiat-
ve and desire to take on tough tasks were given one point on this index.

---

[5]Ibid., p. 252.

However, those who admired such a man for his persistence were not given a point, since that admiration was not regarded as an expression of achievement, but merely of hard work.

The ranking first or second out of a possible six of three characteristics of a job: chances for advancement are good, the work is important, gives a feeling of accomplishment, and high income were potential variables for the index. Both the high ranking of chances for advancement are good and the work is important, gives a feeling of accomplishment were positively correlated with each of the other variables used in the index. However, the giving of a high rank to high income was significantly negatively related to the other two ranking of job characteristics' variables: a result of the positive correlation between the first two variables and the mechanical constraint of ranking among six alternatives. Hence, it was not used as one of the components of the index.

APPENDIX E

MULTIVARIATE TECHNIQUES

Introduction

The strategy of this volume has been to present for each dependent variable some information about its formation and distribution and its relation to the most important explanatory variables, and then to go more directly into a multivariate analysis of the most flexible sort. The procedure is flexible in the following ways:

(a) It does not assume that the predictor variables are properly scaled or their effects linear or additive.

(b) It allows for more than one stage in the causal process, so that a clearly prior set of variables is introduced first, and whatever variation they do not explain is analyzed against a second set of variables.

The investigative technique used in most cases is a searching process that looks for structure, that is, for the definition of a set of population subgroups such that each differs from the rest as much as possible in terms of the dependent variable, is homogeneous within itself, and is large enough to matter.[1]

Since the technique is sequential, both within one analysis and even more in the analysis of residuals at a second stage, it can provide firmer answers to such questions as "Once we take account of age and education, does race matter?"

It combines formal statistics with the common sense of an experienced researcher, since it simulates the procedures of a researcher investigating

---

[1] For a complete explanation, see John Sonquist and James Morgan, The Detection of Interaction Effects (Ann Arbor: Survey Research Center, The University of Michigan, 1964).

a body of data, but, being tireless, does it systematically and with computation at each stage of the proper measurements on which the choices of next steps are based. It is the only multivariate procedure that does not impose the assumption of additivity, and any observer of the world knows that it is full of interaction effects. The effect of education on earnings depends on one's age, the effect of age on hospital utilization depends on sex, and so forth. Most important, economic incentives may affect only those with some freedom to choose how many hours they work, and non-economic motivation may affect only those not dominated by constraints and economic motives. Sometimes any one of several factors may have the same impact: old age, youth, disability, illness, unemployment, or being a single adult with children to care for can reduce the hours a person works for money.

The Computer Program Used

The program operates as follows. For each potential explanatory classification it examines the explanatory power (reduction in error variance) achievable by using that classification. It examines the means of the dependent variable against each explanatory classification in turn. In each case it finds the best way to use that explanatory classification to divide the sample into two parts -- best in terms of the variance explained ("between sum-of-squares").

If the predicting classification has a natural order, the order is preserved, and the number of possible divisions is one less than the number of classes. The machine examines the fruitfulness of isolating the first group from the rest, the first two groups from the rest, the first three, and so on. If the classification has no natural ordering,

all <u>feasible</u> splits are examined. (It can be shown that if the classes
are arranged in order according to the size of the mean of the dependent
variable, then there is never any other more powerful division than one
of those preserving that order.)

Keeping in store the best division on that variable, the process
proceeds to the next predictor, repeats the process, compares the
explanatory power of the better of the two, and preserves that. Then
it proceeds to the third explanatory characteristic and repeats the
process. In any case, the means of the dependent variable for each
class of each predictor are preserved for the printed output at the end.

Having swept through all the predictors and found the best way to
use the best one to divide the sample, the computer then divides the
sample that way, finds the part with the largest remaining unexplained
variability, and repeats the process, examining that part against all
the explanatory variables again.

At each stage after that, the group with the largest remaining
variance is examined and, if possible, divided again. The process stops
when no way can be found to divide any of the groups so as to reduce
the unexplained variance by enough to matter (and to provide some assurance
that the result is not fortuitous). In the present volume with the sample
sizes involved, this has usually been set at 0.5 per cent of the original
total sum of squares (variance). Where the sample used is smaller and/or
the number and flexibility of the predictors greater, even higher cut-off

points are and should be used. For safety, the program also refuses to look at a group that contains less than 1.5 per cent of the total original sum of squares, or fewer than 25 cases, and it refuses to generate more than 50 final groups.

Since the printed output contains, for each subgroup examined, the means of the dependent variable for each class of each predictor, and the explained sum of squares from the best use of that predictor, it is possible to see whether any of the divisions made of the sample had close competition from some other predictor. In that case, the two competing predictors are likely to be highly correlated, and a different sample might well allow the other one to be used. Such close calls are generally mentioned in the text.

Since at least k - 1 divisions are tried for each variable (k is the number of classes of that variable) at each step, it is easy to see that the total branching finally developed is selected from a very large number of possible ones, and cannot be thought of as testing any hypotheses. There are no "degrees of freedom" left in a statistical sense, and no way to estimate the stability of the results over different samples.[2]

---

[2] Tests with the program indicate that the first divisions made in a set of data remain reasonably stable over different samples of the same population, and that the final groups developed tend to be more stable than the particular order of divisions by which they are generated.

Where the dependent variable has a large variance or has extreme cases, the use of reduction-in-unexplained-sum-of-squares as a criterion leads to the isolation of groups with very few cases. We have generally applied the rule that groups of fewer than 25 cases should not be allowed, since they might well be idiosyncratic. Another sample might well lead to a different result. Hence, the figures were truncated, focusing attention on the differences that were both important and likely to exist in the total population.

This problem is not unique to the procedure used here, but arises whenever a body of data is subjected to a large number of analyses, or a large number of explanatory variables are used and then scanned for the "significant" ones. The present formalization of the process merely makes the problem more obvious.

The results of the process are independent of the order in which the variables are introduced, but they do depend on which variables are used, and on the precision with which they measure what we hope they represent. It is always possible that introducing a new variable, or a better measure of one already tried, would lead to new conclusions.

The greatest power of the procedure is its ability to conclude that a particular variable,as measured, does not matter. If that variable is not able to account for any substantial fraction of the variance of the dependent variable, either over the whole sample or over any of its widely different subgroups, then it really does not matter and can be discarded.

A final question is how the process is affected by intercorrelations among the explanatory variables. Multiple regression is frequently described, inaccurately, as "holding other variables constant." The interaction-detecting process used here, since it operates sequentially, actually does take out the effects of variables as it uses them to divide the sample, and analysis of the groups farther down the diagram can show whether the second variable still matters within subgroups divided according to the first. In most cases with correlated variables the answer is no. Hence, whichever of the correlated predictors is the most powerful is actually used, and the other one then drops from sight. Such cases are noted in the text. We regard this as better, in most cases, than the multiple regression procedure, which can best be described as allowing the correlated variables to "share the credit."

If the predictors are having effects at different stages in the causal process, and particularly if there is one clearly prior set that can affect the other predictors but cannot be affected by them, then a two-stage analysis is clearly called for in which we make sure that the effects of the first set are removed first, and the residuals run only against the second set. It is sometimes possible to argue that there is a whole chain of causes operating sequentially, and that the analysis should operate the same way. We have not constructed it to do so, chiefly because there are often uncertainties, because some of our estimates of earlier variables are current responses possibly affected by later events, and because interaction effects may well mean that the prior variables do affect the way later factors work. In general, however, we have put such variables as income in the second stage, for the sake of clearly measuring the potential effects without including spurious effects due to its correlations with education or age or marital status. Hence we are in better shape to answer questions about the possible effects of changing income currently (without changing education which takes much longer).

In some cases, however, the explanatory factors seemed to be operating additively and pervasively in the whole population, and the assumptions of regression seemed appropriate. Even here we avoided the assumption that the effects of each variable were linear, by using "dummy variables" representing membership in the subclasses of each predictor, so that the regression developed its own scaling of each predictor at the same time that it assessed their importance.[3]

Where a variable is assigned to membership in a subgroup, the regression coefficient is an estimate of the effect of belonging to that subgroup if the members of that subgroup were like the total population in their distribution on all the other variables. If the coefficients for any set of subclasses which exhausts the population are constrained so that their weighted mean is equal to the overall average of the dependent variable, then we can compare the actual average effect of each subclass on the dependent variable with this multiple regression estimate of what that average effect would be if one adjusted the group for the effects of its abnormality on all the other variables. And the difference between the actual and adjusted averages is a measure of the amount of intercorrelation among the predictors. If the predictors were completely uncorrelated with one another, the two sets of numbers would be identical, and the unadjusted subgroup average would become an optimal estimate of the effect of belonging to that subgroup.

Clearly, some intercorrelation among predictors must almost always be taken into account. Multiple regression takes account of it by adjusting the estimated mean for any subgroup to take into account disproportionate

---

[3]For an earlier study making extensive use of the dummy-regression approach, see James Morgan et al., especially Appendix E, pp. 508-511.

distributions within the group on other factors, but using estimates of those effects simultaneously adjusted for the composition of groups defined by the other factors. Hence all the adjustments are attenuated, and a variable which would have no relation to a genuine set of residuals is given a weak relation through this procedure.

As we gained experience with regression and the interaction-detecting process, we discovered a number of cases in which a factor which is credited with a mild but significant effect according to multiple regression, proves to have no effect at all once the sample is divided according to one or two other factors, or is shown to affect only one particular subgroup of the sample.

In conclusion, it must be stated that the new program is no substitute for theory, which is required in the selection of the variables and the interpretation of the results. And the findings of this study need to be tested on other samples for stability, on samples from other countries for universality, and on samples later in history for permanence.

APPENDIX F

GLOSSARY OF TERMS

ADJACENT AREA See Location of Residence Relative to Nearest Large City.

ADULT EDUCATION See Education

ALERTNESS OF RESPONDENT, INTERVIEWER'S IMPRESSION OF An overall notation by
the interviewer of the individuals' responsiveness to the questions he was
being asked. Excluded from this measure of alertness were those who had
difficulty answering questions because of language difficulties. (See
Appendix C, p. 454)

AUTOMATIC HOME APPLIANCES NUMBER OF The number of the following three items
to which the family has access: automatic washer, automatic clothes dryer,
or automatic dishwasher. This measure includes those items not only that
the family owns outright, but those to which he has easy access, such as
a washer and dryer located in an apartment building. (See Appendix C,p.418)

BUSINESS OR FARM, WHETHER FAMILY OWNS A determination of whether or not the
family has equity in an income-earning investment. Includes those having
an equity in a business (See Appendix C, Q's. G2-G2a.), regardless of
whether or not they were active in running it. Owning a farm included those
farmers working now and self-employed, as well as those who were retired
farmers or housewives who lived on and did do some work on their farms in
1964. Excluded were farmers who were merely tenant farmers and absentee
landlords.

CENTRAL CITIES See Location of Residence Relative to Nearest Large City.

CHURCH ATTENDANCE A measure of how often the head of the family attends
religious services, regardless of whether or not he has a stated religious
preference. (See Appendix C, p. 452.)

CODING The translation of verbal responses into numerical notation for
puching onto IBM cards (See Appendix B.)

COURSES AND LESSONS See Education.

DEPRESSED AREA, WHETHER Based on whether the county where the interview was
taken was eligible for assistance from the Area Redevelopment Administration.
(See Appendix C, p. 456.)

DISABILITY A physical or mental condition which may or may not limit the
amount of work some member of the family can do. This measure was secured
for the head, as well as other family members. (See Appendix C, p.445.)

DWELLING UNIT A group of rooms or a single room occupied, or intended for
occupancy as separate living quarters, by someone living alone, a family,
or a group of persons.

EDITING A procedure whereby information from the completed interview is
conceptualized into a frame of reference used by the study, done by
reconciling inconsistent responses, assigning missing information and
dollar values to things that the respondent does not know, and performing
some of the more difficult coding operations. (See Appendix B.)

EDUCATION Education of children A measure of education expected for children
of the head of the family now under eighteen, whether children over eighteen
have completed college, and whether or not head of family has children
currently in college.
Hours of courses and lessons The annual hours devoted to furthering education by the head of the family.
Education of head of family and wife A measure of the level of formal
completed education, including the quality of college, if received a
degree from a four-year college. (See Appendix C, pp. 423-424, 425.)
Difference in education between head and father (wife) Education was coded
into eight categories or levels. (See Appendix C, p. 425 for these levels.)
And whether or not there was any difference in education between the head
of the family and his wife or father was determined by the difference in
these bracket codes. A measure of difference was also coded if the completed
education of the head of the family and his wife or father was in the same
bracket, but one did have more formal education that the other.

ETA This is the correlation ratio, which is identical with the multiple
correlation coefficient using a set of dummy variables with no overlapping
between the groups. Its square is the proportion of variance explained by
using the subgroup means of that characteristic to predict the dependent
variable.

EXPLAINED VARIANCE The proportion of the total variance explained by dividing
the sample sequentially into subgroups using, in each step, the most powerful
discriminant explanatory variable. (See Appendix E.)

FAMILY All occupants of a dwelling unit who are related to each other by
blood, marriage, or adoption. The head of the family is the major earner
who either owns the dwelling or pays the rent for it. In the case of a
married couple, the head of the family is always the husband.

FINAL GROUPS These are the groups at the ends of the Figure on which the
explained variance is calculated. They are final groups because they either
did not contain enough variance around their means to be eligible for
splitting again, or no explanatory variable could reduce their variances
enough to make a further division worthwhile, or they contained very few
cases. (See Appendix E.)

HIRING OUTSIDE HELP FOR WORK AROUND THE HOUSE, DIFFICULTY OF An attitudinal
measure of whether or not the family would find it easy or difficult to find
help for the work they now do around the house. (See Appendix C, Q's. C86-C87.)

HOME PRODUCTION Defined operationally as hours spent doing money-saving activities (do-it-yourself) such as painting, redecorating or major house-cleaning, sewing or mending, canning or freezing, and other things that saved money. (See Chapter 9.)

HOURLY EARNINGS The total amount of earned and mixed labor capital income of the head of the family or the wife divided by his or her hours of work for money in 1964

HOURS OF ILLNESS AND UNEMPLOYMENT The number of hours lost from work during 1964 because of illness or unemployment, calculated for head of families, and for wives who worked for money

HOURS WORKED FOR MONEY An estimate of the total number of hours worked during 1964 based on the number of weeks actually worked multiplied by the average number of hours worked per week when working. It thus includes the effects of overtime, second jobs, unemployment, and part-time work. This measure has been calculated separately for heads of families, wives, and for all members of the family including children fourteen or older who worked.

HOUSING STATUS (HOME OWNERSHIP) A family was considered to own his home if he owned it outright, or were buying it. Those who neither owned nor rented were generally those receiving free housing as part of their job compensation. (See Appendix C, Q. B2.)

ILLNESS OF FAMILY HEAD(SICK FOR ONE MONTH OR MORE AND WHEN) A measure of severe illness of the head of the family calculated for those who have ever worked for money. (See Appendix C, Qs. E29-E30.)

INCOME Family Income Money income before taxes received from all sources by all adult family members, and children fourteen or older. (See Appendix C. Q. G6c.)
Mixed labor-capital income All money income from enterprises which involve capital and labor inputs. Money income from farming, unincorporated businesses, roomers, and boarders.
Money income The basis on which all income variables were calculated for this study. It includes all wage and salary income plus mixed-labor income plus capital income plus regular money transfers. This measure was calculated for all family members, including children fourteen or older who received income.

INTERVIEW, CALLS REQUIRED The number of times that the interviewer had to visit the dwelling before securing an interview with the appropriate member of the family. This includes the visit resulting in successful completion of the interview. (See Appendix C, Q. J4.)

JOURNEY TO WORK The number of hours spent during 1964 going to and from one's job, for heads of families in the labor force at the time of the interview and for wives who worked for money during 1964.

LOCATION OF RESIDENCE RELATIVE TO NEAREST LARGE CITY <u>Central Cities</u> of standard metropolitan areas. If a standard metropolitan area has two or more central cities, the largest and any others of 250,000 population in 1960 are designated as central cities.
<u>Suburban areas</u> All urbanized areas in the primary sampling unit and the remainder of any county which includes a central city.
<u>Adjacent areas</u> All territory beyond the outer boundaries of suburban areas within fifty miles of the central business district of a central city.
<u>Outlying areas</u> All territory more than fifty miles from the central business district of a central city.

MEDIAN COUNTY INCOME Data from the U.S. Bureau of the Census on 1959 income of the county in which interview was taken. Used as a measure of the standard of living of the area. (See Appendix C, p. 456.)

OTHER MEMBERS OF THE FAMILY Children, and adults in family other than the head and his wife.

OUTLYING AREAS See Location of Residence Relative to Nearest Large City.

OUTSIDE HELP Aid received by family for things they would otherwise have to do themselves. Includes help doing regular housework, laundry, child care, painting or repairs, lawn care, and time saved by eating out rather than preparing meals at home. Such help may either be free to the family or they may have to pay for it.

PARTIAL BETA COEFFICIENT This is analogous to the usual partial beta co-efficient, except that being based on a set of dummy variable coefficients instead of a variable with an imposed sign, it is always positive. It is a measure of the importance of variables used in multivariate analyses.

PRIMARY SAMPLING UNIT One of 74 areas chosen at the first stage of sample selection. Each of the 12 largest metropolitan areas forms a primary sampling unit; 62 additional units, each consisting of a county or group of adjacent counties, are chosen from outside the metropolitan areas. (See Appendix A.)

REGION A classification of the conterminous United States into geographic areas based on that grouping used by the U.S. Bureau of the Census. (See Appendix C, p. 456.)

REGULAR HOUSEWORK Time spent by heads of families and wives doing meal preparation, regular cleaning, child care, straightening up, and other time spent working around the house. (See Chapter 8.)

RELIGIOUS PREFERENCE A measure of choice expressed by the head of the family; however, it is not a measure of whether or not he actually has membership in the denomination. (See Appendix C, Qs. H23-24.)

SAVINGS LIQUID A measure of savings including checking accounts, savings accounts, and government bonds, and whether or not they amount to as much as two months or more of the family's take-home income. If the family did not have such assets now, they were asked whether or not they had such an accumulation within the last five years. (See Appendix C, Qs. H8-H10.)

SEARCH PROCESS This is a name given to the sequential multivariate analysis used in this study. (See Appendix E. for full explanation of this method.)

SELF-EMPLOYMENT OF HEAD Heads of families who worked were asked whether or not they were self-employed or worked for somebody else. A head of a family who said that he was self-employed was coded as a self-employed businessman only if he had some equity in a business, so that the income he received was mixed labor and capital income, such as in the case of farmers who own their farms. Self-employed professionals, however, were coded as professionals, on the assumption that the selling of their services was really the source of their income, and not the fact they had a capital investment connected with the services they offered.

SIBLINGS, NUMBER, OF HEAD The number of siblings the head of the family had around him when he was growing up, not necessarily how many were currently living. This was also ascertained for the wife of the head of the family. Birth order A code combining both the number of siblings of the head of the family and his order among them. It delineates first whether the head of the family is an only child; oldest with 1 or 2 siblings; oldest with 3 or more siblings; youngest with 1 or 2 siblings; or is neither oldest nor youngest, but has at least two siblings.

SPLIT Refers to a single division of any subgroup using the most powerful discriminant explanatory variable. (See Appendix E.)

STANDARD METROPOLITAN AREA A county or group of contiguous counties (except in New England) which contains at least one city of 50,000 inhabitants or more in 1950. In addition to the county or counties containing such a city or cities, contiguous counties are included if according to certain criteria they are essentially metropolitan in character and sufficiently integrated with the central city. In New England, standard metropolitan areas have been defined on a town rather than on a county basis. (See U.S. Bureau of the Census, Statistical Abstract of the United States, 1956 (Washington, D.C.: U.S. Department of Commerce, 1956), p.4.)

SUBURBAN AREAS See Location of Residence Relative to Nearest Large City.

UNEMPLOYMENT OF FAMILY HEAD, OUT OF A JOB FOR TWO MONTHS OR MORE AND WHEN A measure of unemployment experience excluding reasons of sickness, of the head of the family. It is calculated for those who have ever in their lifetimes worked for money. (See Appendix C, Qs. E27-E28.)

VOLUNTEER WORK Time spent without pay doing work for relatives, church, or charity calculated for heads of families and wives (See Chapter 9.)

INDEX

Variables used as explanatory are indexed where they are used in the text, so if one desires to see what predictive value a certain explanatory variable has, the index gives all the pages where it is so used. The notation "n" indicates footnote, and the notation "t" indicates a tabular presentation, either a table or the figure resulting from the sequential multivariate analysis procedure.